SACRED DISCONTENT

The Bible and Western Tradition

HERBERT N. SCHNEIDAU

UNIVERSITY OF CALIFORNIA PRESS

Berkeley • Los Angeles • London

University of California Press
Berkeley and Los Angeles, California

University of California Press, Ltd.
London, England

ISBN: 0–520–03165–2
Library of Congress Catalog Card Number: 75–18044

Publication of this book was assisted by the American Council of
Learned Societies under a grant from the Andrew W. Mellon Foundation

The author gratefully acknowledges permission to reprint Chapter
One, which originally appeared in *Georgia Review* (Winter, 1974) .

Designer: Dwight Agner
Type face: Linotype Baskerville
Typesetter: G & S Typesetters, Austin, Texas
Printer and Binder: Vail-Ballou Press, Inc., Binghamton, New York

First Paperback Edition 1977

To **HDS—BCS** *in memoriam*

Contents

List of Figures ix

Prefatory Statement xi

One   In Praise of Alienation: The Bible and Western Culture 1

Two   The Mythological Consciousness 50

Three   The Hebrews Against the High Cultures:
Pastoral Motifs 104

Four   The Paradigms of History and Paternity 174

Five   The Bible and Literature: Against Positivism 248

Bibliography 307

Index 321

List of Figures

following page 146

FIGURE 1. Neolithic plastered skull, Jericho

FIGURE 2. "Venus of Willendorf"

FIGURE 3. Palette of Narmer

FIGURE 4. Pregnant woman under reindeer

FIGURE 5. Hybrid bull-man

FIGURE 6. "Dancing Sorcerer"

FIGURE 7. Imdugud

FIGURE 8. Scorpion-man and goat-servant

FIGURE 9. Bull on lyre

FIGURE 10. Mithraic sacrifice

FIGURE 11. "Venus of Laussel"

FIGURE 12. Golden sarcophagus of King Tutankhamen

FIGURE 13. Yahwist landscape: Judean desert

FIGURE 14. Yahwist landscape: Negev

FIGURE 15. Yahwist landscape: Sinai

FIGURE 16. Erotic figurine from pre-Hebrew Palestine

FIGURE 17. Wall painting, Beni Hasan, Egypt: traveling forge?

FIGURE 18. Neolithic tower, Jericho

FIGURE 19. Canaanite Astarte

FIGURE 20. Min, with Astarte on lion, and Resheph on right

FIGURE 21. Another version of Min, with Astarte on lion, and Resheph on right

FIGURE 22. Min-Kamutef

FIGURE 23. Min; vulva signs on kneecaps

Approximate Chronology of Events and Artifacts Mentioned in the Text

Prefatory Statement

The first debt I should like to acknowledge is to the student radicals and counter-culturists of the 1960s. Not that I ever learned anything from their preachifying: on the contrary, their panaceas for society seemed to me facile and shallow when they were not infected by moronic vigilante fantasies. But I was struck by the way our culture treated these garbled denunciations and puerile fantasies as somehow significant, in spite of protestations of contempt. Not only the radically chic, but all of us seemed anxious to show that we could "hear what the youth are saying." No doubt this attitude was compounded of various elements: the Vietnam war was indeed a hideous error, and we knew it all along: other guilts were projected onto this one, and anyhow Americans believe in the wisdom of innocence. But something more was needed for a full explanation. Since I was already convinced that we are a far more Biblical society than we admit, I concluded that underneath what Reinhold Niebuhr calls "the easy conscience of modern man" a latent response to prophetic rhetoric makes us unwilling to shut off even wrongheaded self-accusations. Far more important than our superficial complacency is a fear of missing what might be prophets' messages.

So the recurrent Western habit of self-judgment provided one perspective. Of greater impact, of course, were the insights provided by Biblical scholarship. Anyone who wants to test propositions about the role of the Bible in our culture can avail himself of the fruits of dedicated labor by the scholars and critics; the general ignorance of their work, and the general assumption that we can take the Bible for granted, still astonishes me. I have tried to follow the tenor of Biblical criticism as precisely as I could; some will say I have not been critical enough of certain "Lutheran" prejudices. In reply I can only say that I have been aware of the need to leaven these with other views, just as I have recognized and tried to discount when necessary the romanticism and Jungianism of some of my anthropological sources. But in dealing with this latter distraction, I have often preferred even romantic hypotheses to the abnegations of positivism, for reasons that should become clear. Of course one falls into a certain kind of positivism simply by writing here and now, in the accepted mode. But one does not wish to acquiesce further in it: it is better to be tendentious than to be a positivist.

This study is by nature eclectic, going into a large number of areas zealously guarded by specialists, and I apologize for not mastering all the relevant fields more fully; for I acknowledge that one simply does not see the facts of a field—one lacks the *schemata*—without a certain degree of training in it. But I stand by what I assert in the book; I have certain reasons for believing that my limitations are not crucial to the argument. In fact I think I can bring a certain freshness to some momentous questions just because I am an amateur. If, as Walker Percy observes, "everything is too important to be left to the specialist of that thing," it is because specialists tend to be the prisoners of their hard-won *schemata*. (This problem, that of familiarization, is discussed further in the last chapter.) Nonetheless I read as much specialist work as possible, not only to make my pronouncements more authoritative, but because the whole area and its disciplines are indeed fascinating.

Many people have read the manuscript and I have learned from their evaluations of it, but most of the readings were anonymous, so I can only thank them in general. I must, however, state my gratitude for specific kindnesses from J. Hillis Miller, Hugh Kenner, Donald Pearce, August Frugé, Robert Zachary, Leslie Phillabaum,

Beverly Jarrett, John Irwin, and several students, too many to name. Two former students, now colleagues, must be mentioned: Jesse Gellrich has been extremely helpful, and Walter Michaels has suffered through so much of the book's composition that he deserves a certain responsibility for it. Moreover I am grateful to the Academic Senate Research Committee of the University of California, Santa Barbara, for various grants, and especially I thank the office staff of our English department for performing laborious chores.

Finally I must beg the reader's indulgence for a few peculiar usages, such as capitalizing *Biblical*. There is only one Bible. When quoting it, however, I have used several versions (the Jerusalem, the Revised Standard Version, the New English, and even the King James) as the needs for differing emphases arose. They are all good in different ways.

Santa Barbara, California
January, 1976

Chapter One ⛪ In Praise of Alienation: The Bible and Western Culture

THE CULTURAL IMPERATIVE

What does not change
Is the will to change
—Charles Olson

Modern man, so avid for new information about outer space or inner compulsions, seems relatively incurious about what recent scholarship has to offer on the Bible. His reluctance has its reasons: for the formally irreligious, Bible study is a bore, burdened with the memory of the suffocating pieties of childhood; for believers, on the other hand, there is the fear of reopening settled issues that perhaps cost much pain to resolve. Indeed, Bible-reading frequently does have a troubling effect on calm surfaces. Although the Bible's ideas have been construed into an amazing variety of sectarian beliefs, the very number of these is evidence of their unsatisfying character. Some evangelists are now hawking a vernacular version of the New Testament under the title *Good News for Modern Man*, but we can read it from cover to cover without finding anything to set off a stock market rally. On the contrary, we moderns are like the rich young man who questioned Jesus: when he heard the Good News, he went away sorrowful, "for he had great possessions." The Bible keeps insulting our *amour-propre* by insisting that our proud acquisitions and accomplishments are not so important as we thought, and perhaps are positively unhelpful. Those who consider the Bible irrelevant, written by killjoy fanatics lacking in the cultured graces and urbanities, are dimly recognizing a profound truth: the Bible is not the best book for putting us at ease in the world.

Of course, the Bible is still our all-time best seller, but most of those sales must be for largely ornamental purposes. We hardly know how much the Bible influences us, in the first place because we're not very sure just what is in the book. The Devil in George Bernard Shaw's *Man and Superman* sneers at Milton, who "described me as being expelled from Heaven by cannons and gunpowder; and to this day every Briton believes that the whole of his silly story is in the Bible." But the jibe has a hidden point of which Shaw was unaware, for Milton supplies something that people in general need: mythology. The significant lack of myth in the Bible may have much to do with its unsettling effect.

For the study of literature, it appears, the book is not just an unfailing source of material; in spite of all the tomes that have been written on So-and-so's "use of the Bible," the point is how the Bible uses authors, not vice versa. It would certainly be a mistake to assume that the only importance of the Bible is in the constructions that have been put upon it. These varied interpretations, however, betray in their very restlessness an important symptom of our pervasive cultural amnesia. As the Bible keeps demanding new interpretations, so our culture keeps demanding the uprooting of old forms: perhaps the first point explains something about the second.

The point may be put most simply in terms of ambivalence. We love and hate our culture, and the resultant force is toward change. This ambivalence derives from the Bible. Speaking of the New Testament, Amos N. Wilder observes: "There is a basic anomaly in the relation of the Gospel to human culture, that it both condemns it and nourishes it. The church both denies civilization and creates it." This is part of a larger pattern, for it is also found in the Old Testament, where Israel is commanded to build a just society yet made aware that the foundations of any society whatsoever are without divine sanction. The Bible insists that man is answerable not to his culture but to a being who transcends all culture. Even in his most nationalistic or tribal conceptions, the Old Testament God associates himself with the Children of Israel arbitrarily; he does not choose them because of their merits, nor does he embody their institutions as do other national gods. Instead of praising their culture, he insists that it be reformed; reproaches to Israel are interspersed even among the recountings of the triumphs of Gideon and David. Eventually God allows the nation to be destroyed, raising the hope that its culture may be restored in a purer and more austere form. Western readers have inherited this critical attitude, which eventuates in a pattern of inability to be satisfied with any given state of culture, and a need to keep changing it. As Wilder further remarks, "Christianity attacks human life at so deep a level that it disallows all existing culture."[1] This point is of the essence for a religion which could not find God in the Law or the Temple even though he had ordained them. Yet this negative knowledge is no Christian innovation: the prophets too find a gap between God and the institutions set up in his name, and turn against his cult. Jeremiah denounced ostentatious Temple worship long before Jesus did, and Ezekiel proposed that God had deliberately given Israel bad laws: "which was to punish them, so that they would learn that I am the Lord."[2]

So perhaps the fundamental message of the Bible—that which a literary mind might perceive best, as writers inevitably stand at a certain distance from their cultures and speak in a way meant to transcend immediate conditions—is that of a need for change which

1. Amos N. Wilder, *Theology and Modern Literature* (Cambridge, Mass.: Harvard University Press, 1958), 70–71. Cf. G. Ernest Wright, *The Old Testament Against Its Environment* (London: SCM Press, 1957), 45, 48: "A profound disharmony exists between the will of God and the existing social order. . . . He was no mere personification of group prejudice and ambition; he is portrayed as in continual conflict with the people's desires." And George E. Mendenhall, *The Tenth Generation: The Origins of the Biblical Tradition* (Baltimore: Johns Hopkins University Press, 1973), 15: "Yahweh was not merely a symbol of tribal group interests. Furthermore [the Biblical tradition] illustrates an extraordinarily rare capacity for self-criticism."

2. Jer. 7, 26; cf. Amos 5: 21–26; Isa. 1: 11–17; Ezek. 20: 25–26.

derives from ambivalence toward culture of any kind, but particularly one's own. This is not to suggest that all authors are reformers—
although in Matthew Arnold's "worn phrase," literature is at bottom
a criticism of life—but that literature differs from analogues such
as myth by virtue of its self-conscious relation to culture. In the
Bible this relation finds expression not in a doctrine, still less in a
philosophic position, but rather in a great image—a desolated but
at the same time exalting vision—in which the absolute gulf between
God and his creatures manifests itself. In the societies that we might
call "mythological," including those by which the ancient Hebrews
were surrounded, man's culture and the world of the gods exist in
a kind of cosmic continuum with little or no gap between them;
the stability of these cultures is reinforced by the interpenetration
of the sacred into all areas of life, establishing sanctioned hierarchies
and structures. But Hebrew institutions, even if divinely ordained,
have no inherent sacredness and can always be ultimately questioned. God is no more in them than he is in the idols, or the sun
and moon and stars, or the sacred animals, or the other entities that
the mythological peoples worshiped and the Hebrews abominated.
No Hebrew institution can be sacred, because if so it would become
an idol. Precisely because all beings are creatures of God, they cannot have his sacred status, even if they had certain extraordinary
powers (as the Ark did). For the same reason, the Hebrews have no
divinized heroes. An insight of the late Henri Frankfort shows why
such elements are missing:

> The God of the Hebrews is pure being, unqualified, ineffable. He is
> *holy*. That means that he is *sui generis*. It does not mean that he is taboo
> or that he is power. It means that all values are ultimately attributes of
> God alone. Hence, all concrete phenomena are devaluated. It may be true
> that in Hebrew thought man and nature are not necessarily corrupt; but
> both are necessarily *valueless* before God. . . . "We are all as an unclean
> thing, and all our righteousnesses are as filthy rags" [Isa. 64:6]. Even man's
> righteousness, his highest virtue, is devaluated by comparison with the
> absolute.[3]

3. H. and H. A. Frankfort, John A. Wilson, Thorkild Jacobsen, *Before Philos-*

These words suggest the great image, in which all man's works are dust before the overpowering, irresistible fact of God's existence. Hence, for those Hebrews who had the most direct experiences of their God Yahweh, his mere being left human pretensions in shambles, in the dust—even the most moral ones, and *a fortiori* those in which man takes most pride: his heroism or riches or wisdom, his mighty armies and empires, his massive building projects, his efficient regimentations of the people. All of this is vanity, and a striving after wind, says Ecclesiastes, but the message could come from any book of the Bible.

A most revealing demonstration of this devaluation of cultural attainments is the Bible's treatment of cities, which after all give their name to "civilization." In Genesis, Cain the murderer is the original city-founder, and the Babel story pointedly rejects the great old urban traditions of architectural and astronomical wisdom, which appear to the Hebrews as mere ramifications of the self-deifying pride that is more important to man's buildings than bricks or mortar. A little further in Genesis, Sodom and Gomorrah give a bad name to city-dwelling which continues to resound all through the Bible; we should therefore not be surprised to hear experts tell us that even during the centuries of their highest prosperity the Hebrews were never really urbanized and remained tribal at the core.[4] There are no great Hebrew culture heroes who found cities: in fact it is questionable whether there are "Hebrew" cities at all (or, for that matter, culture heroes in the usual sense). The Bible makes no attempt to disguise the fact that Jerusalem was originally a city of foreigners, Jebusites in this case.[5] The entry into the Promised Land is effected by the destruction of the world's oldest city, Jericho, which stands against the Hebrews as Troy to the Greeks, but not as a prize: all its riches are treated as unclean and

---

ophy: The Intellectual Adventure of Ancient Man (1946; rpt. Baltimore: Penguin, 1961), 241–42.

4. E. A. Speiser in Carl Kraeling and Robert M. Adams (eds.), *City Invincible: A Symposium on Urbanization and Cultural Development in the Ancient Near East* (Chicago: University of Chicago Press, 1960), 245.

5. See II Sam. 5: 6; Josh. 15: 63; Judg. 19: 10; Deut. 7: 1; Gen. 15: 21, etc.

infectious. The notorious laws of holy war, calling for the oblitera-
tion of *everything* in conquered cities (except fruit trees) probably
derives from this attitude.[6] Jericho's massive walls, older in Joshua's
time than the pyramids are now, collapse like cardboard before the
trumpets of Yahweh's army. This fear and hatred of cities cul-
minates in Revelations, where the "eternal city" Rome becomes
Babylon, a symbol of captivity as well as pride. (In apocalyptic
writing the New Jerusalem is not an earthly city at all.) The words
of Jesus continue the ancient tradition: "Woe to you, Chorazin!
Woe to you, Bethsaida! . . . It shall be more tolerable on the day
of judgment for Tyre and Sidon than for you. And you, Capernaum,
will you be exalted to heaven? You shall be brought down to Hades.
. . . Jerusalem, Jerusalem, you that kill the prophets and stone those
who are sent to you!"[7]

Cities are only a symbol of what arouses Yahwist wrath; the most
successful cultures are similarly treated. Egypt is made a mighty
emblem of slavery to culture, and its "divine King," Pharaoh, is
thoroughly worsted in a contest with Yahweh; other empires are
scorned and mocked. Yet the suspicions of man's attempts to build
self-sufficient forms of society turn inward as well as outward; in
the Book of Job, which in many ways is the climax of the Old
Testament, even man's efforts to live in perfect righteousness are
suspect. Any "way of life" is shown to incur pride and error, and
the platitudes of Yahwist society are themselves subjected to searing
mockery. Frankfort's point about the futility of man's righteousness is a key to understanding Job's sense of himself: "Though I
count myself innocent, it may declare me a hypocrite."[8]

Naturally the deepest questionings of culture are found in the

6. Deut. 20. These laws seem barbarous, but help articulate the Hebrew ambivalence toward worldly goods and prosperity. Cf. Habakkuk 2: 5: "Wealth is
indeed a treacherous thing." See the discussion of sacral warfare, pp. 193ff, herein.
    7. Matt. 11: 21–23, 23: 37. Cf. Micah 1: 5: "What is the crime of Jacob? Is it
not Samaria? What is the sin of the House of Judah? Is it not Jerusalem?"
    The reference to Jericho's walls considers them as one typological series,
though, like Troy's, they were rebuilt several times.
    8. Job 9: 20.

prophets, and in the New Testament passages which carry on the prophets' traditions. The prophets portray man in society as greedy, luxury-loving, puffed up with pride, and blind both to his exploitation of his neighbor and to his oncoming destruction. In extreme forms, the prophets' visions develop schizophrenic overtones: men's lives and acts take on a futile, meaningless quality, or seem to be possessed only of a random viciousness and senseless greed.[9] For a zealous Yahwist, as Frankfort says, value ultimately belongs to Yahweh alone; so also with meaning. Of course this vision is not a permanent state of mind: only a few of the prophets can long sustain it, and then only because their experience of Yahweh is so intense that it overbears the depression they feel in looking at their society.

Now the ordinary man in society—and Hebrew society was no exception—cannot live comfortably with the suspicion that his acts are meaningless; therefore, as Isaiah says, he hears but does not hear.[10] He rationalizes the prophetic messages in various ways. What he requires are props for his faltering ideology: in most societies this is the function of myths, which do for the group some of the things that dreams do for the individual—that is, they transform desires and fears, and especially conflicts and contradictions, into mental patterns that can be dealt with, faced up to. This is analogous to the "mediation" that Claude Lévi-Strauss postulates.[11] Myth draws on the symbolic resources of the community, linguistic and other, to cope with the most disturbing questions—such as those of deep contradictions in the culture—or the deepest fears, of

9. For prophetic views of the activities of their fellow men, sample Isaiah (e.g., 1: 3–10, 5: 8–24, 9: 7 ff., 30: 8 ff., etc.); Amos (6 and 8); Micah (2 and 7; 1–4); Zephaniah 3: 1–8; and innumerable passages in Jeremiah. As Hosea notes (9: 7), many of the utterances sound like "raving" to the ordinary man. But Ezekiel, who had long periods of trance and aphasia, seems the most likely target for long-distance psychoanalysis.

See J. Lindblom, *Prophecy in Ancient Israel* (Philadelphia: Fortress, 1965), 197 ff.

10. Isa. 6: 9.

11. See his essay on Oedipus and other myths, "The Structural Study of Myth," in Claude Lévi-Strauss, *Structural Anthropology*, trans. C. Jacobson and B. G. Schoepf (New York: Anchor, 1967), 202–28, esp. 212, 217, 221.

anarchy, pollution, and the like. Myth is a set of familiar paths through confusing, threatening sensations; it links clearings in the psychic jungle. It also links mind to mind; if divorce is "agreeing to disagree," myth can be operationally defined as "agreeing to agree." It is a kind of cultural glue; in this aspect, perhaps, it is to men what mutual grooming is to apes. Freud showed how anxiety dreams "mediate" the individual's fears and desire-conflicts; similar operations are discernible in myth, the cultural dream. Just as human subjects experimentally prevented from dreaming show signs of acute disturbance after a certain time, so cultures deprived of their mythology, as by well-meaning Westerners, may dry up.

The "destruction of religion" among primitive peoples is always cited by experts as a major cause in their extinction in contact with white civilization. Of the Eddystone Islanders Rivers wrote: "By stopping the practice of headhunting the new [i.e., British] rulers were abolishing an institution which had its roots in the religious life of the people. The natives have responded to that by becoming apathetic. They have ceased to increase sufficiently to prevent the diminution of the island's population."[12]

Recently many studies have stressed the usefulness of aggression in stabilizing social structures; hens' pecking orders and baboons' dominance patterns furnish provocative analogies to such groups as the Eddystone Islanders, whose mythology served to order and control the aggression which, when suppressed, may rot the cultural fiber. No doubt similar relations between mythology and violence were a fairly widespread pattern in man's early millennia, whereas in our time unpredictable violence may be linked to instability of mythic beliefs.

The myth, including the story proper and the beliefs implicit in it, supplies to the ideology that enhancement or diminution of the meaningfulness of acts which is critical in the social regulation of individual conduct. Probably myth is the most efficient means man has of stabilizing his societies; its transmissibility guarantees its usefulness. As artifact, all we have left from many societies, it im-

12. Gordon Childe, *What Happened in History* (1942; rpt. Baltimore: Penguin, 1964), 22.

plies cultural traditions just as flint knives and other remains, when closely analyzed, imply technological traditions. If the pottery and implements tell us how the people of a culture made things, myth may tell us how the cultures made themselves. In most societies, probably, the myth is virtually identical with the ideology.

The function of that particular class of legends known as myths is to express dramatically the ideology under which a society lives; not only to hold out to its conscience the values it recognizes and the ideals it pursues from generation to generation, but above all to express its very being and structure, the elements, the connections, the balances, the tensions that constitute it; to justify the rules and traditional practices without which everything within a society would disintegrate. . . . [Some myths] adorn a remote past or future and inaccessible zones where gods, giants, monsters, and demons have their sport; others are content with ordinary men, with familiar places, and with plausible eras. But all these narratives have one and the same vital function.[13]

Or, it may be, the myths do not operate so directly, yet have the same effect: Lévi-Strauss, cutting across the "empirical" tradition in anthropology, asserts that the deeper structures of a culture are not at the observable level, but may be deduced from a distorted reflection in myth: the structures involve "unconscious categories which we may hope to reach, by bringing together domains which, at first sight, appear disconnected to the observer: on the one hand, the social system as it actually works, and on the other, the manner in which, through their myths, their rituals and their religious representations, men try to hide or to justify the discrepancies between their society and the ideal image of it which they harbour."[14] The "unconscious" here evoked by Lévi-Strauss, though not the Freudian

13. Georges Dumézil, *The Destiny of the Warrior*, trans. Alf Hiltebeitel (Chicago: University of Chicago Press, 1970), 3. Cf. Mendenhall, *The Tenth Generation*, 7: "There can be little doubt that the primary social function of the most important myths in antiquity was simply to indicate and promulgate the ultimate metaphysical legitimacy of existing social and power structures."

14. Lévi-Strauss, quoted by Neville Dyson-Hudson, "Structure and Infrastructure in Primitive Society: Lévi-Strauss and Radcliffe-Brown," in Richard Macksey and Eugenio Donato (eds.), *The Languages of Criticism and the Sciences of Man: The Structuralist Controversy* (Baltimore: Johns Hopkins University Press, 1970), 232. Original in *Bijdragen tot de Taal-Land-en Volkenkunde* 116: 53.

one, irresistibly suggests an opening into the vast symbolic world in which we all, to some extent, live and move and have our being, to characterize which the word *irrational* is remote and inadequate: that world of which Freud and others have at least given us glimpses, where (to use an example from Norman O. Brown, following Geza Roheim) the soul may be a penis, or (to use Lévi-Strauss' own example) femaleness may be stench.[15] Mythology appropriates the powers of this dim region for the use of human society, telling of gods, animals, plants, places whose meaning or value in the world of men is drawn from a great reservoir of significations in this realm. Most significantly of all, myth charts paths of meaningfulness among the "systems of difference" which make up a culture, especially in its breeding or laboring aspects. The kinship systems of family, clan, moiety, and tribe, and their counterparts in occupations, crafts, social classes, and functions appear as "givens" in myth, sometimes in coded forms. It would seem that the older theories of myth were not so much wrong as partial: myth does serve to explain the natural phenomenon, to aetiologize the place-name, to rationalize the ritual, to serve as storehouse of the tribal lore. But all of these were aspects of a gigantic project of differentiation and stabilization of culture.

The role of the Hebrew prophets, and of the Yahwist vision which they articulate, is at variance with these functions of myth. The prophets denounce the culture and probe its ideology to the foundations. Instead of imputing sacredness to the various "systems of differences" which make up a culture's kinship or division-of-labor structures, Yahweh obliterates preference: before him, all men and their petty distinctions are as the undifferentiated dust of the desert. The privileged have no privilege, the achievers no achievement. In a sense, of course, the prophets do support their culture and try to save it, but in a most backhanded way, and from a starting point that is the antithesis of all mythology, a sense that the Divine

15. Norman O. Brown, *Love's Body* (New York: Vintage, 1968), 51; Claude Lévi-Strauss, *The Raw and the Cooked: Introduction to a Science of Mythology: I*, trans. J. and D. Weightman (New York: Harper, 1969), 271.

is unknowable—except insofar as he chooses to give messages, through history and through the prophets. Of course the Bible can be used as a culture-supporting myth, but whenever it is, the insidious effect of the Yahwist vision makes the support problematic at best.

It can be put another way. In dreams, one of the deepest terrors is that of isolation and alienation, the fear that all, even loved ones, will turn against the individual and make him the scapegoat (a fear dealt with in Shirley Jackson's story "The Lottery"); in myth, the corresponding fears are of social dissolution and disorder, the distintegration of hierarchy, differentiation, and "degree." The Hebrew prophets begin by embracing alienation, in spite of their fears making themselves scapegoats; then they spread alienation among the people with their visions and sayings; finally, they show a strange equanimity in contemplating the prospect of social disorder. Again Frankfort makes the relevant contrast:

> The abysmal difference between the Hebrew and the normal Near Eastern viewpoints can best be illustrated by the manner in which an identical theme, the instability of the social order, is treated. We have a number of Egyptian texts which deal with the period of social upheaval which followed the great era of the pyramid builders. The disturbance of the established order was viewed with horror. . . . The upshot is unmitigated misery for all: "Nay, but great and small say: I wish I were dead."
>
> In the Old Testament we meet the same theme—the reversal of established social conditions. [Here he quotes as typical the Song of Hannah in I Samuel 2, which celebrates Yahweh's ability to mix rich and poor, powerful and weak, at his whim.] Notice that the last verses state explicitly that God created the existing social order; but, quite characteristically, this order did not derive any sacredness, any value, from its divine origin. The sacredness and value remain attributes of God alone, and the violent changes of fortune observed in social life are but signs of God's omnipotence.[16]

16. Frankfort, *et al.*, *Before Philosophy*, 242–43. Cf. Th. C. Vriezen in *Israel's Prophetic Heritage*, ed. B. W. Anderson and W. Harrelson (New York: Harper, 1962), 128: "Thus Isaiah creates a sense of distance between God and his people. Belief in the fellowship between God and man is the foundation of the prophet's religious ideas; at the same time, he knows that God removes himself from his people, criticizing them as an object, standing at a distance before them."

The prophets vary this theme, with evident relish. In fact, one could say that the indictment of the arbitrariness of social differentiation grows stronger through the Bible. In the New Testament, Jesus sometimes refuses to recognize even those familial distinctions that are the basis of all breeding systems: "Who are my mother and my brothers?" So also with social class: praising Yahweh, Hannah sang "He raises the poor from the dust . . . to give them a place with princes," but in Mary's "Magnificat," "He has pulled down princes from their thrones and exalted the lowly." The motto of the New Testament in this regard might be "The last shall be first." [17]

It would appear that the word that might best describe the thrust of Biblical thought is *demythologizing*. In their attitude toward the practices of their own culture, and even more in their intolerance of the beliefs of the surrounding nations, to which they ascribed many of the most abominable practices, the Hebrew prophets gave voice to a skeptical, often mocking spirit that has long since pervaded the intellectual life of the Western world, visible in forms that vary from austere revolutions in science's hypotheses to the sensational exposé or "debunking." The word *demythologization* has been made known in our times by the thesis of Rudolf Bultmann, that the Christian message needs further translating out of mythological terms and into existential ones.[18] But the scholars who argue that demythologization is something we should, or should not, do to the Bible are wrongheaded: it is something the Bible does to us. The Judaeo-Christian tradition defines itself as opposed to a pagan world which it sees as essentially mythological: "Have nothing to do with godless myths and old wives' tales," Paul warns.[19] A favorite myth of fundamentalists is that the Bible contains no myth—even though

17. "Magnificat," Luke 1: 46–55; on the antinomian theme of last and first, see Matt. 19: 30 and 20: 16; Mark 10: 31; and Luke 13: 30; and, of course, the Beatitudes, esp. Luke's more outspoken version, 6: 20–25. For the prophets, see, *e.g.*, Isa. 3: 1–15.

18. See Rudolf Bultmann, "New Testament and Mythology," and replies to critics, in Hans Werner Bartsch (ed.), *Kerygma and Myth: A Theological Debate*, trans. R. H. Fuller (New York: Harper, 1961).

19. I Tim. 4: 7.

as early as Origen those with more insight have not been scandalized to find it there—but it has long been customary among scholars to distinguish Yahweh from other Near Eastern gods in that in the Bible he has no consort, no pantheon, no adventures, no "mythology." Even when Biblical stories are clearly drawn in parallel to or origin from Mesopotamian versions (*e.g.,* the Flood), the Biblical ones show evidence of having been truncated and denatured precisely of their "mythological" characteristics.[20]

Of course the Hebrews could not, as a culture, avoid having mythology; what society could exist without it? Nor was all of this mythology kept out of the Bible, in spite of apparently vigilant efforts. But whenever mythology developed in Hebrew history, it was inherently more unstable than the mythologies of the surrounding cultures, and those of other cultures generally, because it had a tendency to turn against itself. Its forms had, as it were, short half-lives, because the Yahwist vision was always latent within them, ready to erode the comfortable assumption that they shared in Yah-

20. Hermann Gunkel, at the turn of the century, began using the term *faded myth,* and called such a passage as Gen. 6: 1–4 "nothing but a torso." "The colossal outlines, the peculiarly brilliant colors which characterise these myths in the original form are lost in a measure in the biblical legends of the beginnings of things. The equivalence of the divine beings and the objects or realms of nature, the combat of the gods with one another, the birth of the gods, are some of the features which have disappeared in the version of Genesis." See Hermann Gunkel, *The Legends of Genesis: The Biblical Saga and History,* trans. W. H. Carruth (New York: Schocken, 1964) 14–15. W. F. Albright, in our time, uses the term *archaic demythologizing* for the Hebrew literary process, and traces it from the thirteenth to the sixth century B.C. As a result, "there is no true mythology anywhere in the Hebrew Bible. What we have consists of vestiges," although he acknowledges that there are a great many of those. See W. F. Albright, *Yahweh and the Gods of Canaan: A Historical Analysis of Two Contrasting Faiths* (New York: Anchor, 1969), 183–185. Still more recently, Frank Moore Cross draws the conclusion that Canaanite El-worship was influential in early Yahwism, and this "subdued mythological element . . . breaks out afresh in the cultus and ideology of the monarchy." But prophetic Yahwism, and the conception of history itself, stands "in strong tension" with this. See Frank Moore Cross, *Canaanite Myth and Hebrew Epic: Essays in the History of the Religion of Israel* (Cambridge: Harvard University Press, 1973), esp. 89–90 and 190–91. See also Brevard S. Childs, *Myth and Reality in the Old Testament* (2nd ed.; London: SCM Press, 1962), and John Bright, *A History of Israel* (Philadelphia: Westminster, 1959), esp. 138.

weh's sacredness. Each form of mythologizing aroused its generation
of critics—*i.e.*, prophets—sooner or later. Even such institutions as
the Law, which was manifestly an attempt to stabilize and sacralize
the social ideology and thus substitute for myth, eventually became
liable to demythologization. When Paul determined that the holiness of the Law was contingent and not innate, his work was the
culmination of a long process, a cultural tradition which is, in effect, a culture-questioning tradition.

What would appear to be true, then, of Hebrew society and of
Western society after it, is that it undercuts—or attacks, or interprets—its own myths. In what other cultural tradition is so much
stress laid on such self-analysis? Who else spends so much time uprooting vulgar errors and idols of the tribe? We do not do it for
pleasure; usually the process is discomforting. Yet every Westerner
aspires to the role of the little boy in the story of the emperor's new
clothes. What unites Western culture in all its phases, tying in with
the ambivalence that produces the continuity of change, is a series
of demythologizings and consequent "losses of faith"—some gradual, some traumatic. Nothing is so characteristic of our traditions,
with the result that we can say more truly of Western culture than
of almost anything else, *plus ça change, plus c'est la même chose.*
The Western world, in short, uses up myth at a tremendous rate,
and often has to borrow frantically from other cultures, or to allow
the cultural changes and oscillations that "time and chance" will
bring but which mythological societies will manage to dampen
effectively.

Although in some respects Lévi-Strauss is concerned to have us
recognize our many similarities to mythological or "primitive" cultures, he acknowledges that our attitude toward change makes for
a fundamental difference between what he calls "hot" and "cold"
societies:

> It is tedious as well as useless, in this connection, to amass arguments to
> prove that all societies are in history and change: that this is so is patent.
> But in getting embroiled in a superfluous demonstration, there is a risk
> of overlooking the fact that human societies react to this common condi-

tion in very different fashions. Some accept it, with good or ill grace, and its consequences (to themselves and other societies) assume immense proportions through their attention to it. Others (which we call primitive for this reason) want to deny it and try, with a dexterity we underestimate, to make the states of their development which they consider "prior" as permanent as possible.

. . . .

The object of "cold" societies is to make it the case that the order of temporal succession should have as little influence as possible on their content.[21]

A little further on, he speaks of the "avid need for change characteristic of our own civilization." These needs of a "hot" society may provoke revolution at the most drastic, or faddism at the least. But they also account for the West's rapid evolution, during a few hundred years which are only a clock tick in earth's history, through many different political forms and technological eras.

NEGATIVE KNOWLEDGE

> That God does not have a Being which is analogous to our being, that the word is not a mystical experience, that faith is not an experience and not even something that man is capable of, that God cannot be thought of as substance, that God's work cannot be conceived of as causality, that holy history cannot be thought of as a process—all these gravely passionate negations are simply inherent in the fundamental structure of the Bible.
> —Kornelis H. Miskotte,
> *When the Gods Are Silent*

One of the most problematic areas for Western culture is that of our so-called "traditional" morality. Western tradition is anxious about morality; it even worries about being moralistic. This is understandable, and a Biblical inheritance: not only in the sense that the Bible urges us to be morally strenuous, but because it warns us against identifying morality with culture—which is what is

21. Claude Lévi-Strauss, *The Savage Mind* (Chicago: University of Chicago Press, 1966), 234.

characteristic of a mythological society. The leading institutions of Hebrew life—the monarchy, the commercial and farming establishment, the cult of Yahweh itself—existed not as extensions of Hebrew morality but only side by side with it, and not infrequently opposed to it. Even the family structure was sometimes opposed. This is not to say that morality can be created out of thin air: naturally it presupposes certain cultural habits and ways of thinking. But failure to identify morality with culture is what marks out the Hebrews, and we have inherited this pattern. Thus morality and culture become twin obsessions for us; they cannot fulfill each other. Though we may for everyday purposes act without distinguishing the two, we are significantly unable to tune out recurrent accusations that we have failed in not putting them together. Picture a typical mythological or primitive society: how many of its people will rise up to denounce their own cultures as immoral? But we hear it every day—and have ever since Amos, first of the great "writing" prophets, stood at the shrine at Bethel to bear witness to the hypocrisy he saw there.[22] In societies that don't have a tradition of self-criticism, such acts would seem mad; but we tend to listen, even if we suspect the motives for the act to be power- or notoriety-seeking. Those who tell us that our culture is merely a front for rapacious greed and cruel exploitation might be political charlatans or they might be prophets; how can we tell? (The problem of knowing true from false prophets is one to which the Bible several times addresses itself, never satisfactorily.)

In philosophic terms, what the Bible offers culture is neither an ecclesiastical structure nor a moral code, but an unceasing critique of itself. For this critique a certain cost must be paid: we habitually call this cost "objectivity," but its original name was alienation. This critique was not couched in objective theoretical terms, a mode of discourse unknown to the Hebrews, nor was it arrived at by dispassionate analysis or ratiocination. Rather, it evolved from deliberately chosen and painfully intense experience of alienation: as the

22. Amos 7: 10–17.

prophet's sense of Yahweh weighs him down, he sees man as dust, man's strivings as futility, and he feels chosen, set apart, estranged. Around him he sees his fellow men mill and swarm on their vain errands. He judges his society only by losing his sense of brotherhood with it. He feels isolated (the prophets rarely mention disciples), shut out, terrified at the loneliness of bearing his divine charge. Jeremiah protests: "Ah, Lord Yahweh, look, I do not know how to speak: I am a child!" thereby appropriating the great Hebrew tradition of Moses, Gideon, and other reluctant leaders who have greatness thrust upon them.[23] The prophets look at their culture and see a myth (in our pejorative sense—a usage that compresses the whole process): they can no longer believe in it, for it is a living lie. They speak, but "no one" understands, although the hidden point is that a significant number do understand, do themselves feel alienated enough to make sure the prophets' messages are preserved for the future. The possibility arises of a community of the alienated. But the prophets dramatize their isolation, refusing sometimes even to be called prophet: each mission from Yahweh makes its unwilling executor, like the source of his message, *sui generis.*

In the old world before the Hebrews and other demythologizers disturbed it, the normal mode of knowledge was familiarization: to learn to make a flint knife, to recite oral epic, or to recognize the medicinal plants, you "get to know them" as if they were people. (Much vital learning and functioning still goes on this way; the engineer who keeps a machine running may call it pet names, or bad ones.) In this mainly oral world, knowledge is immediate, intuitive, empathetic, proprioceptive, an analogue of familial intimacy. But in the prophets' experiences we can see the incipient form of a new knowledge, involving dissociation of self: here new terms are needed; even the word *vision* is misleading because of its connotations of mystical union. These prophets know truth because Yahweh's message reveals their fellow men in a new light of de-

---

23. Jer. 1: 6; cf. Exod. 3: 11; Judg. 6: 15; I Sam. 9: 21; etc.

familiarization: a harsh glare in which the prophets, themselves separated from the communal life and the illusions of purpose it cherishes, see men as if they were ants, swarming and scurrying. This vision is the archetype not only of Lévi-Strauss's entomological anthropology, but of so-called objective knowledge in general: that in which the affective element is removed by the observer's self-alienation.[24]

This is not to say that knowledge involving dissociation of self did not exist in the old world before the Hebrews, but as such it was largely institutionalized—in general, in the *rites de passage,* in which visions were sought in alienation induced by self-maiming, drugs, etc., but which always led back to social reintegration; in particular, in the professional sorcerers and shamans, men usually marked out as isolates from early childhood, whose asocial character was part of their power. Shamans are remote, dangerous, sometimes half demonic: their alienation derives from an ability to tap super-human sources of power. In some ways they do indeed resemble the Hebrew prophets: for instance, there is some evidence that their alienation gives them a vision of ordinary men's activities that has a close kinship with the Yahwist one of man's futility. Carlos Castaneda's Yaqui Indian "man of knowledge," don Juan, tries to explain the vision to his interlocutor: "Once a man learns to *see* he finds himself alone in the world with nothing but folly . . . everything becomes unimportant." He develops his alienation into a state of mind which markedly resembles that of Ecclesiastes. "In other words, a man of knowledge has no honor, no dignity, no family, no name, no country, but only life to be lived, and under these circumstances his only tie to his fellow men is his controlled folly. Thus a man of knowledge endeavors, and sweats, and puffs, and if one looks at him he is just like any ordinary man, except that the folly of his life is under control. No thing being more important than anything else, a man of knowledge chooses any act, and acts

24. Lévi-Strauss, *The Savage Mind,* 246. The "two ways" of knowledge distinguished here are, of course, a familiar pairing; Thomas Aquinas calls them knowing *per connaturalitatem* and *per cognitionem*; others use other names.

it out as if it matters to him."[25] But there are major differences, of course, between sorcerers like don Juan and Hebrew prophets: the prophets cannot summon God, but must passively await his Word, while the sorcerers have an armory of devices for getting in touch with power; also the tradition of the sorcerers is esoteric, whereas the Hebrew prophet's whole being, all his acts and all his powers, are devoted to publishing the Yahwist vision to the world. The sorcerer acts as a functionary to his society while concealing his knowledge from it, whereas the Hebrew prophet resists the role of functionary—he does not stabilize his society but tries to change it— while proclaiming his knowledge. It seems that we may say that the Yahwist vision develops out of, but also away from, the visions and experiences of sorcerers. There is certainly sorcery involved in the acts of such prophet-forerunners as Moses, Elijah, and Elisha. But sorcery was rooted out from among the Hebrews, supposedly in Saul's time, as a practice of foreign nations, and all such acts lost the character of belonging to an esoteric tradition.[26] When Amos said "I am no prophet nor a prophet's son" (*i.e.*, not a member of the guild or caste of soothsayers, who were sometimes merely "yes-men" to the king) he made plain the principle that his message could not be written off as the work of any group or class of functionaries.[27] The break was made, and it sent the Western idea of knowledge off on a different road, away from the shaman's vision and toward the scientist's.

For, as our self-critics delight in telling us, we have developed a habit of knowing from "the outside": the analytic, perspectival mode, dehumanized and unfeeling, "scientific" precisely in ignoring the affective relations between observer and observed, in the manner of the prophets. These self-critics also tell us that this lack of affectivity causes alienation; if they were shrewder they would see that

25. Carlos Castaneda, *A Separate Reality: Further Conversations with Don Juan* (New York: Simon and Schuster, 1971) 102, 107.

26. I Sam. 28: 9; but cf. II Kings 23: 24. On shamanism among the Greeks, see E. R. Dodds, *The Greeks and the Irrational* (Berkeley: University of California Press, 1963), Chap. 5.

27. Amos 7: 14. For "yes-men," see I Kings 22: 6.

the alienation is prior, and that what they charge to "logic" or "reason" should really be credited to demythologization. But in either case we are reproached. When D. H. Lawrence called Poe (and Blake, too!) a "ghastly, obscene knower," he was indicting all of us.[28] We listen dutifully to this criticism, and in our so-called "humanist" way, we wish we could restore the comforts of intimacy and affectivity to our intellectual traditions. The necessity of acknowledging our alienation raises guilty phantasms of Nazi scientists using humans as guinea pigs, or white-coated technicians pressing buttons that incinerate cities in atomic holocausts. But while we wring our hands, we fail to see that our willingness to hear the criticisms, and indeed the making of them, is unthinkable without the experience of alienation.

In a distinguished book, *Preface to Plato*, Eric Havelock has demonstrated that a process of alienation and demythologization was effected by Plato in his attack on "the poets," a phrase that seems to have referred to the use of myth as storehouse of cultural knowledge. Professor Havelock shows the ways in which the works of Homer and other poets were used to inculcate social, legal, and moral traditions in Greek schoolboys—all of which depended on the mythopoeic *identification* with the represented characters and situations, "impersonation" in the ancient tradition of knowledge by familiarization. (When we "identify" with characters in literature, we preserve a variant of this usage.) Instead of these ways Plato proposed a dialectical knowledge, dependent on establishing a critical viewpoint, on making the observer examine objectively what he observed, on "separating the knower from the known."[29]

For the philosophical tradition in the West, we may speak of Plato as the inventor of this form of alienation. But the philosophic tradition has until recently depended on the religious: for many centuries, Plato's work was kept alive only indirectly, as an ap-

28. D. H. Lawrence, *Studies in Classic American Literature* (New York: Anchor, n.d.), 82.

29. Eric Havelock, *Preface to Plato* (New York: Grosset & Dunlap, 1967), esp. Chaps. 1, 2, and 11; for the quickest summation, see p. 47.

pendage to Christian ideology. In any case Plato's proposed reforms
were not founded in the conviction that culture was corrupt, as
were those of the Hebrew prophets; the dialogues are exposures of
ignorance, not denunciations of depravity. Plato presupposes edu-
cability and is convinced that those who truly know the good will
desire and practice it. The Hebrew skepticism is far more penetrating. If "the heart is deceitful above all things, and desperately corrupt" education will not improve it. Reforming society by education would have seemed to the prophets only a way to multiply those
who were "wise in their own conceits," and Paul definitively contrasted Greek aspirations toward "wisdom" with "the foolishness
of the message that we preach."[30]

Thus the prophets, who antedate Plato by several hundred years,
retain their priority in the Western development of knowledge by
dissociation of self, and their alienation from culture is the archetype—and remains the precondition—of the "objectivity" about
which we are now so dubious. The Bible, read objectively, tells us
why we read objectively. The importance of alienation is especially
perceptible in view of recent assertions, notably by Lévi-Strauss, that
primitives can have dispassionate ways of comparing and classify-
ing phenomena which deserve the name of *science* no less than our
ways. The difference between their science and ours, says Lévi-
Strauss, is not in the quality of the mental operations involved but
in the realms observed: theirs is a science of sensible properties, of
"the concrete," whereas ours is abstract. *La pensée sauvage* operates
by a "logic of sensations" but produces a taxonomy both practically
and intellectually satisfying: in this connection, myth extends savage
science by ceaselessly rearranging the sensible properties of things,
constantly finding more meaning for them. This practice of thought
implicitly protests "against the idea that anything can be meaningless with which [our] science at first resigned itself to a compromise."
For our science "turned its back" on "what is immediately presented
to the senses": "the qualities it claimed at its outset as peculiarly

30. I Cor. 1: 17–25; cf. Isa. 5: 21.

scientific were precisely those which formed no part of living experience and remained outside and, as it were, unrelated to events."[31] For us science begins by alienating itself from what it studies, which is the reverse of savage familiarization.

Our science resolutely ignores the obviously sensible qualities of things, calling these "secondary," and in working out its methodology it proceeds by what we may call systematic privation or suppression of meaning. Only by shutting out the "illusions" of meaningfulness in sensible properties does the observer isolate the variables or hidden properties he wants to observe. Given this factor in the history of scientific discovery, we can see the aetiology of the unvisualizable, unmodeled universe of modern science, in which man is so alienated he cannot even be an observer, or in which, as with the indeterminacy principle, he mourns because he cannot complete his alienation.

But, it may be objected, the Yahwists are alienated from culture, whereas science is alienated, so to speak, from nature. Yet here too we find Hebrew attitudes analogous, for the appearances of nature were the very stuff of the mythological ideologies that the Hebrews rejected. In setting their faces against the cultures of the surrounding peoples, and in devaluating the old ways of knowledge by familiarization, the Hebrews liberated forces of demythologization which acted against culture and nature at the same time, for these were indeed continuous and interpenetrating in the mythological world. Again the contrary example is the shaman. His sorceries and visions and trances, often involving animals and plants, constantly stress the importance of maintaining the relation between nature and culture. Even his out-of-the-body experiences may emphasize powers hidden in nature which are available to culture through his mediation. In short, he is enwrapped in nature and its personal meaningfulness to him (as functionary not as individual, of course). What Frankfort observes of "mythopoeic thought" serves to indicate the shaman's strengths and limitations: "Though it does not know dead matter and confronts a world animated from

31. Lévi-Strauss, *The Savage Mind*, 21.

end to end, it is unable to leave the scope of the concrete and renders its own concepts as realities existing per se."[32] Because the knowledge is concrete, the myths must be believed, and because they are believed, the shaman's knowledge is power. Another quotation from don Juan signifies a related distinction: "The things that people do cannot under any conditions be more important than the world. And thus a [man of resolution] treats the world as an endless mystery and what people do as an endless folly."[33] Though sorcerer and prophet agree on the folly of man's doings, the Yahwist vision causes a displacement in the location of the "endless mystery": for the sorcerer, it is the world, or nature, but for the Yahwist it is the one God who made that world and is beyond it.

Over the course of time the Hebrews rejected that mythological world "animated from end to end." The Old Testament is relatively silent about the demonic, chthonic powers who populated that world; only in the New Testament, after waves of foreign ideology had washed over the Jews, are demons much in evidence. But Christianity progressively discarded such powers, and thus completed the expulsion from the realm of nature of those forces which were thought to hold it in sacred symbiotic relations with culture. By desacralizing both nature and culture at once, the Biblical tradition prepared us to look at the one "scientifically" and the other "historically," that is, with the disinterestedness that can only proceed from an original alienation. For primitives may have been able to look at nature dispassionately, as Lévi-Strauss implies, but never from a distance: nature for them is either a practical or a symbolic extension of their cultures, as in pharmacology or totemism, respectively. They are unable to set their lives apart from nature, and thus think of it as cultural, in reciprocity often thinking of culture as natural: the Greeks, especially, regarded culture as a kind of growth, an organism developing on nature's principles.[34]

Our difficulty in grasping this point is itself instructive. Because

32. Frankfort *et al.*, *Before Philosophy*, 22.
33. Castaneda, *A Separate Reality*, 265.
34. See Robert A. Nisbet, *Social Change and History: Aspects of the Western Theory of Development* (New York: Oxford University Press, 1969), esp. 9, 21 ff.

of our distance from the mythological world, we think of nature and culture as rather opposed than continuous. Indeed, our ambivalence toward culture may take the form of this opposition: wistful primitivism, which has inspired latter-day prophets from Jean-Jacques Rousseau to Edgar Rice Burroughs, finds its perennial slogan in "Back to nature!" But the Yahwist prophets had no such alternative; going back to nature for them would have meant kow-towing to the mythological cultures around them. Hence we may speak of the role of the Bible in shaping Western man's comparatively ruthless attitude toward nature. Lynn White, Jr., and others have usually cited the command of "dominion" by man over beasts, in Genesis, as the offending clause, but it would make more sense to talk of the whole Hebrew desacralization of nature and the development of knowledge via alienation than of one Biblical passage.[35] The notion would still be oversimplified, for if in Hebrew thought nature is no longer sacred, still it is God's creation, and any attempt to assert rapacious mastery over it would be another impious fruit of man's corrupted imagination. Though it could not be taboo (too dangerous to tamper with), any attempt to master it would be "vanity," emptiness and presumption at the same time. Exploitation of the environment thus had to await a further phase of de-mythologization, which we know as secularism. And so, as well, did the full acceptance of experiment as a method: all of these developments are for better and for worse.

But—to give the argument still another twist—it remains true that secularization is a logical stage of a tradition which continually demythologizes itself; in a sense, the Hebrews invented skepticism. When Elijah taunted the priests of Baal, asking if their god had "gone aside" to relieve himself, or when Jeremiah railed against

35. Lynn White, Jr., *Machina Ex Deo: Essays in the Dynamism of Western Culture* (Cambridge, Mass.: MIT Press, 1968), 85 ff. It is increasingly recognized, to be sure, that primitive nature-worshiping man also scars and defaces his environment, but not without ideological motivations. See, *e.g.*, William L. Thomas, Jr. (ed.), *Man's Role in Changing the Face of the Earth* (2 vols.; Chicago: University of Chicago Press, 1956), Vol. I, esp. the essay by Carl Sauer, "The Agency of Man on the Earth."

those who said to a stone, "My father!" and to a tree, "My mother!" (*i.e.*, worshiped in the Canaanite "high places," hilltop shrines featuring stone and wood pillars that symbolized sexed divinities), or when Paul lectured the Athenians on their perverse polytheism, they set in motion reproaches that would one day be used against the God of their own tradition.[36] From this rebound effect came the "disappearing God," finally the "dead" one, and with him went many of Western man's last restraints. Spoliation of the environment is the cost we have paid, not so much for the material benefits of science, but for the intellectual freedom of emancipation from a personalized conception of nature. The skeptical disbelief that expelled demons could not stop with them; it had to go on to doubt everything in the universe. Is nothing sacred? Not to us. A typical Westerner, initiated into the mysteries, may say "So what?" But more significant than our crassness is our awareness of it.

Still another strange bond between Yahwism and science is suggested by the Hebrew habit of looking to history, or experience, for validation of the prophetic message. Apparently alone among ancient peoples, the Hebrews developed an exaggerated respect for "truth" as we commonly define it now—empirical verification—instead of respecting the "truths" of the mythological world. The latter, useful and valid for millennia of human development, were inadequate to the Hebrews' strange conception of Yahweh's role in history. The Exodus tradition in particular held that Yahweh erupted unpredictably into events, making himself known by "mighty signs and wonders" which cut across and set at defiance regular human expectations: God was known by his arbitrariness (a principle that helps in interpreting Paul's assumptions).[37] The test of validation for Yahwists, therefore, could only be experience, no matter what preconceptions and expectations implied.

Erich Auerbach has made this point quite differently in his treatise on *Mimesis*. In his chapter contrasting the styles of Genesis and the

36. I Kings 18: 27; Jer. 2: 27; Acts 17: 16–34.
37. Romans 9: 14–33. See the discussions in Chapter Four, p. 202, and Five, pp. 299–303.

Odyssey, Auerbach implies that Homer's easy fabulism contradicted no conceptions of truth in the ancient world, whereas the standards of Genesis are at total cross-purposes to them. The Hebrews, he suggests, were haunted by a question doubtless incomprehensible to Homer: did it really happen? Homer unabashedly supplies elaborations that he could not have "known" even if he had been an eyewitness to events. But Genesis reveals an opposite tendency at work (though there are certain examples of elaboration to be found): much is left in the dark.[38] Students of the Bible are regularly amazed by the reticence of the Hebrews to supply pictures or answers about heaven, God's motives, his helpers, etc.; in short, the Bible refuses to speculate about what myth so easily affirms. Obviously an ominous kind of "truth" is involved.

Finally, one cannot help pondering the significance of prophetic knowledge, knowledge by revelation of meaninglessness, in shaping the role of "methodical doubt" for the Western intellect. So many of the culture heroes exalted by our scientism have been doubters and demythologizers—Ockham and Galileo spring to mind, but the list could be expanded to quite useless proportions—that we sometimes forget that even those who seem to us "visionary prophets," like Leonardo da Vinci, usually required a large measure of doubt to free themselves from the myths of their times so that they could go on to create their personal visions. The prophet, he who is "ahead of his time," requires a conviction that his time's beliefs are mostly superstitions. Such foresight is related to Amos' sudden conviction that the "Day of Yahweh"—a comforting belief held by his fellow Hebrews that Yahweh would miraculously intervene to save them from Assyrian armies—was to be instead the day of destruction for the Hebrews: it would be "darkness and not light."[39]

It seems absurd thus to link the Hebrews with science, when

38. Erich Auerbach, *Mimesis: The Representation of Reality in Western Literature,* trans. Willard Trask (New York: Anchor, 1957), Chap. 1. Cf. the role of "violations of expectations" in T. S. Kuhn's *The Structure of Scientific Revolutions* (2nd ed.; Chicago: University of Chicago Press, 1970).

39. Amos 5: 18–20.

they themselves could never have been interested in it and when they appear to think, as they often do, credulously and unscientifically. Perhaps it may be thought erroneous to connect the kinds of alienation involved. Granted, there is an immense distance between a prophet experiencing a conviction that, before Yahweh, much that man considers meaningful is simply vanity, and a scientist making discoveries by disregarding previously meaningful aspects of his experience. But we must remember that the concept of meaninglessness was essentially hostile to the mythological world: the sorcerers and shamans, if they knew it, kept it to themelves, and Socrates was martyred on mere suspicion of suggesting it. We may remember Lévi-Strauss's remark that *la pensée sauvage* protests "against the idea that anything can be meaningless"; this protest is related to the "intransigent refusal on the part of the savage mind to allow anything human (or even living) to remain alien to it."[40] Lévi-Strauss does not go far enough; in mythological thought even stone can live, and spots of ground are meaningful, so our categories of what is human or living are too narrow for the "totalizing" extent of savage meaningfulness.

The cultures around the Hebrews were not savage, to be sure, but they were dominated by the "divinatory" world view. This view, which George Sarton asserts is typical of the ancient world, does not figure significantly in the Bible. Whereas divinatory handbooks and texts are the "largest single category" of cuneiform texts, they do not appear in the Bible: just as prophecy of the Biblical type does not appear in cuneiform. The authorities who make this point, though implying no continuity, make a revealing juxtaposition in going on to explain divination: "The basic assumption of the

---

40. Lévi-Strauss, *The Savage Mind*, 245. Cf. Thorkild Jacobsen, *Toward the Image of Tammuz and Other Essays on Mesopotamian History and Culture*, ed. W. L. Moran (Cambridge, Mass.: Harvard University Press, 1970), 60–61: "For our modern inability to understand myth is very largely our inability to 'commune' with matter and the powers that inform it. . . . There is, then, truly no other way toward understanding myths either as myths or as literature than the laborious one of trying to recapture the lost unity of the human soul with the universe as matter and phenomenon."

mantic, or divinatory, Weltanschauung is diametrically opposed to that of modern science."[41] Clearly it was necessary, for the growth of Western science, that the divinatory world view be demythologized; the Bible performed this task for our culture.

If it is ironic that the Hebrews stand as precursors to science, the long warfare of science with theology is simply an extension of that irony, compounded by the fact that "science" and "history," once antagonists to myth, have become thoroughly mythologized themselves. Would we deny the existence of "culture heroes" created by scientism? Or that the average man's idea of science is anything but mythical? V. Gordon Childe remarks that "few of us have any better grounds for believing in germs than for believing in witches."[42] The lifeblood of the Western ideological tradition continues to flow in systolic-diastolic rhythm. Man cannot live without myth, and—in the West at least—he cannot live with it.

DEMYTHOLOGIZING AND CULTURE

Civilisation is hooped together, brought
Under a rule, under the semblance of peace
By manifold illusion; but man's life is thought,
And he, despite his terror, cannot cease
Ravening through century after century,
Ravening, raging, and uprooting that he may come
Into the desolation of reality:
Egypt and Greece, good-bye, and good-bye, Rome!
          —W. B. Yeats, "Meru"

In assessing the Yahwist attitude toward culture, we must remember the situation of Israel among its neighbors: the ones, bearers or satellites of high and mighty cultures whose deep-rooted traditions

41. William W. Hallo and William Kelly Simpson, *The Ancient Near East: A History* (New York: Harcourt, 1971), 158. Cf. George Sarton, *A History of Science* (2 vols.; New York: Norton, 1970), I, 91.

The traditional derivation of science from Ionian philosophy is not in question, of course; the aim is simply to emphasize the catalytic role of Biblical thought.

42. Childe, *What Happened in History*, 23.

went back beyond the Stone Age, and the other, a puny band of shepherds and farmers identified more as a tribe than a nation, who for a brief time developed a second-rate empire when the greater powers were in decline. Just over the horizons of Israel to the northeast and southwest were Mesopotamia and Egypt, sites of the oldest and most formidable civilizations in the world. The Hebrew kingdom itself was situated among the so-called Canaanites, whose culture was strongly influenced by Egypt and Mesopotamia and whose influence on Israel, in turn, was the dread of good Yahwists. Almost everywhere the Hebrews looked they were surpassed by impressively cultured neighbors. These seemingly timeless civilizations represented the distillation of millennia of human experience which had eventuated in a sedentary, agricultural, city-building, and "mythological" way of life. The Hebrews, on the other hand, cherished a seminomadic self-image that aligned them, indirectly and with important reservations, with the traditional enemies of city-dwellers, the barbarian nomadic raiders. The possibility exists that the Hebrew hostility toward city-centered culture represents a phase of a great cultural dialectic rooted in the time of man's emergence as a tribal being. This dialectic between sedentary and nomadic peoples dominated the history of Central Asia, and the Near East, for many millennia. Those feelings of the emptiness of human achievement which the Yahwist prophets focus upon and articulate might have roots not only in the publication of certain previously esoteric traditions of shamans or sorcerers, but also in the contempt of the austere and fanatical nomads for the materialistic, pleasure-loving, and vulnerable cities which they harassed and looted. But the Hebrews cannot be written off either as Bedouin (who did not then exist as such) or as mere reactionaries: something greater than that is here.

Like many of the groups with nomadic origins, the Hebrews underwent the process of sedentarization with mixed feelings, but they seem to have been fanatical in preserving the memory of their anti-urban background—and what is more important, they made a written record of their ambivalences. Because of this tenacious preservation of traditions, they gained a reputation even in their own time for fierce exclusiveness; they are the people who violate the norm of cultural conciliation and assimilation in the Near East. Whereas most other sedentarized groups tended to become linked to one of the mighty civilizations, the Hebrews remained hostile even when they borrowed from other cultures; a significant proportion of them kept up a resistance to the inevitable acculturation that enabled the nation, to some degree, to have culture and reject it too.

The breakaway of the Hebrews from the cultural patterns of their time is symbolized in their intransigent refusal to use or create images. Image-worship was a practice that brought the mythological community together, in all senses, and gave articulation and support to the ideology. Frankfort remarks on the "shattering boldness of a contempt for imagery at the time, and in the particular historical setting, of the Hebrews." He derives it once again from the consequences of the Yahwist vision: "Every finite reality shrivelled to nothingness before the absolute value which was God."[43] Or, to use Paul's conception, no creature can contain its creator. Whereas mythology seems to ask for images as concrete embodiments, Hebrew ideology had to do without such focusing points. Pompey's conquering legions, according to Tacitus, found that the Holy of Holies held no awesome image, but was merely an empty room: "The shrine had nothing to reveal." No doubt they felt swindled.[44] This emptiness forecasts the *via negativa*, which the Middle Ages credited to Dionysius the Areopagite, and points further to great negative knowledges of recent times.

It has been remarked that the Hebrews had a culture only in the anthropological sense, not in the Greek sense of a set of institutions that train up the potentialities of the person. They had no artists, few craftsmen, and no indigenous ways of producing diplomats, statesmen, or military leaders. This was not entirely because of incapacity. The Yahwist attitude suggests that the Hebrews would have been unable to accept culture-training institutions. For the one

43. Frankfort *et al., Before Philosophy*, 242.
44. Moses Hadas (ed.), *Complete Works of Tacitus* (New York: Modern Library, 1942), 662 (History 5:9).

medium tolerated by them—literature—had an intense though narrow development, to which their music was an adjunct, in the service of the overriding religious conception of Yahweh. Literature provided the one form in which Yahweh could be envisioned: all other forms, including the shrines, the priesthood, and the rituals themselves, were suspect. Thus the Hebrews became the People of the Book, an attribution that has some bearing on the provenance of literature in the West.[45] Even more interesting than this obvious connection is the relation between literature and certain kinds of negative knowledge. If "art is a lie that makes us realize truth," as Picasso and others have said, then literature and its "fictions" are even more obviously indebted to this principle.[46]

To return to Israel and its neighbors, this picture of fanatical exclusiveness presupposes an opposition in the background, a set of tendencies against which the prophets had to fight. There must have been, at any given moment, a good number of Hebrews who desired more acculturation and more intercourse with their cultured neighbors. The impulse toward syncretism, toward hedging one's bets by offering sacrifices to other gods as well as Yahweh, must have been powerful in a people surrounded by superior cultures, and this is of course why the Yahwist vision was expressed by the prophets in such uncompromising terms. For the prophets the concept of culture represented not only the foreign influences that threatened to dilute Yahwism, but also the attitudes of those Hebrews who were most ripe for such seductive appeals. The rich, successful, and sophisticated—such as they were—were the most likely to support and continue Solomon's program of importing "culture" for Israel, with its notoriously idolatrous consequences. (Solomon is, of course, the figure of ambivalence *par excellence* in the Old Testament: on the one hand a symbol of wisdom and the prosperity that goes with wisdom; on the other hand, a symbol of the idolatry and infidelity that follows prosperity: "when Solomon grew old his [foreign] wives swayed his heart to other gods." The denunciations

45. Even though the phrase was Mohammed's.
46. Richard Ellmann and Charles Feidelson (eds.), *The Modern Tradition: Backgrounds of Modern Literature* (New York: Oxford University Press, 1965), 25.

of his excesses retroactively planted in Deuteronomy 17:14–20 and
I Samuel 8:4–18 should be consulted, as well as the condemnation
of his idolatries in I Kings 11:1–13.) If there were few apostates in
Israel, there were many whose vision of Yahweh could never be as
intense or as exclusive as that of the prophets. These were ready to
compromise; they could make use of the mythology of other religions to shield them from the devastating character of pure Yahwism, which was far too demanding for citizens of a mildly prosperous little nation desirous of more of the world's goods. Hence the
"whoring after other gods" that so revolted the prophets.

Just as the prophets discerned, culture always entailed foreign
ways, though the Bible's writers could not know just how much of
Hebrew culture was borrowed from others. They had no sense, for
instance, that the early legends of Genesis had Mesopotamian originals, or that the Mosaic laws owed much to Hammurabi and other
Near Eastern precursors. They were even unaware that their language was simply a dialect of Canaanite. In the same way, probably,
Isaiah and Ezekiel had no sense of compromising with mythological
thought when they wrote of their visions of Yahweh in imagery
(cherubim, etc.) ultimately deriving from myth.[47] Myth cannot be
kept out; driven away, it returns from every side. Since the Hebrews
were not insulated against foreign contacts, they picked up myth
from other nations without noticing it. Indeed, their ambivalences
left them with so little culture of their own that the Hebrews had
need of much foreign borrowing. When David wanted to learn
military strategy or Solomon wanted a temple built, they went to
foreigners. (It should also be remarked that the Hebrews were never
merely xenophobic; they were remarkably protective of the aliens,
the *gerim*, living among them.)[48] Thus came about the peculiar
blend that is Hebrew culture: hostile to foreign influence, yet composed of borrowed bits and pieces. The impress on our civilization

47. Isa. 6: 1–7; Ezek. 1; cf. Revelations, *passim*.
48. Exod. 22: 20, 23; 9; Lev. 19: 9–10; Deut. 10: 18–19, 24: 17 and 21–22,
27: 19.

of this pattern of ambivalent borrowing has been as fateful as that of the original ambivalence out of which it develops. For a long time Western culture felt itself embattled among pagans, as an after-image of Israel's isolation. Yet even at the height of its pride it displayed an inordinate interest in things of other peoples. In contrast to civilizations indifferent to what "barbarians" have or do, we study other cultures: and while proclaiming our superiority on the one hand, we expropriate on the other. We are constantly tempted to fill in what we see as cultural gaps with ideas from other cultures: recent artists and poets have been especially prone to look to "the wisdom of the East" or to primitives for revitalization of their modes, but even at a deeper level our culture shows that blended character typical of the Hebrews, raised several powers. As V. Gordon Childe remarks, "If our own culture can claim to be in the main stream, it is only because our cultural tradition has captured and made tributary a large volume of once parallel traditions."[49] Thus, one of the subtlest influences of Hebrew culture on the West has tended to disguise or obscure that influence itself. By facilitating our borrowing from other cultural streams, whose material remains so far overshadow their own, the Hebrews have hidden themselves under our noses, as it were, in our search for our ideological ancestors.

The interplay of cultural ambivalence with the desire for stability, complicated by the problem of foreign influence, produced a predictable pattern in Hebrew history, which is adumbrated in the rhythm of events in the book of Judges.[50] Established in the Promised Land, the nation grew fat and prosperous, which led to syncretism and intercourse with foreign cultures. As what must have seemed an inevitable consequence of foreign intercourse, invasion or other disaster followed. Typically the nation was saved by the spontaneous rise of charismatic leaders (paradigms for the later prophets) who stemmed the invasion and led a return to exclusivist

49. Childe, *What Happened in History*, 29.
50. See Judg. 2: 11–19.

Yahwism: at which point the cycle started again. At length, impatient of the risks in this arrangement, the country turned to kings: but the stability thus provided gave a fatal dose of prosperity. Grown finally too insolent, the now-divided nation was overrun and decimated; a few survivors of these cataclysms lived precariously in exile, clinging to their separatist traditions. From one group of these remnants, a band of fanatical Judahites, we have inherited the whole Biblical tradition.[51] The descendants of these Judahites, now called Jews, have survived innumerable variations of these cycles, using their ambivalent traditions of adaptation and alienation. Unique among peoples, they treasure in exile a document that tells them how richly their ancestors deserved their disastrous fate. Even a writer bent on proving that the Hebrews were mainly syncretists comments: "That constantly recurrent national apostasy should be made the leit-motif of an entire literature is something unparalleled in antiquity; it requires explanation."[52] With no culture of their own that cannot be carried with them, and with their technique of borrowing from the surrounding culture while remaining aloof from it, the exiles display a remarkable gift for survival. The Egyptians, Assyrians, and the rest are long submerged, but the Jews keep coming up to the surface of history.

Christianity is of course another story. While the restored Jews of the Hellenistic and Roman periods quarreled about how to resist new waves of foreign oppressors, the Christians came up with the novel solution of conquering them from within. To do this they became "all things to all men": the apostles learned to speak not only in the pagan tongues but in the *lingua franca* of the myth-

51. It is not generally recognized that the Bible is a Judahite document. This can only have increased concentration on the themes of ambivalence toward prosperity and toward worldly glory or preference, since Judah was the "junior partner" of the two kingdoms, and the Northern Kingdom (Israel, Samaria, etc.) was the apparently favored. The theme of the "Younger Son" in Genesis (Jacob over Esau, etc.) and elsewhere has been interpreted to signify 1) the Hebrews *vs.* other nations, 2) Judah surviving Israel, 3) Christians over Jews, 4) Protestants over Catholics.

52. Morton Smith, *Palestinian Parties and Politics That Shaped the Old Testament* (New York: Columbia University Press, 1971), 47.

ological consciousness. They went out to meet the Gentiles on their own ground, and in doing so made out of Christianity a gigantic mythological structure whose saints, feasts, cults, and concepts have long been known to have pagan origins or parallels. So striking were the similarities between Christianity and the mystery religions that some fathers explained them as the work of mischievous demons who forehandedly put out spurious imitations in order to confuse the Christian claim to truth.[53] Instead of treating myth with monolithic hostility, some Christians began to view their religion as the myth to end myths, that which completes and subsumes all the partial truths of pagan myth and philosophy. Hence came about Catholic Christianity's well-known ability to ingest pagan cults, in both the Old and the New World.[54] The early Church absorbed a whole body of Greco-Roman mythology, allegorizing it into moral precepts.[55] This Church, built partly in the image of the Roman *imperium*, was fortunate enough to deflect the demythologizing energies latent within it toward the doctrines of rivals and heretics. As Paul Tillich points out, in this period "all dogmas were formulated negatively, that is, as reactions against misinterpretations."[56] Tertullian against Marcion, and the rest, all made use of the weapons of demythologization in the cause of orthodoxy. Meanwhile the Western Church was spared such literal-minded attacks on mythology as iconoclasm, and in consequence lasted for more than a millennium, internalizing Yahwist upsurges by establishing such culture-questioning institutions as monasticism and pilgrimages. This Church made itself dependent both on those who led the *vita activa* and the *vita contemplativa*, mollifying both supporters

53. Thomas B. Falls (ed.), *The Writings of Saint Justin Martyr*, in *The Fathers of the Church: A New Translation* (Washington, D.C.: Catholic University of America Press, 1948): *The First Apology*, Chaps. 23, 54, 62; *Dialogue With Trypho*, Chaps. 69, 70.

54. See Frank Waters, *Masked Dancers* (Denver: Sage, 1950), Chap. 3.

55. For the history of the various mythographic traditions, see Jean Seznec, *The Survival of the Pagan Gods*, trans. Barbara F. Sessions (New York: Harper, 1961).

56. Carl E. Braaten (ed.), *A History of Christian Thought* (New York: Harper, 1968), xiii.

of culture and those who wanted to withdraw from it. There is no
more ingenious way to hold ambivalence in suspension.

In many ways medieval Europe was as mythological as a society
can be, yet it held on to the essence of Yahwism with a central
principle that might give some pause to determined secularists: if
you weren't worshiping the true God, they thought, you were surely
worshiping some false one; if you were not pursuing the highest
good, you were bound to pursue some contingent one (since everyone pursues *some* good), thus elevating it out of its sphere and
making an idol of it. For all the interleaving and buttressing of a
hierarchical society in the Middle Ages, its ideology retained a self-
distancing dynamic.[57]

Cracks in the structure eventually appeared. In retrospect Ockham's nominalism seems the most important: this was a patent demythologization, denying the reality of "universals" and criticizing
the multiple entities assumed by the mythological mind. In the
same era a tradition of crying out on social abuses grew up, following the great precedent of the Hebrew prophets; and these twin
strands led to Martin Luther's great work of demythologization.[58]
His attacks, propagated by generations of Bible-reading reformers,
soon spilled over from the doctrinal and ethical into secular areas.
The rise and fall of political-economic and philosophical-scientific
doctrines and critiques in the last few centuries of Western history
appears, in consequence, to be a pattern of the careers of various
short-lived myths, substitute religions in fact. This inference has
been drawn before; here it is most useful to explain the instability
of these doctrines. If latent Yahwism is present in all Western ideologies, naturally they eat themselves up sooner or later, no matter
how ambitiously mythological they may become.

The most recent and most convulsive effort of secular demythologizing, no doubt, is nihilism in all its many forms. Nihilism is

57. Augustine, *On Christian Doctrine,* trans. D. W. Robertson, Jr. (New York:
Bobbs-Merrill, 1958), 88 (III.10). Similar formulations are echoed by Boethius and
many others.

58. See G. W. Owst, *Literature and Pulpit in Medieval England* (2nd ed.;
Oxford: Blackwell, 1961), esp. Chaps. 5 and 6.

willing to lose everything for the sake of doing away with myths wholesale; yet it cannot avoid creating its own mythology. Indeed nihilism resurrects a nineteenth-century myth, that of the autonomous consciousness. This is the mind that believes itself to be the origin and judge of its own "reality," the master of its fate, the captain of its soul. With the decay of the idea that "losses of faith" were trials sent from God, some began blaming them on the meddling intellect. As the mind accepted this blame, it also began to congratulate itself on its ability to meddle, to see through things. Thus arose the perverse cults of demythologization, which bore fruits not only in nihilism but also positivism, empiricism, and other derivations: all of these mimic the dissolvent action of the original. What could show the power of the Biblical influence on Western tradition better than these sincere forms of flattery?

The prevalent contemporary form of nihilism is not the showy destructiveness of Antonin Artaud, but our assumption that the mind is the arbiter, even creator, of all values. J. Hillis Miller defines its inevitable emptiness: "Nihilism is the nothingness of consciousness when consciousness becomes the foundation of everything."[59] When we slip into this assumption, values become the froth of desires. But even desires cannot escape the suspicions of the doubting mind. How do I know what I really want? Am I just imitating another's desire, like a child who wants a toy only when the others want it too? Desire too can come to seem arbitrary, like all the other projects of culture.

A naive version of the mythology of demythologization of course underlies all "humanist" traditions, producing an appearance of progress in the quest of stripping away illusions, veils, myths to reach reality. In our time it has become painfully obvious that "progress" is one of those illusions, yet each reformism—political, sexual, hallucinogenic, or whatever—covertly assumes it as a model. The telltale nihilist complication in each of these schemes manifests itself in their frenzy for change in Western society. It is as-

59. J. Hillis Miller, *Poets of Reality: Six Twentieth-Century Writers* (Cambridge: Harvard University Press, 1966), 3.

sumed that the "ferment" of proposals must ultimately be creative, and a simpleminded syllogism has pervaded our lives: things could be improved, therefore any change will be for the better. This amounts to making an idol of Western cultural dynamism. Yet it is very hard for Americans, even "conservatives," to resist subscribing to the myth of change. Satisfaction with "the way things are" today is unimaginable, even heretical.

Precisely because we are so conscious of the arbitrariness of culture, our grasp of continuities in our own is important. We are not Promethean heroes, and cannot create all our values anew at each moment; we could never get through the morning if we tried. Since we must imitate, it behooves us to think carefully about our models. If we try to remake our culture at will, nihilistically, we usually wind up copying its more meretricious forms.

The Biblical attitude may condemn culture, but it also nourishes it, as Wilder remarked. The use of the term *ambivalence* is thoroughly justified. Hence the peculiarity of Westernism is to project an attitude that stresses contempt for "the world," but refuses to withdraw from it or to be unconcerned about it. Western tradition has not only avoided the quietism and asceticism of certain Eastern traditions, but has in fact constructed powerful, dominant societies whose ideology belittles their power and condemns their dominance as a standing temptation to pride. Thus each successive form of this culture is eroded from within by the culture-questioning forces it contains, yet typically each form is succeeded by a still more powerful one. Successors often gather energies out of the old forms and borrow new institutions, just as did the Hebrews. The range of flexibility and experiment is wide compared to that in more self-satisfied societies, and this leads to worldly success of the kind that exacerbates the prophetic impulse, which starts the whole process over again. It is prosperity, not poverty, that causes social criticism and, ultimately, revolutions.

Surely, it is tenable to maintain that Western civilization has propagated itself so dynamically because the essential mistrust of culture at its heart has prevented it from giving itself too unreservedly to any of its successive forms. Like other genetic structures, cultures live by flexibility: not by adapting too successfully to a given environment but by maintaining a certain reserve. Species that adapt too well die off with environmental change: in the alienated tradition, the failure to integrate with nature or to perfect the culture yields long-term success in surviving—the Jews themselves are the most obvious example.[60]

Because no culture enables us to reach God, we are free to shape it to human rather than cosmic aspirations. This entails constant dissatisfaction, since human desires are less easily satisfied than the cosmos, but it also gives our culture its dominant character. To use another biological analogy, alienation and demythologization are to culture as oxygen is to life. We are told that oxygen cannot have been in the atmosphere when life arose, because it is too corrosive for the earliest fragile protoplasm: but when life grew sturdier oxygen became an invaluable catalyst to the rise of dominant forms. Perhaps the Yahwist vision would have been too harsh for publication in early societies, which needed myth instead. But we have learned to thrive and grow dominant on our ambivalence. It has speeded up our cultural evolution—to what some today feel is an intolerable tempo.

One of the forms of our discomfort, entirely predictable in view of the background of ambivalence, is a nagging guilt about the power and success of the West. We must face the painful fact that Western culture is fast extinguishing all others. There is some tendency to regard the peoples of the East, or the Third World, as rival forces, but these are simply the latest people to be Westernized; they take their place in a long procession, some of whom came to harass and remained to pray. Whether the industrializing of these peoples is done by capitalists or Communists doesn't matter. What

60. Whereas the "Mousterian" culture survived in relatively static traditions (see note 55 to Chapter Two), the Jews survive change. Their longevity in adversity reminds me of bristlecone pines, the longest-lived beings on earth, which thrive on cold, arid heights where little else can even grow. See David Muench and Darwin Lambert, *Timberline Ancients* (Portland, Ore.: Charles H. Belding, 1972).

is communism but a Western idea? R. H. Tawney called Marx the last of the Schoolmen, because of his idea of the just price: but he is even more obviously a son of the prophets, who bitterly denounced economic exploitation.[61] It has been suggested that his conceptions of revolution and the proletariat are suspiciously like those of Armageddon and the Saving Remnant. More to the point, his indictment of the arbitrariness of economic systems is another in the long series of demythologizings of culture.

The debate about the virtues and vices of Western civilization, having forgotten its Biblical origins, is now conducted in political terms which either applaud or deplore the fact that the Western way of life is the most dominant and irresistible the world has ever known. It has eviscerated its competitors; none is left to stand against it except in a few desert or forest redoubts. Those are not Oriental robes the Chinese leaders are wearing; the ubiquity of Western costume, even in proletarianized form, is as sure a clue as industrialization itself to the triumph of what Lévi-Strauss calls "monoculture." Christian missionaries were enough to coerce the native cultures of most areas; more intransigent societies have fallen to political persuasions. In *Tristes Tropiques* Lévi-Strauss uses the white man's diseases as metaphors for his effect on previously well-adapted primitives: but the native's diseases barely slowed down the white man's march. Lévi-Strauss, in one of his roles, is a kind of missionary in reverse—or, more exactly, he is an entomologist describing a beautiful butterfly we are about to step on. But even he is obsessed with the indeterminacy principle: he knows that the very process of observing the natives deforms their culture. The anthropologist has the same effect as the missionary: both bear the germs of change, as lethal to primitives as smallpox.[62]

Dominance, as the prophets would be the first to remind us, does not imply righteousness; and to some of us, indeed, it automatically

61. R. H. Tawney, *Religion and the Rise of Capitalism* (New York: Mentor, 1947), 39. The work of Karl Löwith illuminates the Christian background of Marxism and, indeed, of secularism (see note 3 to Chapter Four).

62. Claude Lévi-Strauss, *Tristes Tropiques*, trans. John Russell (New York: Atheneum, 1970), 51, 341, *et passim*.

means the opposite. Self-hatred, the morbid allotrope of self-criticism, arises all too easily from the interaction of alienation, ambivalence, and guilt feelings caused by Western dominance: unassuaged by effective mythology, these forces may enter into lethal psychic combinations. Our tradition is not an easy one to bear, and those with least insight into its origins often feel its burdens as deficiencies in themselves, which is painful enough, or may project these feelings onto various scapegoats, which is more dangerous. No doubt our self-critics are right to point out that Western life is not psychologically comforting. In mythological societies, we may well believe, there is significantly less feeling of randomization, rootlessness, isolation, and meaninglessness: myth "mediates" the fears that cause these, whereas alienation exacerbates them. Not without reason do the British call a psychiatrist an "alienist." Judged in this aspect, our society may seem a cruel, competitive struggle—not only in its economics; many of our emotional traditions too are zero-sum games, demanding a loser for every winner. In a mythological society, for instance in the Middle Ages, each man's function in the community protected him against disturbing feelings of insignificance. In the post-Renaissance West, function is not enough: we are driven by the need to feel superior, ahead of the rest. Thus, to use G. K. Chesterton's phrase, Western society, which had been a dance, became a race, with plenty of psychic casualties and dropouts. We have become almost accustomed to experiences of despair and depression, so much so that psychologism has become a disease in itself, and we talk knowingly of the abyss of absurdity on the brink of which human actions are conducted. Erich Fromm long ago pointed out that suicide rates were highest in our most progressive, humanist countries—*i.e.*, those in which the "vanity of human wishes," the emptiness of anything man can do or want, reveals itself with the least religious mediation. In those most demythologized societies, only the myths of progressivism itself stand between man and revelations of meaninglessness, and they are thin veils: as John Stuart Mill and others have found. Even prosperity works against these societies, for the Biblical heritage, even when unacknowledged, firmly associates prosperity with guilt; no wonder we can't stand it.

If the most Western of countries are those with the highest incidence of psychic disturbance, the most "mythological" segments of our society show how an acceptance of relatively static conditions may lessen such problems. These segments have always existed in the countryside (*pagan* means "villager"). Lévi-Strauss comments on the use of his methods for a field study of a village in northern Burgundy: "Even in our historical societies there exist small pockets of phenomena where things more or less function as they do in non-literate societies."[63] Such pockets could be found in the American South, too, and in other regions, holding out against the alienating effect of industrialism.

Which is not to say that only in these rural areas do we find myths in Western thinking. Roland Barthes has recently devoted a number of two-page essays to various French myths: two pages is all they deserve, for they are all feeble. Still, if myth is a network of semiconscious assumptions and values that permits social actions, or more precisely a coding of that network, we must have it. Barthes' remarks are worth noting (his example is a magazine cover showing a black colonial soldier saluting the French flag):

> Myth does not deny things, on the contrary, its function is to talk about them; simply, it purifies them, it makes them innocent, it gives them a natural and eternal justification, it gives them a clarity which is not that of an explanation but that of a statement of fact. If I state the fact of French imperiality without explaining it, I am very near to finding that it is natural and *goes without saying*: I am reassured. In passing from history to nature, myth acts economically: it abolishes the complexity of human acts. . . . It establishes a blissful clarity: things appear to mean something by themselves.[64]

Many of these predicates apply to ancient and primitive myth too, although we have only to think of the compromised character of

    63. "Interview: Claude Lévi-Strauss," trans. Peter B. Kussell, *Diacritics*, I (Fall, 1971), 49.
    64. Roland Barthes, *Mythologies*, trans. Annette Lavers (New York: Hill and Wang, 1972), 143.

"French imperiality" to see the difference. Barthes' work implies that Western man may have *more* myths, quantitatively, than others, because the transience of them requires that they be constantly replaced.

From its own attitude to itself, conditioned by the Bible's warnings against pride and self-aggrandizement, proceeds Western culture's characteristic pattern: on the one hand dynamic and dominant, on the other hand restless and unfulfilled; on the one hand self-transforming, on the other self-destructive. If we honor inventors and innovation, we also succumb to making change an end in itself; if we dream of Utopias, we are also driven by Faustian desires. With our own culture we may experiment comparatively freely, create new ways of doing things and borrow others, but we may never rest in any achievements, for at bottom we cannot wholly believe in them. The cities of America, most Westernized and Bible-reading of nations, are symbols: always in a boom-bust cycle, either growing or decaying. The Biblical hostility to cities erodes our confidence in them, but this drives us into still more frenzied building and achieving.[65] The Western psyche, to borrow a phrase, has the iron constitution of the chronic invalid. It enjoys poor health.

SELF-CONSCIOUSNESS AND THE FALL OF MAN

> The self does not come into being except through our comprehension of it.
>
> —Bruno Snell

In these psychologistic times it is hard to find anyone who'll say a good word for alienation, but those who join the choruses of complaint should explain how our society is conceivable without it. For instance, our way of life requires the synergistic potentialities of great cities, since the Biblical tradition produces ambivalence that issues in frantic efforts to remake them constantly, and aliena-

---

65. See Lévi-Strauss, *Tristes Tropiques*, 101, 100: "The cities of the New World have a perpetual high temperature, a chronic illness. . . . They are built for renewal, and the sooner the better."

tion is necessary equipment for life in them. One must learn to *shut out* stimuli in a city; those who come to them from less alienated societies suffer "culture shock." A look of indifference, or better, hostility, is required protection on a city street; those who never "want to get involved" are simply overtrained.

In America, many of us grew up not in large cities but in close-knit communities, approximations of those "pockets" of mythological life to which Lévi-Strauss referred. Which of us goes back, except in fantasy? Have we forgotten why we left in the first place, to escape from the stifling and repressive potentialities of *communitas*? The struggle for independence has perhaps been made too easy, and produces stiflings of its own. But it remains the dream of Western men and nations. It is, in effect, the most honorific form of alienation. Familiarization, as the word itself reveals, implies familial interdependence; breaking free of dependence on our families is necessarily estrangement: some have compared children leaving home to divorce. The words of Jesus to his mother at Cana were "Woman, what have I to do with thee?"[66]

The great inventions with which we associate modern life—the automobile, telephone, television, skyscraper—facilitate "communication" by minimizing personal involvement. These instruments of alienation create new opportunities for deracination, a Hebrew invention as important in the history of mobility as the wheel itself. Much might be said, also, about the concept of responsibility, that lubricant which keeps the wheels of the bourgeois world turning, and its derivation from a kind of self-alienation. And, of course, there is our well-known alienation from our bodies and their by-products: neurosis in this mode is the price of sanitation.

There is a more serious and far-reaching implication in self-alienation, in that it makes us self-conscious. Western man is often accused of having an exaggerated sense of "the self," of being too self-centered, too given to constructing mythologies of individualism. Many thinkers have equated self-consciousness with the Fall: but it is, more precisely, the flaming sword turning every way that prevents our going back to the Eden of primordial community.

66. John 2: 4.

Some have gone so far as to talk about Western man's "invention" of the self. That stresses the mythological character of the concept; on the other hand, some inventions have turned out to be discoveries.

Whatever the case, the rise of the mythology of the individual depends to some extent on the compromising of the old mythology of the community and its culture. Thus the Bible lays the groundwork for this most Western of concepts, and its image of the prophet estranged from his culture has shaped the adversary role that Lionel Trilling notes as peculiarly that of modern writers:

> In its essence literature is concerned with the self; and the particular concern of the literature of the last two centuries has been with the self in its standing quarrel with culture. We cannot mention the name of any great writer of the modern period whose work has not in some way, and usually in a passionate and explicit way, insisted on this quarrel, who has not expressed the bitterness of his discontent with civilization, who has not said that the self made greater legitimate demands than any culture could hope to satisfy.[67]

This notion provides the evidence that the Biblical message registers sharply on the literary mind, and that this advocacy has had great success, for what Trilling lists as a prerogative of writers has been claimed as a general privilege. Just at that point in history where everyone in the West is at least potentially an individual, someone with a capacity for transcending his culture, hostility toward culture has compromised itself by becoming fashionable. There is now an ignoble repetitiveness in intransigence, like the compulsory individualism of mod costume which produces a certain sameness.

When the concept of the self turns into that of the autonomous consciousness, we might well want to abolish it. But is this a necessary transformation? For light here we might turn to Reinhold Niebuhr, in his defense of the Biblical ideology published as *The Nature and Destiny of Man*.[68] There he demonstrates the difficulties that Western man gets himself into when he tries to define himself

67. Lionel Trilling, *Beyond Culture: Essays on Literature and Learning* (New York: Viking, 1968), 118.
68. Reinhold Niebuhr, *The Nature and Destiny of Man* (2 vols.; New York: Scribner's, 1964).

outside his Biblical heritage. Niebuhr's points are especially cogent in discussing the recent deterministic views of man. These share one characteristic: they all present a problem to themselves. The more they claim to explain, the more inconceivable it is that they should explain it: for if we are all bounded by our animal natures, or class interests, or psychic archaisms, how can anyone step outside the circle to become aware of this and tell us the news? And how can we respond? If self-deception is so regular, how can we who discuss these theories ever overcome it, even temporarily? We might be able to believe that Darwin, Marx, and Freud were correct—except for the existence of Darwinism, Marxism, and Freudianism. In short, Niebuhr feels about such philosophers the way Byron felt about Coleridge "Explaining Metaphysics to the nation/ —I wish he would explain his Explanation." [69]

This paradigmatic paradox—if thinking is an illusion, how did John B. Watson think of it?—in Niebuhr's hands is more than a stick with which to beat simpleminded behaviorisms. He makes it a challenge to our sense of limitations: "If one turns to the question of the value of human life and asks whether life is worth living, the very character of the question reveals that the questioner must in some sense be able to stand outside of, and to transcend the life which is thus judged and estimated." In some sense: even suicide, for Niebuhr, is a way of asserting a capacity for self-judgment which may cut across the negativity of the judgment. The philosophical counterpart of suicidal self-hatred is a doctrine that overtly or covertly judges man to be "evil": a judgment we hear most often, these days, from apocalyptic political or ecological fantasists who portray man as essentially a greedy wrecker. Yet, as Niebuhr asks, "How can man be 'essentially' evil if he knows himself to be so? What is the character of the ultimate subject, the quintessential 'I,' which passes such devastating judgments upon itself as object?" [70] This quintessential I, whether it be a Western invention or not, is a capacity for thinking about the self that is "unnat-

69. Lord Byron, *Don Juan*, I, II ("Dedication").
70. Niebuhr, *Nature and Destiny*, 2.

ural" in at least some senses of the term. Man exhibits a unique self-consciousness even in asserting himself to be a mere animal. This faculty would seem to deserve a place with language and tool-making as definitively "human" characteristics. In Yahwist teaching, man's evil propensities are redeemed only by this capacity for self-judgment, but it is enough to put him a little lower than the angels.[71]

Even those philosophies that have asserted that man's powers are godlike may fail to do justice to this unique capacity, asserts Niebuhr, citing rationalism as an example: "The rationalists do not always understand that man's rational capacity involves a further ability to stand outside himself, a capacity for self-transcendence, the ability to make himself his own object, a quality of spirit which is usually not fully comprehended or connoted in '*ratio*' or '*nous*' or '*reason*' or any of the concepts which philosophers usually use to describe the uniqueness of man."[72] Of course Niebuhr does not shrink from couching his argument in terms that suggest Christian concepts: he believes that words like *spirit* and *soul* have more than a vague sentimental meaning. But the inescapable point of his remarks for us is the notation that self-transcendence consists of a "subject which can make itself its own object." That formulation describes, manifestly, a process of self-alienation, a turning of oneself into a strange and unfamiliar object which can be known, and judged, in our alienated Western way. We come to the fullness of self-awareness that characterizes the Western heritage only by becoming strange to ourselves. In contrast to those societies in which there are virtually no selves, but only parts of a group which function together more or less harmoniously, Western tradition insists on the uniqueness of each individual and stresses his transcendence, of his society and ultimately of himself. There is no way to evade the fact that the foundation of all these capacities for transcendence is in alienation. In the mythological world there seem to be many forces operating to diminish the possibilities of individualistic ide-

71. Ps. 8: 5.
72. Niebuhr, *Nature and Destiny*, 4.

ologies: naturally so, since in these societies even the potentiality of individualism is a threat to the social stabilization, the "coldness," that minimizes change.

The modern pessimistic philosophies, with their scorn for the myths of the autonomous individual, are full of ironies. For one thing, they derive from the era of bourgeois individualism which they denounce. This parallels the fact that they adopt the point of view of the autonomous consciousness in order to pronounce that all of us have determined consciousnesses. But the major irony is that they recapitulate, in their attempts to be "Copernican Revolutions" against man's pretensions of disinterested autonomy, the Yahwist vision. The first demythologizings evoke the latest ones: both see culture as arbitrary, full of random scurrying and striving; both tell us that man twists his natural motivations into grotesque parodies. Psychoanalysis is peculiarly close to the original: Freud derives civilization from a primal murder, just as the Bible derives it from Cain. The patient on the couch is an image of demythologization; the doctor interprets the dream on the spot and short-circuits it, preventing its growth into myth.[73] In short, the Bible explains more about Freud than vice versa.

The personal life of every Westerner still reverberates with some of the effects of the great "losses of faith." From the time we are disabused about Santa Claus, we are open to sudden revelations of meaninglessness or arbitrariness. The range of these experiences runs from blighting despairs to strenuous conversions, from John Stuart Mill's realization of the emptiness of his beloved projects to Pascal's "faith born out of despair."[74] Sooner or later we are afflicted

73. In *Structural Anthropology*, 175 ff., Lévi-Strauss presents the image of psychoanalyst as shaman. These are two planes cut through the same operation.

74. Cf. T. S. Eliot, "The 'Pensees' of Pascal" (1931), in *Selected Essays* (New ed.; New York: Harcourt, Brace, 1960), 366: "A moment of Jansenism may naturally take place, and take place rightly, in the individual; particularly in the life of a man of great and intense intellectual powers, who cannot avoid seeing through human beings and observing the vanity of their thoughts and of their avocations, their dishonesty and self-deception, the insincerity of their emotions, their cowardice, the pettiness of their real ambitions."

Ferdinand de Saussure's dictum (sometimes called "the enabling act of structuralism") that the relation between signifier and signified is *arbitrary*, is still

by the feeling that nothing matters, or "makes any difference," *i.e.*, that we are unable to supply the differentiations which in primitive cultures are articulated by myth, so that our lives and purposes are reduced to entropy. We may flee to various cults, but doubt will have its turn at those. Thus latent Yahwism works within us, leavening all the lump. We are condemned to freedom, not because God is dead but because he is very much alive, as an agent of disillusionment in a basic sense. In this condition, it is not remarkable that we are nihilistic: what is remarkable is that we can become aware of it and can acknowledge intermittently the "nothingness of consciousness when consciousness becomes the foundation of everything." So with all self-deceptions: their extent is not as remarkable as our awareness of them. We have reached out for the apple of self-knowledge, and in doing so have alienated God, nature, and each other; but by pressing our self-awareness to its extreme, where we become alienated from ourselves, we find that this is not the end of the story. The Fall is only the beginning of the Bible. To be thus "decentered" (and, as I shall try to show, to be acutely conscious of the fictionality of things) is the precondition of insight: thus it is a *felix culpa*, good news for modern man of a somewhat unlikely kind.

---

another reappearance of prophetic insight: see Fredric Jameson, *The Prison-House of Language: A Critical Account of Structuralism and Russian Formalism* (Princeton, N. J.: Princeton University Press, 1972), 30–31.

Chapter Two ✦ The Mythological Consciousness

TRANSMISSIBILITY AND SYNCRETISM

The politeness of these savages in conversation, is indeed, carried to excess, since it does not permit them to contradict or deny what is asserted in their presence. . . . [A missionary, disgusted with this habit of his Indian hearers, said:] "What I delivered to you were sacred truths; but what you tell me is mere fable, fiction, and falsehood." The Indian offended, replied, "My brother, it seems your friends have not done you justice in your education; they have not well instructed you in the rules of common civility. You saw that we, who understand and practice those rules, believed all your stories, why do you refuse to believe ours?"

—Benjamin Franklin

In the fields of law, politics, economics, literature, cultus, and even of the affective and conceptual life, Israel was heavily dependent upon and thoroughly a part of her environment. One can, therefore, single out point after point where the Old Testament was a part of its world. Yet the astonishing thing is that far more basic resemblances exist between the religions of the ancient world than exist between the Bible and any one of them.

—G. E. Wright

Do not adopt the ways of the nations.

—Jer 10:2

We can reconstruct the "habits of mind" of the societies surrounding the Hebrews from ancient records and from parallel evidence gathered among so-called primitives, and from the Hebrew opposition to those habits of mind. The Hebrews habitually defined themselves negatively, by their differences from their neighbors; thus the Bible's denunciations and disbeliefs are an inverted source of our knowledge of how these neighbors thought. The mythological beliefs and Hebrew oppositions form a figure-ground pattern which, like some puzzle pictures, is reversible: each, as background, brings the other into clearer articulation.

One primary attribute of mythology is its communicability and tendency to spread. Without this it could not perform its great twin function of differentiation and stabilization within cultures, for these roles depend on its ability to penetrate everywhere, reach everybody in every generation. Language is the great original "system of difference" which reaches and brings together all members of a culture; myth, a special kind of language, supports many other "systems of difference" (kinship systems, geographics) which allow the culture to elaborate itself. But myth's ability to permeate barriers of strangeness or distance, transcending even that of language, gives it an intercultural as well as an intracultural function: it opens channels between cultures as well as within them. Myths seem to pass between certain kinds of cultures even through the most evanescent contact, almost as if they were infectious. That this is so of the stories themselves suggests that the cultural structures to which they pertain have a homologous relationship in the transmitting and receiving cultures, and further that the beliefs which they reflect (and which, following good Western usage, we may equally call "myths") perhaps have basic interchangeability. Perhaps a general "consciousness" underlies societies with similar mythological patterns in spite of their manifest ethnographic variety.

Like blood, or diseases, or money, or gifts, or women in primitive kinship systems, myths must circulate to function, regardless of whether they have a particular content (*i.e.*, message) to carry.[1] All

1. For a brief statement of the usefulness of "systems of exchange" in primi-

these are forms of communication, and communication invariably has at least two aspects: not only does it transmit information, but it also serves a phatic function, simply keeping channels open. When we say people are "not speaking," we don't mean they have nothing to tell each other. Those overly impressed by this fact conclude that all language is merely verbal behavior; but it is equally plausible to say that all behavior is merely a kind of language. Behavior and anything else we can understand comes to us in the form of signs in systems, not intelligible in themselves but only against differentiated elements of the system. If myth-telling is seen as a form of behavior, it is still dependent on a peculiar quality of structural memorability.

Lévi-Strauss insists that the transmissible part of the myth is not so much the story but a structure underlying it. He observes that myths are relatively undeformed by translation, and are felt to be myths in whatever language they appear. To him this implies a resolution of the problem of versions: there must be an essential structure which persists through them all, which can transcend the various languages and perhaps the changing arrangements of the narrative, too. Thus, he says, we don't have to find *Ur*-versions, nor do we have to find separate meanings for the various narrative frameworks, which after all in oral tradition would be so easily permuted. By isolating the essential structure, we can find the meaning; more to the point here, we can see the intercultural element, the really transmissible part.[2]

The ancients themselves have left us plentiful evidence of the results of transmissibility in the widespread religious phenomenon of syncretism. Many ancient men merged their cults and mytholo-

tive societies, see Marshall D. Sahlins, *Tribesmen*, Prentice-Hall Foundations of Modern Anthropology Series (Englewood Cliffs, N. J.: Prentice-Hall, 1968), 10 ff. Basically the point is that these systems work against an anarchic paranoia in which all neighbors are seen as potential enemies; exchange delineates the range of nonenemies. The precept goes back to Marcel Mauss and beyond. See also Lévi-Strauss, *The Savage Mind*, 109.

2. These assertions are made in the Oedipus essay, "The Structural Study of Myth," Lévi-Strauss, *Structural Anthropology*, 202–28, esp. pp. 206, 213–15, and 226.

gies with those of neighboring peoples, without signs of struggle or embarrassment. The most impressive ancient civilizations—Greece, Egypt, Sumer—show traces of having been built up by this practice, so that the law of their birth might be a rule of combination: cult + cult + cult = culture. In the world around the Hebrews, this tradition manifested itself in pantheons, differentiated collections of gods. Some pantheons arose through conquest, the invaders placing their gods over those of the conquered, but even in such processes parallelisms must have been important. Originally unrelated gods may become familial: frequently, the more powerful god becomes a son, while the lesser "father" retires or, as the scholars say, becomes otiose; to make this credible, family resemblances must be found. In any case there is reduplication and recombination, a flowing and shifting of identities and essences, that embodies the readiness of the mythological consciousness to "believe everything" or, more precisely, to assent to multiple truths even when these appear, to us, to be self-contradictory. The Indians of Ben Franklin's little story are paradigmatic: they gravely assented to the white man's creed as simply another truth, which could coexist with their own. What Franklin took to be politeness was in fact the mythological principle of *assent*. As Barthes noted, "Myth does not deny things."[3]

Thus, even where the ancient world did not create pantheons it loved to discern essential identities between gods, as Bruno Snell observes:

To the Christians who landed in America the gods of the Indians were of course idols and devils; to the Jews the gods of their neighbours were

3. Barthes, *Mythologies*, 143. For a brief presentation of the prevalence of syncretisms among the Hebrews' neighbors, esp. Egyptian-Canaanite (of Seth with Baal, Hathor with Anath, etc.) see John van Seters, *The Hyksos: A New Investigation* (New Haven, Conn.: Yale University Press, 1966), 173 ff.; cf. John A. Wilson in Frankfort *et al.*, *Before Philosophy*, 41, where he speaks of Egyptian "catholicity and syncretism" coexisting with contempt for foreigners, and p. 59, where he says that "the Egyptian accepted various myths and discarded none of them." See also W. F. Albright. *From the Stone Age to Christianity* (2nd ed., 1946: rpt. New York: Anchor, 1957). esp. pp. 190, 212–214, 224. "The impact of this cultural internationalism on the religion of Western Asia was prodigious" (p. 212).

enemies of Yahweh. But when Herodotus visited Egypt and encountered
the native deities, it never occurred to him that he might not find Apollo,
Dionysus and Artemis there too. Bupastis translated into Greek is none
other than Artemis (2.137), Horus is called Apollo, and Osiris is Dionysus (2.144). Just as the Egyptian name of the king sounds different in
Greek, as his insignia deviate from those of a Greek or a Persian King . . .
so also the Egyptian gods are not identical with those of the Greeks, but
they are easily "translated" into the Greek tongue and into Greek ideology. Not every nation calls all the gods its own; Herodotus found some
barbarian gods for whom he was unable to cite a Greek name; those gods
were to be regarded as barbarian *par excellence*.[4]

Particularly in the ancient Mediterranean and Near East, avidity
for parallelisms was a rule with few exceptions. The most successful
of all these cultures, Rome, practiced syncretism on a massive scale
and divided labor so often among the multiplied gods that they
eventually erected a *dea cloacina*, goddess of the sewer. The Canaanites, among whom the Hebrews lived, had a particularly syncretistic culture, dominated at different periods by Egypt, Mesopotamia,
and Anatolia.

Of course the Hebrews present the relevant contrast. They failed
to understand the multiplicity of mythological "truth." The ubiquity of parallelisms, syncretisms, and pantheons demonstrates that
the Hebrew habit of lumping all other peoples together as "Gentiles" or "the nations" had a certain validity; at first it may seem
an extreme ethnocentricism, in which all foreigners look alike, but
it cannot be written off as mere nationalism or xenophobia; neither charge gets to the real insight. The Hebrews were probably
less xenophobic than the typical mythological society, since they
cherished fewer illusions about the finality of their own culture.
Hebrew separatism obliquely recognizes the fact that among both
their cultured neighbors and the more primitive peoples many traditions had penetrated from prehistory, some of them going back
as it were to Olduvai Gorge. Over the span of a million years or
more, these traditions had spread and recombined in powerful new

4. Bruno Snell, *The Discovery of the Mind: The Greek Origins of European
Thought*, trans. T. G. Rosenmeyer (New York: Harper, 1960), 24.

forms, especially among the high cultures of Egypt, Mesopotamia, and the Levant, acquiring a terrific psychic momentum; yet in the Hebrews these traditions met only stubborn resistance. It was against the observances of these almost timeless ideas that the Hebrews turned their faces.

The question may well be asked here: if the Hebrews' own culture was mostly a product of diffusion (see Chapter One on their borrowings), and if cultural diffusion was regularly associated with syncretism and mythologization, how were the Hebrews able to make an exception of themselves? Or, to put it another way, how real were their proclaimed differences from their neighbors?

Among Biblical and Near Eastern scholars the topic has been recently much debated, and many scholars are now ready to backtrack on some previously assumed differentiations which the Bible, as all agree, exaggerates. To cite three examples, it is now asserted: 1) that not only does Hebrew culture and language derive largely from Canaanite, but Hebrew hostility toward Canaan portrayed in the Bible was exaggerated by propaganda in the postexile period, when intermarriage was prohibited and complete separatism enjoined in an effort to reclaim Palestine from a "mixed" population; 2) that there are Mesopotamian and other precedents for such Hebrew "inventions" as the belief that God operates in history; 3) that an opposition between prophet and priest, thought to mark a self-critical Hebrew attitude setting them off from other peoples, has been overdrawn.[5] There is corrective value in all such revisions, but two points must not be swept away: first, for the history of the West, Biblical ideology is more important than factual Hebrew history, and the exaggerations of Israel's differences in the Bible are themselves the cause of Western developments; second, a

5. For the first point, see M. Smith, *Palestinian Parties and Politics*. For the second, see *e.g.*, Bertil Albrektson, *History and the Gods* (Lund: Gleerup, 1967). The third point has been widely discussed; Frank Moore Cross is the latest to criticize "antinomian" and "Lutheran" prejudices against the priestly and cultic (in *Canaanite Myth and Hebrew Epic*). Yet even Smith recognizes that the work of, *e.g.*, Aubrey R. Johnson, asserting that Israel's were in effect *cultic* prophets, is untenable (M. Smith, *Palestinian Parties and Politics*, 8–9).

whole series of ambivalences on such matters as cults, images, kingship, prosperity, and culture must still be explained. It has long been conceded that most Hebrews at any given time were likely to have been strongly tempted to join their pagan neighbors in syncretizing, but something held many back. The separatism of the postexilic years cannot have sprung full-grown from nothing; it presumes long-smoldering oppositions to acculturation and mythologization. In monarchic times syncretism flourished at court and the prophets of Yahweh were reduced to a handful, yet a powerful mistrust of neighborly exchanges must still have been latent among the population. When Jehu ended the dynasty of the Omrides, he did so in the name of zealous Yahwism, and crusaded against Baal: he cannot have invented this cause single-handed.[6]

Most of the historical evidence suggests that the Canaanites and other peoples in the area made no great point of "differences" from their neighbors, so the Hebrews would certainly be unusual in that respect. If neither nationalism nor xenophobia gives a precise description of their attitude, what was its rationale? The Bible stresses the point that Hebrew opposition to other cultures derived from fear of apostasy. So while syncretism worked as a unifying force among the neighboring peoples (perhaps in the same way that totemism tends to mollify the xenophobia of primitives, as Lévi-Strauss notes)[7] the Hebrews were repelled by the practice. But they did not proceed from a conviction about their own superiority: the prophets were always at pains to assure the people that they did not deserve their election, that God had chosen them arbitrarily, to manifest his power, not theirs. All human merits and distinctions were trivial before God in any case (a tradition that leaves us with an ambivalence toward even the most meritorious "works") , and a people who vaunted their superiority were riding for a fall.

The question of Hebrew difference naturally leads to the ques-

6. Cross, though a critic of the antinomian attitude, concludes that whereas early Israel absorbed mythic elements without danger to itself, "by the ninth century B.C. . . . Israel had become vulnerable to a less wholesome syncretism," so that a "battle against syncretism and Ba'alism" had to be "mounted by the prophets of Yahweh" (Cross, *Canaanite Myth and Hebrew Epic*, 190–91).

7. Lévi-Strauss, *The Savage Mind*, 166.

tion of Western difference. As the prophets would warn us, we should beware of letting the differences between Western and mythological ways of thought become part of an invidious debate about superiority. But this warning should apply equally on both sides: fatuous self-criticism is no better than fatuous self-praise, and to exaggerate other societies' merits at our expense is foolishness. A slightly disguised way to attack our own traditions is to deny all differences between us and the primitives: but to say "there's no difference" makes one. What other society so regularly encourages the detection of the hidden ethnocentric premises in its own ideology? Indeed, all such assertions of nondifference, whether between man and man or between man and nature, are self-contradictory: the vantage points assumed by the makers of such statements belie the assertions.

Once, Western man lazily and egocentrically ascribed his own ways of thought to ancients and primitives (children, too, used to be considered compact adults). Then Lucien Lévy-Bruhl told him savages were prelogical, which was still egocentric but at least recognized a difference. Now we have Lévi-Strauss to tell us that we don't think any better than savages, which may be true, but is not grounds for denying that we think differently. The synapses and cortical configurations of all men are likely to be pretty much the same, and as for cranial capacity, Neanderthal man equals us. But to assume that we all use these capacities to produce the same ideology is simply more laziness; in the ill-concealed relish with which sophisticated men expose the "savageness" of their fellow Westerners, we see the familiar spectacle of the autonomous consciousness lecturing the determined consciousness.

True, we have been misled by a spurious analogy with evolution and maturation into believing that ours is the "normal" way to think: that is, that all peoples if not stunted or misdirected would think as we do. Up until recently all Western students of myth, including Ernst Cassirer and Bultmann, have been bedeviled by the lingering aftereffects of this assumption. Actually, however, evidence is piling up that it is the mythological consciousness, in all its variations, that is "normal": or, as Kornelis Miskotte puts it,

"Paganism is the religion of human nature as such, always and everywhere."[8] Western thinking is strange, aberrant, and requires arduous training, as our children find out. Hence Western education can never be "naturalized," in spite of the dreams of Utopian reformers. The manic Western stress on education reveals the actual situation, for the "natural" tendencies of children, which we laboriously curb, are clues to the mythological consciousness: unfortunately in the past this fact has seemed to confirm our assumption that savages were childish. What we must face now is the fact that for most of human time men have thought in a way foreign to ours. Our way of thinking is very late indeed; it dominates only the tiniest fraction of human time. Though full of promise, and danger, it has not yet really been tested, not in the sense that myth has been. It should be clear that mythological thinking, though not "natural" in the biological sense, is an elaboration of normal human reactions to an environment. What we see in children—a tendency to personalize things, an intense interest in the animal world, in alimentary and reproductive systems, and so on—can be found in most mythological ideologies too.

No form of cultural thinking can be wholly natural. As soon as humans are aware of themselves in societies, they have already separated from nature. This entering wedge of alienation can be blocked in "cold" societies, which seek to inhibit further separation from nature by projecting back all their structures and folkways to natural sources and analogies. Such societies look to nature to systematize their patterns of differentiation. The difference of nature from culture is "mediated," or made into a symbiosis. Thus a typical pattern, as in South American myth, is for humans to receive fire as a gift from the jaguar. The mythological consciousness consists of an ideology that seeks validations from nature by retrojecting culture back into it. Here we can see the continuity beween Lévi-Strauss's Bororo and ancient Sumer or Egypt.[9]

8. Kornelis Miskotte, *When the Gods Are Silent*, trans. J. W. Doberstein (New York: Harper, 1967), 9.

9. Frankfort says of Sumer and Egypt that "the two peoples agreed in the

Probably the most striking fact about Hebrew ideology in its context is that it claims nothing from nature: all origins, if they come into question, are from Yahweh, who is beyond nature. This disparity from the normal pattern shows up in the difficulty of using structuralist analysis on the Bible. Fortunately, here a disciple of Lévi-Strauss has opened the way for us. Edmund Leach, a Cambridge anthropologist (but not a follower of Jane Harrison *et al.*), has tried out his methods on the Old Testament. The unevenness of his results is outweighed by his rehearsals of the arguments against his project, in which he notes that Lévi-Strauss himself is notably reluctant to embark on such a task:

[Lévi-Strauss] advances the rather curious proposition that Old Testament mythology has been "deformed" by the intellectual operations of Biblical editors and he seems to imply that, on this account, a structural analysis of such materials must prove to be largely a waste of time.

. . . .

When Lévi-Strauss says that the Biblical texts have been "deformed" he presumably means that the intellectual operations of the Biblical compilers have operated in conflict with the randomized non-intellectual workings of the structure of ancient Jewish culture, thus making the latter indecipherable.[10]

These "intellectual operations," clearly, are the processes of elaborating discontinuity that we may call demythologizations. Such operations obscure the essential structures otherwise visible through the "randomized" and widely circulated myths. Leach, interestingly, chooses to regard them only as inconveniences, and Lévi-Strauss's hesitation as mere timorousness. He proceeds undeterred, but we may note his fair-minded recitation of the argument for differentness:

---

fundamental assumptions that . . . society is embedded in nature, and that nature is but the manifestation of the divine. This doctrine was, in fact, universally accepted by the peoples of the ancient world with the single exception of the Hebrews" (*Before Philosophy*, 241).

10. Edmund Leach, *Genesis as Myth and Other Essays* (London: Cape, 1969), 29–30. Leach is right to see a paradox in Lévi-Strauss's reluctance, but in a larger sense it is wholly fitting that the Bible should be his "blind spot": for if he analyzed it he might have to acknowledge his debt to the Yahwist vision.

The critics, Paul Ricoeur in particular, have posed the question whether the apparent success of Lévi-Strauss's method has not depended upon the kinds of material to which it has been applied. Taking the particular case of myth interpretation, Ricoeur has noted that although Lévi-Strauss first illustrated his technique by reference to the Oedipus myth he has never again committed himself to the interpretation of mythical materials derived from any of the historical societies of Western civilization. All his later and more detailed analyses have been concerned with the myths of a "totemic" kind from very primitive sources, that is to say mythologies in which there is a notable confusion between human beings and animals but which are characterized by the absence of any setting within an historical chronology, real or imaginary.[11]

These "totemic" characteristics are the definitive marks of a mythological consciousness: the "notable confusion," as it seems to us, between animals and humans derives from putting culture back into nature, while the absence of chronology signifies the attempt to freeze states of development. Leach is misleading us, however, when he suggests that these characteristics are typical only of "very primitive" societies: we will find them in the ancient Near Eastern civilizations as well.

THE COSMIC CONTINUUM: ANIMALS

[For primitive and ancient men] the inner bonds between the animate and inanimate worlds, between men, animals, plants, matter and the cosmos were never sundered. . . . Their reverence for the animal reflects their reverence for everything imbued with life.

—S. Giedion

In the mythological world all visible and invisible realms are directly related: gods, men, and nature interpenetrate and are mutually accessible. The prehistoric veneration of animals is an eloquent witness of this belief, but also shows why it is misleading to think of the world of myth as a three-decker universe, gods above men who are above animals: in fact, strong evidence suggests that the

11. *Ibid.*, 27–28.

real "confusion" in myth is between animals and gods. The combination of fear and admiration in which ancient men held animals undoubtedly amounted to worship, without a touch of our patronizing sentimentalism. G. Rachel Levy, who has written the most powerfully suggestive scholarly exposition of the mythological consciousness in *The Gate of Horn*, goes so far as to speculate that men "quite naturally felt themselves inferior to the perfected species who were at home in [their environment]."[12] To be more exact, man is the only species capable of envying the strength, speed, or fertility of others. Man is not physically inferior to many animals, and he outranks all in his versatility: he is the only animal that can run several miles, swim a lake, then climb a tree. Nonetheless his self-consciousness may make him feel inferior. Hence it was more arrogant of men than condescending to include in some of their mythologies a primordial time in which "men married animals" and thus founded the various totemistic clan systems, etc. In these myths men appear as fortune-hunters after heiresses: from these alliances, they say, came all human power and knowledge. We shall return to these marriages shortly.

The animal-man-god interpenetration is the key to many of the most important ramifications of the mythological consciousness: not only man's attitude toward nature but also his reverence for sacred power—particularly the linked powers of fertility and fatality, or what we now call sex and aggression—and for sacred space were involved in the relationship symbolized by the cave-art portrayals of large and powerful animals. The first exercise of the human imagination in seeking the causes of things tended to focus on these impressive beings. Even man's treatment of his own dead may have been predicated on this relationship.[13] Certainly belief in metamorphosis is related to the animal cult: men who can change

12. G. Rachel Levy, *The Gate of Horn*, later published under the title *Religious Conceptions of the Stone Age and Their Influence Upon European Thought* (1948; rpt. New York: Harper, 1963), 23. The original title will be cited hereafter.
13. See below, p. 82. There is also, of course, a well-known association of animal bones, skulls, etc., often arranged as if for cult or ceremonial purposes, with early human burials.

into beasts can gain control of their powers. Finally, the great
dream of the mother goddess, which dominated the Near East for
many centuries and about which the silence of the Bible speaks volumes, was originally related to the animal cult through the fertility theme.

Significantly, pre-Hebrew Palestine yields abundant evidence of
the prevalence and continuation of local animal cults and their relation to fertility worship. According to Emmanuel Anati, the art
of the early culture called "Natufian" has overtly sexual representations linked to animal themes. He comments:

We shall find that in later periods animal figurines are frequently connected with rites invoking both abundance of the earth and the fertility
of women. In Neolithic times and thereafter both kinds of fertility are
frequently interrelated, and this conceptual association between the
mother-of-man and the mother-earth has been the basis for many mythologies. . . . Natufian art also shows that the concept of fertility had become very broad and complex, and had been extended from woman to
the earth.[14]

The connection between woman and earth and animals typically
resulted in an ideology we may call "autochthony." In a way it is
synecdochic for the whole mythological consciousness, as later discussion will indicate.

Obviously ancient man managed to conceal through ideology any
incipient sense of alienation from the world of the animals. In fact,
as a rule he did not conceive of a world in which any parts were
alienated from each other: all the phenomena conceivable to the
archaic mind were interwoven in elaborate and fantastic ways, with
mythology as the primary vehicle of linkage. But the Hebrews
acknowledged great alienations at the core of their beliefs; they
granted the realm of the sacred only to Yahweh and had only a
problematic and ambivalent mythology to stabilize their society's
internal and external relationships. We find in the Bible a great
ban of silence or execration on such themes as relations with ani-

14. Emmanuel Anati, *Palestine Before the Hebrews: A History, from the
Earliest Arrival of Man to the Conquest of Canaan* (New York: Knopf, 1963), 161.

mals, magical powers, matriarchal divinities or societies, autochthony, and metamorphoses.

For the Hebrews, the whole complex of mythological ideas could
be seen by looking toward Egypt, the country of the bitter memories
of slavery, for the showpiece of ancient culture was also the land
that most tenaciously preserved the tradition of the mythological
continuum, especially in the form of animal worship. From his
study of art and beliefs in Egypt, S. Giedion draws these conclusions:

Among the most notable [of man's primeval beliefs] was the role of the animal, venerated throughout prehistory as a being mightier and more beautiful than man. The constancy with which this veneration persisted side by
side with the worship of anthropomorphic deities—the transmutation of
animals into deities and deities into animals, and the granting of immortality to animals through mummification—bears witness that at no time during the entire Egyptian period was the prehistoric bond with the animal
severed. . . . In other words, the acceptance of the relation between society
and natural species, the reverence for the animal, was maintained, as A. R.
Radcliffe-Brown (1952) has found it maintained among primitive peoples
today. . . . We of today, with our firmly anchored acceptance of the
supremacy of man and his dominion over plants and animals, our religion
based on the Book of Genesis and our logic based on the Greeks, find
Egyptian ideas as illogical as they are untenable: such as the identification
of the god of creation (Atum) with a lizard or the identification of the
sun-god (Ra) with a dung beetle. That this identification of the highest
gods with the most insignificant creatures was possible at all betokens an
imagination rooted in a world closed to us, a world in which an unbroken
cord linked creature with creature, expressed not only as a pictured representation but as a sacred reality. Only if we understand the religious
conviction that no discrimination was conceivable within the realm of
animate matter can we comprehend that an insignificant insect and the
cosmic godhead could be one and the same.[15]

The "confusion" that meets the eye of the modern observer of
Egyptian religion is not a mere appearance; there is a real (if not
absolute) difference between ancient thinking and ours. For the

15. S. Giedion, *The Eternal Present*, Vol. II, *The Beginnings of Architecture*
(2 vols.; New York: Pantheon, 1964), viii, 30, 31. Hereinafter cited as *Eternal
Present*, II.

Hebrews, in contrast to the Egyptians, the bonds between creatures became bounds, structural repetitions of the separations between God and all his creatures. There is a world of difference, literally, between Yahweh and Atum. Fitful efforts to restore the sense of continuity in times nearer our own could not erase these bounds; they produced not continuum but hierarchy: the closest Western analogy is the Chain of Being, linked but disparate strata of existence.

When the Hebrews broke with the traditions of their hated Egyptian overlords, they sundered the cosmic continuum. But they felt more liberation than loss, for there is a parallel between the Exodus from slavery and the breakaway from myth. Harmony with nature entails bondage as well as security: we may remember Frankfort's remark that mythical thought is bound to the "scope of the concrete."[16] In rejecting Egypt, with its high culture and animal-headed gods, the Hebrews chose freedom, at a cost recognized in the "murmuring" traditions of Exodus and the following books, in which the hungry fugitives yearn to return to the cooked food of Egypt. But Moses the prophet refused to go back to the gods of culture and nature, giving allegiance instead to a mysterious power who entered the world at will but was never bound to any of its forms, be they ever so mighty. In this choice of painful freedom originated our inheritance of alienation and ambivalence.

To augment this point we might consider what the world would have been like without the Hebrews. Henri Frankfort asserts that the dynamic norm of the ancient mind and world is the unalienated "I-Thou" relationship:

The world appears to primitive man neither inanimate nor empty but redundant with life, and life has individuality, in man and beast and plant, and in every phenomenon which confronts man—the thunderclap, the sudden shadow, the eerie and unknown clearing in the woods, the stone which suddenly hurts him when he stumbles while on a hunting trip. Any phenomenon may at any time face him, not as "It," but as "Thou." In this confrontation, "Thou" reveals its individuality, its qualities, its will. "Thou" is not contemplated with intellectual detachment.[17]

16. Frankfort et al., Before Philosophy, 22; see note 32 to Chapter One.
17. Ibid., 14. The terminology of "I and Thou" was made current, of course,

The difference between "Thou" and "It," as Shaw said of the difference between a duchess and a flower girl, is not how they act but
how they are treated. Our habitual treatment is "subject-object,"
not "I-Thou": we may turn anything into an "It." But for those
growing up in non-Western human groups, it is more natural (habitual) to see all entities as personal beings and wills. As Frankfort
says, the ancient and primitive mind "looks, not for the 'how,' but
for the 'who,' when it looks for a cause. . . . When the river does
not rise, it has *refused* to rise."[18] We should be clear here: "I-Thou"
thinking is not natural in the same way that an animal instinct is,
but surely it represents a normal human reaction to the terrifying
prospect of a depersonalized universe. The commonest form of ex-
tending "Thou-ness," probably, is seen in the phenomenon of treating animals as family members (a process that may have been needful in early domestication, preserved in trivial form in our treatment
of pets). Especially in hunting societies, as Rachel Levy points out,
a personal relationship to the animal is a key part of the ideology:
the prey may be called "elder brother," for instance.[19] But as Frankfort indicates, "Thou-ness" may be extended beyond the animal
realm. Don Juan, reported by Carlos Castaneda, tells us: "In order
to see plants [in their secret being] you must talk to them personally.
. . . You must get to know them individually; then the plants can
tell you anything you care to know about them."[20]

   Obviously this mythological ideology raises problems for itself: if

---

by Martin Buber, whose work of that title (1923; rpt. New York: Scribner's,
1958) explores an appropriation of this category for the Judaeo-Christian tradition. But its original locus, as Frankfort implies, was the world of myth.
   18. Frankfort *et al.*, *Before Philosophy*, 24.
   19. Levy, *The Gate of Horn*, 26. See also Jacquetta Hawkes, *Prehistory*, Vol. I,
Pt. I of UNESCO, *History of Mankind* (New York: Mentor, 1965), 289: "An
interesting sidelight on the growth of animal cults of a more or less totemic kind
is provided by the experience of two German refugees who decided to live alone
in the African veldt as hunters. They discovered that after a year or so of this
hunting existence, they not only dreamed nightly of animals but also of themselves turning into animals. Primitive man does not dissociate the dreaming from
the waking world, and it is easy to see how dream experiences could . . . shape
totemic beliefs."
   20. Castaneda, *A Separate Reality*, 117.

everything is potentially his brother, what is man? We may reflect here on Lévi-Strauss's wry observation in *Tristes Tropiques* about the early explorers of America: "Whereas the white man took the Indians for animals, the Indians were content to suspect the white men of being gods."[21] The white explorers, whose reluctance to count the Indians as human beings was, by the way, based upon the Bible's omission of them from the list of human peoples (Gen. 10), could not of course find room for them as gods. That they thought the Indians to be animals does them little credit, but it does us no more to see this simply as an insult: the Indians would not necessarily have taken it so. Lévi-Strauss tells us that the Indians' mistake does "more honour to the human race," demonstrating that he understands his own point only imperfectly. As a Jew he ought to have more insight into why Western tradition is on guard against glorifying the human race. Is anthropocentric pride somehow superior to ethnocentric? In his clearer moments Lévi-Strauss is tacitly guided by his Biblical heritage, which condemns all kinds of pride impartially.

But the real problem comes from the contradictions involved in trying to maintain that man is "natural," and again Lévi-Strauss illustrates the problem: he himself seeks to follow the example of Rousseau, who on hearing reports of gorillas chose to regard them as men, rather than exclude any possible variety of man from his sense of brotherhood. In so doing Lévi-Strauss inevitably falls into sacramentalizing the primitive, in spite of tortuous attempts to avoid it. In the antepenultimate chapter of *Tristes Tropiques*, "The Apotheosis of Augustus," he describes how he struggled to visualize a concept of "the passage from manhood to divinity" by writing a play about the deified Roman emperor. Leaving aside certain ironic complications, here is the gist:

Augustus, left alone on the stage, finds himself faced with an eagle: not the conventional eagle, divinity's attribute, but a wild creature, evil-smell-

---

21. Lévi-Strauss, *Tristes Tropiques*, 80. It is worth noting, however, that the Indians' means of testing their identification consisted of drowning white captives and then watching the corpses for signs of decay.

ing and lukewarm to the touch. It is, none the less, Jupiter's eagle; the same who carried off Ganymede after a bloody combat in which the boy struggled in vain. Augustus can hardly believe his ears when the bird explains to him that his divinity will consist simply in immunity to the feeling of repulsion which overcomes him, as a man, when the eagle draws near. He will know that he is a god not because of any inner radiance or any capacity to work miracles, but because he will endure without disgust the nearness of a wild creature which will smell disgustingly and cover him with its droppings.[22]

This insight into the ideology of the cosmic continuum is dramatic in the best sense; it not only avoids clichés about divinity, but manages to suggest that it is right under our noses, stultified though they are. Instead of unstopping our ears to the music of the spheres, Lévi-Strauss opens our nasal passages. Moreover, this insight picks up another theme of the book, that of the ministrations of nature which, because of alienation and repulsion, we fail to recognize: *e.g.*, the worms that infest a wounded man's hand turn out, providentially, to save the man an amputation or death by eating away the gangrenous flesh from the wound as it putrifies.[23]

No doubt Lévi-Strauss's unwritten play was efficaciously caused by his struggle with his own repulsions, which—being those of a fastidious Frenchman living "in the bush"—must have been considerable. The eagle in the play pointedly remarks to Augustus that "any patch of ground will seem to you good enough to lie on: you will not think of it, as you do now, as prickly, swarming with insects, and certainly infectious." But here we find a theme that complicates the first one. Elsewhere Lévi-Strauss tells us that his favorite Indians, the Nambikwara, are among the only ones in South America so primitive that they don't even make hammocks. They sleep on the ground, and the other Indians call them a name expressing that fact.[24] So they are animals among other animals, and yet, as the eagle asserts, they are also gods. But in this equation the human is left out: only a god or an animal can be wholly free from alienation.

22. *Ibid.*, 378.
23. *Ibid.*, 348.
24. *Ibid.*, 378 and 268–69.

Thus Lévi-Strauss in effect acknowledges the inevitability of man's alienation as a function of his self-consciousness. When the psalmist wrote, "What is man that Thou art mindful of him?" he implied that God's mindfulness of man was a mystery, but a being who is aware of himself in this way is not the same as other creatures: he is "a little lower than the angels."

To us the Nambikwara seem neither animals nor gods, but children, who are also unfastidious about nature. Indeed the love of children for pets, zoos, bugs and worms, and even animal cartoons expresses one of the obvious roots of the mythological consciousness. We would be mistaken to impute stunted growth to the Nambikwara—though Lévi-Strauss reluctantly suggests they may be decadent—[25]but we would be equally wrongheaded to assume that their habits reveal the "natural" or "true" state of man, and still less any "sacramental" state. Their ideology avoids the problem of self-consciousness by imputing a vaguely human quality to everything: in other contexts, we would call it "the pathetic fallacy."

Here the ironies in *Tristes Tropiques* turn back on themselves, for it is not so much a book that establishes a new view of "primitives" as an expression of the dilemma of secularized but self-critical Western man. Lévi-Strauss will not admit that the assumptions of his own criticisms are taken ultimately from the prophets. He tries to argue that self-castigating insights in the West derive solely from "remorse."[26] If we criticize ourselves more harshly than any other society, we must deserve it: the implication is clear, though not overly logical. But in fact are we not more open than most societies? Straying from strictly defined folkways is virtually unthinkable in "archaic" societies, except for irregular deviant groups. If these societies develop few traditions of self-criticism, is it not because they sense that their kind of stability can tolerate no question-

25. *Ibid.*, 271.
26. *Ibid.*, 388; cf. p. 78. To be sure, he contends that the value of criticism (and anthropology) is not to have us live up to "natural man" as a standard, but to help us "disentangle" ourselves from our society in order to envision a just one. Yet his belief that Rousseau is the source of this insight is curious, to say the least. See Octavio Paz, *Claude Lévi-Strauss: An Introduction*, trans. J. S. and Maxine Bernstein (Ithaca, N. Y.: Cornell University Press, 1970), 101.

ing of social patterns? Whereas our culture, following the Hebrews, seems to have learned to find a certain stability in self-questioning, balance in motion, permanence in change. Our symptomatic sin is rapacity, the typical excess of a society that cannot curb the projects of desire by establishing narrow changeless channels for them. For us, as Ivan Karamazov says, all is permitted: and our remorse is not so much real guilt as anxiety over this vertiginous freedom.

In evading these points Lévi-Strauss follows Rousseau into another profound error, that of contrasting the "indolence of the primitive state and the questing activity to which we are prompted by our *amour-propre*."[27] Why should self-satisfaction cause questing? Surely it would rather cause indolence. Our *amour-propre* is in fact most precarious, and the questing like the remorse comes mostly as an over-compensation.

Lévi-Strauss can no more come to terms with these contradictions than with his own "objectivity." He wants to be the pure scientist, rebuking Western society for its alienations, but he cannot admit that alienation is part of the process of being able to detach ourselves from our society so as to see the values in the others.

SACRED SPACE AND AUTOCHTHONY

> Mountains and creeks and springs and waterholes are, to [the Aranda native], not merely interesting or beautiful scenic features . . . they are the handiwork of ancestors from whom he himself has descended. He sees recorded in the surrounding landscape the ancient story of the lives and deeds of the immortal beings whom he reveres; beings, who for brief space may take on human shape once more; beings, many of whom he has known in his own experience as his fathers and grandfathers and brothers, and as his mothers and sisters. The whole countryside is his living, age-old family tree.
>
> —T. G. H. Strehlow

27. Levi-Strauss, *Tristes Tropiques*, 390. In the end, what we see in Lévi-Straus is the pattern Paul de Man calls "blindness and insight." See Paul de Man, *Blindness and Insight: Essays in the Rhetoric of Contemporary Criticism* (New York: Oxford University Press. 1971), esp. 14–19.

Lévi-Strauss, who quotes this passage, remarks that its author was "an ethnologist born and brought up among the natives, speaking their language fluently and remaining deeply attached to them. He can be suspected of neither incomprehension nor ill-will."[28] Strehlow's words show us why the cosmic continuum does not stop at "animate matter," but goes on to affirm that stone and soil can have life and sacredness. If this seems extravagant, we can remember Thorkild Jacobsen's remark that our trouble in understanding myth stems from "our inability to 'commune' with matter and the powers that inform it." He goes on: "In the world of myth there is one common level of dignity and the powers in things are not stripped, by being of things, of claim on our emotional response. Rather, these powers in things and phenomena have their own dignity on a par with, often even higher than, that of man."[29]

Loving and detailed knowledge of their environmental landscapes by primitives and ancients is well known. The Bushmen are said to know "every bush and stone, every convolution of the ground," and to have names for every food place, however sparse, in "an area of hundreds of square miles." One commentator on them observes: "They do not read or write, but they learn and remember. If all their knowledge about their land and its resources were recorded and published, it would make up a library of thousands of volumes. Such knowledge was as essential to early man as it is to these people."[30]

For Lévi-Strauss such knowledge expresses an innate tendency to classify and systematize which goes far beyond the demands of immediate need or use, and so a connection between landscape and

28. Lévi-Strauss, *The Savage Mind*, 235–36.
29. Jacobsen, *Toward the Image of Tammuz*, 60–61; see note 40 to Chapter One.
30. Elizabeth Marshall Thomas, quoted and elaborated by John E. Pfeiffer, *The Emergence of Man* (New York: Harper, 1969), 135. Cf. G. S. Kirk, *Myth: Its Meaning and Function in Ancient and Other Cultures* (New York and Berkeley: Cambridge and University of California Presses, 1970), on "charter myths": "When the Trobriand islanders tell each other myths about clan origins, they are not only instructing the adolescents in the essentials of the tribal tradition, they are also restating, often on a solemn and regular occasion, their claim to particular ancestral lands and objects. Their tribal ancestors were literally autochthonous; according to the origin myths they emerged from the earth at the very spot at which the tribe is centered" (p. 256).

sacred order is in his view a typical development. "A native thinker makes the penetrating comment that 'All sacred things must have their place.' . . . It could even be said that being in their place is what makes them sacred for if they were taken out of their place, even in thought, the entire order of the universe would be destroyed. Sacred objects therefore contribute to the maintenance of order in the universe by occupying the places allocated to them."[31] If this argument is too abstract to explain what he calls "mythical geography and totemic topography," we can easily think of more empirical motivations.

Man in his early forms had to respond to territoriality in the animal, quite apart from any question of his own instincts. Whether hunter or collector he adapted very watchfully to the patterns of animal movements and to the establishments of ranges and lairs, for defensive reasons at the very least. Long before he hunted the great herd animals, he had to know their movements to avoid trailing predators. As variety in diet developed, immediate interest in a broad range of animals and plants multiplied and demanded still more careful sensitivity to locale and landscape. But Lévi-Strauss is probably right that the immediate interests would have been dwarfed by intellectual ones. With the curiosity typical of primates but magnified in man, the early hunters in thousands of years would observe all that was observable in their habitats and would accumulate the knowledge through speech and finally through myth, where the features of the landscape become sacralized.

In one sense, ancient religion is a form of geography. As a rule it organized space into sacred configurations, to which our notion of neutral rectilinear dimensions is wholly foreign. The nuclei are, or become, shrines, altars, oracles; and these sometimes form a network of chthonic cults, venerations of ground-dwelling or place-bound spirits and demons, such as Jane Harrison found to underlie the Olympian pantheon.[32] Before Zeus and his relatives came, Greece was full of sacral powers embodied in groves, springs, and

31. Lévi-Strauss, *The Savage Mind*, 10.
32. See Jane Harrison, *Prolegomena to the Study of Greek Religion* (1903; 3rd ed., 1922; rpt. New York: Meridian, 1955).

caves. The detritus of these traditions lay scattered long after the Olympians absorbed most of their functions: the *genius loci* was acknowledged to the end of classical paganism, and beyond. Some evidence points to the origin of the cults of place in primeval caves, which seem to have been thought to be pockets opening directly into a realm of mysterious power. With these sites as nodes, the whole landscape could be transfigured in association with them.

Very likely the veneration of caves sprang from the fact that powerful animals used them. The Greek word *ethos*, which came to mean "personal behavior-pattern" or "influence of character," and is of course the root of the word *ethics*, originally may have meant "the 'lair' or 'haunt' of an animal," according to Eric Havelock.[33] Paleolithic man's motivation for seeking cave-dwellings would then seem to have more to do with appropriation of the animals' mysterious powers than with a simple need to get out of the rain. The caves (and the hearths, dancing-floors, burial places, and storage-pits that were later established within them) must have been laden with sacred significance: all such areas were enclosures of magic powers. Almost all scholars infer the existence of elaborate rituals in the caves, and most connect the cave-art with these. Rachel Levy extrapolates persuasively from these early practices, linking up shrines, altars, labyrinths, temples, and finally pyramids and ziggurats as forms of the cave *redivivus*.

The cave is a direct link to the animal tradition of the mythological consciousness, but springs and groves too would be chthonic. As Lévi-Strauss insists, savage thought is systematizing and totalizing, and religious mythology may inform every feature of the landscape. "In this respect the Penobscot of Maine . . . interpret all the physiographic aspects of the tribal territory in terms of the peregrinations of the civilizing hero Gluskabe and other mythical personages or incidents. An elongated rock is the hero's canoe, a streak of white rock represents the entrails of the moose he killed, Kineo mountain is the overturned cooking pot in which he cooked his meat, etc."[34] Hence the giant-in-the-landscape traditions that James

33. Havelock, *Preface to Plato*, 63.
34. Lévi-Strauss, *The Savage Mind*, 166

Joyce and William Carlos Williams worked into *Finnegans Wake* and *Paterson* respectively are traces of a widespread habit of the human mind.

Even in the relatively demythologized Western culture, we find enough vestigial remnants of attitudes proper to sacred space to infer what it must have meant to mythological man. Our monumental building, though secularized, owes much to the techniques discovered by early man to make his sacred places permanent fixtures: the erection of great stones, the "megalithic" technique that produced Stonehenge, is an ancestor of the ingenuities by which we built, first, cathedrals, and, later, skyscrapers and other monuments intended to designate the seats of power and to overawe the populace. An ironic completion of a cycle is effected by at least one serious proposal for the redesign of cities: in this plan, all houses and buildings would be buried in artificial hills, and would have hillside entrances, to provide the benefits of city and rolling parkland in the same place. In effect we would return to the caves.[35]

Our emotional attachments and repulsions to places tell us on what psychological events the ideology of sacred space was founded. Ancients and primitives might want to know why we don't recognize that such states as vertigo on heights, claustrophobia, and agoraphobia (fear of open spaces) testify to the psychic powers of location in landscape. The fact is that we do mythologize space, but individualistically and in unstable, short-lived forms. Changing tastes in where to live, how to garden, where to find recreation, and how to travel all represent mythologizations, but relatively unsystematic ones. During the "Dark" and Middle Ages the rectilinear four points of the compass were somewhat redeemed from barren neutrality by sacramental mythology. The North was the land of devils and witches, the South the direction of Grace; the East was the land of births and origins, and the West of course decline: "to go West" still may serve as a euphemism for *die*. In many areas of medieval Europe, mythologization went far beyond this.[36]

35. Pfeiffer, *The Emergence of Man*, 445.
36. See, for some medieval legends, George Every, *Christian Mythology* (London: Hamlyn, 1970), esp. 115–20. Cf. Paul Shepard, *Man in the Landscape: A*

But the Hebrews fought against this sacramental tradition of ancient man. Yahweh, who was never localized, claimed the whole of the Promised Land as his (Lev. 25:23), and thus dispossessed all the chthonic spirits. (Some of the legends of Genesis seem to reflect his earlier absorption of a few of the better-known *elohim* or local deities.) Holy ground occurs only where, and when, he appears. Neither Sinai nor the Temple represents more than a halfhearted attempt to give Yahweh a local habitation; ambivalence toward the latter will be discussed later. In short, there are only the slightest traces of a chthonic aspect to Israel's tradition, and these are almost exclusively pre-Exodus: on the other hand, many signs of compulsive "displacement" and decentering occur. In the Deuteronomic reform of 621 B.C., even orthodox Yahwist shrines in the countryside were declared idolatrous, because they reflected the pagan practice of venerating sacred places.

A variant of the ideology of sacred space especially fateful for the Bible is the concept of autochthony, which arose out of the "confusion" of earth's fertility with that of women and animals. Literally the belief is that man can be born out of the ground, but the more prevalent forms stress the belief that conception takes place in a woman largely or entirely through the agency of particular sacred places or plants, or spirits belonging to them. Some present-day examples are given by Lévi-Strauss in *The Savage Mind*:

[The Arabanna believe that] in mythical times (*ularaka*) the totemic ancestors placed the spirit-children (*maiaurli*) in the totemic places. The Aranda have an equivalent belief. But, whereas among the Aranda the spirits regularly return to their place of origin to await a new incarnation, Arabanna spirits change their sex, moiety, and totem at each successive incarnation. . . . [Among the Aranda] totemic affiliation is deter-

---

Historic View of the Esthetics of Nature (New York: Knopf, 1967), esp. 38 ff.; Shepard's remarks on Christian voyaging could be extended by the use of such works as Carl Sauer's *Northern Mists* (Berkeley: University of California Press, 1968) and others. Also, Giedion should be consulted (*Eternal Present*, II, 436 ff.) on the vertical as the sacred; and Lévi-Strauss, in *Tristes Tropiques*, 126, makes several illuminating comments. Finally, it would be easy to show how the Mercator and similar maps have governed our expectations (by contrasting Buckminster Fuller's Dymaxion map, for instance).

mined not by a rule of descent but by the place at which a woman happens to be when she becomes conscious of her pregnancy.

. . . .

In Aurora, on the other hand . . . the future mother . . . believes that a coconut, a bread-fruit tree or some other object is mysteriously connected with the child, who will be a sort of echo of it. Rivers found the same beliefs in Mota where many people observe food prohibitions because they believe themselves to be an animal or fruit which their mother found or noticed while she was pregnant.[37]

The examples irresistibly suggest that hackneyed jokes about the offspring of women psychically influenced by animals or events (a fat man's mother must have been frightened by an elephant, etc.) probably derive from late-blooming folk beliefs once held quite seriously.

The concept of autochthony gave rise to an anthropological controversy as to the existence of groups ignorant of the facts of physical paternity. Edmund Leach surveys the evidence, under the provocative title "Virgin Birth," and concludes that "theology" rather than "ignorance" produces native belief that copulation is not the efficient cause of childbirth.[38] (Man is a species, in contrast to animals for whom "one copulation may, and usually does, secure a whole litter of offspring," in which "ten or a hundred matings may take place with only a single offspring [or none]. . . . Thus in man the continuous sexual life [as opposed to estrus cycles] is secured at the expense of about a hundred times as much production of sperm by the male and a hundred times as much sexual activity as is needed for the reproduction of a species with a cyclical mating activity." Man's "sperm-redundancy" is enormous. Hence the assumption that spiritual factors are determinative in conception and childbirth would certainly seem natural to pre-scientific man. Even Charles Darwin believed that conception was the action of masses of sperm.[39])

37. Lévi-Strauss, *The Savage Mind*, 81, 76.
38. In Leach, *Genesis as Myth*, 94, 108–10.
39. C. D. Darlington, *The Evolution of Man and Society* (New York: Simon and Schuster, 1969), 48–49 and 64.

As Leach puts it, "From many sources we learn of legends, traditions, ritual practices which seem to imply a belief that women may
sometimes be made pregnant by means other than insemination by
a human male. . . . If we are to understand such stories we need to
consider them all together as variations on a single structural
theme."[40] If there is only one structure to these stories, autochthony
might well claim a place as a unifying element, and would often
lead to mythological statements that man is born out of particular
spots of ground. Thus autochthony could not only rationalize much
fruitless intercourse, but it could also explain the differences between people of different regions.

Autochthony must have received powerful reinforcement from
the development of agriculture, and it cannot be coincidental that
in the Bible farming is not a gift but a curse. Although almost all
the Hebrews in historical times were farmers, their preferred self-
image was that of seminomad shepherds. At the Fall, God deprives
the soil of creativity, so that its fruits can be brought forth only
precariously, with grueling labor (the old Hebrew territory was
the least arable in the Palestine area). But autochthony has roots
that precede agriculture; not only is the magical fertility of soil observable in the case of wild plants, but worms and other small creatures can also be "observed" being born out of the Great Mother.
(As we know, this belief—with the help of Aristotle's authority—
slipped into Western tradition and persisted past the Middle Ages.)
To include human birth among the powers of "significant soil" is
simply an extension enshrined in many familiar mythologies: in the
Greco-Roman stories of Cadmus and Deucalion, men grown from
stone or dragons' teeth spring out of the ground, and Lévi-Strauss
suggests that the whole "Theban" complex of myths concerns this
belief.

In analyzing the Oedipus myth central to this complex, Lévi-
Strauss carefully dissociates the validity of his method from that of
his interpretation, asserting that his "demonstration" is like that
of the "street peddler, whose aim is not to achieve a concrete result, but to explain, as succinctly as possible, the functioning of the

40. Leach, *Genesis as Myth*, 107, 109.

mechanical toy which he is trying to sell to the onlookers."[41] Nonetheless, his conclusions can hardly be casual. He proposes that the "persistence" and the "denial" of "the autochthonous origin of man" are two of the four elements that hold one another in tension in the essential structure of the Oedipus stories:

The myth has to do with the inability, for a culture which holds the belief that mankind is autochthonous (see, for instance, Pausanias, VIII, xxix, 4: plants provide a model for humans), to find a satisfactory transition between this theory and the knowledge that human beings are actually born from the union of man and woman. Although the problem obviously cannot be solved, the Oedipus myth provides a kind of logical tool which relates the original problem—born from one or born from two?—to the derivative problem: born from different or born from same? By a correlation of this type, the overrating of blood relations [incest, suicidal loyalty to family, etc.] is to the underrating of blood relations [patricide, fratricide] as the attempt to escape autochthony is to the impossibility to succeed in it.[42]

This analysis would suggest that the stories are related to a crisis, a cultural watershed in which autochthony was losing relevance. The solution to the problem was a myth: the anguish of "what to believe?" was assuaged by a subtly compelled assent to contradictions. In contrast, the Hebrews don't try to hold contrary beliefs in suspension. Instead of mediating with a myth, the Bible insists on deracination from the spirit of place. Perhaps it is indicative that in the Septuagint, the Greek translation of the Old Testament, the word *autochthon* designates the hated "native," *i.e.*, Canaanite.[43] The Hebrews carefully and revealingly preserved traditions emphatically asserting that they were not native to the Promised Land, but were journeyers to it.

THE CULT OF THE DEAD

In terms of major cultural achievements, perhaps the most important of late glacial times was the sudden emergence of a belief

41. Lévi-Strauss, *Structural Anthropology*, 209.
42. *Ibid.*, 212.
43. William F. Albright, *Archaeology and the Religion of Israel* (New York:

in a life after death, which is recorded for the prehistorian in the many burials of the dead with accompanying clothing, decoration, food and weapons.

—J. N. Coles and E. C. Higgs,
The Archaeology of Early Man

> I have not eaten any bread of mourning;
> I have consumed nothing that was unclean;
> I have offered nothing to the dead.
> I have obeyed the voice of Yahweh my God
> and I have done all as you commanded me.
> —Deut. 26:14

For primitive man at least, a cemetery is a preeminently sacred and fertile place. As Strehlow's work indicates, sacred geography is likely to be part of a monumental recycling ideology, in which the ancestors embodied in landscape return in the form of near relatives. Since these ancestors are often totemic or animal, the cosmic continuum shows itself in still another form. Here it reconciles chronology as well as ontology, turning what would be for us a "historical" or diachronic problem (the ancestors) into a synchronic one. The ancestors continue to exist, and become functioning parts of the great mythological system. Time as well as space is a sacred continuum. Eras are inalienable from each other, not separated by unbridgeable gaps: what the ancestors did then, the native does now. "In his myths we see the native at his daily task of hunting, fishing, gathering vegetable food, cooking, and fashioning his implements. All occupations originated with the totemic ancestors; and here, too, the native follows tradition blindly: he clings to the primitive weapons used by his forefathers, and no thought of improving them ever enters his mind."[44] Lévi-Strauss comments on such use of the past by "cold" societies: "There is indeed a before and an after, but their sole significance lies in reflecting each other."

Anchor, 1969), 122–23, 210. See also, on Hebrew resistance to sacred places, Walter Harrelson, *From Fertility Cult to Worship* (New York: Doubleday, 1969), 36–37.

44. Lévi-Strauss, *The Savage Mind*, 235. Cf. Ezek. 20:18—"Do not live by your ancestors' standards, do not practice the observances they practiced, do not defile yourself with their idols."

As Barthes put it, myth turns history into nature, making established orders seem inevitable and unquestionable.[45] The mythological consciousness worships nothing remote; our sense of the distant past appears to reflect an alienated sense of history.

Other authorities comment that "cold" societies look beyond appearances to a "hidden, timeless world" where the ancestors validate relations with nature. The native undergoing initiation "seeks to integrate himself, not merely into contemporary society but into the company of his ancestral spirits, and at the same time to enter into close communion with the underlying realities of his physical environment."[46] The cosmic continuum unites nature, and culture with nature, through the ceaselessly reborn ancestors. Myth is the vehicle for all the unifications, and it transmits social structures or breeding systems that appear as configurations of relationships among ancestors. Thus the "cold" society projects an image of perfect self-sufficiency, while the changes and borrowings that follow from cultural diffusion are retrospectively validated by new variations on ancestral themes in myths. The cult of the dead validates and symbolizes the whole process.

Perhaps the most expressive symbol of this unity of concepts is the Australian *churinga*, as described by Rachel Levy:

The churingas [are] incised or painted objects of wood or stone which were believed to hold in union divinity, animal and man—including the recent dead and those awaiting incarnation—and were shown to every initiate. . . . [They] were slabs of wood or stone within which the spiritual body of the "eternal uncreated" ancestor had been distributed when he touched the earth. They contained the souls of the unborn, and their presence in the waterhole, rock or tree, which was the point of divine entry to this world, caused passing women to conceive.[47]

Thus the cult of the dead merges with autochthony. Such mergers are latent in any case throughout the varying forms of the mythological consciousness.

45. Barthes, *Mythologies*, 129.
46. Grahame Clark and Stuart Piggott, *Prehistoric Societies* (Harmondsworth: Penguin, 1965), 106.
47. Levy, *The Gate of Horn*, 37, 46.

The contrast to Hebrew society is stark. Hebrew attitudes toward such recycling were, at the most generous, ambivalent and, at the least, fiercely hostile; as the epigraph shows, they proscribed funerary cults. Yahwism rejects the culture-supporting, nature-embracing, space-sacralizing, and ancestor-reviving consciousness in general and in each particular. There are indeed traces of ancestor cults in some texts, especially in the Machpelah traditions, but these are comparatively demythologized. The key point is that the Bible insists that no one knows where Moses is buried.[48] For the Hebrews to discover (or create) the place would have meant an irresistible temptation toward all the mythologizing processes, beginning with a cult for the mighty hero. But they were not allowed to know where it was: perhaps the most decisive of all their negative knowledges. The lost or empty burial-place is a symbol that unites the two Testaments.

Many scholars have suggested a potential connection between careful and elaborate burial—signs of which go back beyond *homo sapiens* to Neanderthal man or earlier—and the belief in survival of ancestral spirits in particular places. Before the various Lands of the Dead were conceived, sacred spots—especially caves—contained the ghosts: as these places formed networks of chthonic cults, it would be assumed that the great realm of earth into which they commonly opened was the actual repository. (Our equivalent for place-bound ancestral spirits is again a joke-cliché, the haunted house: no doubt such staples of humor play for us the "mediating" role toward psychic problems that myth played for earlier men— another sign of the hard times on which mythology has fallen.) The form of many Paleolithic burials suggests a connection between the sacredness of the burial spot and the fertility-power of rebirth: corpses are bound in fetal positions, often stained with red ochre to restimulate blood or life. (Some suggest that the binding is not to induce birth, but to prevent the dead from threatening the living: but in either case the dead come back to life.) For these peoples "Mother Earth" was no figure of speech.

48. Deut. 34: 5–7. Significantly, they also had no cult at Sinai.

In general scholars agree that death was not "natural" for primitive man, but a positive force erupting into an otherwise endless existence. Thus it was a power to be worshiped, just as was fertility, and must similarly have been originally the prerogative of large dangerous animals. Hence the great doubleness or "ambiguity" of the sacred, the sense that the giving and taking of life were bound up together, reflected in sacrifice and related forms. Certainly by hunting times man had begun to envy the lethal powers of the animal-gods.

But this force of death does not extinguish beings; it only translates them into another state. The continuum concept works against total extinction: even the humblest animals were often thought to have surviving souls. For inextinguishability primitive man had plenty of evidence, most clearly in dreams: there the dead do after all appear, acting often in strange ways that betoken their new form of existence. The famous dream in the *Iliad,* in which Patroclus visits Achilles to give instructions and warnings, may be an archetype of human experience, for the dead in dreams often bring messages from the spirit world.[49] And since messages we hear in dreams often "come true," in one way or another, the powers of the spirit world (and the possibilities of divination) are triumphantly validated.

In many primitive ideologies the powers of these spirits of the dead convey the fact that they have themselves become numens. Actual worship of ancestors as gods is not universal, but in the parts of the world that gave birth to the Bible the sacredness of the afterlife dwarfs that of the present life, particularly in mighty Egypt. Typical of the fantastically elaborate mortuary cult of Egypt was the necropolis, the city of tombs. The very cosmology of Egypt explains why many Egyptians in fact spent their lives in virtual servitude to the dead. Once again, the Egyptians carried on the primeval tradition with fervent care and great elaboration, and their anxieties about its continuation caused them to exaggerate it and finally to rigidify it.

49. *Iliad,* XXIII, 59–107. The appearance of the dead in dreams of the kind described by Jacquetta Hawkes (note 19), involving human-animal metamorphosis, might contribute still more to totemic concepts.

The animal cult was involved in the mortuary cult too: S. Giedion links the "reverent" animal burials of the Magdalenian period (preserved in bone engravings that go back to a period before any depiction of human burials) with animal mummification in Egypt. Precisely because animal mummies are so numerous, they have been slighted by archaeologists, says Giedion: "The excavators simply leave them among the rubbish." But in some sites animals were buried with greater care than humans and were "richly accompanied with grave-utensils." Another relation of the two cults is found in the practice of including animal-symbols among the grave-utensils: "The frog—like the snake—being a chthonic creature seemingly emerging from the earth, was a symbol of nascent and ever-renewed life. Its great fertility bound it to the goddess of birth, and possibly to the fertility-god Min. When placed in a grave it gave assurance of life in the hereafter."[50] Other cultures had other chthonic animals: in some places the mud-loving pig, which may partly explain the Hebrew abhorrence of pork. The snake needs no further comment than the Eden story.

Egypt's example was a powerful deterrent to the growth of potential Hebrew burial cults. But Palestine itself was full of survivals of such practices, perhaps going back to the Stone Age of Mount Carmel. Not too many miles from this mountain is Jericho, the world's oldest town. When Kathleen Kenyon supervised excavations there, she found striking emblems of the worship of the dead:

In the debris beneath the floor of one of the houses of the Pre-Pottery B stage [ca. 7000–6000 B.C.] there came to light a deposit of seven human skulls. Later two other similar skulls were found in another room of the same house. The lower part of these skulls had been covered with plaster, moulded into the likeness of human features. Each head has a most individual character, and one cannot escape the impression that one is looking at real portraits. The eyes are inset in shells. In the cases of six of the heads, the eyes are made of ordinary bivalve shells, with a vertical slit between two sections giving the appearance of the pupil. The seventh head had cowrie shells, and the horizontal opening of the shells gives him a distinctly sleepy expression. [In other parts of the world cowrie

50. Giedion, *Eternal Present*, II, 33, 41, 35.

shells are fertility symbols, seemingly because of their resemblance to the female vulva.]

. . . .

Moreover, as successive layers were excavated in all the different areas, skeletons were found from which the cranium had been removed. Though a corresponding number of plastered skulls was not found, it is clear that the removal of crania from burials was a regular practice; it is possible that they were removed to some central repository or shrine, which has not been located. It is therefore clear that the Jericho skulls are those of venerated ancestors and are not trophies.[51]

Some authorities may have been cautious at first about Miss Kenyon's conclusions, but none suggested real alternatives. That the skulls might have been war-trophies Miss Kenyon discounted because "too much loving care had been spent on them." Similarly, although they show amazing artistic skill, "totally unexpected at so early a date," merely aesthetic motives can be ruled out. Only in our alienated world has art been divorced from religion.

Why were heads particularly revered, aside from the preternatural human fascination with the face and its wonderfully expressive musculature? Among other possible causes, one tradition is especially relevant: the eating of brains. Although ancients did not share our belief that the brain is the sole intellectual-emotional organ, some evidence of great antiquity suggests that brains were consumed in order to give the dead and the living an interpenetrating identity. Lévi-Strauss refers to the possibility among today's primitives that "cannibalism and necrophagy are based upon the wish to annex for oneself the merits and capacities of the dead";[52] the

51. Kathleen Kenyon, *Archaeology in the Holy Land* (New York: Praeger, 1970), 52–54. The association of cowrie shells with fertility has been noticed before; see E. H. Gombrich. *Art and Illusion: A Study in the Psychology of Pictorial Representation* (2nd ed.; Princeton, N. J.: Princeton University Press, 1961), 110. Also, it has been suggested that possession of these skulls might have to do with title to land: see Kent Flannery in Peter J. Ucko, Ruth Tringham, and G. W. Dimbleby (eds.), *Man, Settlement and Urbanism* (London: Duckworth, 1972), 29. If so they might be related to the Biblical *teraphim,* Rachel's "household gods" that she stole, presumably, to aid an inheritance claim. In I Sam. 19:13 Michal uses the *teraphim,* covered with goats' hair, as a facsimile of David in bed: that might fit the idea of a skull on some kind of base. See fig. 1.

52. Lévi-Strauss, *Tristes Tropiques,* 217; cf. 385-86.

practice also gives a new form of life to the dead: it expresses the recycling ideology.

F. M. Bergounioux has this to say about Choukoutien, site of the cave of the early hominid "Peking Man":

Skulls and jaws are present in such large numbers that one is led to assume that they were carried there intentionally. Furthermore, in four of these the occipital part was raised by successive fractures, as if there had been an attempt to reach the brain. This suggests funeral rites of the type known as "two stage," which were still observed among the Buginese on the south coast of the Celebes, before their conversion to Islam in the eighteenth century. The body of the deceased was carried far from the dwelling and left out in the open, sheltered from beasts of prey. When the body had dried out, the head could be detached easily, without the need even to cut the cervical vertebrae. (No vertebrae were found at Choukoutien.) The skull was then solemnly carried to the village, carefully washed, and became a kind of protective divinity of the family of the deceased . . . the brain was devoured by those who wished to assume the virtues and merits of the dead man.[53]

Another authority, Alberto C. Blanc, notes further parallels in Borneo, Melanesia, and New Guinea:

In certain tribes of New Guinea a newborn child receives a name only after the killing and beheading of a man whose name is known. The father or a near relative mutilates the base of the skull of the victim, extracts its brain, bakes it with sago, and eats it, after which the infant may bear the name of the dead one. The mutilated skull is kept as a sacred object. . . . This gruesome custom is practiced by tribes that are not particularly bloodthirsty or aggressive and have rather high morals; the ritual cannibalism is performed as a strict obligation toward the community, on the one hand, and the new born, on the other. When the Dutch government tried to stop this tradition, the tribes revolted. Their argument was: "We have to give names to our children, and how could we handle it otherwise?"[54]

Blanc believes that the ancient "Mousterian" culture, which we associate with Neanderthal man, may have preserved ritual brain-

53. F. M. Bergounioux, "Notes on the Mentality of Primitive Man," in Sherwood L. Washburn (ed.), *Social Life of Early Man* (Chicago: Aldine, 1961), 114.

54. Alberto C. Blanc, "Some Evidence for the Ideologies of Early Man," in Washburn (ed.), *Social Life of Early Man*, 126.

eating for a quarter of a million years, giving us a titanic demonstration of the freezing power of the "cold" society: "The 'Mousterian' culture has persisted, practically unchanged, for a long time, while the somatic characters of the races that produced it have evolved and changed very definitely during the same period of time. In other words, the cultural features of the 'Mousterian' culture appear to have been far more stable than the somatic features of their bearers."[55] It is wrenching for us to try to think of culture in terms of such eons. We may go from horse-cart to moon-rocket in less than a century, but our way is still unproved: it must bow in awe before ways of thought that stood the test of such unimaginable stretches of time. Indeed the mythological consciousness, in examples like these, seems able to abolish time, or at least make it stand still.

MEGALITHISM

> In ancient times, building was considered a sacred task. . . . Building linked man with god.
>
> —S. Giedion

In his earliest work with structures of rearranged stone, man "confused" the activities of burial, food-preparation, ritual enactment, and provision of shelter. These ideologically continuous practices were organized around sacred sites, marked with stones, in the caves. Later men re-created the cave outdoors with special techniques for raising giant stones, "megaliths," into erect positions; these techniques were invented and passed on before writing and make no use of the wheel, metals, or other technological advances without which we could not dream of duplicating such feats. Over and over around the globe these mighty labors took place; the techniques involved were presumably passed around by the sacred transmission vehicle, myth.

It was once believed that the megalithic structures must have been, in effect, unsophisticated copies of more advanced construc-

55. *Ibid.*, 131.

tions like the pyramid and ziggurat. Mediterranean trade and influence is known to have extended to northern Europe, where some of the most impressive of these structures are, at a very early date: therefore it was assumed that megalithism was a late-comer. But this assumption has recently been challenged, for new methods of radioactive dating, adjusted by tree-ring chronology, suggest that the European megaliths are older than the pyramids.[56] Exactly what the "megalithic culture" in prehistoric Europe was, and whether it passed on building techniques to the rest of the world, is not positively known. But Stonehenge is in any case a mind-boggling example of the open-air temple that appropriates the chthonic functions of the cave and "confuses" them with astral powers. We know now that Stonehenge and other sites were complicated astronomical observatories. Still more important, the megalithic erections signify a formidable new development in the primeval conceptions of sacred space: for the first time, man was able to *impose* a permanent configuration to dominate the landscape. Though ties to nature were still close, they were more obviously honorary; and human will became a heightened power, along with human pride. In fact megalithism represents a new phase of alienation, requiring still more mythological energy to hide it.

The great megalithic forms express the combining of traditions in various ways. Rachel Levy asserts that a dolmen is "at once a table of offering and an earth-covered gateway to the world of the dead." Many of the structures are explicitly tombs; others are *hypogea*, sacred cellars that sometimes become independent structures, with chthonic association. Miss Levy connects all of the forms with stone altars rising out of the earth. The oil or blood poured over altars symbolizes, she says, the great function of taking life and giving it— back to the earth, and to the worshipers as well—in the typical sacrificial enactment of the "ambiguity of the sacred." She also compares the stone structures to pillars and columns, and relates these

56. See Colin Renfrew, "Carbon 14 and the Prehistory of Europe," in C. C. Lamberg-Karlovsky (ed.), *Old World Archaeology: Foundations of Civilization* (San Francisco: Freeman, 1972), 206–207. See also Colin Renfrew, *Before Civilization: The Radiocarbon Revolution and Prehistoric Europe* (New York: Knopf, 1973).

in turn to sacred trees and even stalagmites in caves. In Palestine, where dolmens and altars also occur, the Canaanite shrines contained stone pillars embodying male divinity (*massebôth*) and wooden poles embodying female divinity (*asherim*).[57]

The connection between stone and sacred fatality is not hard to grasp, since stone is so obviously a source of weaponry, but we may have some trouble linking stone to fertility concepts. Yet it is widely attested in myth; again Deucalion comes easiest to mind: the stones flung over his shoulder sprang up as men. The South Pacific and Middle America were especially fertile in groups of men who identified themselves, and their reproductive powers, with stone. Very likely some of these traditions grew out of cults of stone implements whose original use had been forgotten. As the material with which man had hacked his way to ascendancy and civilization over a million-year period, stone could easily become generalized as an object of worship. Rachel Levy notes that some Papuans "keep large stone axes (whose practical use is forgotten) as fertility charms."[58] Decorative stone axes were used for ritual purposes in many societies long after flint had been replaced by metal. Sometimes the relations between ritual and practical uses became weirdly backward. In the Mesopotamian delta, where there were no stones or metal, men made and venerated clay models of axes, "which copy stone forms which themselves reproduce types proper to cast metal."[59] (These nonfunctional axes betoken the conservatism found in "cold" societies: sacred materials and techniques persist even when conditions change and they are no longer suitable. Grahame Clark and Stuart Piggott find, in the cut and joining of early Scandinavian clothing, "a textile-made garment still preserving, in its anomalies of pattern, complications necessary only in the skin prototype.")[60] Per-

57. See Levy, *The Gate of Horn*, 126, 106, 124–29; also, Roland de Vaux, *Ancient Israel*, Vol. 2, *Religious Institutions* (2 vols.; New York: McGraw-Hill, 1965), 285–86. The megalithic remains may have contributed to the Biblical legends of giants in the land (Anakim, Nephilim, etc.): see Gen. 6:4, Deut. 2:10 and 20–21, 3:11. Anati discusses megalithism at length in *Palestine Before the Hebrews*.

58. Levy, *The Gate of Horn*, 152. In several mythologies, "Flint" is a living being: cf. Frankfort *et al.*, *Before Philosophy*, 144–46.

59. Clark and Piggott, *Prehistoric Societies*, 179.

60. *Ibid.*, 309.

haps the clearest case of human embodiment in stone is that of the *churinga*, mentioned earlier. Lévi-Strauss insists that "each chu-ringa represents the physical body of a definite ancestor and genera-tion after generation, it is formally conferred on the living person believed to be this ancestor's reincarnation."[61] Rebirth of the an-cestors, once again, is the primary purpose of human fertility as mythological societies conceive it; though there be strength in num-bers, these societies rarely seem interested in increasing the popula-tion simply to promote "growth." Thus the *churinga*, though stone (or sometimes wood), is a fertility object *par excellence*: it fulfills the primary need of revivifying ancestors. By similar processes, per-haps, the great stone slabs of megalithic building became identified with fertility powers.

At first we may be surprised at the combination of chthonic and astral traditions in the megalithic cults. We are used to a notion of religious "evolution" that sharply distinguishes between earth-gods and sky-gods. But for ancient man these realms were not separately compartmentalized, but rather continuous. In many cosmologies, the sun and stars emerge from the earth and go back to it each day. Second, the collection of lore that became astronomy and astrology originally was tied to natural cycles of growth, just as farming and calendrical astronomy were to become intricately related later. The transition from the hunting rituals of the cave to the farming rit-uals of the open spaces doubtless involved the new astral lore; ac-cording to Rachel Levy, in Malekula and some other societies evi-dence shows that "the hunters' rites for promoting animal fertility and destruction have obviously been extended to assist the oscilla-tion of the seasons."[62] (Again the basic conservatism of the myth-ological consciousness shows through: the changes from hunting to farming were in fact revolutionary, but the preservation of ritual makes them appear continuous.) Recently a highly respected his-torian of science, Giorgio de Santillana, has lent his authority to the assertion that myth is basically a set of variations on themes

61. Lévi-Strauss, *The Savage Mind*, 238.
62. Levy, *The Gate of Horn*, 152.

provided by archaic but precise astronomical knowledge, especially the theme of the precession of the equinoxes.[63] Most students of myth doubt such sweeping claims on their face, remembering Max Müller's sun-myths; but whatever the truth Santillana's researches strongly suggest that the astronomical sophistication of certain esoteric traditions and societies in the ancient world far exceeds our patronizing expectations. Few doubt any longer that precise and complex observations and computations can be passed through generations without the use of alphabetic writing. It may be that many cultures supported and stabilized themselves with star-lore we can only laboriously re-create. Still more recently, Alexander Marshack has interpreted marks on Paleolithic bones as evidence of lunar-calendrical notation. Both hypothesis and evidence are under debate, yet many lines of speculation seem to be converging on a much earlier date than is generally assumed for ancient "writing."[64]

Because of its power to unite the chthonic and astral realms, the megalithic structure was often conceived as a world-tree, rooted in the earth and branching into the sky. Rachel Levy notes of the Sumerians:

At Nippur the temple was called "The House of the Mountain," but also, as at Larsa and Sippar, the "Bond of Heaven and Earth"; and because the king represented the God, his palace in Babylon was called "The Bond." . . . This bond, like the tree-pillar, connected the Heaven and Earth, and the Ziggurat was thus conceived as a kind of Jacob's ladder whose pathways were external, a stairway later mounting in a spiral from stage to stage; the Megalithic way of approach to the divine state here lifted toward the sky.[65]

At the same time the ziggurat commemorated the "lost ancestral mountain," on whose hilly flanks took place the so-called Neolithic

63. See Giorgio de Santillana and Hertha von Dechend, *Hamlet's Mill: An Essay on Myth and the Frame of Time* (Boston: Gambit, 1969).

64. See Alexander Marshack, *The Roots of Civilization: The Cognitive Beginnings of Men's First Art, Symbol, and Notation* (New York: McGraw-Hill, 1972).

65. Levy, *The Gate of Horn*, 169. It may be worth noting that the word *pharaoh* comes from a word meaning "great house." See Frankfort *et al.*, *Before Philosophy*, 85. This forecasts the imperialization through monumental building discussed in Chapter Three herein.

revolution (domestication of animals and plants, techniques of settled life) which allowed civilization to emerge later in the river
deltas; it also symbolized the " 'place of fertility' over a vast hollow,
the primeval cave where the dead dwell." [66] Thus the ziggurat foreshadows the cosmology of Dante's *Commedia*, which is our closest
approach to a mythological universe. Like the Tower of Babel, the
ziggurat therefore serves as an all-embracing image of the ideology
of the naturalizing cultures which the Bible rejected. No doubt
great traditions of esoteric knowledge, astronomical and other, faded
out when Bible prevailed over Babel. But—because of our alienated habit of seeking lost knowledge—they are not wholly gone.

MOTHER GODDESSES AND METAMORPHOSIS

My mistress with a monster is in love.
                                              —Puck

Fertility rites and symbols are too consciously involved in every concept of the mythological consciousness to need much outlining
here. In one sense, it suffices to say that the Bible sets its face against
all such practices and beliefs. Yahweh was the Father without a consort, one more in the series of great absences and emptinesses that
mark the true Biblical tradition. Fertility was in his mysterious
asexual control; no rites could induce it, though it might on rare
occasions be begged from him by sufficiently humble supplicants,
like Hannah. On the other hand he might grant it to a skeptic like
Sarah.[67] All the pagan idols and practices to induce and ensure (and
limit) fertility were banned and condemned by the Law. If we find
them popping up occasionally in the stories of David and others,
this only shows how hard a task Yahwism had in eradicating these
symbols: except in times of religious crisis, some of the population
would hoard little fertility idols, just as some Westerners today
keep rabbits' feet.[68]

66. *Ibid.*, 168: see the whole of that chapter.
67. I Sam. 1–2:21; Gen. 18:9–15.
68. I Sam. 19:11–17 (see above, note 51), Judg. 18:14, etc. For associations with
kings and sacrifice, see Hosea 3:4 and other prophetic texts.

Two issues in the fertility-concepts of the mythological consciousness are especially important for full understanding of the Biblical
context and reaction, and both of these have been strangely slighted
in the scholarly literature. The reason is not hard to grasp: both
involve what could be called bestial sodomy.

The earliest human figurines in Paleolithic art, by all accounts,
are almost invariably female. To this class of objects belongs the
well-known and representative "Venus of Willendorf," an appealing
but enormously obese little statue who coyly displays her mam-
moth bosom and *mons veneris*.[69] The pendulous breasts and bloated
hips make it hard to decide whether or not she is enormously pregnant, though most interpreters think she is. There is no face, no
hands or feet, but the head is covered with an abstract pattern that
may have some resemblance to ritually dressed hair. She is the
power of fertility in limestone form, shaped in the image of a
child's vision of the pregnant mother.

Aside from anthropocentrism, there is no reason to assume that
she has been made pregnant by a man. If the cultures that produced these figurines were autochthonous, as seems likely, then she
probably represents not fertility in general but the fertility of a particular place, which may have been sacralized as the lair of a powerful animal. There are images in the cave-art and other signs suggesting that the Venus-figures might actually have been thought of
as impregnated by animals. (We remember Leach's remark that
we have abundant evidence of beliefs "that women may sometimes
be made pregnant by means other than insemination by a *human
male*"—my italics.[70]) What more literal form could appropriation
take than a vision of marriage with animals?

We know what the animals do, what are the needs of the beaver, the bear,
the salmon, and other creatures, because long ago men married them and
acquired this knowledge from their animal wives. Today the priests say we
lie, but we know better. The white man has been only a short time in

69. See fig. 2. See discussions in Clark and Piggott, *Prehistoric Societies*, 70 ff.,
and Hawkes, *Prehistory*, 277 and 187. See Levy, *The Gate of Horn*, s.v. "Great
Mother," etc.

70. See note 40, above.

this country and knows very little about the animals; we have lived here thousands of years and were taught long ago by the animals themselves. The white man writes everything down in a book so that it will not be forgotten; but our ancestors married the animals, learned all their ways, and passed on the knowledge from one generation to another.[71]

This American Indian ideology seems related to those in present-day Australia and the ancient Near East, and in these ideologies animal marriage is a great sign of favor. The divine king in historic Egypt and Africa regularly claimed animal ancestry, as does the shaman wherever he occurs. In the well-known "palette" of Narmer, who is usually regarded as the first king of united Egypt, he is shown wearing a distinguishable tail. Narmer may have been preceded, however, by a king known to us only as Scorpion. Even the Romans, so much nearer to us in sensibility, were careful to provide Romulus and Remus with a she-wolf for a mother. Scipio Africanus claimed that his real father was a python, and this story was considered "aristocratic," probably because Alexander's mother said that he'd had similar begetting. (King Arthur's father was a "Dragon.")[72]

Thus animal marriage was a link to the primeval orderings of things, and those early figurines of pregnant human females who lack human consorts may have been married to the giant beasts on the cave walls. Only a few extant images seem unmistakably to represent such unions: one is a fragment of bone-engraving showing a pregnant woman lying on her back, next to the legs of a standing animal.[73] One of Rachel Levy's schematically reproduced cave-drawings seems to show a male and female about to copulate in animal attitudes; she calls it simply a "ritual dance"—true, no doubt, but not the point. Elsewhere she alludes skeptically to the "erotic" interpretation of certain drawings involving animals, but she does go so far as to suggest that in certain rituals "a 'sacred mar-

71. Lévi-Strauss, *The Savage Mind*, 37. As usual, myth is to primitives what writing is to the West: the latter is the Biblical paradigm.

72. For Narmer, see fig. 3. For Scipio *et al.*, see Darlington, *Evolution of Man*, 258, and Philip E. Slater, *The Glory of Hera: Greek Mythology and the Greek Family* (Boston: Beacon, 1968), 43 ff. Slater makes the obvious connection with maenadism.

73. See fig. 4.

riage' was performed on behalf of the beasts."[74] Surely it is equally likely, if the humans were in the cave to get hold of the animal powers in the first place, that such rituals were not so much intended to increase the animals as to effect through the women the rebirth of the ancestors who were, in many cases, totemic and half or wholly animal.

Miss Levy does tell us that in Athens the wife of the *archon basileus* mated Dionysus in a building called "the cattle shed." She quotes Jane Harrison: " 'The conjecture lies near to hand that in bygone days there was a marriage to a sacred bull.' "[75] The impelling evidence toward such conjectures is the population of mythology—especially Greek, Egyptian, and Sumerian—by hybrid creatures, mixtures of man and beast (or god). Queen Pasiphae, along with Io, Leda, Europa, and other heroines, becomes more interesting by the moment, and the "ox-eyed" Hera of Homer deserves new scrutiny, for her epithet may as easily mean "ox-faced." If so she is clearly the Greek equivalent of the Egyptian Hathor, who had the body of a woman and the head of a cow.[76]

Our automatic response is to find this topic repulsive, but we find that normative human attitudes do not agree with ours. In fact, repeated Biblical warnings instruct us against such "confusion" (Ex. 22:18; Lev. 18:23, 20:15–16; Deut. 27:21). Against what were the Biblical writers legislating, if the ritual miming of ancestral animal marriages were not a regular feature of pagan practice? In fact, this form of sexuality has always been known, especially in rural areas, and in those is considered about as abnormal as masturbation. On the other hand, the regularity of this animal-human interpenetration provided another demonstration of the unnaturalness of the naturalizing ideology. For nature does not exhibit such sexual intercourse between widely different species. Once again, man's anxiety about his potentialities for going beyond the forms

74. Levy, *The Gate of Horn*, 43–44.
75. *Ibid.*, 103.
76. For Hathor, see Giedion, *Eternal Present*, II, 77, 32, and Levy, *The Gate of Horn*, 119.

and habits of nature reveals itself in his projections, in this case of his sexual drives, back into nature: here in a grotesquely literal way. As usual the attempt to unify man and nature belies itself.

The great theme of metamorphosis throws light on these animal-human unions. Again, the conventional interpretations of cave-drawings are in question: Rachel Levy and others typically interpret figures combining human and animal features as "masked dancers." In many cases, however, this is manifestly impossible. There are two or three examples at least of "bisons with human hindquarters." The bison parts are almost certainly real bisons, not masks. In one, below the human knee a hoof seems to emerge: Giedion notes that this "hybrid continually changes its animal and human form from part to part and limb to limb."[77] We know that masked dancers often depicted such hybrids, but are the drawings merely depictions of depictions? Are they not more likely images of humans who can metamorphose into animals, the mythological offspring of the animal ancestors?

In the best-known example, the so-called "Dancing Sorcerer," several animals are combined on a human armature.[78] The horns and ears are reindeerlike (though one horn uncannily resembles an emerging hand), the eyes and beak (?) owllike, the tail horselike and the genitals too dangling to be normally human, perhaps feline. The hands look as if they're metamorphosing into flippers. A dancer could with immense trouble disguise himself in such a way, but the back of the figure is turning into the outline of a real stag. (The cave-artists must have been as finely attuned to animal outlines as aircraft spotters are to airplane shapes.)

By mythological expectations, the unions of humans with animals might produce human beings who can transform themselves into many shapes. In the ideology, these abilities are never wholly lost. Sorcerers and shamans, including Don Juan, claim the power to turn into animals. Metamorphosis emphasizes not the monstrosity of hybrids but the kinship that underlies all forms of life. Actual ob-

77. Giedion, *Eternal Present*, II, 61: see fig. 5.
78. See fig. 6; Hawkes, *Prehistory*, 186, and Levy, *The Gate of Horn*, 22–23.

servable metamorphosis, as in the life cycles of chthonic animals and insects, could only reinforce the idea that shape-changing is one of the powers occurring in the natural world. The interchangeability of forms, at its origins a key to autochthonic ideologies, recurs in many variants in later philosophies. Even Apuleius, though he treats it as a punishment, draws on the archaic traditions: whereas Ovid makes it the unifying theme of his "lost worlds." (Such forerunners of Western literary attempts to revive "myth" bear a similarity to the mystery cults and syncretized religions—Orphism, Mithraism, Gnosticism—and other attempts to revive the traditions of the slowly decaying mythological consciousness, which was being choked in the growth of syncretism, the very power that had spread it so far.[79])

Another twist on the conception is worth noting for its grim overtones. If animals and humans do not really mate, they do often eat each other, another visible sign of continuity. Funerary rites at the Neolithic settlement of Çatal Hüyük, as described by James Mellaart, featured "wall-paintings of vultures with human legs" attacking headless bodies; real skulls were found in baskets below large sculpted bulls' heads protruding through the walls. Here the conception seems to be that the carrion animals (and perhaps priestesses in vulture costume) assist the passage of the humans to death and rebirth; in other shrines goddesses are shown giving birth to rams' and bulls' heads. Mellaart's description of the variety in the art found at this site draws attention to the double aspect:

Scenes of life on one wall contrast with scenes of death on the other. A huge bull's head is frequently found emerging from the wall above a red

79. We meet here for the first time a paradox of success/failure often discussed later: the ingestion of new energies in Hellenistic syncretism finally satiated and then deracinated it. See, *e.g.*, Henry Bamford Parkes, *Gods and Men: The Origins of Western Civilization* (New York: Vintage, 1959), who notes that novelties in Hellenistic style "would not have happened if the traditional Hellenic culture had retained its vitality and its capacity for assimilating alien immigrants and resisting or absorbing alien influences" (p. 354). For a less pejorative view of Hellenism, however, see Frederick C. Grant (ed.), *Hellenistic Religions: The Age of Syncretism* (New York: Bobbs-Merrill, 1953). See also notes 1 and 2 to Chapter Three herein.

painted niche, perhaps symbolic for the netherworld. Other heads accompany the bulls and breasts are frequently shown in rows. In other cases women's breasts are carefully portrayed, but incorporate the lower jaws of wild boars, the skulls of fox, weasel or the griffon vulture, unmistakable symbols of death. Equally symbolic is the combination of bull's horn and woman's breast, both symbols of life.[80]

He also hypothesizes that all the female representations are one goddess with three aspects (youth, pregnancy, death) and that the male representations, animal and human, refer to two aspects of this goddess' consort: in his older form he is often portrayed on a bull, or "as a bull's or ram's head." Finally, the goddess also appears "as a stalactite or concretion with a human head which probably emphasizes her chthonic aspects related to caves and underworld."[81]

This goddess would appear to have a parallel among the "Stone Men" of Malekula (where corpses are also decapitated), whose Le-hev-hev is "sometimes imagined as a Rock, can be crab, spider, or megalopod, but is chiefly a formless evil, like the Babylonian Tiamat—the chaos which Marduk caught in his net of ordered creation."[82] (But she is also associated with boar and hawk.) Her function is to devour the dead who do not know how to complete a certain labyrinthine design, yet she also seems to have some role in rebirth. Here the fertility-fatality complex, or the ambiguity of the sacred, is mediated by the principle of metamorphosis.

Some similar ambiguity may underlie the Sumerian Imdugud, a lioness-headed eagle.[83] It forecasts the type which became a Mesopotamian specialty—winged lions and bulls, cherubim, sphinxes, and the like. Such beings are at once chthonic and astral, and also combine fertility and fatality. In addition to these, Mesopotamia presents us with an unusual variety of combinations: in one striking image from Ur, perhaps an illustration for the Gilgamesh epic, a scorpion with a human head is attended by an upright goat with

80. James Mellaart, *Earliest Civilizations of the Near East* (New York: McGraw-Hill, 1965), 96–97; cf. p. 101.   See also Mellaart's *Çatal Hüyük: A Neolithic Town in Anatolia* (New York: McGraw-Hill, 1967).

81. Mellaart, *Earliest Civilizations*, 96, 92.

82. Levy, *The Gate of Horn*, 155.

83. See fig. 7, and Giedion, *Eternal Present*, II, 55 ff.

human arms.[84] Hybridization and metamorphosis are strangely mixed here.

For the Bible the most immediately relevant Mesopotamian motif is the bull-man. His human features are not always noticed; I have long been familiar with a certain Sumerian bull, but for years I overlooked the fact that he has a human beard.[85] The cylinder-seals are especially rich in bulls and bull-men. The Bible itself tells us of the ubiquity of bull-divinities in the area. Having learned nothing from the story of the Golden Calf, if they knew it, the kings of Israel after Solomon worshiped Yahweh enthroned on bull-pillars (see I Kings 12:32), a common form from Çatal Hüyük to Canaan (whose El was also "father bull"). The more fiercely exclusivist Judahite writers condemned the northern compromise with idolatry, but the real point is that the bull-divinity association was so ingrained that the northern kings seem to have felt innocent of apostasy.

It has been suggested that the original domestication of cattle may have been for religious not nutritional purposes. We know now that "domestication" is a most problematic concept, perhaps usually involving magic and ritual.[86] In any case, the bull-cult continued for centuries to be the most familiar symbol of animal-power worship in the Mediterranean area. We know of its enthusiastic practice in Crete, where the Minotaur story is laid, and we know its importance in revivalisms like the cult of Mithra: when slain, Mithra's bull sprouts grain from its tail.[87] The bull was a useful choice for symbolism; he is at once a breathing image of raw and lethal force, yet manageable with relative ease. The cults could thus have long and varied developments with real animals in the rites: sometimes sacri-

84. See fig. 8.
85. He is part of the lyre on which the scorpion and bull-men appear; see fig. 9. The lyre is from the "Great Death Pit" of Ur.
86. See Carl Sauer, *Agricultural Origins and Dispersals* (New York: American Geographical Society, 1952), 84–96, esp. 88–93. The concept is discussed in Chapter Three herein.
87. See fig. 10; for a set of useful illustrations, see Arnold Toynbee (ed.), *The Crucible of Christianity* (New York: World, 1969), 248–52, and the discussion on p. 254.

ficed, sometimes merely worshiped, or in the version that survives today, engaged in ritual combat. The most tantalizing evidence comes from Crete, where we find representations of young dancers flinging themselves over the bull's back, jumping through or holding on to the horns. (The horn is of course a symbol of the power-source; nothing expresses the antiquity of the fertility-fatality complex better than a gravid "Venus," carved on a cave wall, holding a horn: perhaps the source of her pregnancy.[88]) The clue to the Cretan practice, or its rationale, may be in a figure interpreted by Rachel Levy as another "masked dancer": a being with human legs, insectlike abdomen, and bull forequarters is doing a backbend, so that it resembles the leaping youths, but is in effect jumping through its own horns![89] Clearly metamorphic, the figure brings us back with renewed curiosity to the Minotaur. If the labyrinth was not a place where captive maidens were turned loose to be found and trampled by a real bull, then perhaps its ritual involved a *hieros gamos* with the bull or even a bull-masked priest. In either case the girls were probably insensible of their privilege of serving as avatars of great Pasiphae. But Theseus was probably less a rescuer than a forerunner of Mithra, an appropriator of bull-power, in the original myth.

THE LOST WORLD

We do not trust the metamorphic nature of landscapes and bodies, being a literary rather than mythologically oriented people.
—Paul Shepard, *Man in the Landscape*

As poet I hold the most archaic values on earth. They go back to the Neolithic; the fertility of the soil, the magic of animals, the power-vision in solitude, the terrifying initiation and rebirth, the love and ecstasy of the dance, the common work of the tribe. A gas turbine or an electric motor is a finely-crafted flint knife in the hand.
—Gary Snyder

88. See fig. 11; Levy, *The Gate of Horn*, 59–60; and Chapter Four, herein, p. 229.
89. Levy, *The Gate of Horn*, 227–33.

Why "myth" has been so appealing to poets, since the late eighteenth century especially, is obvious. To discover myth is to apprehend a sense of hidden significance and continuity, to feel that one is stumbling on a treasury of lost and fascinating symbols, or even to discover that the whole world is a system of correspondences: in short, myth tantalizes us with the suggestion that the world is a language which, when illumined, we can learn to read. And, of course, the treatment of nature and man and god as a continuum helps resolve the poets' form of the perennial Western philosophic dilemma of subject and object: specifically, how can the individual subject have anything valid to say about what is outside him? Even fragments of the mythological ideology can help heal this alienation. But the most revealing use of myth by poets is as disguised criticism of their own society, for to affirm myth is to rebuke the West. Charles Olson puts most of the uses together in recommending what he calls "objectism," which is "the getting rid of the lyrical interference of the individual as ego, of the 'subject' and his soul, that peculiar presumption by which western man has interposed himself between what he is as a creature of nature (with certain instructions to carry out) and those other creations of nature which we may, with no derogation, call objects."[90] Here Olson, the most myth-minded poet of our times, chides alienation as presumptuous, which varies slightly from the usual condemnation of it as a curse. And he does not, like Lionel Trilling, frame the quarrel as one of self *vs.* culture: he goes a step further and sees that such an antinomy is precisely what is typical of our culture. But he takes the prophet's stance all the same.

There are obvious dangers in omnibus treatments of myth, whether by me or by the poets: here I may note simply that in taking myth as

90. Robert Creeley (ed.), *Selected Writings of Charles Olson* (New York: New Directions, 1966), 24 (originally published in 1950). Here Olson foreshadows the structuralist attack on "the subject": and even though he speaks in the name of "myth" and "nature," he helps make it clear that all such self-criticisms in the Western tradition recapitulate the prophetic denunciation of man's pretensions to autonomy. Lévi-Strauss says he believes the "ultimate goal of the human sciences to be not to constitute, but to dissolve man" (*The Savage Mind*, 247), and similar statements are made by Michel Foucault and Jacques Derrida. They are all indebted to the Yahwist vision.

a whole, the poets (and I) repeat the Hebrew pattern of lumping together "the nations." Of course the mythological ideology, either in my version or Gary Snyder's, never existed in the form of one particular group embodying all the traits—unless the recurrent myth is true, that all prehistoric belief and knowledge consisted of fragments left over from a lost Atlantis or other *Ur-kultur*.[91] The discovery of this source would be fascinating, but would not alter the Bible's role in relation to myth. Paul could denounce pagans with perfect assurance that they had all made variations on one mistake, exchanging the glory of the immortal Creator for a multitude of created forms.

The world of the pagan mind seems to us a glowing, magical, harmonic one. As with Christendom in the Middle Ages, each society, though using the forms differently, typically totalized them into comprehensive systems. There was an answer for every question: or if not, the question could be sacralized into a mystery, or a myth. There was intimate, marrow-deep communion with the natural world and with the lost dead. Relatively few agonies of choice, few worries over personal behavior were necessary. Every thing and person had a place, and there was a place for everything, which as Lévi-Strauss noted is what makes things sacred: "if they were taken out of their place, even in thought, the entire order of the universe would be destroyed."[92] (In the next chapter the repressive potentialities of this belief, and the revolutionary impulses of those who don't "know their place," are explored.)

By now it is commonplace to remark on what mythological thinking could do for us: give us back a sense of landscape, eliminate our waste-disposal problems, and so on. But the mythological consciousness is certainly more important than that. It tells us more than we can easily understand about our internal and external milieu, the great oceans of sensation and consciousness in which we swim. Contemplation of it lets us rest from our fretful desire to know what we are—until we remember that a being who can affirm that he is

91. See William Irwin Thompson, *At the Edge of History* (New York: Harper, 1972), Chapter 6.
92. Lévi-Strauss, *The Savage Mind*, 10.

continuous with nature in a sense places himself beyond it by that affirmation.

Having deprived us of such myth, the Bible proves to be a key to its recovery. There were other demythologizers—perhaps Akhenaten and Buddha and Zoroaster, certainly Plato and Mohammed—but none so singlemindedly contemptuous of so many hallowed traditions as the Bible-writers. By reacting so violently to them, they enable us to isolate these traditions from their natural surroundings and to study them in detail. Here the Bible's function is like that of infrared aerial photography.

In the millennia around 10,000 B.C. man began to make the Neolithic revolution. The arts of civilization slowly emerged, and man after this revolution was a very different being from the one who lived before. Yet no records indicate much awareness of change. Continuity remained the ruling principle. Only in retrospect did men have some dim sense that things had been different in an earlier time; certain creation myths enshrine this sense. However, civilization and violent change feed on each other. The walls of Jericho and Troy, once down, are soon rebuilt on the same spot, and soon pulled down again. Destruction opens the way for new creation. The ancient civilizations we so admire were built by change: but they, like Lévi-Strauss's "cold societies," effectively disguised the fact. A Sumerian legend told of a fish-man rising "from the primeval waters to teach them civilization, 'after which nothing further was invented.' "[93] Once again the myth of origins from nature signals the attempt to freeze development. In the earlier world, conservation had to be the first thought in every enterprise: it was more important to remember and pass on a tradition of getting an edge on a flint ax than to invent a new and simpler way of doing it: some tool-making traditions lasted hundreds of thousands of years. After 10,000 B.C. new ways of doing all things became feasible and desirable, and the high cultures throve on these, but redoubled their awe of the principles of con-

93. Levy, *The Gate of Horn*, 91. The quotation is from Berossos, who is late, but A. Leo Oppenheim suggests that the myth may be traced back to Sumer. See Oppenheim's *Ancient Mesopotamia: Portrait of a Dead Civilization* (Chicago: University of Chicago Press, 1964), 195, 365.

servation and continuity. Their anxiety about the top-heavy growth
of the superstructures of their monumental cultures expressed itself
in a frenzied attempt to multiply continuities with nature; hence
they elaborated to the point of grotesquerie the basic beliefs and
observances of the earlier mythological consciousness. The Hebrews,
on the other hand, could never convincingly project their ideology
back into nature, and thus they had a dissatisfaction with culture
that was different from the anxiety of the more sophisticated countries. Instead of affirming continuities, they began to explore the
ways man could adapt himself to nature and culture without being
in real harmony with either. We have adapted ourselves to this pattern of discontinuity: that is our "difference."

The Neolithic revolution, as Piggott and Clark point out, did not
inevitably lead to civilization as we know it. The emergence of the
high cultures "can hardly be attributed to the inevitable working out
of any common set of social, economic and technological factors. . . .
Civilizations are the exceptions."[94] We are the greatest exception, the
most uncentered aberration. In elementary school textbooks each of
the high cultures—Sumer, Egypt, Greece, Rome—was a stepping
stone toward ourselves; but though we have borrowed from them, we
know now that our appearance in the world was not a matter of
progress or maturation. Nor did the decay of myth in the Hellenistic
world mean that people were growing up and needed it no longer.
The growth of the emperor-cults is revealing: in his lifetime Augustus was deified in Egypt and other parts of the empire, but not at
Rome until after his death; after that restraints fell away, and the
emperors became divine kings similar to ancient African and Asian
ones.

We have not grown up either, but we have developed the Hebrew
possibilities into disciplines that are often useful, though sometimes
destructive. Specifically, the most comforting achievement of our own
civilization is its arrival at a point where we can begin to recover the
traces of the world the Hebrews overturned. Our tradition is not
condemning itself when it does so, especially when it acknowledges

94. Clark and Piggott, *Prehistoric Societies*, 148.

its losses. Certainly, just as we cannot see myth clearly without the Hebrew reaction, so we cannot fully appreciate the Bible and its legacies to us without recovering as much of the lost world as possible.

The specialisms that aid us to read "the forgotten language" are not privileged to exempt themselves from blindness, pride, and error; yet the self-critical instinct of our traditions can serve as counter-balance. We hear it said that we know more about Homer than Aristotle did, and we certainly know more about the Hebrews than they themselves did. Let us be tempted to a sense of purpose rather than pride in these accomplishments; then we can recover the lost world, without patronizing it and also without sentimentalizing it. Our way of thought, though raw and untested by the standards of mythological time, is also brash enough to proceed undaunted in piecing together the incalculable eons of prehistory from a few frag-ments of bone, flint, pollen, and coprolites. The techniques of sci-ence, rooted in alienation, prove to be the indispensable guides back past the flaming sword and into the remains of Eden. Perhaps some-day it will be maintained that the most important development of consciousness in the twentieth century had to do not with moon walks or atomic bombs, but rather with the new availability of an adequate sense of prehistory. Whereas our fathers and grandfathers had caveman fantasies, we have important opportunities for insight: we are able to locate ourselves more precisely than any previous gen-eration of humans. Credit must go to the restlessness, the "questing," that proceeds not from our *amour-propre* but from the conscience-searching taught us by the Bible. Its role in our widening awareness of the archaic world, if ironic, is not the less catalytic.

Chapter Three ⛪ The Hebrews Against the High Cultures: Pastoral Motifs

RIGIDIFICATION IN THE HIGH CULTURES

[Jewish customs], which are at once perverse and disgusting, owe their strength to their very badness. . . . Among themselves they are inflexibly honest and ever ready to show compassion, though they regard the rest of mankind with all the hatred of enemies. They sit apart at meals, they sleep apart, and though, as a nation, they are singularly prone to lust, they abstain from intercourse with foreign women; among themselves, nothing is unlawful. Circumcision was adopted by them as a mark of difference from other men. Those who come over to their religion adopt the practice, and have this lesson first instilled into them, to despise all gods, to disown their country, and set at nought parents, children and brethren. Still they provide for the increase of their number. It is a crime among them to kill any newborn infant. . . . The Jewish religion is tasteless and mean.

—Tacitus

Whereas the Hebrews saw around them people who worshiped unholy powers like the dead, fertility goddesses, sacred animals, stocks and stones, the typical Gentile saw the Hebrews (later the Jews) as refractory, fanatical exclusivists who refused to accede to cosmopolitan culture or to worship the powers that be. Though not perfectly informed on all points of Jewish belief, Tacitus expresses the natural attitude of the Hellenistic-Roman mind toward these puzzling people. His sensibility is injured by the failure of the Jews to acknowledge the superiority of syncretism, and their concept of a morality above culture and family appears to him a wicked counsel intended to subvert the *pietas* which was the foundation of Roman society. Both Jews and Christians were accused by Romans of being dangerous atheists: so they were, in a mythological view. Tacitus' scorn for Jewish opposition to infanticide is most revealing of all, with its casual indication that the ancient mind had frozen itself into observing archaic and barbarous rites. The infanticide that was normative in Paleolithic hunter-collector bands with limited food supplies had persisted into agricultural societies and had become sacralized, in this case with a eugenic rationale. For the Hebrews it was child-murder, a symbol of the depraved superstitions in which, as they saw it, the pagan mind was sunk.[1]

By Tacitus' time the freezing power of "cold" societies had produced a pattern of such rigidifications and degenerations. What had

1. On infanticide, one estimate is that it was practiced on 15–50 percent of the births in pre-agricultural societies. See Richard B. Lee and Irven De Vore (eds.), *Man the Hunter* (Chicago: Aldine, 1968), 11. On Jews and Romans, see A. N. Sherwin-White, *Racial Prejudice in Imperial Rome* (New York: Cambridge University Press, 1967), 86–101. He makes the point that hostility to Jews was expressed more often culturally than politically, thus involving Greeks more than Romans. The Roman authorities had little to fear from Jews; but those concerned with Hellenistic culture saw a more ominous threat, as well they should. See also Michael Grant, *The Jews in the Roman World* (New York: Scribner's, 1973), esp. 34.

Yet even Tacitus had some grudging respect for the Jews' reverence for their imageless god: this point is made by Jérome Carcopino, *Daily Life in Ancient Rome*, ed. Henry T. Rowell, trans. E. O. Lorimer (New Haven, Conn.: Yale University Press, 1940), 124. His tolerance reflected the decay and petrifaction of syncretism referred to in Chapter Two, which allowed Jews and Christians some success in proselytizing among the more troubled. They did best where culture and tradition were weakest: as A. D. Nock says, "It should be borne in mind that the majority of the early converts were town dwellers and therefore not particularly interested in agrarian rites (*pagani* means backwoodsmen), and again came from a social stratum which had not old and dear traditions. The issue was very much one of tradition. So in the fourth century we find the antithesis of the pagan aristocracy of Rome and the Christian bourgeoisie of Milan," Nock, *Conversion: The Old and the New in Religion from Alexander the Great to Augustine of Hippo* (New York: Oxford University Press, 1933), 227.

See also Kraeling and Adams (eds.), *City Invincible* (196) on the clash of "hither-worldly" with "prophetic" ideals in the Hellenistic city.

happened can be summarized thus: the anxieties attendant on the beginning of civilization, and the hidden sense of alienation in the early societies of Sumer and Egypt, caused these societies to make frantic efforts to encompass and appropriate all the naturalizing traditions of the precivilized ideologies. But the very ideological power —in myths and other forms—of civilization made these traditions into petrified forms, which eventually lost their vitality. The Hellenistic age was full of examples. The inclusivist spirit of syncretistic mythologizing itself had been perverted into a gluttonous appetite for novelty by the spread of great empires and the consequent compromising of religions everywhere. The imperial conquerors often allowed free practice of local worship, but unhesitatingly uprooted troublesome cults or demanded conversions if it suited them. Worse than forced conversion, however, was the deep psychic dislocation wrought by shifting populations. Whether due to deportation, migration to great cities, or other causes, the world after Alexander was filled with displaced persons: and only peoples like the Jews, deracinated rather than autochthonic, could (and did) prosper in exile. The result was an abiding malaise under the veneer of cosmopolitan culture.[2] In its last exfoliations, pagan religion was reduced to decadence or revivalism. Mystery cults and exotic salvationisms temporarily revived religious feeling and assuaged the malaise, but throughout the whole period of decay we can see the once-vital forms stiffening.[3]

2. Cf. Martin P. Nilsson, *A History of Greek Religion* (2nd ed., 1952; rpt. New York: Norton, 1964), 298: "The world of culture was shaken to its very foundations by the religious crisis, and the population of the cities also became involved in its after-effects; the bankruptcy of the state religion deprived men of faith in their gods and made them turn instead to gross superstition and to the new and vigorous deities introduced from abroad." See also W. W. Tarn, *Hellenistic Civilisation* (London: Arnold, 1952), 337 ff., and M. Rostovtzeff, *The Social and Economic History of the Hellenistic World* (New York: Oxford University Press, 1941), 63–73.

It must be admitted that the Jews of Palestine, in the Hasmonean period, adopted such imperial tactics as forced conversions. Thus they came to have Herod for a ruler.

3. The comparison of mystery religions to revivalisms, Methodist or Salvation Army type, is made by Ronald Knox, *Enthusiasm: A Chapter in the History of Religions* (New York: Oxford University Press, 1950), 27–28.

These disruptions, insofar as they were the result of expansionist imperialism, had roots that went back more than two millennia, to the first great "conqueror," Sargon of Akkad. Sargon's invention, the standing army, was to be the basic imperial tool for enslaving other peoples and uprooting their cultures.[4] But imperialism was itself only part of the spreading pattern of rigidifications, which set in when the great ancient cultures became urbanized to the extent that social classes had to be separated by decree. Such laws symbolize the loss of the sense of place and community, the autochthony which was the precondition of the mythological societies. These laws were promulgated by the temple authorities, the priestly castes, with the goal of preserving the mythological communality of the society, but the result was undermining of temple authority and the cohesiveness of the society. Robert M. Adams, an authority on early urbanism, hypothesizes "that forces inherent in temple control, some of them only coming into being in societies already integrated by temple leadership, gradually weakened the foundations on which temple supremacy rested. . . . Thus in a sense, an era of temple dominance —however 'classic' its religious or artistic expression—may be viewed as a transitional period necessary for the emergence of social groups and concepts profoundly at variance with those reflected in the traditional homogeneity and group solidarity of folk-village life."[5]

Ancient civilizations were usually the victims of their own success, as the Hebrew prophets saw. Their prosperity became their pride, and toppled them: in a typical pattern, their wealth attracted large hordes of foreign invaders, who for a time might furnish labor, mercenary armies, and even new energy—Sargon himself was descended from Semitic invaders who had breathed new life into a waning Sumerian society—but imperial success attracted either more vicious invaders or rival empires, who eventually brought down these

4. Giedion, *Eternal Present*, II, 18. See also Henri Frankfort, *The Birth of Civilization in the Near East* (1950; rpt. New York: Anchor, n.d.), 82 ff., Oppenheim, *Ancient Mesopotamia*, 154 and 403; Hallo and Simpson, *The Ancient Near East*, 57 ff.

5. Robert M. Adams, "Some Hypotheses on the Development of Early Civilizations," in Mark P. Leone (ed.), *Contemporary Archaeology* (Carbondale: Southern Illinois University Press, 1972), 361.

great nations in their pride. Though we associate these empires with fatal opulence, their very statecraft, that which had made them great, was equally the cause of their fall: as their bureaucratic and military regimentations grew more efficient they grew more brittle, and their hierarchies became top-heavy. The pervading contempt of Hebrew prophets for the achievements of culture appears in part to be a response to their sense of this inverse relationship between worldly success and durability.

If we survive our own depletions of resource, it will be because we have failed to freeze ourselves into a "cold" society and have retained that ambivalence that feels like discomfort but makes for adaptability. The dangers of prosperity threatened the ancient cultures precisely because they overadapted to immediate conditions and erected their heritages into rigid traditions. In adapting the ideology of the mythological consciousness to high-culture environments, the early civilizations gained great psychic energy, but in the process they twisted the beliefs into weirdly petrified shapes, which became heavily superstructured and rootless. The animal cults of a cultured Egyptian, after all, were not founded in the same intimacy as were those of Pleistocene man. All of the traditions mentioned in the last chapter—worship of animals, necrolatry, etc.—underwent petrification, but some of the most visible distortions can be observed in monumental building, legacy of the earlier megalithism.

Megalithism was a striking occurrence in human history because of the uncanny remains it has left antipodally scattered from Easter Island to the British Isles, but these included more than big stone ruins and geometrical alignments that tantalizingly suggest arcane astronomical lore.[6] This wondrous achievement of ancient man also bequeathed a heightened emphasis on human will and pride, forecast in the very structures we boggle at now. Megalithism represents

6. The reference is to the hypotheses put forward by Gerald Hawkins, Alexander Thom, and others. See, *e.g.*, Gerald Hawkins, *Stonehenge Decoded* (New York: Dell, 1965). Renfrew observes (Renfrew, *Before Civilization*, 222) that Hawkins' arguments "for at least some of the alignments are now widely accepted" in spite of this book's "sensational and slipshod" nature.

One theory holds, by the way, that the standing stones were buried in earth mounds.

the twin possibilities of imposing regimentation on a culture and self-glorifying monuments on a landscape; the very permanence of the stones is ominous as well as awe-inspiring. No doubt the cultists who designed Stonehenge did not think of their temples as man-made, and proclaimed the roots of their stones in the soil: for in the ideology of autochthony, nature indifferently makes trees, rocks, and men come out of the ground. Yet even in the collective will that made such feats of manpower possible we can perceive a discord with the agencies of nature. Even if all the megalithic erections were labors of love, still they point forward toward authoritarian ordering of workers—eventually captive and slave—in the high cultures. The very efficiency with which the ancient tribes focused their energies would sooner or later make centralization of power seem desirable to imitate such feats, and soon the centralized leadership would want to take active control of the "division of labor" so as to produce specialized castes and classes. The megalithic cultures no doubt required priestly guilds, in whose keeping were the myths that enshrined the cult and its lore. In these provisions we see the origins of the Egyptian scribal secretariats. In the end not only "labor" but all the tribal functions would be divided and ultimately rigidified.

In Palestine itself, the great walls of Jericho (*ca.* 8000 B.C.: "megalithic" by courtesy) are representative. A leading scholar remarks: "The prodigious labour involved in the erection of these defences implies an ample labour force, a central authority to plan, organize and direct the work and an economical surplus to pay for it."[7] This economic surplus had not merely to pay for the work; it had to be wealth worth defending. So even in this early era, not only before the wheel but before pottery, we must speak of leisure and luxury, and of the required imposition of authority, as preconditions of the building process.

In Egypt, these social conditions are implicated by the vast imposing pyramids. The slavery of most live Egyptians to a few dead ones allowed the techniques of stone building and social regimentation alike to be diverted into the raising of giant repetitive tombs. The

7. Mellaart, *Earliest Civilizations,* 36.

vulnerability of this form of mythologization is evident: in spite of massive walls and ingenious devices, which must have pretty well tied up the nation's engineering talent, the monumental structures could not keep determined tomb-robbers away from the treasures of these men who believed themselves to be gods. We moderns have been deprived of many gaudy sights by tomb-robbers, but we cannot fail to be struck by the demythologizing character of their acts: like Death in Richard II's image, they bore through castle walls with little pins, to put an end to royal dreams of immortality.[8]

The pyramids are more impressive for what they conceal than for what they display; metaphysically, they announce a permanence, but inside they are full of dead men's bones and all corruption, even if embalmed. The uselessness of the contents reproaches the pretensions of the builders. To some extent, all monumental building expresses this complex: though impersonal, the Acropolis bespeaks a similar imposition of human will upon the landscape, and by Yahwist moral logic, at any rate, ruin is its appropriate condition. As Rachel Levy and others have noted, the Mesopotamian ziggurat commemorates the "lost ancestral mountain," and there is an abundance of legends insisting that the gods themselves designed these temples; but these attributions cannot conceal the aspirations of the human builders, so clearly highlighted in the Babel story.[9] Over and over again the Hebrew vision penetrated through such imposing facades to the pride, and mortality, of the men behind them: they saw through the emperor's new vesture of stone. Even in the traditions about Solomon and his temple, such demythologizing scrutiny is evident. Solomon himself, if the account is accurate, was seized by doubts as to whether God would dwell in a house built by man:[10] the force of the Hebrew insight into the emptiness of monumental building prevented Solomon from indulging in most of the usual self-deifying activities of Near Eastern monarchs, in spite of his obvious tendencies in that direction.

This insight of the Hebrews goes back to the time of their coales-

---

8. *Richard II*, III, ii, 196–70. Note that the Bible is silent on pyramids.
9. See note 66 to Chapter Two, herein; cf. Giedion, *Eternal Present*, II, 231–38.
10. I Kings 8:27.

cence as a people, perhaps, but it must have been confirmed by their observations of many kings who degenerated into types of Shelley's Ozymandias. It is worth noting that most scholars date the Hebrew Exodus from Egypt in the time of Rameses II, who was the original of Ozymandias, and inordinately devoted to such works as colossi of himself. In fact his reign, typified by the giant replicas of his own image at Abu Simbel, caps an era of glorious building in Egypt; temples at Luxor, Karnak, Abydos, and Thebes, together with a host of lesser works, testify that the pyramid builders had worthy successors at this time. (Moreover, the Ramesside era is marked by increasing subservience to the dead and to a priestly bureaucracy: both anathema to Hebrews.)[11]

Had the Hebrews not had a long tradition of ambivalence toward culture, they might perhaps have been overawed by the spectacular monuments and sacralized social system of Egypt, as presumably were many of their fellow Asiatics, whose assimilation into Egyptian life was another feature of this same period. In that time there were many Josephs: scholars note the "rising importance in the government of foreign-born or foreign-named officials and courtiers, mostly from the Semitic populations of Palestine and Syria."[12] The stage was set for Exodus by migrations of Semites to Egypt, in search of food perhaps, and many prospered there; but deep hostility to Egyptian life kept some—the ideological nucleus of the Hebrews—from immersion and disappearance in the population. They kept their character, significantly, by insisting that they were shepherds, "for every shepherd is an abomination to the Egyptians" (Gen. 46:34); they retained their identity at the cost of being stigmatized. Even Joseph, though in effect the ruler, had to eat by himself. The pastoral badge that allowed these Hebrews to evade the sacralized social system bespoke not only an alien's occupation, but also a religious declaration of noncompliance: it was itself a demythologization.

Even though monumental building in Egypt seems to have preceded large-scale urbanization, we connect these grandiose achieve-

11. Hallo and Simpson, *The Ancient Near East*, 275–78. "Ozymandias" was apparently the name used for Rameses II by Diodorus Siculus.
12. *Ibid.*, 276.

ments with great cities, and so did the Hebrews. In the Bible cities
are made to symbolize the self-aggrandizement of their leaders and
the concomitant social injustice. Long before there were any emperors as such, the evolution of cities, for all the benefits it brought, was
moving into patterns that forecast the later imperial abuses. Soon
after they began, the cities of Sumer underwent "massive structural
changes," according to Adams:

Perhaps most obvious is an increasing emphasis on militarism, reflected in
the construction of fortifications; in the mustering and equipping of large
bodies in militia; in the emphasis on martial equipment in the so-called
"Royal Tombs"; and in a host of myths, epics, and historical inscriptions
recounting the internecine struggles of the city-states themselves. Responsibility for the conduct of military affairs was lodged not in the older,
economically and ritually oriented, institutions of the temples but in the
newly emergent dynastic state. And closely linked to the latter was the
increasing stratification of the society at large. This involved, *inter alia,*
the decay of kin-based social units; increasing concentrations of private
wealth in land; and the employment of modest numbers of war captives
and other slaves not only for household service and agricultural subsistence, but also for commodity production.[13]

Soon after these developments the cities became incurably expansionist, and each fell after a brief period of dominance.

The patriarchal narratives of Genesis may well portray a people
taking part in great population movements westward, *circa* 1800–
1700 B.C. To such wanderers, the royal cities they had left or passed
would seem full of enslaved and regimented people. In Babylon, in
the name of the god Enlil, the priests had promulgated a law pre-
scribing that a son must follow his father's trade.[14] The great law
codes of the early Near East, though they expressed many admirable
values, and must have served as curbs on kings to some extent, in
fact were all symptoms of an enforced rather than engendered social
organization. Such laws, though they procured stability for a time,
sooner or later became part of the pattern of rigidification. When
the cities grew complex, their rulers were irresistibly tempted to

13. "Patterns of urbanization in early Southern Mesopotamia," in Ucko,
Tringham, and Dimbleby (eds.), *Man, Settlement, and Urbanism,* 742–43.
14. Darlington, *Evolution of Man,* 99.

impose on them models of the great cosmic continuum, so dear to the mythological mind, in the form of social hierarchy. So at the time of their highest development, a "fundamental tenet of the world-view of the Mesopotamians was that human society was an exact replica of the society of the gods, with the temple tower, or *ziggurrat,* constituting a tangible link between heaven and earth."[15] The great mythological project of differentiation, giving value and meaning to the different functions, kinship systems, etc., of the tribe, can be turned into a rationalization of the guild and class systems fixed by law. In Mesopotamia, many forces seem to have converged in rigidifying the social structure thus set up. As usual, these forces include the most ingenious and successful innovations of the societies: for instance irrigation. We already know that irrigation eventually ruined the grainfields it had originally made possible: its consequence, due to the peculiarities of the Mesopotamian soil and water table, was salinization, which sterilized the land.[16] But now we can also see that it had a similar effect socially. Adams concludes that "by engendering inequalities in access to productive land, irrigation contributed to the formation of a stratified society. And by furnishing a reason for border disputes between neighboring communities, it surely promoted a warlike atmosphere that drew people together in offensive and defensive formations."[17] Militarism tied together the network of forces that made failure inevitable even while producing success: the dynastic kingships, which had originated in the need for war-leaders, solidified their control while temple leadership eroded.

Thus, even with the best of intentions, rulers and sages seeking to

15. E. A. Speiser, "The Biblical Idea of History in its Common Near Eastern Setting," in *Oriental and Biblical Studies: Collected Writings of E. A. Speiser* (Philadelphia: University of Pennsylvania Press, 1967), 190. Lewis Mumford (in Kraeling and Adams [eds.], *City Invincible,* 7) says that such a "fusion of sacred power and secular power . . . produced the nucleus of the city." He proceeds to analyze cities as "power machines."

16. Oppenheim, *Ancient Mesopotamia,* 41; cf. Thorkild Jacobsen and Robert M. Adams, "Salt and Silt in Ancient Mesopotamian Agriculture," *Science* 128 (November 21, 1958), 1251–58.

17. In Ucko, Tringham, and Dimbleby (eds.), *Man, Settlement, and Urbanism,* 744.

preserve the forms of the archaic mythological communities succeeded only in erecting petrified mummies of them. The centralization of power was a key symptom. In many ancient societies, elaborate decorations and complex honorific rituals were lavished on
rulers in response to deep spiritual needs of the people; the felt
identification between society and ruler made this natural. But
aggrandizement of the king's powers, especially his military ones,
made for machinelike nations. Such societies can produce great
works, but their very productivity and efficiency open them to abuse
by rulers flattered into megalomania by fawning counselors, or allow
them to be used for expansionist ventures by an alliance of merchant
and warrior groups. When the interests of enough privileged classes
and self-seekers combine, the result is imperialism, internal and
external. The proletarianization of city-dwellers may coincide with
demands for fresh captive labor and for booty from neighboring
cultures. While the king is busy on his campaigns of conquest, his
servants use the slaves sent home to erect the palaces, temples, tombs,
colossi, and other emoluments that imitate the great standing stones
of megalithism. Autochthony degenerates into a compelled allegiance
to the city-state: archaic reverence for sacred space becomes a slavish
awe of mighty cities, temples, and tombs. These societies undergo a
"centering" around the great city and its supposed permanence.[18]

18. The use of the term *centering*, recalling certain concepts in the work of,
e.g., Mircea Eliade, is prompted by that of Jacques Derrida, who looks at philosophy as a series of imperial theologizations. The imperial cities, whose massive erections were designed to overawe the citizenry, and keep them in mental
subjugation to the culture, were another example of success/failure; as they
grew more polyglot and syncretistic, and the citizens were exposed to more and
more exotic cults, an inevitable demythologization took place: it became possible to doubt whether any of the cults or myths were valid. Of course this made
the ruling classes redouble their efforts to solidify their own cults, with resulting petrifaction. The Roman emperor, for instance, became more and more divinized; elsewhere, while old "cults of the cities" persisted among the aristocra-
cies, the urban proletariats became readied for conversion to Christianity. See
Chester G. Starr, *A History of the Ancient World* (New York: Oxford University Press, 1965), 605. Meanwhile, something nearer the old autochthonous
idea persisted in the countryside. "Anyone who really wishes to understand the
religion of antiquity should have before him a clear and living picture of the
antique landscape, as it is represented, for instance, in certain Hellenistic reliefs and Pompeian frescoes. It is saturated with religion in a manner quite for-

The reactions of Yahwists to these empires and their leaders became increasingly scornful through the course of history. When they entered the land of Canaan under Joshua, the Hebrews identified themselves as natural enemies of the Canaanite city-states, ruled by petty monarchs. Joshua had the necks of captive kings ground underfoot, and then had the degraded men hanged: the worst of executions, reserved for those "accursed of God" (Josh. 10:24–27; cf. Josh. 8:29; also see Deut. 21:22–23). After settling in as a nation, on land won where the Canaanite chariots could not operate, the Hebrews found that they had chosen an area which was a bottleneck, the mouth of a strategic funnel, right in the path of any aspiring conquerors of the then-known world. The activity of the prophets was called forth by threats of conquest; they chided the Hebrew kings and people for offending Yahweh by trying to play the game of power politics, and thus making Israel into a petty principality rather than an elect nation. Calling on the Yahwist heritage of ambivalence toward culture and all its works, which was of course sharpened by natural hostility to the alien conquerors, the prophets used the looming images of the kings of Assyria and Babylon to give hair-raising vividness to their message that Yahweh was set on chastising Israel. Yet Isaiah proclaimed that the king of Assyria was merely an instrument of divine wrath agains the Hebrews, "the rod of my anger, the staff of my fury," and ridiculed him while simultaneously using him as a bogeyman: "Does the axe claim more credit than the man who wields it?" (Isa. 10:5, 15)

Delight in the humiliation of foreign kings is a leading Biblical theme, culminating in the book of Daniel. This collection of visions is presented as the work of a legendary seer who is supposed to have served successive emperors during and after the Babylonian captivity of the Jews; actually it is mostly an allegory designed to foment Jewish opposition, two centuries later, to still another ruler (Antiochus

---

eign to us. One could hardly have taken a step out of doors without meeting a little temple, a sacred enclosure, an image, a cult-pillar, a sacred tree. Nymphs lived in every cave and fountain. . . . This was the most persistent, though not the highest, form of antique religion; it was the form which gave way last of all to Christianity" (Nilsson, *A History of Greek Religion*, 118–19).

Epiphanes, a successor of Alexander's *diadochi* who governed the
Syrian or "Seleucid" part of the world-empire). The visions, with
their theme of the transience of empires, are received with improb-
able gratitude by the mighty kings, who supposedly acknowledge
Yahweh's control over them and over history when Daniel is able to
interpret their dreams and omens. The most famous vision is of a
great colossus with "feet of clay": the cliché originally signified the
waning of empires and their fall (Dan. 2:41), to be replaced finally
by the messianic kingdom of heaven. Daniel is shown to outlast all
the emperors he served, as well as all the enemies who sought to discredit or destroy him; though his attitude toward the emperors is
respectful, they are firmly demythologized and put in their mortal
place.

With these passages as indices to their contempt for imperial
authority, we can see why the Jews gave the Roman Empire so much
trouble, out of all proportion to their numbers and military strength.
Until finally crushed and dispersed in the second century, the Jews
were a recurrent plague to the Caesars, infecting the eastern part of
the empire with disorder, for they could see Rome as only one more
in the series that began with Akkad and ran through the Seleucids.
What the Roman emperor represented to Jews and early Christians
needs no demonstration: many lost their lives for resisting his cult.
One of the major ironies of history is that the Roman emperor
eventually became an official Christian: this is paralleled by the fact
that the royal house of Assyria, after it had dwindled into a minor
state, became converted to Judaism.[19] We might reflect here on the
fact that other parts of the empire treated the Caesars as divine even
before this worship was allowed at Rome: the emperors were flattered into making gods of themselves. As Lévi-Strauss sees in his
visionary play "The Apotheosis of Augustus," such deification ex-
propriates the great mythological identification of nature and divinity: by proclaiming themselves gods, these men attempt to disguise
the imposition of their wills on the world by founding their existence in "the order of things."[20] They want to seem not only irresist-

19. Hallo and Simpson, *The Ancient Near East*, 143.
20. George Mendenhall traces the pattern back to "Bronze Age religious ide-

ible, but cosmically given, *de rerum natura*. (Barthes' example of present-day mythology, we remember, was "French imperiality," also striving to be taken for granted.) This arrogance is the height of Ozymandian petrifaction, and the stones that supposedly give permanence to the mortal bodies of the rulers now are fittingly defaced by the forces of erosion and decay. In memory these rulers are only instances of the familiar theme of the transience of princes; Hamlet in the graveyard sings a ditty the author of Daniel would have liked: "Imperious Caesar, dead and turned to clay / Might stop a hole to keep the wind away."[21] The emperors' self-aggrandizement reveals the essential self-contradiction of the mythological consciousness, in yet another way: man cannot find himself in nature, either as continuous with it, or as established by it. The author of Daniel gave an ironic twist to the theme of imperial expropriation of the state of nature that makes a suitable complement to Lévi-Strauss's image of Augustus: one of the monitory punishments of Nebuchadnezzar was a sudden loss of reason, so that he "ate grass like the ox," while "his

---

ology," where the king's building of "temples, palaces, [and] fortifications," along with his subsidization of "a sumptuous and expensive art in ivory, gold, and silver" was designed "to convince the peasants they should be proud to have such a king. His prestige was based on divine right; his power derived from the gods whose rituals he supported both in the building of elaborate temples and in the maintenance of a complex priestly organization, and of course from an army and often a navy." Finally he co-opted the whole cult: "I maintain that the original and extremely old fertility cult has in all our written sources been politicized—that is, the old beliefs and myths have been readapted to show that the whole mythical process of fertility and power, the complex of powers and forces beyond the control of man, have actually been delegated to the king who exercises them as the chosen of the gods." Mendenhall, *The Tenth Generation*, 222–23.

See also Thorkild Jacobsen's sketch of Mesopotamian kingship in his *Toward the Image of Tammuz*, 132–55, especially the last pages: "The rulers of Akkade extended the pattern of primitive monarchy to cover an empire. Their huge standing army was used both for conquest and for garrisoning a network of army posts along the major highways of the empire." Meanwhile Sargon and his successors began to style themselves *dingir* or "god"—"the king was raised under Naram—Sin to the status of personal god of the capital"—and later ages took the final steps toward overt deification. Jacobsen concludes that the Assyrian revival of the Akkadian pattern "made first the Persian, later Alexander's empire possible," and that this was a "major conditioning factor behind all of the following Hellenistic and Roman history."

21. *Hamlet*, V, i., 200–201.

hair grew as long as eagle's feathers, and his nails became like bird's claws" (Dan. 4:30).

To complement the figure of the bestial emperor, the Bible repeats ceaselessly the anti-urban theme: the Old Testament passages against Sodom and Gomorrah, Babylon and Nineveh may be typified by Ezekiel's denunciation of the riches, commerce, and arrogance of Tyre. After listing all the glories, pomps, and wealths that will be no more when she is destroyed, Ezekiel accuses the prince of Tyre of the final sin: "Because you try to think the thoughts of a god I will bring strangers against you, the most ruthless of nations, who will draw their swords against your fine wisdom and lay your pride in the dust. . . . Will you dare to say you are a god when you face your assailants?" (Ezek. 28: 6–9; Yahweh of course is speaking.)[22]

Such oracles become images in the New Testament, in which Jesus at Jerusalem, Peter at Rome, and Paul everywhere proclaim the meaninglessness of culture's ambitions. John on Patmos envisions Rome as Babylon:

The kings of the earth who committed fornication with her and wallowed in her luxury will weep and wail over her, as they see the smoke of her conflagration. They will stand at a distance, for horror at her torment, and will say, "Alas, alas for the great city, the mighty city of Babylon! In a single hour your doom has struck!"

The merchants of the earth also will weep and mourn for her, because no one any longer buys their cargoes, cargoes of gold and silver, jewels and pearls, cloths of purple and scarlet . . . [here follows a catalogue of goods reminiscent of Ezekiel's.] "Thus shall Babylon, the great city, be sent hurtling down, never to be seen again! No more shall the sound of harpers and minstrels, of flute-players and trumpeters, be heard in you; no more shall craftsmen of any trade be found in you; no more shall the sound of the mill be heard in you; no more shall the light of the lamp be seen in you; no more shall the voice of the bride and bridegroom be heard in you!" (Rev. 18:9–23)

The real Babylon had already fallen, as foretold by Isaiah and Jeremiah; the latter had said "marmots and jackals shall skulk in it,

---

22. Ezekiel's catalog of the goods and stuffs in which Tyre traded is so detailed and exhaustive as to amount to an ethnographic report (see his Chap. 27).

desert-owls shall haunt it, nevermore shall it be inhabited by men" (Jer. 50:39); by A.D. 363 it had become a zoo.[23] The lesson was clear: "Worthless now is the thing for which the nations toiled; the peoples work themselves out for a mere nothing" (Jer. 51:58).

In his "eschatological discourse" (Mark 13, Matt. 24, Luke 21), Jesus had warned that not a stone of the Temple would be left standing: this prophecy knits together the Biblical symbolism that appears in the stories of Babel's tower and Jericho's walls. The only thing stones can do, in the Bible, is *fall*. Thus the hostility to what began with megalithism provides the image for many demythologizing energies. Yet the antipathies that fuel them go back to a time even before megalithism, to a time before kings, and cities, and history.

SHEPHERD AND FARMER: THE CULTURAL DIALECTIC

> Pastoralism is more than an economy or even a way of life. Like hunting, it is a collection of images about the world which need not be practical in the usual sense to be valid.
>
> —Paul Shepard, *Man in the Landscape*

> All through history, from Abraham to Mao, prophets have left the city behind them to insist upon a vision of things greater than they are; but in the double nature of all phenomena, the abandoning of the city for the wilderness is also the pattern of madness: the psychotic leaves the social structure of sanity. From the psychotic's point of view, one could paraphrase Voltaire to say that sanity is the lie commonly agreed upon. Those left behind in the city define themselves as responsible and sane and see the wanderer as a madman. The wanderer defines himself as the only sane person in a city of the insane and walks out in search of other possibilities. All history seems to pulse in this rhythm of urban views and pastoral visions.
>
> —William Irwin Thompson,
> *At the Edge of History*

Millennium after millennium, the descendants of Pleistocene man lived in a way that causes us to label him a "hunter-collector." Cer-

---

23. James Wellard, *By the Waters of Babylon* (London: Hutchinson, 1972), 18.

tain cultural tangents thrust out from this pattern, but no great fixed rifts between forms appear to have developed before the "Neolithic revolution," *i.e.*, the long span of time preceding 5000 B.C. when agriculture, domestication of animals, and other arts slowly began and were combined into patterns of settled life. Clashes may have occurred, but little evidence survives even to hint at these encounters. When we come to the time of plant and animal domestication in the Near East, however, we can see a dialectical pattern emerging, though it is never one of simple thesis and antithesis between two styles of life. "Now Abel became a shepherd and kept flocks, while Cain tilled the soil." The basic distinction between shepherd and farmer in the ancient Near East, we know now, is only partly represented by the fratricide of the Cain-Abel story: we find a smoldering hostility always latent in this relation, but it stems from interdependence. Most of the time the ruling pattern was symbiosis, each way of life giving something to the other. The exchange was not restricted to milk and grains; there was psychic symbiosis too, in which mutual opposition may have served as a defining and stabilizing element.

This division cannot be thought of as having a fixed historical "origin," but rather appears again and again as a fissiparous tendency in the fluid evolution of culture. Carl Sauer, perhaps the most famous American geographer, simply gives expansion as an efficient cause: "As the numbers of people and stock increased, herdsmen and herd moved farther and farther away from the villages and became more permanently detached from the settled lands. This about describes the roots of pastoral nomadism. . . . The original and absolute pastoralists can scarcely be said to exist or ever to have existed; they derive from a farming culture in which livestock was an original element."[24]

The fact is that we have only a few tantalizing hints from ancient sites that can allow us to visualize the origins of this process any more completely. At one Natufian settlement, a midden containing

24. Sauer, *Agricultural Origins*, 97. Some still argue for pastoralism preceding agriculture: see Robert Raikes, *Water, Weather, and Prehistory* (London: John Baker, 1967). But most now believe that pastoralists could not evolve directly from hunters. See Darlington, *Evolution of Man*, 78–81.

bones of many animals surprisingly lacks those of sheep, perhaps indicating a taboo which in turn may indicate some cultural clash reflected in ideology; at another site, in Iran, a pastoral economy took over so completely, after an agricultural phase, as to indicate some potent ideological development requiring a splitting-off from the usual mixed economy.[25]

With the beginnings of Mesopotamian urbanism, fissiparous specialization seems to have increased as a consequence of the very success of the cities, so that in part they were responsible for an ever-increasing pastoralism. Adams mentions this fact, at the same time noting the pastoral associations of an old Sumerian land-name that just might have something to do with Genesis: *edin* was the term for the steppe between the Tigris and Euphrates, or rather between the cities clustering along these and their associated watercourses.

At still greater distances from the cities, land in many cases apparently passed out of cultivation altogether. The high *edin* is perhaps the best example of great steppe marches that were formed in this way along the frontiers between periodically contending city-states. Such zones had the secondary advantage of serving as buffers, augmenting a defence in depth against overland military encroachments. Much increased in size over earlier scattered pockets of steppe-land, they also provided a base of operations for non-sedentary, perhaps ethnically distinct, herdsmen who were increasingly less dependent on their close symbiotic ties to cultivators.[26]

In other words, the organizing of the cities affected the configuration of the land in a double way, providing pockets of concentration and large open areas too. The latter appeared wherever agriculture moved on to more efficiently irrigated sites. Other factors, as we shall see, also accelerated the spread of pastoralism.

The notion that the herdsmen of the *edin* may have been "ethni-

---

25. See Mellaart, *Earliest Civilizations*, 24; Kent V. Flannery, "Origins and ecological effects of early domestication in Iran and the Near East," in Peter J. Ucko and G. W. Dimbleby (eds.), *The Domestication and Exploitation of Plants and Animals* (Chicago: Aldine, 1969), 82–85.

26. In Ucko, Tringham, and Dimbleby (eds.), *Man, Settlement, and Urbanism*, 744. On the older idea that *Eden* meant "delight," see Shepard, *Man in the Landscape*, 65; cf. Jacobsen, *Toward the Image of Tammuz*, 8 and 137; he calls it both "broad grassy steppe" and "open desert."

cally distinct" raises the possibility that even at this early date, clan-breeding systems could serve to reinforce the cultural dialectic. Sauer also mentions the possibility, noting that the Semitic (and later the Hamitic and Indo-European) pastoralists may first "have lived on the fringes of the older, unnamed agriculturalists, perhaps as hunters and collectors who gradually learned the arts of tillage and stockrais-ing."[27] But even if we try to imagine the results of fissiparous special-ization *within* racial groups, it is obvious that inbreeding would soon form new subgroups. Cain and Abel are brothers, but their "descen-dants" head in different directions. In short, it is certainly possible that evolving groups branched off early enough, and decisively enough, to provide the later Near East with peoples whose memorial traditions identified them predominantly with one way of life or the other, even when in fact they practiced both ways or lived in co-operation with their ideological opposites.

We do know that in early Sumer the division had been mytholo-gized, in forms that undoubtedly influenced the Biblical symbolism. In some myths the division has a hopeful note, with some realization of the role of the city in mediation and exchange between occupa-tions. "Not surprisingly, one of the recurrent themes in early myths is a rather didactic demonstration that the welfare of the city goddess is founded upon the harmonious interdependence of the shepherd and the farmer."[28] In other myths, the division appears to be mainly amusing. But in still others the more serious aspects come forward, in contests and conflicts between shepherd-gods and farmer-gods. Dumuzi, whom we know as Tammuz, seems to have been the chief Sumerian shepherd-god, although there was also a Dumuzi in the cowherds' pantheons, and others in those of marshmen and orchard-men: testimony to the fissiparous tendencies in the "division of labor" against which syncretizing mythology would serve as counter-force. The famous Sumerologist Thorkild Jacobsen has concluded that the Dumuzi worshiped by shepherds was specifically an incarna-

27. Sauer, *Agricultural Origins*, 96.
28. Robert M. Adams, "The Origin of Cities," in Lamberg-Karlovsky (ed.), *Old World Archaeology*, 140.

tion of fertility in sheep, "the divine power to produce lambs and milk in the ewes in springtime." How this conception conflicts with agricultural values he demonstrates in the myth in which Dumuzi is slain by the storm-deity Bililu:

When the milking season ends and Dumuzi, the power in milk, is no more, his death can be laid to the thunderstorm, to Bililu and Girgire. That they should figure as enemies and killers of Dumuzi is understandable enough, for as is well known milk tends to curdle and sour in a thunderstorm. On a different level the bitter and deep antagonism between shepherd and farmer, which is ever present in ancient cultures, would, of course, make the assumption of enmity between Dumuzi and the agricultural deities of rain and thunder both natural and readily acceptable.[29]

What was life to the farmers, the rainstorm, was death to the shepherds' most cherished food. Thus at an early date the patterns that would form the Biblical symbolism were already present in a mythology from which the Hebrews are known to have borrowed repeatedly (the Eden story, the Flood story, etc.)

From many authorities we receive warnings against romanticizing this conflict between shepherd and farmer. It appears that this was a typical excess of simplistic nineteenth-century views of the origins of Israel, in which monotheism was traced to the simple life and stark environment of the Bedouin, or "true" nomads. Whether this view is wholly devoid of insight is a separate question, but certainly it has been established that the Hebrews, when we know them as such, were never true nomads, so that the equation *Beduinentum = Jahwismus* is invalid.[30] Some revisionists would go further: for instance, George Mendenhall, a noted authority, states flatly that "there is no justification for concluding that a radical contrast existed between the shepherd culture and that of the village."[31] Yet the symbolism, both in the Bible and in mythology, surely implies this contrast. How can we

29. Jacobsen, *Toward the Image of Tammuz*, 29, 57, 59.

30. The flat equation is by Samuel Nystrom, *Beduinentum und Jahwismus: Eine Soziologische Religiongeschichtliche Untersuchung zum Alten Testament* (Lund: Gleerup, 1946).

31. George Mendenhall, "The Hebrew Conquest of Palestine," in Edward F. Campbell, Jr., and David Noel Freedman (eds.), *The Biblical Archaeologist Reader III* (New York: Anchor, 1970), 103.

account for it? Mendenhall himself suggests the solution when he goes on to say that "it is between the city and the village that the primary contrast of ancient times lies, not between the village farmer and the shepherd who may be typically bloodbrothers."[32] What we are really dealing with in most of the symbolism, then, is the problem of opposition to the values of the city. The antithesis is symbolized by the shepherd rather than the farmer, naturally, for the cities until the time of their imperialist expansions were only enlarged farming communities anyway. So the shepherd stands for a rebuke to urban values, while the farmer stands for acquiescence in the whole commercial structure of civilized life: he might as well be a merchant. (The Hebrews felt a smoldering opposition to merchants; the name, *Canaan,* of their detested neighbors seems to have been a word for *merchant,* from their trade in royal purple dye—note the imperial connotations.[33] The Phoenician and Carthaginian offshoots from Canaan give rise to the stereotype of the far-ranging and shrewd

32. *Ibid.*, 105. The story of Lot and the angel who lets him flee Sodom to Zoar indicates perhaps that city/village distinction.

33. See Martin Noth, *The Old Testament World,* trans. V. I. Gruhn (Philadelphia: Fortress, 1966), 50–53, and his *The History of Israel* (New York: Harper, 1960), 142; also Yohanan Aharoni, *The Land of the Bible: A Historical Geography,* trans. A. F. Rainey (London: Burns and Oates, 1966), 61–62. Ezekiel's gloating over the trade that will end when Tyre falls is typical. Even today, pastoral contempt for mercantile values prevails in some societies, though it now seems a reactionary gesture. Paul Shepard's comparison of pastoralism to hunting as an impractical, sentimental image of resistance to human innovation is revealing: "Pastoralism shares profoundly with hunting the consciousiness of a world not made by man, where the fragile tent and footprint in the sand are gone tomorrow" (*Man in the Landscape,* 52). He goes on to point out that both resist the prospect of the "year-round drudgery" of agricultural life, and of course the coerced "work" of commercial societies: "Except for hunting, pastoralism is the only life in nature without arduous labour." Hence, as he says, the literary forms of pastoral stress "freedom to discourse, think, make music, dance, and make love" (*Man in the Landscape,* 75).

This leads to ironic complications: for although hostility to "the work ethic" or "rat-race" is highly visible in today's pottery-making, bead-stringing variations on pastoralism, historically pastoral has been informed by a contrast between aristocratic idleness and "honest" labor. See the epigraph to the last section of this chapter. But both sides of the ambivalence toward "work" are culture-questioning.

Speiser (*Oriental and Biblical Studies,* 104) says that early Hebrew did not even have a word for "merchant." See Hosea 12:8–9, and the note in the Jerusalem Bible.

Semitic trader, a role into which the Jews stepped, ironically, in the Diaspora.)

The shepherd-farmer mythology, whatever its historical origins, then can be seen as a symbolic node likely to have preoccupied those who wanted to remember or invent traditions that placed them in opposition to cultured neighbors; for these the shepherd could become a potent signifier of independence, austerity, loyalty, and content. Mendenhall himself provides the most suggestive aetiology of this usage in his analysis of the Hebrew Conquest of Palestine as an anti-urban revolt.

Mendenhall's analysis may have started from his sense that the Biblical symbolism of pastoral life was overgrown to the point of distorting historical facts. Clearly the symbols—sheep and tent and wilderness, as well as the shepherd himself—have assumed a life of their own in the Bible. Yet the evidence, as Mendenhall sees it, indicates that the Hebrews were a group whose opposition to the city implies not complete separation but rather a significant experience of city life:

> One may begin by discussing the concept of "withdrawal." There can be no doubt that the conditions of urban society, in antiquity as also today, resulted in the disvaluation of that society on the part of groups and individuals. The code of Hammurabi already [*i.e.*, long before the Conquest] must make provision for the situation in which a person states, whether overtly or in effect, "I hate my king and my city." By this hatred, he has renounced any obligation to the society in which he formerly had some standing (if not status), and has in turn deprived himself of its protection. This is all that is meant by the term "Hebrew," *Hab / piru, 'Apiru,* which recurs in many sources from 2000 B.C. to its last occurrences in the Hebrew Bible about the time of David, who was himself a Hebrew in this sense when he was fleeing from King Saul. . . . In other words, no one could be born a "Hebrew"; he became so only by his own action, whether of necessity or by the inability any longer to tolerate the irrationalities of the society in which he was born.[34]

Not all scholars would agree with Mendenhall's analysis of the term *Hebrew,* but surely this hypothesis gives an enlightening emphasis to

---

34. Mendenhall, "The Hebrew Conquest," 105–10.

"withdrawal," which must have included demythologization of king, city, and culture. For a group to outlaw itself (outlaws are those who forfeit the law's protection, so that like Cain they have to fear being killed without legal reprisal) would require a rationalization based on moral imperatives, in which a useful motive would be returning to the life of the fathers. We can embellish Mendenhall's picture simply by looking at the narratives about Abraham, a dropout from Ur, "the city," one of the most sacred of the old Mesopotamian centers.[35] Abraham's tribe bypasses the loci of culture, obeying obscure religious behests and vague promises. Very possibly his entourage contained some of alien lineage who yet considered themselves Semitic seminomads (as some hippies of today believe themselves to be reincarnated American Indians, perhaps).[36] In any case the group's values seem derived from a deep disaffection with the cities, and they take up the image of shepherds as peaceful wanderers in search of a land of milk and honey, emblematic pastoral foods. The stories of Genesis refer to farming, and perhaps even caravaneering, as well as to keeping flocks, but the patriarchs always call themselves shepherds.

According to another expert, A. Leo Oppenheim, the pattern of withdrawal into pastoral life and the attempts to stem it played a role in developing expansionist and imperialist tendencies in the cities.

Difficult economic and political situations were liable to crowd out of the cities such persons as delinquent debtors, power groups defeated in intra-city striving, defectors from the great organizations, and others. In the open country, they joined the inhabitants of abandoned villages and settlements who had been driven into a seminomadic way of life by the deterioration of the soil, the breakdown of facilities for irrigation, or be-

35. Mendenhall believes that the "Conquest" was a peasant's revolt rather than an invasion, but he does agree that it was "a religious revolution" involving a "systematic, ethically and religiously based, conscious rejection of many cultural traits of the Late Bronze Age urban and imperial cultures," such as "kingship, art, professional military, temples" (*The Tenth Generation*, 12 and n.). Even Israelite law, he argues, "presupposes a violent rejection of the highly stratified society of Late Bronze [Age] Canaan" ("The Hebrew Conquest," 111).

36. Thompson, *At the Edge of History*, 27.

cause they had rebelled against taxes and rents. The number of these was increased by infiltrating groups from the mountains and the deserts around Mesopotamia. . . . The most effective remedy against these potentially dangerous elements were projects of internal and frontier colonization which only a powerful king could set afoot. The inscriptions of such kings speak triumphantly of the ingathering (*puḫḫuru*) of the scattered, the resettling (*šušubu*) of the shiftless on new land, where the king forced them to dig or re-dig canals, build or resettle cities, and till the soil, do *corvée* work [and make bricks without straw, perhaps]. We shall see how the situation just outlined, characterized by the tension between city and open country, contributed to the curious lack of political stability in Mesopotamia.[37]

Again the success/failure pattern is evident: as the kings succeeded in regimenting the dissidents, they created top-heavy empires open to further withdrawal and even attack by nomadic elements. So the tension could suddenly assume vaster proportions, and the symbolism be even more dramatically fixed.

Even if, as Mendenhall asserts, the so-called Hebrew Conquest was really a "peasant's revolt against the network of interlocking Canaanite city states," it is clear that the revolutionaries adopted the pastoral symbolism as a rallying cry.[38] Exodus speaks of a completely different tradition, but it too was an enactment of rebellious "withdrawal" with powerful pastoral overtones: whatever the historical validity of the story, the nomadic trek of the runaway slaves was made to bear a pastoral stamp through the wilderness symbolism. (The prophets sometimes spoke of the wilderness period as a period of special intimacy, a honeymoon, between Yahweh and his people.)[39] So from Genesis we have the tradition of shepherds leaving the city in search of pasture, and from Exodus the fugitives going into and through the desert to face the challenge of being Chosen. Adams' view would suggest that there were good economic reasons why fissiparous specializations and withdrawals proliferated

37. Oppenheim, *Ancient Mesopotamia*, 82–83.

38. Mendenhall, "The Hebrew Conquest," 107.

39. See esp. Jer. 2:2: "Yahweh says this, I remember the affection of your youth, the love of your bridal days; you followed me through the wilderness, through a land unsown." See also Hosea 2:16–17.

and became a historical pattern that was mythologized for various purposes; Mendenhall's view implies that the shepherd-farmer symbolism bespeaks a deeper psychic conflict. In either case the challenge and opposition to civilization is manifest, and the symbolic memorialization of the conflict becomes more important in retrospect than its presumable origins, though there may still be more insights to be gained by considering those.

In the Bible as we have it, the symbolism is nearly unequivocal. The first shepherd is Abel, type of the Just Man in later theologizations, while Cain the agrarian murderer is associated with varied arts and crafts bespeaking culture. Through a conflation of legends —there is some evidence that he was originally a hero, perhaps even a nomadic one—Cain is made the first city-founder.[40] His own outlaw wandering is not the Biblical ideal, but a repudiation, reinforced by the story of Ishmael, of the savage and intractable Bedouin, the true nomads called "wild asses of men," "whose hand is against every man."[41] Never does the Bible have anything good to say about this dangerous intransigence: naturally not, since the hard fact was that the Ishmaelites, Amalekites and Midianites, typical nomad raiders, harassed and looted Hebrew settlements until the time of the monarchy. However, though these nomads are condemned, and provide in the Gideon story the one instance where the symbolism is reversed, so that the Hebrews are symbolized by barley with the tent as the symbol of their enemies, they are still recognized, significantly, as kindred peoples: black sheep in the family, as it were.[42]

What the Bible praises is the way of life of the sheepherding semi-

40. It has been speculated that his "mark" was originally not that of a fugitive, but of the first Yahwist. Later prophets may have been "marked" men (see 1 Kings 20:42, etc). *Cain* means "smith" in Semitic languages, indicating that he was the eponymous ancestor of the Kenites, nomadic metal workers for whom Moses worked as a shepherd. By Biblical reckoning he lived with them from youth till his eightieth year: the "Kenite hypothesis" concludes that Moses must have learned Yahwism from them. See the discussion by S. H. Hooke in *Peake's Commentary on the Bible*, ed. Matthew Black and H. H. Rowley (Rev. ed.; London: Thomas Nelson, 1962), *s.v.*, "Genesis IV." See also Lindblom, *Prophecy in Ancient Israel*, 67–68.

41. Gen. 16:11–12.

42. See, *e.g.*, Judg. 6–8 and Ex. 17:8–16, but also Gen. 25:1–18.

nomad, not that of the camel-riding Bedouin: the distinction is vital, for many reasons. For instance, the use of the wilderness in the pastoral symbolism implies the attitude not of the desert-dweller but of domesticated man. It is not the utilitarian at-homeness of the Bedouin, but the awe and fear of men for whom the desert was danger, but also refuge and not infrequently the scene of theophany, that shapes the desert symbol in the Bible. The story of Hagar illustrates a gradation within the attitude: in Chapter 16 of Genesis, Hagar flees from the persecution of her mistress Sarah and goes instinctively to the desert: but in Chapter 21 she is driven away, with her newborn son, and she helplessly awaits death for them both in the desert, only to be saved by the appearance of God's angel. The first tradition is more nomadically oriented, but in the second another kind of refuge is suggested: though the desert is a place of despair, its uncanny and terrifying aspects can make it the proper locus for the miraculous manifestation of God's power.

Small wonder that the great shepherds in the Bible after Abraham are persistently associated with a period of exile in the wilderness. Moses is forced to become a shepherd of the flocks of Midian, having fled Egypt for doing righteous murder: in the desert he experiences the most important of all theophanies, that of the burning bush. David the young keeper of flocks, who uses shepherds' weapons in combat with giants, merges typologically with David the outlaw fleeing from unjust Saul, hiding in desert caves. In the popular mind this fugitive period would be the likely time for David to compose the best-known of all Psalms, the Twenty-third: "The LORD is my shepherd; I shall want nothing. . . . I fear no evil, for thou art with me, thy staff and thy crook are my comfort."

Finally, the prophets associate themselves with the wilderness. Amos, first of the great writing prophets, identifies himself as a humble shepherd (and fig-dresser) of Tekoa, a small town with an adjacent wilderness named for it. Quite possibly this claim makes reference to the wilderness aura associated with Elijah, whose food and clothes were pastoral symbols, imitated by later prophets and recapitulated in the animal-skins and the locusts-and-honey diet of

John the Baptist. Jesus' nomination of John as Elijah was a piece of Scriptural interpretation.[43]

Jesus in the Gospel of John says: "I am the good shepherd: the good shepherd lays down his life for the sheep" (10:11–12). This motif was so popular in early Christian art that its exemplars outnumber even those of the Crucifixion.[44] But pastoralism for Jesus was wholly symbolic; in life he was a carpenter, and his parables are full of agricultural imagery reflecting the relatively fertile soil of Galilee: the only experience in the Gospels approaching pastoralism was the retreat and temptation in the wilderness. But that was enough, for it was typologically linked to Elijah's withdrawal to the wilderness in flight from the persecution of Jezebel.[45]

This humble but not simple symbolism may well turn on a passage in the story of David as king, in which he proposes to build a temple for Yahweh. Yahweh refuses; though Solomon later does build a temple, we know to what end Solomon came—idolatry. The terms of Yahweh's refusal to David are what is especially revealing: "I have never stayed in a house from the day I brought the Israelites out of Egypt until today, but have always led a wanderer's life in a tent" (II Sam. 7:6). Yahweh's self-description, as the prophet Nathan delivers it, links the Ark in the wilderness with pastoral life and implies an obvious transition to the metaphor of leaders as shepherds. Actually this image was common in the ancient Near East; Pharaonic regalia included a shepherd's crook as well as a cattle-flail.[46] The Bible does not openly acknowledge the ubiquity of this metaphor, though in a sense it provides a reverberation for the theme that the shepherd may be a potential leader or king (Moses and David again). Perhaps too there was some awareness of it behind

43. Matt. 11:7–15. On the "wilderness of Tekoa," see II Chron. 20:20; cf. Amos 7:14–15 and 1:1. Again see Lindblom, *Prophecy in Ancient Israel,* 66.

44. For a discussion of early Christian art, see André Grabar, *Christian Iconography: A Study of Its Origins* (Princeton, N. J.: Princeton University Press, 1961), esp. 11 and 132.

45. I Kings 19.

46. See fig. 12. John A. Wilson says that "a shepherd's crook is one of the earliest insignia of the pharaoh and is the origin of one of the [Egyptian] words meaning 'to rule'" (Frankfort *et al., Before Philosophy,* 88). It was equally ancient in Mesopotamia.

the prophets' repeated denunciations of Hebrew kings as "bad shepherds": if so, the prophets were saying that the kings had become indistinguishable from other Oriental despots, when they should have retained the pastoral values of early Israel, those of "good" shepherds.[47]

Further in the same speech Yahweh refers to the leaders of Israel as shepherds, implying that David is their symbolic culmination who was prepared for kingship by his pastoral responsibilities: "I took you from the pasture, from following the sheep, to be leader of my people Israel."[48] Yahweh dethrones the mighty and exalts the humble, raising a mere shepherd-boy to be king and to conquer those who would enslave his people. Shepherds, so scorned by sophisticated folk that Egyptians will not even eat with them, are fitting symbols of the people of Israel, a puny people who outlast and humiliate tyrants and oppressors.

When the Philistine threat to Israel proved too strong for the irregular charismatic leadership of the Judges, necessitating a king with a standing army, the new need clashed with the old antimonarchic traditions (see especially I Sam. 8). Both Saul's and David's accessions were controversial; even after David had turned the tables on the Philistines, making vassals of them and most of the other neighbors, there was a recurrent cry of factions against his house: "Every man to his tent, O Israel! We have no portion in the house of Jesse."[49] Which is remarkable, considering that at this time all the best people had long been living in houses. For an even more striking pastoral anachronism, we may look at the famous line in John's Gospel, "The Word was made flesh and dwelt among us"; the verb for *dwelt,* literally translated, means "pitched his tent." Not surprisingly, in Luke the announcement of the divine birth is made first to shepherds.[50]

---

47. See, *e.g.,* Ezek. 34: "Shepherds ought to feed their flock, yet you have fed on milk, you have dressed yourselves in wool, you have sacrificed the fattest sheep, but failed to feed the flock. . . . You have ruled them cruelly and violently" (3–5). Milton transposes this complaint from kings to churchmen (pastors) in *Lycidas.*

48. II Sam. 7–8.

49. II Sam. 20:1; cf. I Kings 12:16.

50. John 1:14 (see the note in, *e.g.,* the Jerusalem Bible); Luke 2:8–20.

In at least one instance the pastoral symbolism was strong enough
to create what may have been a cultural back-formation. Several
times in the Old Testament we hear of a clan called the Rechabites,
identified as very zealous Yahwists. They made the pastoral ideas a
rule of life, forbidding themselves any participation in farming,
commerce, or even property-owning: no houses, no wine (which
could be associated with Canaanite ways, as in the story of drunken
Noah), only sheepherding as a means of subsistence. Their putative
ancestral lawgiver had told them that "you must live in tents all
your lives, so that you may live long on the soil *to which you are
alien.*"[51] The italicized words imply a conscious hostility to autochthonic ideologies. Evidently the Rechabites had developed an exas-
perated contempt for all aspects of sedentary life. They were of
course not typical of all Hebrews, but rather the fundamentalists of
their day. Do their precepts distort the meaning of the pastoral
symbolism, or merely throw it into higher relief?

Similar questions could be asked about all the post-Hebrew groups
who withdrew to the desert as a spiritual retreat, notably the Qumran
Community of Dead Sea Scrolls fame. And later there was Christian
monasticism. Some scholars, who are rightly skeptical about the so-
called "desert ideal," warn us against misreading the Old Testament
by projecting these later developments back into it.[52] This is a good
point, for the desert is not idealized, only used as an image of contrast to culture, in the Bible. Yet even the fanatical monks of the
Thebaid can tell us something by the way they lived out their own
ambivalence toward culture: in their case, the milieu was that of the
post-Hellenistic cosmopolis, so rootless as to give rise to all kinds of

51. Jer. 35:7; see the whole chapter, and II Kings 10:15. I Chron. 2:55 links the
Rechabites to the Kenites; they must represent, literally or symbolically, the old
seminomadic tradition. Cross points out that the association of Moses with Kenites
or Midianites is the more believable because it survived the later polemics against
Midian (Cross, *Canaanite Myth and Hebrew Epic*, 200). The Rechab who appears
in II Kings 10:15 represents "zealous" Yahwism; the heroine Jael of the Song of
Deborah is the wife of a Kenite. Thus several signs point to a Kenite-Rechabite
traditions as "plus Yahwiste que les Yahwistes."

52. See Shemaryahu Talmon, "The 'Desert Motif' in the Bible and in Qumran
Literature," in Alexander Altmann (ed.), *Biblical Motifs* (Cambridge, Mass.: Harvard University Press, 1966), 31–63. Mendenhall is also contemptuous of what he
calls the "Bedouin mirage."

excess. They remind us of the fatuous atavism of many dropouts and commune-dwellers today, with their literal-minded interpretation of the Biblical precept of withdrawal.

As Mendenhall says, participation in life may become "too much" for some people in any culture, but certain conditions—especially cosmopolitanism and stratification in societies—are bound to exacerbate the psychic stresses. The pattern of flaws of the later empires is a retracing of the problems of the early cities. Adams remarks on the "essentially artificial character" of Sumerian cities, pointing out that the advantages of urbanism were great only for a privileged minority, and that "the greater part of the population was tied to the city only under varying degrees of duress"; this sounds like the decadence of Rome itself.[53] The Hebrews trained themselves to resist empires by developing a pattern of opposition to early cities: so the essential continuity here runs from Rome back not only to Akkad, but all the way to Jericho: a span of almost ten thousand years in which the success / failure pattern of the cities was repeated by the empires, while the Biblical precept of being in but not of the world was formulated.

Faced with the regimentation of city life, the Hebrew recourse was to withdraw, at the behest of a god whose most remarkable characteristic, in the early conceptions, is that he is a god of people rather than of land. Albrecht Alt, in his influential work on patriarchal religion, finds the mobility, landlessness, and cohesiveness of the early Hebrew tribe reflected in the traces of the "God of the Fathers." After reviewing the evidence he concludes: "All this implies that the seeds of a completely different development from that of local and nature gods were implanted at the very inception of the cult: the god was not tied to a greater or lesser piece of earth, but to human lives, first that of an individual, and then through him to those of a whole group."[54] The God of the Fathers was first the God of *a* father—

53. In Ucko, Tringham, and Dimbleby (eds.), *Man, Settlement, and Urbanism*, 743. Mendenhall's "tenth generation" concept amplifies this view, asserting that the Hebrew polity, "the kingdom of Yahweh" (see my Chapter Four on how this succumbed to the early monarchy), was the key event in human history.

54. Albrecht Alt, "The God of the Fathers," in his *Essays on Old Testament History and Religion*, trans. R. A. Wilson (New York: Anchor, 1968), 54–55. The essay dates from 1929.

Abraham, Isaac, or Jacob—and then of the tribes who traced their descent, accurately or not, from these. Mendenhall may be right that one had to claim the status of "Hebrew," and the term may have been used, at various times, to designate wanderers, brigands, slaves, and all sorts of landless and *declassé* peoples: but many of these could unite as *Bene Yisrael,* sons of Jacob, the patriarch identified (in what the great scholar Gerhard von Rad thinks is a primal "cultic confession") as a "wandering Aramaean."[55] If this was the earliest such passage, the very first lesson of the Hebrew catechism was that of seminomadic origins. Their god was unlocalizable and alone; he had no original cult centers and no role in pantheons of syncretized deities.

One famous artifact that bears on this problem is the "Merneptah Stela," a Pharaonic inscription boasting of victories in the Syria-Palestine area about 1230 B.C.: of the several worsted peoples on the list, Israel is the only one "which is written with the determinative of people rather than land."[56] In other words Israel alone is designated by tribal name rather than place-name. Some scholars conclude that the Hebrews simply had not yet completed the Conquest, but would it not be more likely that they were continuing to identify themselves with the condition of landlessness, with all that it implies?

Although there are strong indications that seminomadism was a real factor in the Hebrew background, it is possible that their memory of these traditions was mostly an invention; the symbolism was powerful enough in the Near East to have persuaded the Hebrews to adopt it. In a similar way, though it is all but certain that they were never real nomads, they could feel the force of nomadic traditions. Even from the extreme nomads they could take some values, while rejecting the predatory raiding that the desert peoples practiced. In this sense Henri Frankfort's words are revealing even though at first they seem inapplicable:

55. Gerhard von Rad, *Old Testament Theology,* trans. D. M. G. Stalker (2 vols.; New York: Harper, 1962), I, 122 ff.

56. James B. Pritchard (ed.), *The Ancient Near East: An Anthology of Texts and Pictures* (Princeton, N. J.: Princeton University Press, 1965), 231 n. See also

It seems that the desert as a metaphysical experience loomed very large for the Hebrews and coloured all their valuations. . . . The settled peasant's reverence for impersonal authority, and the bondage, the constraint which the organized state imposes, mean an intolerable lack of personal freedom for the tribesman. The farmer's everlasting preoccupation with phenomena of growth and his total dependence on these phenomena appear to the nomad a form of slavery. Moreover, to him the desert is clean, but the scene of life, which is also the scene of decay, is sordid.[57]

Notice that Frankfort does not assert that the Hebrew experience of the desert was *historical*: rather he calls it "metaphysical." Such "metaphysical" experiences, like any myths, can of course be far more important than the verifiable facts of history. As to the likelihood of the Hebrews being affected by such experience, we have indications that the whole of the ancient Near East, compared to other areas, was tinged with nomadic values. It may be that autochthony never took hold quite so deeply or widely there as in other early centers; in any case, given the perennial instabilities of the cities, complicated by the gigantisms that were part of a frantic effort to compensate for these instabilities, we find that autochthony by the time of later Egypt and Babylon had declined into chauvinism, as part of the general petrifaction of mythological traditions: so even at the height of their success, these empires were in ideological decline relative to nomadic values.

This distinctive pattern of the Near East has been pointed out by Carl Sauer in studies of the origins of domestication: he came to believe that there was indeed a worldwide cultural dialectic between "peasant and pastoral ways," but that the ancient Near East was primarily and above all pastoral.[58] Sauer suggested that the earliest origins of agriculture must have come among deeply sedentarized

---

D. Winton Thomas (ed.), *Documents from Old Testament Times* (New York: Harper, 1961), 137–41 and opposite p. 182.

57. Frankfort *et al.*, *Before Philosophy*, 246–47. Here again the Bedouin contempt for the farmer's "slavery" reflects the hostility to labor emphasized by Paul Shepard. But unlike the Bedouin, the Hebrews resisted becoming raiders who took by plundering what they scorned to work for: the ideology of holy war militated against accumulation of spoil.

58. In Thomas (ed.), *Man's Role in Changing the Face of the Earth*, 56 ff.

people, likely to be shore-dwellers, perhaps in Southeast Asia; that these starts grew into what he called "hoe culture," integrated rather than specialized, raising "diverse assemblages of useful plants" rather than great fields of one crop; and that this pattern is typical of East Asia, Africa, and the pre-Columbian New World. Against this he contrasts the Near Eastern culture of fissiparous specialism, calling it "the other ancient trunk whence spring the sowers, reapers, and mowers; the plowmen, dairymen, shepherds, and herdsmen. This is the complex already well represented in the earliest Neolithic sites of the Near East."[59] These practiced specialist farming, which is a matter of "seed production of annuals, cereal grasses in particular," while the nonspecialist "hoe cultures" are represented typically by "maize-beans-squash" or other complexes grown all together. To us this latter is more like gardening than farming, and indeed Sauer notes that our attitude comes from the former, from the Near Eastern "ancient trunk": "Our Western know-how is directed to land use over a short run of years and is not the wisdom of the primitive peasant rooted to his ancestral lands."[60] The Bible has helped give to Western society the pattern in which place-rootedness is relatively insignificant. The point is perhaps crucial, for the domestication of cereal grasses, wheat, and barley seems to have been made possible by taking the wild weedy progenitors away from their native habitats and forcing an artificial growth pattern on them by transplantation. Hence our attitudes toward agriculture, in spite of the Biblical down-playing of the farmer, are, like our ambivalence toward cities, an offshoot of the pastoral symbols and tensions in the Bible. Having transmitted this Near Eastern pattern to us, with reinforcement from the other Mediterranean cultures who also practiced specialist cereal farming, the Bible is in the ironic position of having its ambivalence toward culture come to be symbolized by what was, in the ancient context, the symbol of culture itself. For most of our pastoral values find more practicable images in farming than in shepherding. Many of our urbanites have a real or fancied nostalgia for "turn-of-the-

59. *Ibid.*, 58.
60. *Ibid.*, 57–58.

century rural America," which is in effect a displacement of the pastoral opposition along a spectrum of life-styles. Every now and then one of them may actually take a vacation down on the farm, barely conscious of those roots of his impulses that stem from the clash of Yahwism with culture.

Moreover, as Sauer points out, the economic-ecologic pattern of land use in the Near East made the spread of pastoralism inevitable. An increase in desiccation in the area over several millennia has long been noticed, sometimes explained by climatic factors; but pastoralism itself was the cause of much of this desiccation, with the consequence that more and more land fell out of cultivation and was turned over to grazing. For sheep, as every reader of cowboy stories knows, tend to destroy ground-cover and thus spread desiccation. Combined with the fact that grainfield agriculture wears out the soil's nutrients, this would explain the aridization of Near Eastern lands, without any postulation of climatic change. Sauer points out that such "xerophytism of vegetation" (desert plants taking over from more lush growth) and production of barren, lifeless areas took place all around the Mediterranean, accounting for the dunes and wastes of the Sahara and Arabia which contrast so vividly with the relatively life-filled American deserts, where sheepherding is less than two centuries old.[61] So pastoralism feeds on itself: wherever it gains a foothold, it acquires more and more land from agriculture. This tendency of pastoralism to spread must have been a factor, multiplied by rigidification in the higher cultures, in the viability of pastoral symbols and values for the Hebrews, leading to their "metaphysical experience of the desert."

Some of the other cultural out-thrusts that broke off from the original Near Eastern "trunk" can also be revealing. "Spreading into the steppes of Eurasia, the culture lost its tillage and became completely pastoral, with true nomadism."[62] Thus even the horse-nomads of Central Asia can illumine the cultural dialectic, in much the same way as the values of the Bedouin do: for the notable hos-

61. *Ibid.*, 60–61.
62. *Ibid.*, 58.

tility to urban civilization of the Mongols, Tartars, and others represents a fierce variant on the Biblical pattern. These ferocious tribesmen did not give much importance to moral denunciations, but
their corrective function was felt by ancient writers, who saw in
them "the scourge of the Lord, sent for the chastisement of ancient
civilizations."[63] They too were demythologizers by implication:
"When the sedentary and often decadent communities yielded under
his onslaught, the nomad entered the city and, when the first few
hours of massacre were over, without any great difficulty took the
place of the rulers whom he had defeated. Unabashed, he seated himself upon the most time-honored and exalted thrones—as grand
khan of China, king of Persia, emperor of India, or sultan of Rum—
and adapted himself accordingly."[64] (Of course the impudent horse-
nomads who so cynically seated themselves atop archaic mythologized power structures had a tremendous military advantage: the
mounted archers dominated Asia for so long that the Czar tried to
use them against Napoleon in 1807.)[65] Yet the horse-nomads too
formed a kind of symbiosis with their victims. René Grousset compares the relations between the two to the "feelings of a capitalist
society and a proletariat enclosed within a modern city."[66] Hostility
can easily result from mutual dependence, even to the point of
fratricide.

Still another permutation, in Africa, develops aristocratic overtones that are not entirely irrelevant to Western thought though
barely visible in the Bible: in some versions of the pastoral hostility
to sedentary culture, feelings of innate superiority prevail. This
example is that of the Hamites, of whom a noted Egyptologist remarks: "The cattle-breeding nomad is a specific type of African
Hamite whose natural vigour and resolute character acquired
through his struggle for existence equip him to become a nation-

63. René Grousset, *The Empire of the Steppes: A History of Central Asia*,
trans. Naomi Walford (1939; rpt. New Brunswick, N. J.: Rutgers University Press,
1970), vii.
64. *Ibid.*, ix–x.
65. *Ibid.*, xi.
66. *Ibid.*, ix. Sahlins (*Tribesmen*, 33–34) mentions Owen Lattimore's thesis that
pastoralism in East Asia was sometimes a "by-product of imperial civilization

builder ruling over racial groups of agriculturalists."[67] From the Sudan and Sahara to what is now Burundi this symbiosis still occurs, unhappily now issuing in horrible civil wars as modern political ideas reach into these areas. The few real fratricidal conflicts of ancient days are dwarfed by today's.

In spite of the ever-present hostility, it must be reaffirmed that the original patterns of symbiosis and dialectic were crucial in the opening up of Western Asia to civilization. Anthropologists have hardly begun to study the ways in which farmers and herdsmen served as catalysts for each other's activities in forwarding the Neolithic revolution. One benefit that has long been recognized is that the herds served as "storage" for the extra grain, so that in the recurrent rainless "lean years" they could be eaten. "Archaeological and ethnographic evidence suggest that plant cultivation and animal herding, far from being two separate subsistence activities, are interrelated in ways which help 'bank' surpluses and even out the erratic fluctuations of the Near Eastern environment."[68] Pastoralism could also have helped in the exploration and opening up of new areas for cultivation, at first. Other effects of this kind are just beginning to be described in research.

New light on the uses of nomadism is suggested by the activities of an African tribe described by an anthropologist: "Nomadic movement therefore may be said to provide a means for the regular positive affirmation of multiple enduring social ties and for the easy segregation of conflicting individuals from each other; the value which Hazda place on movement as such, on movement more frequent than can be explained on ecological grounds alone, is related to its importance for every individual Hazda as a means through which his or her social ties may be manipulated without strain."[69]

---

rather than a direct product of neolithic evolution": against a "dominant and exploitative Chinese civilization," it was "an act of resistance, even of freedom."

67. Hermann Kees, *Ancient Egypt: A Cultural Topography,* ed. T. G. H. James, trans. I. F. D. Morrow (Chicago: University of Chicago Press, 1961), 22–23.

68. Kent V. Flannery, in Ucko and Dimbleby (eds.), *Domestication and Exploitation,* 87.

69. James Woodburn, "Ecology, nomadic movement and the local group," in Ucko, Tringham, and Dimbleby (eds.), *Man, Settlement, and Urbanism,* 205.

This conclusion can easily be transposed to Genesis, where we notice conflicts between the tribes of Abraham and Lot, Jacob and Laban, Jacob and Esau, being mediated by nomadic movement. In fact if we give Mendenhall's hypothesis of "political and subjective withdrawal" its completion in actual physical movement, and add the thought that such kinship-oriented movement would create and reinforce the breeding patterns that gave rise to clan and tribal systems, we may see a whole new dynamic in Genesis and Exodus. Lévi-Strauss and other anthropologists, in showing how the machinery of totemism is deployed for the purpose, have proved the importance of differentiating symbolisms in breeding structures.[70] Equally provocative is the corollary that such withdrawals may have been an important social mechanism for avoiding conflict and allowing the sites of early settlements to develop. Adams' remark on the usefulness of the *edin* as a buffer zone between Sumerian cities comes to mind.[71]

On the whole the picture of symbiosis, reinforcement, stimulation, and synergy forms a fascinating anthropological problem, one necessary for understanding the tangled roots of our civilized ways of life. The interplay is complex, but we must begin with the divisions. Most obviously, we should strive to understand the "mental universe" of pastoralists and those who elaborate pastoral traditions. One aspect of direct significance for the Bible is the way in which a seminomad's view of "nature" differs from the farmer's. Surely this goes far toward explaining why Hebrew ideology is so much less nature-oriented than those of mythological peoples, and why the Bible lays such stress on the unnaturalness of Yahweh's appearances: the celebrated theophanies, especially in Exodus, seem to use the phenomena of nature as mere masks, and to call attention to this fact. The burning bush, it has been suggested, might be explained by sunset light coming through scrubby red desert growth, and the plagues and Sinai appearances might have such natural explanations

70. See "Totem and Caste" in Lévi-Strauss, *The Savage Mind,* and Claude Lévi-Strauss, *Totemism,* trans. R. Needham (Boston: Beacon, 1963).
71. See Note 26 above.

as micro-organisms or vulcanism, but these explanations are beside
the point: for the Bible makes it clear that these are all signs that
point beyond the natural order, even where that order includes what
we would call the miraculous.[72] We are not being invited to contem-
plate the powers of nature, as we are by mythology: another realm
of existence altogether is what is suggested. Yahweh is not incarnated
in the appearances, nor do they function as symbolic keys to him:
they are neither continuous with him in any sense, nor analogous to
his essence. The "cosmic continuum" is deliberately broken, the
forms are arbitrary signals, and the arbitrariness is the point. Elijah
at the cave on Horeb is confronted with a mighty wind, an earth-
quake, and a fire: but Yahweh is in none of these. Only when he
hears a gentle breeze (or "still, small voice") does Elijah cover his
face and go out to speak with God.[73] Baal would have been in a
storm, but Yahweh is in the least remarkable of sounds; similarly,
he chooses an insignificant nation to be his Elect. The hostility to
natural forms is elucidated by Frankfort's words: "The farmer's
everlasting preoccupation with phenomena of growth and his total
dependence on these phenomena appear to the nomad a form of
slavery."[74] So they seem to have been interpreted by Yahweh himself, so to speak, whose attitude toward the forms of growth or other
natural appearances is perfectly consistent with nomadic values.

The nomadic sense of growth, form, and nature as something to
be free from helps explain both the Hebrew resistance to autochthony and the Biblical connection between physical "withdrawal"
and freedom: for in fact the Hebrew verb meaning *to leave* means
also "to go free."[75] Nomads have sacred space too, but not a farmer's
kind, not a kind which would lead to the autochthonic or at least
nativistic ideologies of the early empires. The habit of movement itself, the mental set required for the readiness to undertake it, should
be studied as a dynamic force in opposition to the early civilizations.

72. See D. M. G. Stalker in *Peake's Commentary, s.v.,* "Exodus VII–X."
73. I Kings 19.
74. See Note 57 above.
75. Speiser, *Oriental and Biblical Studies,* 202.

It created a sacredness of spatial emergence rather than one of continuity, and it leads eventually to the great literary theme of the journey or quest, including picaresque versions which are full of implicit social criticism.

THE DESERT AS THE OTHER

> Yet I am Yahweh, your God since the days in the land of Egypt; you know no God but me, there is no other saviour. I pastured you in the wilderness; in the land of drought I pastured them, and they were satisfied.
>
> —Hos. 13:4–5

> Yahweh says this: I remember the affection of your youth, the love of your bridal days: you followed me through the wilderness, through a land unsown.
>
> —Jer. 2:2

> A voice cries, "Prepare in the wilderness a way for Yahweh. Make a straight highway for our God across the desert."
>
> —Isa. 40:3

Yahweh, unlike the nature gods of the pantheons, is fittingly found in the wilderness, as opposed to the cities, marketplaces, or grainfields: the unearthly landscape of the desert is not God's "home" but a scene appropriate to him, for he too is unearthly. It may be that *djinn* and other desert demons are relevant to the ideas behind certain Biblical passages (especially Exodus 4:24–26, where Yahweh tries to kill Moses), but Yahweh is not a "desert god," for he is not localizable anywhere.

The desert is always just over the horizon in the Fertile Crescent, which stands centered in the Old World arid belt that runs from the Sahara to the Gobi. Especially in Palestine itself, the desert is never far out of sight, or mind. A finger of wilderness thrusts up from the Negev into the Jordan Valley, along the side of the Dead Sea, itself another awesomely unnatural entity; the landscape around the edges of Palestine is one altogether beyond both nature and culture. Frankfort characterizes the Hebrews as living "between the desert

and the sown, between the most fertile of lands and the total negation of life, which, in this remarkable corner of the earth, lie cheek
by jowl."[76]

Frankfort goes on to remark that the cost to the Hebrew of withdrawing from urban-agricultural values is loss of "the bond with
the phenomenal world":

In fact, he gains his freedom at the cost of significant form. For, wherever
we find reverence for the phenomena of life and growth, we find preoccupation with the immanence of the divine and with the *form* of its manifestation. But in the stark solitude of the desert, where nothing changes,
nothing moves (except man at his own free will), where features in the
landscape are only pointers, landmarks, without significance in themselves
—there we may expect the image of God to transcend concrete phenomena
altogether.[77]

No image could be made of Yahweh, Frankfort suggests, precisely
because of this loss of "significant form" from nature. But notice
that the experience of the desert he describes is that of a seminomad: to Bedouin, as to Don Juan in Mexico, the desert is full of
immanent "power spots," the landscape is mythologized, and is
neither lifeless nor terrifying. But to the seminomad who must live
next to it yet could not flourish on it, the desert's formlessness could
suggest that aspect of the numinous that Rudolf Otto called the
"Wholly Other."[78] Ultimately, it is the discontinuity of the desert
with the usual forms of life that could give the paradox of a concrete image of transcendence.

The handiest way to visualize the relevance of the desert in this

76. Frankfort *et al., Before Philosophy*, 246. Martin Noth in *The Old Testa-
ment World* summarizes many important points about Palestinian geography.
Standard works on the subject include George Adam Smith, *The Historical Geog-
raphy of the Holy Land* (1894; rpt. of 25th ed. [1931] New York: Harper, 1966);
Denis Baly, *The Geography of the Bible* (New York: Harper, 1957); Aharoni, *The
Land of the Bible;* and the several good Bible atlases.

77. Frankfort *et al., Before Philosophy*, 247. See also Eric Voegelin, *Order and
History*, Vol. I, *Israel and Revelation* (Baton Rouge: Louisiana State University
Press, 1956), 113.

78. Rudolf Otto, *The Idea of the Holy*, trans. John W. Harvey (1923; rpt. New
York: Oxford University Press, 1958), 25–30. Shepard uses the phrase "otherness
of the desert," in his *Man in the Landscape*, 51.

sense is to look at pictures of Sinai, or the Negev, or the Judaean wilderness where Christ went to be tempted and where Bishop Pike went to die.[79] A few examples will show what Frankfort means by "the desert as a metaphysical experience." The morphology of desert forms, such as they are, plays preternatural variations on our sense of landscape. The earth looks broken and carved, as if by giant hands—a consequence of the type of erosion that takes place in arid lands. The crags and outcrops, antithetical to the rounded and harmonious forms of a landscape we can live in, attract us precisely because they are alien, not familiar: as Frankfort says, they are "the total negation of life."

Let us avoid confusion: there is nothing morbid or death-centered about Yahwism; such a term could be used of the Egyptians, perhaps. The desert symbolism does not embrace the values of death, which would be something different from negating life: the desert is a standing demythologization of those powers that myths worship as "life," "nature," etc. In myth death is something positive, and is not in any sense a demythologizing of life: in Egypt death was the primary realm of mythic activities.

We can see this contrasting or negating function as the basic structure of the whole pastoral symbolism, as it is of many intellectual forms. The structural linguists have long since shown the defining value of opposition, and Lévi-Strauss has found mythological and totemic thought built on the basic principle of binary opposition.[80] In various ways antithesis has been postulated as a "law" of

79. See figs. 13–15.

80. See the works of Roman Jakobson, especially his work with C. G. M. Fant and Morris Halle, *Preliminaries to Speech Analysis: The Distinctive Features and Their Correlates* (Cambridge, Mass.: MIT Press, 1969) and his "Linguistics and Communication Theory," in *Selected Writings*, Vol. II (4 vols. projected; The Hague, Mouton, 1971), esp. 571. Milka Ivić, *Trends in Linguistics*, trans. Muriel Heppell (The Hague: Mouton, 1965), says that "Jakobson's descriptions of distinctive features, on which depends the establishment of phonemic oppositions according to the principle of binarism, have been carefully elaborated and today are already classic" (p. 145). He adds that "in fact all information theory rests on the application of this principle" (p. 226). Lévi-Strauss's debt to Jakobson is well known and fully acknowledged. His analysis of the Oedipus myth into "bundles of relations" recalls Jakobson's definition of a phoneme as a "bundle of distinctive

human thought, precisely because it is so useful. There are special reasons, however, for suspecting that the principle of opposition was heightened and dramatized in the ancient Near East, going back to the cultural dialectic and symbiosis between agricultural and pastoral ways. A sense of conflict that is recognized as somehow both dangerous and stimulating seems to pervade the thought of the area; it must stem from a recognition that the whole spectrum of life, once civilization had been introduced, depended on the violent clashes which engendered change. Perhaps there was some sense of the feeling Reinhold Niebuhr saw behind Greek tragedy, that there can be no creation without destruction.[81] For, as remarked before, civilizations thrive on change, although the early ones tried to muffle their awareness of the fact; the pervasiveness of the pastoral symbolism and associated complexes throughout the area might well signal an underlying anxiety about this needful conflict.

The desert plays a part in the history of the Near East that uncannily suits the role of great opposite, enhancing and threatening man's life at the same time. There was an older theory that the advance of the desert, an increase of aridization drying up former jungles, was the efficient cause of civilization, forcing scattered bands of people to come together in oases and river-valleys until a "critical mass" was assembled that could make the leap to domestication, division of labor, etc. We need not subscribe to this oversimplified picture, especially since the climatic evidence is not agreed upon, but we can easily see that once civilization did begin in the river-valleys the deserts did much to protect it. The great deserts and the associated mountain chains that flank Egypt and Mesopotamia would serve as both gates and barriers. They can be crossed by purposeful journeys for trade and immigration, but they discourage

---

features." (See Lévi-Strauss, *Structural Anthropology*, esp. 225.) Lévi-Strauss treats binarism as universal, but even so we might find greater and lesser employments of the law. See Ecclus. 33:15: "This is the way to view all the works of the Most High; they go in pairs, by opposites."

81. Niebuhr, *Nature and Destiny*, I, 10–11. Obviously this sense of conflict is too deep and ambivalent to be explained by more simple theories such as Toynbee's "challenge-and-response."

casual encroachment by hordes of strange humans, animals, or plants. Where forests or grasslands would have given too easy acess to invaders of various kinds, so that the early city-dwellers would have had to spend inordinate time on erecting barriers, the desert allowed entry in the early stages only to enough invaders to serve as a challenge: or even to be assimilated. Thus in a sense the desert provided a quality control: the nomads who came to raid and in many cases remained to settle had to be an ambitious and hardy breed; not just any backwater tent-dweller would do.

The desert's service in this way points up its simultaneously life-supporting and life-negating function. The fact that the desert is a highly selective environment and that only organisms of great adapt-ability can survive on it is obvious in the case of humans, but also critical in the case of plant growth and early agriculture. It is being increasingly recognized that, for their origins, our important cul-tivated plants were required to be ecological disturbers and invaders, to have weedy tendencies. The necessary variation and hybridization for the evolution of "noble grasses" into cereals cannot have taken place where native flora had worked out a systematic balance: man, or rivers, or fire must make "scars" on the earth where the plants we desire can gain a foothold. "Cultivated plants and their ancestors are, from one point of view, nature's misfits. They cannot form a part of climax vegetation but must needs take advantage of dis-turbed open soils or rocky areas of such poor soil quality that noth-ing without the tenacious powers of quick growth and ability to store large quantities of food could survive."[82] A persuasive hypo-thesis for the origins of "hoe culture" is the so-called dump-heap theory: on middens and refuse piles the weeds that are ancestral to valued plants will spring up, and these weeds provide the necessary hybridization with closely related forms that precedes the appear-ance of the great food-storers. In the alluvial deserts of Egypt and Mesopotamia, the rivers in uncontrolled flood leave mudbanks and floodplains suitable for hybrid development. But the origins of

82. J. G. Hawkes, "The ecological background of plant domestication," in Ucko and Dimbleby (eds.), *Domestication and Exploitation*, 29.

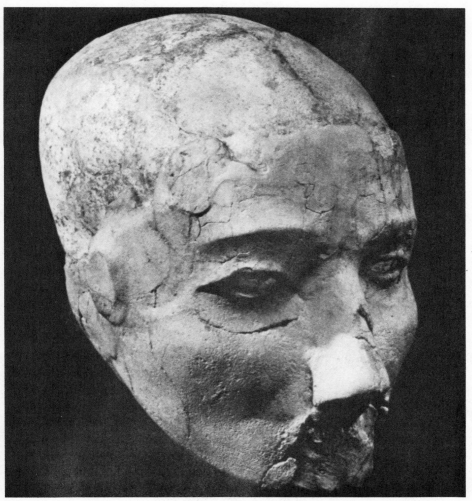

FIGURE 1. Neolithic plastered skull, Jericho. See page 82.

FIGURE 2. "Venus of Willendorf." See page 91.

FIGURE 3.   Palette of Narmer. See page 92.

FIGURE 4. Pregnant woman under reindeer. See page 92.

FIGURE 5. Hybrid bull-man. See page 94.

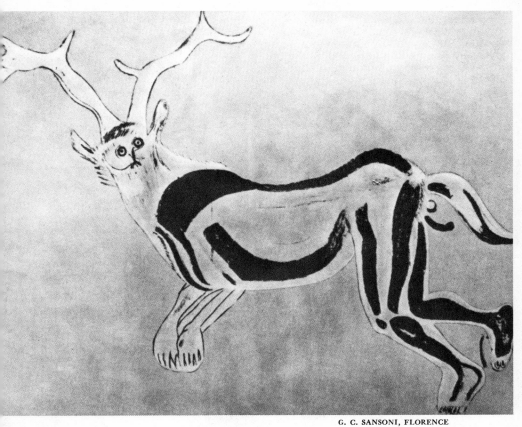

G. C. SANSONI, FLORENCE

FIGURE 6. "Dancing Sorcerer" (watercolor copy). See page 94.

FIGURE 7.   Imdugud. See page 96.

FIGURE 8.   Scorpion-man and goat-servant. See page 96.

FIGURE 9. Bull on lyre. See page 97.

FIGURE 10.   Mithraic sacrifice. See page 97.

FIGURE 11. "Venus of Laussel." See page 98.

FIGURE 12. Golden sarcophagus of King Tutankhamen. See page 130.

FIGURE 13. Yahwist landscape: Judean desert. See pages 143–44.

FIGURE 14. Yahwist landscape: Negev. See pages 143–44.

FIGURE 15. Yahwist landscape: Sinai. See pages 143–44.

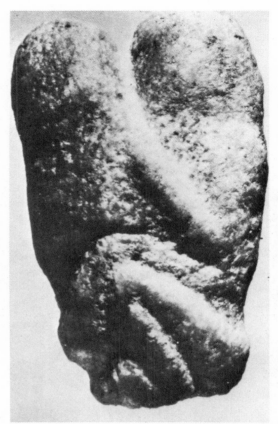

FIGURE 16. Erotic figurine from pre-Hebrew
Palestine. See page 152.

FIGURE 17. Wall painting, Beni Hasan, Egypt: traveling forge? See page 190.

KATHLEEN M. KENYON

FIGURE 18. Neolithic tower, Jericho; part of wall older in Joshua's time than pyramids are now. See pages 191 and 6.

FIGURE 19. Canaanite Astarte; cf. figures 2 and 11. See page 225.

FIGURE 20. Min, with Astarte (as *Qudshu* or "Holiness," deity of cult prostitutes) on lion, and Resheph on right. See pages 239 and 240n.

FIGURE 21. Another version of Min, with Astarte on lion, and Resheph on right.

FIGURE 22. Min-Kamutef. See page 239.

FIGURE 23. Min; vulva signs on kneecaps.

APPROXIMATE CHRONOLOGY
Of Events and Artifacts Mentioned in the Text

6,000,000–1,000,000 B.C.—Emergence of "man"

3,000,000–500,000 B.C.—"Peking man," remains at Choukoutien (brain-eating?)

250,000–50,000 B.C.—Neanderthal man, "Mousterian" culture (definite brain-eating)

60,000–50,000 B.C.—Indisputable evidence for burial of dead, often arranged with animal bones and (at Shanidar cave, at least) with flowers

30,000–12,000 B.C.—Cave art, such as "Dancing Sorcerer"; Venus-figurines, bone-engravings such as "Woman under Reindeer," also calendrical marks (Marshack)

12,000–8000 B.C.—Neolithic revolution of domestic arts, preconditions of urbanism; beginnings of wheat/barley and sheep/goat domestication

8000 B.C.—Jericho, oldest town, emerges from pre-Hebrew cultures of Palestine. Ancestral skulls; erotic figurines?

6500 B.C.—Çatal Hüyük in Anatolia, Old European culture in Balkans (Marija Gimbutas)

4800 B.C.—Oldest megaliths in Brittany

4000 B.C.—Emergence of Sumerian culture (Invention of wheel, etc.)

3100 B.C.—Traditional date of first writing, in Sumer; rise of Egyptian culture; use of bronze

2800 B.C.—Stonehenge

2600 B.C.—Date of Gilgamesh? Age of pyramid-building

2300 B.C.—Sargon of Akkad invents standing army; emperors as gods

1800 B.C.—Hammurabi

1700 B.C.—Abraham? Withdrawals of partially assimilated Semitic and other elements from Mesopotamian cities; Hyksos in Egypt

1350 B.C.—Akhenaten; Habiru a problem

1290–1230 B.C.—Rameses 11 (Ozymandias)

1250–1230 B.C.—Probable date of Exodus from Egypt; Song of Miriam?

1200–1190 B.C.—Philistines (among "Sea Peoples") repulsed from Egypt, settle in Palestine, bringing iron weapons; domestication of camel?

1100–1025 B.C.—Period of Judges follows Hebrew conquest of Palestine; Song of Deborah?

1040–1010 B.C.—Eli, Samuel, Saul

1010–970 B.C.—David; captures Jerusalem about 1000

970–931 B.C.—Solomon, Temple, chariot army; after his death the united kingdom again becomes two, Israel (North) and Judah (South). J? Court Historian?

885–874 B.C.—Omri; height of Israel's power; Assyria begins to rise

874–853 B.C.—Ahab, Jezebel, Baalism, Elijah

841–814 B.C.—Jehu, usurper of throne of Israel, slaughters Baalists

760–740 B.C.—Amos, Isaiah, rise of "writing prophets"

721 B.C.—Conquest of Israel (North) by Assyria; deportation of Ten Lost Tribes

687–642 B.C.—Manasseh king of Judah; pagan cults, even male prostitutes in Temple; martyrdom of Isaiah?

640–609 B.C.—Josiah, Yahwist reaction; Deuteronomic reform; revision-editing of historical books? 621 is traditional date of finding of "book of the Law" (Deuteronomy) in Temple

606 B.C.—Assyrian empire overcome by Babylonians

598–586 B.C.—Judah succumbs to Babylonians; deportations; Ezekiel

539 B.C.—Cyrus of Persia conquers Babylon, allows Jews and others to return to native lands

490–440 B.C.—Battles of Marathon, Salamis, rise of Athens

336–323 B.C.—Alexander the Great

175–163 B.C.—Antiochus IV Epiphanes; Daniel

63 B.C.—Pompey takes Jerusalem; the empty shrine

44 B.C.—Julius Caesar assassinated

37–34 B.C.—Herod the Great

7/6 B.C.–30 A.D.—Life of Jesus

50–67 A.D.—Letters of Paul

65–100 A.D.—Gospels

wheat and barley were not here: they began up the "hilly flanks" of the mountains around the Fertile Crescent, in Anatolia and Iran, and were then imported to the floodplains, probably in stages. Very likely these weedy grasses were harvested wild up in the hills for a long time, and then some of their seeds sprouted when taken to rocky ledges, leading to enough hybridization for cultivation to begin. Then they might be moved again, each invasion of an ecological niche giving them a new advantage, and finally they were taken to the desert, where they could dominate immediately when supplied with water from irrigation. Large-scale agriculture could never have contended, at this date, with rain forest or even grass-land: primitive plows and hoes are not strong enough. But the desert, once watered, was like truly virgin soil, especially alluvial desert where rivers cut a swathe through native vegetation. Every Californian knows the phenomenon: sandy, scabby-looking, and apparently lifeless soil which with a little water will grow varieties of plants in great abundance. The Imperial Valley, a rich site formerly desert, recapitulates the early Near Eastern patterns.

Edgar Anderson, who has summarized some of these points in his handy *Plants, Man, and Life*, also observes that insects and other enemies that keep plants in check in their native places are effectively countered by moving the plants to alien areas. As he says, most of our American cash-crops are Asian in origin.[83] What better new locale for keeping down insects and rodents than a desert? So the desert's harshness gives tended crops a great head start.

Both the weedy hybrids that are the basis of our agriculture and the primate hybrids that we are ourselves have a tendency toward flourishing in opposition to other varieties of life, rather than the habit of fitting quietly into ecological niches. This tendency is exaggerated by Western man, but true of all: Anderson contends that the history of weeds is the history of man.[84] We, like weeds, want to dominate not integrate: we too are "nature's misfits." Consequently

---

83. Edgar Anderson, *Plants, Man, and Life* (1952; rpt. Berkeley, University of California Press, 1967), 187.
84. *Ibid.*, 15.

the desert's fundamental hostility to life is good for man too. Aridity is healthful for us, since it reduces what we must contend with, especially micro-organisms. An excess of water, as in the tropics, means an excess of life forms to be combated: and man is debilitated by germs or parasites or pests, or by the struggle against them. Where there is fever in the ground, man's life is short and only great fecundity keeps his settlements going. But where genetics combines with aridity, some astonishing life-spans are reached, as by the famous Russian peasants of the Central Asian arid belt. In such areas, if a man can survive the various threats of childhood and young manhood, he can prolong his life amazingly. This may even be part of the explanation of the mythological life-spans of Genesis. We know of several other factors tht might have been involved, *e.g.*, confused chronologies, as in ancient king-lists, where for instance a discrepancy in a king's dates may be remedied by having him reign from one date to the other, sometimes hundreds of years apart. Also playing a part is the Hebrew concept of "corporate personality," in which many generations will be referred to by the name of the tribal ancestor: see Judges 1:3, where Judah and Simeon are said to converse, though they lived 500 years before and obviously their tribal councils are meant. The name *Israel* itself is an even better example. But given the possibilities for life-spans in arid regions, Methuselah might not be as far out of line as we tend to think.

For the early civilizations, the epidemiological advantages of the desert were largely offset by the great rivers themselves: they carried all kinds of parasites and other disease vectors.[85] No doubt one of the factors in the growth of sedentarism was the accommodation of the population to parasitic and endemic diseases through breeding patterns. For the established populations, natural selection would have helped build relative immunity: individuals with resistant genes would propagate; those without would die off early. But then

85. See Darlington, *The Evolution of Man*, 40–41, 651; also Deut. 7:15, 28:60, and Amos 4:10. These passages make it clear that the "plagues of Egypt" were originally suffered by the Hebrews, not the Egyptians.

we can see even more clearly why nomads would fear sedentary centers, for they would be unprotected populations. Even today, some nomads move whenever disease breaks out: they associate all illness with places.[86] So this healthy fear would further stretch the tensions that produced the symbolic clash of shepherd with culture. Culture means growing—too many things growing to suit nomads. No wonder for them the pullulating life of the floodplains was (in Frankfort's words) "sordid," "a scene of decay."

It also happens that man possesses a body-cooling system that allows him to work in heat that would enervate most animals, if by foresight he has arranged for sufficient water: so here is another advantage he would have in the desert. (Sheep too can thrive in heat unbearable for other animals, for their air-trapping fleece is an insulator that can keep body temperature forty or more degrees cooler than the outside air.) [87] If we add together all the advantages that can come into play on the steppe or desert, we can understand why the beginnings of settlement flourished on their edges and why pastoralism increasingly encroached on these lands. But the basic advantage for man is simply his adaptability, the capacity he has for dealing with a variety of conditions. Early man established himself in many types of environments, including jungles: this demonstrates the quality. But it would also follow that man would flourish best where this adaptability could come most fully into play. What environments would best serve to bring it out? Sauer thinks of the seashore, while most contemporary biologists seem fascinated with the image of man the hunter on the African savannas.

But surely the best of all worlds for man would be "rift valleys" or other faulted zones with greatly varied landscapes, where rivers, mountains, and plains or deserts are pushed close together by tectonic forces. East Africa, land of the savannas, is at one end of the "Great Rift Valley": the other end is the Jordan Valley of Palestine.

86. James Woodburn, in Ucko, Tringham, and Dimbleby (eds.), *Man, Settlement, and Urbanism*, 204.
87. Kent Flannery remarks that the dominance of sheep (and barley) in the Near East results from their tolerance of heat and salinated land: Ucko and Dimbleby (eds.), *Domestication and Exploitation*, 91–92.

Such broken landscapes are places where we find many traces of early man: East Africa and Palestine are two of the richest sites. On the other side of the Fertile Crescent, where up to now we have found most of the earliest remains of animal and plant domestication, a similarly rifted landscape presents itself. Because of late Pliocene folding, Iran was shoved closer to Arabia; then Mesopotamia slowly sank in the middle of the crunched area. "The result was an area in which altitudinal differences produce a great number of contrasting environments in a relatively limited geographic area . . . [including] high plateau (c. 5000 ft.), intermontane valleys (1500–4000 ft.), piedmont-steppe (600–1000 ft.), and alluvial desert (100–500 ft.)."[88] Once again the role of contrast seems to be crucial: if we remember the point that man is the only animal that can run fast, swim far, then climb a tree, and extend this to complicated conditions, we can see why. In fact the earliest village sites are often found on the borders of climatic and vegetational zones: e.g., where oak-pistachio forest meets steppeland, in Iran. Such borderlands would be ideal places for working out the systems of symbiosis when early "herder castes" broke off from agriculturalists.

In judging the importance of variety in terrain, more than just adaptability is involved: it may have been the complicated demographic problems arising from the intersection of "optimal" hunting areas with "marginal" ones that gave rise to cereal-eating and cultivation in the first place.[89] Hunting peoples normally feed themselves quite well, and would have needed no new food sources; but if some areas were so good that the population rose fast, and the surplus people moved to handy "marginal" areas, a need might arise to cause experimentation. So the interplay of adaptability, inventiveness, and environment full of contrasts may well have caused the beginnings of the world as we know it: though cultivation might well have arisen from ritual needs, not biological ones. In any case, in the lands where it happened, the proximity and usefulness of the desert seem to have been always a part of the formula.

In the nineteenth century, Ernest Renan and others guessed that

88. *Ibid.*, 73.
89. *Ibid.*, 76.

the monotony of the desert had something to do with monotheism. In fact they cannot have been wholly wrong, if Frankfort's points about "the desert experience" are valid: yet far more important than monotony, in the whole tangled history of early civilization and the ambivalence toward it that gave Yahwism its distinctive character, is the variety of the landscape where the desert intrudes. By itself the desert would have led to nothing; in combination with valleys, meadows, plains, and ultimately cities, it produced a formidable set of developments. Everywhere it furnished the frontier that could serve as barrier, gate, refuge, irrigated cropland, and so on. The peasants of Egypt and Sumer hated and feared it, just as they did the nomads on it; but their grudge must have concealed some sense, however dim, that their own cultures had come into being partly through its agency. Hermann Kees, the Egyptologist, notes with irony when "settled people began to hate the desert from which their ancestors came."

It was a foreign land and it was contrasted unfavourably as the "red" with the "black" fertile soil which gave Egypt its name *Kemet* ("the Black"). Similarly the free nomads of the desert profoundly despised the *fellaheen* tied to the soil. Everything that comes from the desert, everything that moves about in it is sinister to the peasant's eyes, even if it is only so peaceful and harmless an animal as the dainty gazelle or the fleet hare.[90]

In Mesopotamia, desert raiders were often pictured as demons from the underworld. The depth of the sundering in spirit between the people of the two ecologic zones is increased by the cheek-by-jowl layout of the two: except for the delta itself, Egypt is only a thin strip of arable land hemmed in by desert, and the desert intrudes in a similar way on Mesopotamia. So the two ways of life, like the two landscapes, lay locked in hostile embrace, and we now dig out their traces and live out their attitudes.[91]

In the midst of these tensions we find innumerable signs of the

90. Kees, *Ancient Egypt*, 36–37.
91. See John A. Wilson in Frankfort *et al.*, *Before Philosophy*, 47: in Egypt "the same hieroglyphic sign was used for 'foreign country' that was used for 'highland' or for 'desert'. . . . Thus the Egyptian pictorially grouped the foreigner with the beast of the desert and pictorially denied the foreigner the blessings of fertility and uniformity."

Hebrew consciousness coming to birth. If "Eden" was borrowed by them from the *edin*-steppe of Sumer, it was charged with pastoral connotations; likewise, the play on words that occurs as Adam emerges from the ground (*adamah*) may hark back to the practice of calling the desert "the red," for *adamah* is apparently related to the word for "red," as for instance in *"Edom"*: supposedly from Esau's hair. (Esau even eats Jacob's reddish [*adom*] soup.) Thus man, whose name and life are of the (red) ground, is set in a (steppe) garden, provided with a miraculous source of water (Gen. 2:6). But he sins and is driven out to be a farmer. His sons form the first symbiosis, but only the shepherd's offerings please God, whereupon the farmer murders his brother: perhaps, it has even been suggested, this was originally a tale of ritual sacrifice to increase the fields' fertility— human sacrifice for that purpose being well known in the ancient world.[92]

Eden, like the *edin*, is between the Tigris and Euphrates (Gen. 2:10–14) and there is no going back there. The land of promise, of milk and honey, is Palestine, equally permeated with the tensions between pastoral and cultured ways. On the one hand, if Sauer's suggestion is correct that the Near East as a whole is more pastoral than peasant, Palestine would be the nearest thing to an exception, for the chthonic associations of the land of Canaan go back to the ritual burials of the cave-dwellers of Mount Carmel. Here, at Natufian sites, are found some of the oldest traces of fertility-animal-earth cults, as described by Emmanuel Anati: one suggestive artifact may be the world's oldest erotic figurine, a portrayal of copulation no doubt good for fertility.[93] The Natufians may well have been a forager-fisher culture like those that Sauer postulates as the originators of "hoe culture"; they were at least semisedentary before agriculture even developed. Megalithism had a very early foothold in the land; many rude structures survive. The very brokenness of the landscape, and the intrusion of the desert, made groves, springs, and

92. See S. H. Hooke in *Peake's Commentary*, *s.v.*, "Genesis IV." On *adom*, see Albright, *Yahweh and the Gods of Canaan*, 140.
    93. See fig. 16.

oases the early sites of chthonic cults. "It is a remarkable fact that the spring at Jericho, which became the site of the oldest known town, appears to have been revered from early times."[94] In short Palestine was superbly equipped to be a fit prize for Hebrew conquest: its local mythologies, cult sites, city-states, and farming-commercial culture, imitative of and much dominated by Egypt and Mesopotamia, represented all that against which the Hebrews thrust themselves. The antiquity of chthonic Canaan, expressed in its culture, made it a defining opposite for Hebrew aspirations. The story of their sojourn in it is one of constant struggle against the idolatrous temptations of the chthonic, naturalistic religion of the Canaanites.

On the other hand, evidence exists to suggest that Palestine was often in the hands of pastoralists and had suffered several such invasions before that of the Hebrews. Gaps in archaeological records at many sites are interpreted by some investigators to signify periods of nomadic conquest. We believe that the people the Bible knows as "Amorites" were the latest to sack the cities of Palestine, about 2300 B.C., before the Canaanites and Hebrews came.[95] Perhaps this was part of a cyclical or even ritual pattern of invasion and sedentarization: Palestine's geography may have made it desirable and accessible to recurrent waves of nomads. The succession of settlements at Jericho, as at Troy, indicates that these cities "fell" not once but many times: and each time new creation would arise out of destruction. Surely the access to Palestine of these nomads was enhanced by the penetration of the deserts into the area. Whereas in one context the desert around the oasis of Jericho served as defense, in another context—*i.e.,* when the nomads grew better organized—the desert served as a highway, and as a refuge where nomadic forces could withdraw if necessary. Joshua's army could have used the same pattern, as could all "Hebrews" before or since. At about the same time that Jesus retreated to the wilderness where John the Baptist and

94. Sonia Cole, *The Neolithic Revolution* (London: British Museum, 1967), 58.
95. See Kathleen Kenyon, *Amorites and Canaanites* (London: British Academy, 1963), 76; also her "Jericho" in D. Winton Thomas (ed.), *Archaeology and Old Testament Study* (Oxford: Clarendon, 1967), 266–69.

the Qumran Community flourished, Herod constructed what he thought was an inaccessible and impregnable fortress in the desert at Masada. (A supremely determined Roman army later proved him wrong.) Herod was not a Hebrew; he didn't understand, as T. E. Lawrence did later, that the desert was for mobility.[96]

If we weigh all these facts, hypotheses, and symbols together, certain conclusions are inescapable. The pastoral motifs that have such force in the Bible derive their significance from the emergence of what we call civilization, but what they portray is the contingent nature of it. The precise nature of the definition that the shepherd and desert give to the city by opposing it is one that reminds us, through images of civilization's fragility as well as those of its oppressiveness, that it is not at all "in the order of things." Though the pastoral symbolism does not recognize nature as an antidote to culture, it does emphasize the sense in which urban culture took a turn away from the older way of things, in which culture had been integrated with nature, and which before 10,000 B.C. had served man for over a million years. Man as hunter-collector and forager-fisher was all the world knew of him for the vast majority of human time. Then a set of circumstances fell together, and he began to do quite different things and live in different ways: some of these carrying the seeds of specialization out beyond the tribal "division of labor," so that the possibilities of withdrawal and conflict appear. When fissiparous specialization begins, the integrated culture is called in question, and pastoral symbolism arises to oppose those who substitute regimentation for integration.

The respected prehistorian Stuart Piggott concludes that "all my study of the past persuades me that the emergence of what we call civilisation is a most abnormal and unpredictable event, perhaps in all its Old World manifestations ultimately due to a single set of unique circumstances in a restricted area of western Asia some 5,000 years ago. . . . It is, I would rather suggest, the non-civilised societies of antiquity that were the norm" of humanity.[97] Surely it is fitting

96. See pp. 54–58 in Toynbee (ed.), *The Crucible of Christianity*.
97. Stuart Piggott, *Ancient Europe: From the Beginnings of Agriculture to*

that two foods, wheat and milk, which symbolize the new way, leave traces of their difficult adaptation on the species that has thrived on them: they still cause the commonest allergies, suggesting a reservoir of intolerance in the human population.[98] The development of these products of the agricultural and pastoral innovations was fateful for us in many senses: not only did it stimulate the possibilities of growth and break forever the demographic patterns of the old way, but also it rendered a return to natural ecology impossible.

Starting with a relatively stable configuration of plant and animal species at 10,000 B.C., early cultivation took two genera of cereal grasses [wheat and barley] and two genera of small ungulates [goats and sheep] out of their habitat and artificially increased their numbers while they underwent a series of genetic changes, many of which were favourable from man's standpoint. These favourable changes made feasible a still greater investment of human labour in the cereals and caprines, and a greater artificial expansion of their range at the expense of other species. At this point, the ecosystem was no longer cybernating, or "stable."

This writer, Kent Flannery, concludes that "return to a wild resource economy would have been nearly impossible."[99] Civilization was off and running on its creative-destructive pattern, fueled by the new foods.

The inhabitants of Sumer and Egypt must have been troubled by their own sense of deviation from the old ways; this would explain their frantic efforts to elaborate a naturalistic ideology, resulting in the rigidified traditions spoken of earlier. The more insecure they felt, the harder they would try to justify their way and place of life as given, normal, natural, that to which all should aspire. The pastoral complex contradicts this effort and demythologizes its ideological products, pronouncing the urban way of life provisional and

Classical Antiquity (Chicago: Aldine, 1965), 20. New arguments against "diffusionism" (see Renfrew, *Before Civilization*) may require some revision in such statements: but the point about the abnormality of civilizations remains valid.

98. See John Yudkin, "Archaeology and the nutritionist," in Ucko and Dimbleby (eds.), *Domestication and Exploitation*, 549. In fact milk does not "have something for every body"; populations must adapt to it genetically. In the fecund populations of the Far East and tropical Africa they did not do so.

99. Ucko and Dimbleby (eds.), *Domestication and Exploitation*, 95.

conventional instead of cosmically centered. It has no need to call for the utter destruction of civilization, being neither nihilistic nor even revolutionary in the political sense. It serves, rather, as culture's *memento mori*, bidding us remember our ends and our beginnings.

The sense of conflict underlying the symbolism in part manifests a sense that civilization, because of its need for change, profits by opposition. In part the pastoral symbolism replaces the "cybernetic" effects of natural checks and balances. The city-states, and then the empires, rise and fall, but this success / failure pattern is disastrous only for those who put all their eggs, as it were, in one basket. The implicit demythologizations in Western culture minimize psychic overinvestment in a fixed form of life; consequently the ambivalence latent in the pastoral symbolism has been on the whole good for us, or at least has helped us stay out of static patterns leading to decadence. The allergies caused by the shepherds' and farmers' foods, milk and wheat, are symbolic of more than the "unnaturalness" of the bases of civilized life: these breakfast foods of ours get us going, for they represent all the factors synergizing in the development of civilization that can produce rapid, sometimes gigantic growth on the one hand and dysfunction on the other. They stand for that speeding-up of cultural evolution that has been carried to its extreme in Western industrialized societies: each advance bringing new costs, each disaster new opportunities for creation. We, and our forms of culture, live and change at what for archaic men would have been an inconceivably hectic pace. The Mousterian culture, which persisted in essence even while its people were mutating somatically, is at the farthest possible remove from our style of life.[100] That kind of culture might as well have been God-given: but our own efforts to appropriate a similar rationale for our own forms of life are feeble and intermittent, precisely because the Bible gives us, in such insistent symbolisms as the pastoral complex, unavoidable images of culture's contingency and of the psychic withdrawal that results in a continuity of change. No Westerner is ever wholly a

100. See Note 54 to Chapter Two herein.

citizen of his own time and place; other ideals, looking forward or backward, draw him on, and the pastoral symbolism reminds him that it is this decentered condition, not the givenness of his immediate society, that is a necessary constant for him.

LITERARY PASTORAL

The long vogue of the pastoral suggests that it is connected with a universal impulse of the human mind.

—Harold Jenkins

Pastoral—a puzzling form that looks proletarian but isn't.

—William Empson

The literature that we call pastoral derives specifically from Virgil and some other classical authors, although pastoral theorists, aware of a debt to the Bible, used to point to some of the Psalms as crowning achievements in the genre. As poetry it has been of minor importance since the Renaissance, but a reflective look at the tensions and issues involved in the pastoral symbolism of the Bible convinces one that pastoral is not just a quaint kind of poetry that imitated classical works; the essential themes have spread far and wide, appearing in a great number of major works of literature. That pastoral is more than a limited genre is the position of William Empson, whose *Some Versions of Pastoral* takes a suggestively comprehensive viewpoint. Though he does not trace the form back to the Bible, Empson finds pastoral in a number of diverse texts ranging through Shakespeare's histories to *Alice in Wonderland*. Obviously one does not have to use the regular machinery—shepherds with oaten flutes, laurel wreaths, and so on—to be making use of pastoral attitudes.[101]

101. Besides William Empson, *Some Versions of Pastoral* (1935; rpt. New York: New Directions, 1960), see the survey by Harold E. Toliver, *Pastoral Forms and Attitudes* (Berkeley: University of California Press, 1971), and a collection called *Pastoral and Romance: Modern Essays in Criticism,* ed. Eleanor Terry Lincoln (Englewood Cliffs, N. J.: Prentice-Hall, 1969). A handy anthology of the traditional poems is Frank Kermode (ed.), *English Pastoral Poetry: From the Beginnings to Marvell* (London: Harrap, 1952). See also Raymond Williams, *The Country and the City* (New York: Oxford University Press, 1973), for a broad view of the antithesis in English literature.

In the great age of poetry when those motifs seemed alive, and not mere machinery, pastoral was the form recommended to the poet beginning the climb up the ladder of Parnassus, so as to follow the example of Virgil. Much of the poetry thus produced was at best apprentice-work, naturally, but in the hands of masters like Spenser the form was amazingly flexible and effective. The hallmark of the best pastoral was its infusion with Christian issues. Of course the values of classical pastoral diverged from those of the Bible, but the Renaissance desire to mesh them produced some viable syntheses. The most notable success harmonized classical *otium,* the ideal of the simple retired life, with Biblical mistrust of worldly striving and success. Hallett Smith, the authoritative critic, cites what we might call the four freedoms of Christianized *otium*: freedom from envy and care, freedom from the consequences of the life of pride, freedom to do what you like in near-perfect leisure, and freedom from what the Elizabethans conceived as the most fascinating and appalling of moral temptations: the "aspiring mind." Though the tyrant Nimrod, to whom Babel was ascribed, was often named as the first sinner in this kind, Milton could later use the idea as an inspiration for Satan. "The central meaning of pastoral," says Smith, "is the rejection of the aspiring mind."[102]

Much pastoral poetry in this vein was a criticism of courtiers by each other. When the feudal structure decayed, a courtier ceased to be typically a great marcher lord with an independent power base, and became something much nearer a middle-class man on the make. So the repeated warnings against aspiration and ambition, and even the tradition of "dispraise of the court" itself which grew up in consequence, were part of the courtly game. But at its best pastoral was considerably more than finger-waggling at one's rivals and opponents. Beneath the criticism of the aspiring mind lay an insight into the infinitude of human desires: so that the obverse of pastoral, in

102. Hallett Smith, *Elizabethan Poetry* (1952; rpt. Ann Arbor: University of Michigan Press, 1968), 10–11. *Otium* also implied the positive benefits of leisure for creativity and education (school comes from a Greek word meaning *leisure*) that is emphasized by Paul Shepard's remark that pastoral, as a life without "arduous labour," gave "freedom to discourse, think, make music, dance, and make love" (see note 33 above) and, of course, make poetry.

this sense, is the myth of Faust. The inability to be satisfied by any created thing—the literal endlessness and therefore emptiness of desire—was both empirically evident in this age, and an image for its people of the abyss of Hell. This at least was directly from the Biblical tradition, expressed in the forceful terms of the prophets. It becomes obvious here that the Bible was not just an auxiliary source of pastoral images, but the power that allowed the form to seize the imagination of the Christian West.

In this regard Christopher Marlowe's works are especially interesting, first because he could write charming pastoral lyrics, second because he was fascinated by Faust and by that apologist for the aspiring mind, Tamburlaine. Some have thought, indeed, that Marlowe's fascination was excessive, that he was of the devil's party and knew it, so that the professions of orthodox morality in the plays are mere sops for the gullible. However, other readings make Marlowe a subtle but not rebellious participant in the traditions of his time.[103] No doubt he, like Shakespeare, saw the emptiness in his own culture, but we need not postulate any deep cynicism to explain that: the Bible itself, of which both authors display rich knowledge, is the best source of insight into the vanity of all societies and all their strivings. True, what Marlowe does with Tamburlaine offers certain satiric possibilities in the light of pastoral's anti-imperial overtones, for here we have a shepherd who conceives the most grandiose of ambitions and turns himself into a tyrannical conqueror. (Of course Tamburlaine is a demythologizer too, of his victims.) Yet in essence this is only a permutation on the theme of the fallen or strayed shepherd: and for this theme classical myth augmented the Bible by offering the figure of Paris, who was tending flocks when he made his fatal judgment. In the mythographic tradition of the Middle Ages and Renaissance, Paris' choice of lust over wisdom and domesticity was an analogue of the Fall of Man, to be interpreted in its light. He should have remained a shepherd, a symbol of Edenic content, leisure, and responsibility.[104]

103. See, *e.g.,* Douglas Cole, *Suffering and Evil in the Plays of Christopher Marlowe* (Princeton, N.J.: Princeton University Press, 1962).
104. See H. Smith, *Elizabethan Poetry,* 3–8.

On the issue of *otium* versus the aspiring mind, classical and Biblical values made a fairly stable combination. The Biblical restrictions still allow for the possibility of right action and just achievement, even for fame, under the qualification that justice can only be sought in orientation toward God, not toward the world; in spite of the inevitable transience of the earthly city one must always strive toward the Just City. There are tensions here, which are precisely those of Western culture, but we have thrived on them just as Elizabethan pastoral used to. However, more basic disjunctions arise in some of the other marriages of Biblical and classical values. In one of the most obvious cases, the classical Golden Age makes an insecure union with the Biblical Paradise, leading to confusions centering on the idea of innocence.

The classical *topos* of the Golden Age, before what Ovid calls "amor habendi" came into the world, suggests a basic continuity of man and nature which is a legacy from the mythological consciousness. Although the Eden story can be brought into analogy with this *topos,* we know that Biblical thought was debarred from envisioning man as essentially continuous with nature. Even in Eden, though there is no disharmony, man is different from and above the other creatures, and in the late version he is said to be made in God's image.[105] Of course the Garden has been a great and fruitful myth in the West; and it was given further Biblical support from a pastiche of texts, including some passages in the Song of Songs, Isaiah's Song of the Vineyard, and some Psalms. Nonetheless, one of the enduring and revealing results was that a stress was laid on the idea of innocence in the Eden story that has very little textual support. Complicated concepts of the purity of life before the Fall, which by the way is not a Biblical term, are almost entirely theologizing elaborations. As far as innocence is concerned, the hypothetical author we call "J" who dramatizes this story deals only with the shame of nakedness that comes after disobedience. J's interest was

105. According to the "documentary" hypothesis accepted in some form by most scholars, Gen. 1–2:4a was written fairly late compared to the "J" material of 2:4b–4, etc.

elsewhere; most of his emphasis is laid on the "curse on the ground," on agricultural and human fertility, which is part of God's punishment of man. He even overdetermines this motif, giving it another causation in Cain's murder of Abel. Somewhere there was a conscious effort by J or one of his sources to repudiate autochthonic ideology: no spirit children or spirits of corn can inhere in accursed soil. On the other hand, J does not affirm that the soil was magically fertile before the curse, any more than he affirms that man was immortal. If anything is magical in J's Garden it is the mysterious "fountain" or "flood" or "mist" of Genesis 2:6; the tendency to see earth as commonplace and water as miraculous is a legacy of the arid lands and is oriented away from autochthony.[106]

Certainly J leaves the door open for later theologizations, especially the fateful one linking sexual desire to death as twin intruders into Eden. This eventually made way for the Western idea which has been called "the invention of childhood," in which maturation into genital sexuality entails a poignant loss of innocence, even a kind of death. (Empson elucidates this as a pastoral theme in *Alice in Wonderland*.)[107] Yet real innocence in the Bible is something quite different; it occurs not in Eden but in the Peaceable Kingdom forecast in Isaiah 11:6 ff.

> Then the wolf shall live with the sheep
> and the leopard lie down with the kid;
> the calf and the young lion shall grow up together,
> and a little child shall lead them.
>
> .   .   .   .
>
> The lion shall eat straw like the cattle,
> the infant shall play over the hole of the cobra,
> and the young child dance over the viper's nest.
> They shall not hurt or destroy in all my holy mountain.

106. *Paradise* could originally have meant "garden"; an oasis in the desert? See Shepard, *Man in the Landscape*, 65. Shepard also points out that the Septuagint (Greek) translation heightened the emphasis on the curse on Nature, providing Christian theology with its great rationalization for rejecting mythologization of Nature, the concept of *natura deprivata per peccata*.

107. Empson, *Some Versions of Pastoral*, 256–57; cf. pp. 268–69.

Isaiah's vision explicates the root meaning of "innocence," *in-nocens,* not harmful or hurtful, and sees nature not as such but as *transformed,* into a shepherd's dream in which predators do not threaten the flock or the little boys who often watched them alone. (Remember that David overcame "both lion and bear" before Goliath.)[108] Once again the symbol of pastoralism is the shaping force for a key Biblical idea. The ultimate source of Isaiah's vision was the Sumerian myth of Dilmun, a place where "the wolf snatches not the lamb," and sickness and aging do not occur. Interestingly, Dilmun is also a source for Eden, for it is basically an arid Paradise with a miraculous source of water: this motif may be an oblique recognition of the connection between aridity and longevity.[109]

Two important conclusions follow from Isaiah's vision: 1) what is required for the Peaceable Kingdom is the abolition of "Nature red in tooth and claw," so the natural order is in effect rejected in favor of something quite unearthly; 2) this vision is laid in the future, not in the past. Here the Bible and the classical sources are going in opposite directions. Whereas the pagan world was settled in inevitable nostalgia, looking to the past for its ideal, the Hebrew conception of history opens toward a vague but fulfilling future. Moreover, the pagan concept is still tied to the tendency of the mythological consciousness to see all things in eternal patterns: the Golden Age could return only as part of a repetitious cycle.[110] Biblical thought, for all its mistrust of culture, sees the reality of civilization's changes and movements: the world is open for creativity—though this too can become debased into an idea of progress. In any case, Biblical innocence is not analogous to that of the child; and our sense of the word—a virginal prepubescent ignorance of the facts of life—is

---

108. I Sam. 17:34–37.

109. See Samuel Noah Kramer, *Sumerian Mythology* (Rev. ed.; New York: Harper, 1961), 55–56, and his *History Begins at Sumer* (New York: Anchor, 1959), 143–49; and Thorkild Jacobsen in Frankfort *et al., Before Philosophy,* 170–74. Jacobsen identifies Dilmun with Bahrein Island, but Kramer suspects it was in Iran or even in the Indus Valley: see Kramer's *The Sumerians: Their History, Culture, and Character* (Chicago: University of Chicago Press, 1963), 281–84.

110. E.g., Virgil, *Eclogue IV*.

rather unhelpful, a sign of the confusion resulting from the effort to entwine the divergent Biblical and classical world views.

A closely connected confusion involves our neoprimitivist sacralization of nature, which has enough problems in itself, but has also led to the trivialization of pastoral. The clash is already evident in the comparison of the Golden Age to Eden: one essentially accepts the "cosmic continuum" while the other rejects it. But the real problem comes later, culminating in the eighteenth century. Interestingly enough, what happened is paralleled in pastoral itself. Erwin Panofsky long ago pointed out that Virgil was responsible for much sentimentality about nature in pastoral, through his utopianizing of "Arcadia" into the type of the *locus amoenus*. For those who lived in the real Arcady, in Greece, it was "a poor, bare, rocky, chilly country, devoid of all the amenities of life and scarcely affording food for a few meager goats": a typical result, in Sauer's view, of overgrazing. Virgil added the amenities, changed the goats to sheep, and transferred the idyllic landscape which had been a background decoration in Greek-Sicilian pastoral to a region described by some as a desert. "It was, then, in the imagination of Virgil, and of Virgil alone, that the concept of Arcady, as we know it, was born—that a bleak and chilly district of Greece came to be transfigured into an imaginary realm of perfect bliss."[111] This explains much about the trivialization of pastoral, though it was left to the eighteenth century to make Arcadia the home, in effect, of the Noble Savage, and to impute a reality to these myths quite foreign to classical or pastoral intention.

Pastoral has become known as an indulgent and escapist fantasy, largely because it was reduced through Arcadian sentimentalization to a simple antithesis between nature and culture. While pastoral was being written and read by generations who grew increasingly less aware of the complexities of its background, another powerful force made itself felt: this was the sanctifying of nature, as part of a disease of Western metaphysics, inherited largely from the Greeks, which typically begins with an overvaluing of one term of a duality

111. "Et in Arcadia ego," reprinted in *Pastoral and Romance*, pp. 28–29.

at the expense of the other. What were originally defining oppositions became moral hierarchies: the old Gnostic habit of treating body as inferior to soul (or mind), foreign to the Bible, repeats itself, so that even qualities as abstract as internal and external or profound and superficial are treated as if they were Good and Evil. (Reason and passion, like written and oral, went through a complete evolution, being reversed in value.) The natural began in contradistinction to the artificial, but the latter now suffers the taint of being unreal. In the seventeenth century *artificial* could mean simply "made by art" without all the contempt we now pour on it, whereas *natural* did not have its present unequivocally honorific value. (In fact a "natural," in terminology which finally became obsolescent in the nineteenth century, was an idiot.) [112] Though nature was a great force, only someone like Edmund in *King Lear* would worship it; its chief lesson, as in Shakespeare's great pastoral comedy *As You Like It,* was to teach the uses of adversity. The "sermons in stones" do not flatter any illusion of comfortable continuity with nature. This is not simple Arcadian pastoral; in the play the "golden world" is an untrue rumor, while the forest is several times called a "desert." [113] Before the Renaissance, images of life in the wild tend to be even more unflattering. Bewildered by the epigones of Romanticism, we may imagine that the sojourn of Tristan and Isolde in the forest was some kind of idyll: but the point is that only fools and outlaws live in the forest, and that the lovers were in peril of their souls. Even on into the early eighteenth century, "nature" meant something far more comprehensive than the countryside, and mountains were not scenic but rather blemishes on earth's surface. [114] We have been taught our attitudes by the

112. See O.E.D., *s.v.,* "natural," "artificial."

113. See *As You Like It*: the "golden world," I, i, 107–11: "desert," II, i, 23; II, iv, 67; II, vi, 16; II, vii, 110; III, ii, 119, etc. Cf. Jacques at II, v, 53–54: "I'll go to sleep, if I can; if I cannot, I'll rail against all the first-born of Egypt." True, the forest presents a world of idealized justice where wicked, usurping brothers repent: but this is manifestly a purging of civilization, not a Shangri-La to be desired for its own sake.

114. See Marjorie Hope Nicolson, *Mountain Gloom and Mountain Glory: The Development of the Aesthetics of the Infinite* (Ithaca, N. Y.: Cornell University Press, 1959).

Romantics, not without benefits, but at the cost of blurring the great Biblical distinction between nature and divinity.

Having written a chapter in praise of alienation, and having expanded a few pages back on how man flourishes by disturbing ecology, it behooves me not to sound like a propagandist against environmentalism. Cleaning up our wastes is good even for "business," and only our defective system of cost-accounting obscures this fact; obviously one must oppose freeway mania when the state highway department, to say nothing of oil and concrete industries, becomes a vested interest. Nonetheless, the debate today is full of fatuous oversimplifications, which Edgar Anderson disablingly points out. The first chapter of his *Plants, Man, and Life* is called "Man and His Transported Landscapes" and concerns the fact that many of the rural scenes and vistas we prize are artificial, just as is the freeway. For thousands of years man has "carrie[d] whole floras about the globe with him" and "now lives surrounded by transported landscapes. . . . Many roadside and dooryard plants are artifacts. An artifact, by definition, is something produced by man, something which we would not have had if man had not come into being. That is what many of our weeds and crops really are."[115] As anyone who has seen industrial horrors would, we must urgently press for the preservation of wilderness, and we must immediately place political checks on our Western momentum toward rapacity; but we must not support these laudable causes with bogus salvationisms that sacralize the so-called "natural" into something untouched by human hands. The observation that man is the unnatural animal, one of "nature's misfits," remains valid for all of us, especially, but not only, Westerners. If, as our self-critics insist, we cannot even recover as much communion with nature as primitives have, the attempt at it is hypocritical as well as futile.

Ironically, the Bible's hostility to mythologizations serves as a cause for the proliferation of such ideologies among us, for its demythologizing action constantly creates a psychic power vacuum. Since it is perhaps impossible to have thought without myth, we

115. Anderson, *Plants, Man, and Life*, 9.

supply ourselves with substitutes to assuage our alienation whenever we wear out some governing idea; having freed ourselves from the traditions of myth that our ancestors worshiped for countless centuries, we are under pressure to accept ersatz versions. Fortunately demythologizing corrects the errors it caused, and the poverty of these substitutes is readily exposed.

What happened to pastoral poetry is instructive; as it was reduced to nature *vs.* culture, it grew banal and insipid, despite occasional bravura feats, so that in Dr. Johnson's judgment the form was "easy, vulgar, and therefore disgusting."[116] Dwindling further, it gave rise to topographical poems, and then to poems in praise of humble occupations, sometimes written by the workers themselves: the advent of such as Stephen Duck, the Thresher Poet, caused a prominent literary historian to write: "The idea of learning as essential to a poet perished in the eighteenth century."[117] The decline is paralleled and pictured in the canvases of certain French painters, whose coy scenes, fleecy with clouds, display vapid aristocrats masquerading as countryfolk. This particular cult led to Marie Antoinette tricked out as a milkmaid, a spectacle which is said to have helped cause the Revolution.

In more than one way it is ludicrous that pastoral should ever have come to stand for the sentimental ideal of Nature. In its Biblical context, the landscape associations are with desert or with steppe, marginal grazing land that the layman cannot tell from desert anyway. Neither farmer nor shepherd represents the life of nature; the nearest approach to that, in a text relevant to the Bible, is the wild man Enkidu in *Gilgamesh,* no pastoral figure.[118] That savage form of life was a curiosity, something fit for a zoo, even in early Sumerian times. Farmer and shepherd together stand for a way of life rapidly and irreversibly moving away from nature; their opposition

116. Samuel Johnson, *Lives of the Poets,* "Milton" (in discussing *Lycidas*), page 112, in the Oxford World's Classics edition.

117. George Sherburn, in Albert C. Baugh (ed.), *A Literary History of England* (New York: Appleton, 1948), 1103.

118. Translations of this part of *Gilgamesh* appear in N. K. Sandars, *The Epic of Gilgamesh* (Baltimore: Penguin, 1960), 60–67; Alexander Heidel, *The Gilgamesh Epic and Old Testament Parallels* (Chicago: University of Chicago Press, 1949), 19–32; Pritchard (ed.), *The Ancient Near East,* 42–50.

stands for discord and contingency in the new way, but not for any return to savagism. True, pastoral opposition was bent against the ideology of the city-states, which included frantic attempts to expropriate nature; but insofar as this is relevant, it is the city that stands for nature, with the shepherd against it! The nomadic contempt for the forms of growth and nature, symbolized in Yahweh's unnaturalness, is the key; Yahweh, though he will accept the title of shepherd and wanderer, never appears in any natural guise and cannot underwrite any associations between pastoralism and nature.

The basic point, again, is that the pastoral symbolism has no meaning as a positive ideal, but, like the very elements of language themselves, signifies through its patterns of opposition. Even the most elementary sounds of a language are heard only in contradistinction to sounds they are not; it is questionable whether there are sounds distinguishable in themselves, and certain that there are none with meaning in themselves. Surely the point is equally true with ideas. Even in its most generalized and insipid form, as meaning merely ruralism, pastoral should retain the character of an opposite: the word *country* is derived from the Latin *contra,* "against."[119] The attempt to make nature ideal in and of itself is bound to force it beyond the realm of ideas altogether, to promote it to the status of the sacred, in which realm alone can things have meaning of themselves. Pastoral has no such pretensions; its point is derived from the fact that shepherds represent a scorned way of life, not a sacred one. If Yahweh allows himself to be styled tent-dwelling wanderer, that does not express his essence; it defines him only in that it differentiates him from other gods, who dwell in temples and are seen in the powers of nature.

An equal mistake was made by romanticizing theologians who postulated a "desert ideal"; in the Bible, the fearful and repellent aspects of the desert are never blurred out, and no prophet seriously proposed that the people of Israel should go marching off into the wilderness to regain a lost purity.[120] There can be no ideals to be

119. O.E.D., *s.v.,* "country."
120. See the criticism of the "desert ideal" by Talmon, "The 'Desert Motif' in the Bible and in Qumran Literature," in Altmann (ed.), *Biblical Motifs.*

desired for their own sake in Biblical thought, other than Yahweh alone, for even righteousness and justice are configurations of his will. Thus there literally can be no hypostasis to sacralize. As the use of pastoral symbolism by prophets in antimonarchic passages shows, the whole dynamic of the motif is one of opposition. We think of Samuel with Saul, Nathan with David, Elijah with Ahab, and so on: these defining oppositions were ignored by the monarchs at their peril.

Finally, the most ludicrous aspect of pastoral's decline into propaganda for "the natural" is that it is one of the most artificial, indeed contrived, forms ever used. Even in its Biblical origins it was not spontaneous, but memorial. There is no touch of realism in pastoral literature: its flaunted symbolic quality is crucial to the effect. The fact that it could deal with real issues, especially ecclesiastical controversies, only makes the point clearer: the lack of realism made pastoral so flexible that it could be used for all kinds of allegorical encoding, from Platonized theology to personal love-messages. The swain's simple song can effectively signify a great many things, but one thing it does not mean or resemble is a real shepherd's song. (In *As You Like It* and some other works, "real" shepherds appear for satiric contrast.) "The shepherd in pastoral is, strictly speaking, never a shepherd. He is a musician, a poet, a prince, and a priest."[121] No divergence from the Bible needs to be explained here, for there isn't any. The Elizabethans were quite aware that Moses and David were not "real" shepherds, any more than was Paris, or for that matter Jesus. That the symbolism in the Bible is as fully conventional as it was later is tellingly demonstrated by the example of Isaiah, whose great vision of innocence in the Peaceable Kingdom takes an overtly pastoral form, and who prophesied that Immanuel, the promised child, would feed on shepherds' foods, curds and honey.[122] Isaiah was no shepherd: he was a city man, perhaps even a Temple official. The whole effect of the seminomadic traditions espoused by the withdrawing Hebrews, from whichever cities or

121. Introduction to Lincoln (ed.), *Pastoral and Romance*, 2.
122. Cf. Isa. 11:6 ff., 7:15–25.

empires, depended on their being memorial: not really a "return to ancestral ways" but an announcement of the badge, or totem, under which disaffiliation was taking place. Pastoral is a reminder to society not to puff itself up, but it does not urge a primitivist or regressive revolution.

The artificiality that inheres in pastoral of course leads to trouble, like the degeneration into the picturesque among the French painters. Even in the Renaissance there were reactions against the excesses of Arcadianism, sometimes satiric, sometimes deadly serious. One recent analyst traces the latter kind to the influence of an Italian poet, Mantuan, whose works were so popular among Elizabethans as to be a staple in English schools; he attempted reform by writing a more sharp-edged and overtly Biblical form of pastoral. Where the Arcadian pastoral held conflicting values arising from Biblical and classical streams in a kind of counterpoise or abeyance, in Mantuan the "confrontation of disparate values involves a polemical antagonism of opposites."

Mantuanesque pastoral thus takes pastoral's criticism of the city and transmutes it into an attack on the life of the World, takes pastoral's portrayal of the irrationality of love and transmutes it into a contrast of secular love and Christian love, takes pastoral's tension of values and transmutes it into a vices-and-virtues antagonism. Pastoral's criticism of values and its reforming impulse are modified according to the polemical and doctrinal interests of Mantuanesque pastoral. . . . Whereas the Arcadian tradition creates, or attempts to create, a world in which man's instincts and desires for *otium* can be satisfied, Mantuanesque pastoral creates a largely predatory world from which only religion and eternity promise relief: the city, the court, Eros, all are instruments of the devil preying upon man, luring him to the loss of his soul; and against these vices there can be no ambivalence.[123]

Mantuan took his Bible rather seriously, which was fitting since he was a monk (whose real name was Johann Baptista Spagnuoli) embroiled in the ecclesiastical controversies of his time. Certainly he served to remind his contemporaries, if they needed it, that a "pastor" is a shepherd, that a bishop's staff is a shepherd's crook, and

123. Patrick Cullen, *Spenser, Marvell and Renaissance Pastoral* (Cambridge, Mass.: Harvard University Press, 1970), 3, 25.

so on. It is no accident that the most famous English pastoralists—
Spenser, Marvell, Milton—were up to their necks in the raging theological struggles, and civil wars, of the time.

Mantuan's impulse to reform pastoral by turning to essentially
medieval forms—the psychomachia or war of vice and virtue, the
hortatory contrast of cupidinous and charitable love, and so on—is
intriguing, for among other things it raises the question of why pastoral poetry was comparatively insignificant in the Middle Ages.
Equally with the Renaissance, this era revered Virgil, as pagan
prophet of Christianity, as sage, as magician, above all as poet. Why
did its poets not imitate him? Perhaps the answer has to do with the
presence of pastoral *institutions* in the Middle Ages: pilgrimages,
monasticism, and all the forms of the contemplative life, were ways
of withdrawal. When these were abolished as parasitic and superstitious, there was an eruption of pastoral values in literature: the
equation is dangerously simple, but perhaps valid in this case. At the
same time, the medieval tradition of pulpit oratory against ecclesiastical abuse and neglect underwent such a burgeoning as to spill over
from sermons into poems, farther-reaching vehicles.[124] It is natural
to speak of churchmen, good or bad, as shepherds, going back to
Jesus' distinction between the Good Shepherd and the Hireling or
Mercenary (see Chaucer's lines on the Parson). So the Middle Ages
may have some part in pastoral after all: one might even compare
Chaucer's gentle mockery of the "lover's malady" suffered by woebe-
gone Arcite with Rosalind's good-humored but unsparing dissection
of love as madness in *As You Like It*; both are in the mode of the
pastoral "palinode," the song in rejection of love.[125]

The more recent history of pastoral is a mixed prospect. It survives as an important element in many works, in spite of general
trivialization. How subtle its influence can be is suggested by Emp-

124. The pulpit tradition is described by Owst, *Literature and Pulpit in Medieval England*. It might be noted that the word *anchorite,* so relevant to the
Middle Ages, comes from a verb meaning "to withdraw."

125. *Canterbury Tales*, 1 (A), 1355–79; *As You Like It*, III, ii, 376–80; cf. IV,
i, 85–98. Of course, too, such quests as Gawain's for the Green Knight involve the
theme of "spatial emergence" that relates to pastoral while deriving power from
the quest-motif in myth.

son's analyses. For instance his handling of the black humor about sex, growing up, and death in *Alice in Wonderland* opens several vistas: these filiate and ramify, as he shows, into a set of attitudes toward the "conventions" of polite society that is profoundly harmonic with the whole pastoral outlook.[126] Charles Dodgson took advantage of the "invention of childhood" to make his demythologizing foray into manners: his formula, as Empson puts it, is that the child as swain is the child-become-judge. Perhaps Empson is overzealous in relating the tensions of the work to Dodgson's personal problems as an Oxford don with strange compensations for repressed sexuality; these are surely efficient causes, but what they provoked Dodgson to see, at least to see in his art, was a set of insights belonging to a most ancient pattern. As Empson says, what psychoanalysis, rightly used, discovers in this work is not "a neurosis peculiar to Dodgson," but rather a shift onto the child of "the obscure traditions of pastoral." The sexual dilemmas and contradictions of Western culture are merely synedoches for our uneasy compromise with "natural" life in all realms. So the child's encounter with the conventions of "breeding" entails all the problems of convention itself, and of culture.

Empson notes that "the whole book balances between the luscious nonsense-world of fantasy and the ironic nonsense-world of fact"; this is a fitting way for modern pastoral to appear, challenging the nothingness of human affairs that are taken so overseriously as are those that elaborate themselves after the invention of "fact" (in the seventeenth century).[127] Moreover, the book (like the epigraph to an earlier section) reminds us that he who would withdraw is bound to seem psychotic, as he judges the culture to be: Empson says that "it is the ground-bass of this kinship with insanity, I think, that makes it so clear that the books are not trifling, and the cool courage with which Alice accepts madmen that gives them their strength."[128]

Many of the points in Empson's essay could be transposed usefully

126. See note 107 above.
127. See Hugh Kenner, *The Counterfeiters: An Historical Comedy* (Bloomington: Indiana University Press, 1968), 60–67.
128. Empson, *Some Versions of Pastoral*, 281.

to works where the use of childhood is similar: *Huckleberry Finn* is an obvious example, among all those classics of American literature that D. H. Lawrence discovered to be subversive tracts masquerading as "capital books for boys." Huck ends up lighting out for the territory ahead of the rest, because of his experience of "sivilization": it is the pattern of withdrawal in a painfully obvious form. Americans always tend to be literalistic Bible-readers.

But the dispersal of pastoralism into all sort of new embodiments has not been without its drawbacks. Whereas the eighteenth century had Stephen Duck and Marie Antoinette, we have a host of banal imitations of what Empson sees as the convention of "putting the complex into the simple." Phrased that way, pastoral is obviously the formula for most popular entertainment: the situation comedy, the comic strip, the Western or crime or spy story—though some can be interesting in their kind. Then too we have radical chic, and pre-faded blue jeans, and Nazaritically long-haired rock stars who lay up treasures on earth by hymning the Rechabites of our time.[129] These permutations, seen in the long view, are inverse testimony to the tautness of the moral issues which pastoral raises: substitutes that turn the form into bland comedy, romance, or morality play—the three staples of entertainment and politics—are much easier to face than the issues themselves.

For if we see pastoral clearly we see the challenge to itself that Western culture always carries with it: that of facing, by reminding ourselves of the possibility of withdrawal, the contingency, the arbitrariness, the metaphysical emptiness of any systematizing of human dispositions that we might call culture. This is why pastoral cannot really be politically revolutionary: no achievable society could escape its demythologizing scrutiny, none could reach "givenness." The possibility of opposition and withdrawal makes meaningless culture's attempts to make itself permanent, in whatever political form, for this quest involves sacralization as surely as does the eleva-

129. See Jean Shepherd, "I Hear America Singing, or 'Leaves of Grass' revisited, like," reprinted in Edward Quinn and Paul J. Dolan (eds.), *The Sense of the Sixties* (New York: Free Press, 1968), 139–48. It is surely right that someone named Shepherd have the last word on this topic.

tion of Nature. Ironically, though withdrawal makes sacralized culture meaningless, it gives provisional culture the only meaning we can grasp, through the defining power of opposition: by unmasking culture as contingent, it helps us change it and give it the meaningfulness of adaptability.

Chapter Four 🌾 The Paradigms of History and Paternity

THE BIBLICAL AND WESTERN CONCEPTIONS OF HISTORY

The Bible is first and foremost a unique distillation of history. . . . All the other aspects of the Scriptures are subordinated to this central theme.

—E. A. Speiser

In fact, the first people to feel deeply about their own past in a specifically historical sense, and therefore the first people to produce real historians, were the people of Israel.

—J. H. Hexter

The distinction of the Hebrew habit of finding their God active in history, as against the pagan conception of the divine immanent in nature, has become commonplace. Reexamination of the problem has led to the conclusion that the Biblical concepts and themes forming what we call history had traceable Mesopotamian ancestry; in other words, the development owes something to the sojourn of the Hebrew ancestors among the cities of Sumer and Akkad. Nonetheless, the Hebrew-pagan distinction remains valid, and any further blurring might be seriously misleading. E. A. Speiser, one of the authorities who established the relation of the Mesopotamian idea of history to the Bible, still believed that the Hebrews were the people "to make history in more ways than one." The pagan contribution was limited to the belief that the gods intervened in men's affairs, especially with disasters: no concept of purpose was developed. "In terms of a philosophy of history, the past was desperately important to be sure [to the Mesopotamians], but only as a check against the recurrence of previous disasters. It was not a positive factor in the understanding of the present or a more confident facing of the future."[1]

Making the distinction firm is a matter of some importance, since the enormous debt of Western civilization to the very concept of history is generally acknowledged, or sometimes bewailed. If the habit of thinking about history had come to us in a secular form, instead of the Biblical one, we would have been very different. The salvationist residue in our concept of history is evident in the way all factions in the political spectrum claim history for their side. Both Adolf Hitler and Fidel Castro, in defending their first, abortive coups, asserted that history would "absolve" them. Conservatives claim that respect for history would quiet student radicalism; yet all radicals follow in the wake of Marx who in effect deified the historical process. Meanwhile the nihilist who wants to free himself from tradition pays tribute to the power of the idea of history by complaining of its stranglehold on us all. As I have pointed out elsewhere, his position has curious similarities to that of the rugged-individualist entrepreneur: for instance, Henry Ford, for whom history was bunk.[2] This recurrent Western desire to want to be free from history, or to put a stop to it, flares up in times of political disorientation. In itself antihistorical, it derives from those developments within the Hebrew idea of history which produced apocalyp-

1. Speiser, *Oriental and Biblical Studies*, 188, 192–93. The orthodox contrast is succinctly summarized in C. A. Patrides, *The Grand Design of God: The Literary Form of the Christian View of History* (London: Routledge, and Toronto: University of Toronto Press, 1972), Chap. 1, with useful bibliographical notes. Patrides' interest, however, is in specifically Christian concepts and their literary offshoots: he slights somewhat the Biblical matrix. For a sample of recent challenges to the orthodox contrast, see Albrektson, *History and the Gods*.

2. In Herbert N. Schneidau, "The Age of Interpretation and the Moment of Immediacy: Contemporary Art vs. History," *ELH*, XXXVII (June, 1970), 312.

ticism. Norman Cohn and Karl Löwith, for instance, have demonstrated the striking likenesses of Communist and Nazi visions to the doctrines of revolutionary medieval millenarians, which in turn were based on the Bible.[3] The expectation of the coming of the Kingdom of Heaven, crucial to the New Testament, was the firstfruits of Jewish apocalyptic, but not the last.

We struggle with our own history in a way not adequately comprehended in any of the dry rationales for history as an academic discipline. The fact is, as many radical academics have brightly discovered, that disciplines such as history and science are not fundamentally "objective" at all, but bear many marks of their polemic origins in Hebrew denunciations of pagan ways of living and knowing. Secularization has somewhat obscured these marks, giving rise to tenuous rationales about "learning from the past." In reality we don't learn much, certainly not enough to account for the immensity of the effort; nor does any of us really believe in Ciceronian rotundities about history being the trainer of the mind, the guide to life, the light of the age, and so on. In some way, and even more when we do it in political or humanistic terms, we all search the past for meaning in the image of the Hebrew prophet searching for God. What we want is transcendent—not just more meaning to add to that we have already, but the key to the code.

The tenuity of the humanistic rationale for the veneration of history is exposed by Lévi-Strauss in the last chapter of *The Savage Mind*, which takes the form of an argument with Jean-Paul Sartre about the implied inferiority of primitive thought. As usual the best thrusts are against Western follies, rather than in support of savage achievements. Lévi-Strauss seeks to demonstrate the contradictions in our "mystical" conception of history, though what he really shows is its power over us. He notes that for Sartre, and for many Western thinkers, "history plays exactly the part of a myth."[4]

3. Norman Cohn, *The Pursuit of the Millennium* (2nd ed., New York: Harper, 1961); Karl Löwith, *Meaning in History* (Chicago: University of Chicago Press, 1949), esp. 44 ff., 65. Löwith helpfully elaborates Hermann Cohen's belief that history was a "product of prophetism" (p. 17), thus is relevant everywhere in this chapter.

4. Lévi-Strauss, *The Savage Mind*, 254. Cf. Voegelin, *Order and History*, Vol.

Skewering the naive hope that we can shore ourselves up against history's ambiguities with piles of diligent research, he notes simply that an infinite labor would be self-defeating: "A truly total history would confront [us] with chaos . . . [and] would cancel itself out—its product would be nought." The burden of history is interpretation; no matter how neutral the historian's position he can never be neutral enough; merely in selecting the facts an indeterminacy principle enters. "History is therefore never history, but history-for."[5] And so, with these and other arguments, Lévi-Strauss sets about to demythologize history itself. His assertion that overvaluation of "the diachronic" pervades our culture, giving rise to illusions of continuity which we would call superstitious among savages, gives us an important clue: history is becoming myth when it affirms continuities, but has another role when it sets times apart from each other and stresses their alienation. Hebrew history does both, but perhaps its resolution was to find continuity in discontinuity, in the acts of God related, finally, only by his ultimately inscrutable will.

We can pursue this point by making a discrimination between *history* and *the past*, as for instance in J. H. Plumb's popular book, *The Death of the Past*. On the one hand, as Plumb puts it, "The past is always a created ideology with a purpose, designed to control individuals, or motivate societies, or inspire classes. Nothing has been so corruptly used as concepts of the past." He might as well have used the term *myth*, though if he had it might have reminded him that the use of a mythical past by a cold society is not usually "corrupt" or maleficent, and that he reveals his essential Westernism by emphasizing that aspect. On the other hand, he does recognize that the process peculiar to the West is that of history as demythologizer: "The critical historical process has helped to weaken the past, for by its very nature it dissolves those simple, struc-

I, *Israel and Revelation*, 124: "Israel alone had history as an inner form, while the other societies existed in the form of the cosmological myth. History, we therefore conclude, is a symbolic form of existence, of the same class as the cosmological form; and the paradigmatic narrative is, in the historical form, the equivalent of the myth in the cosmological form."

5. Lévi-Strauss, *The Savage Mind*, 257.

tural generalizations by which our forefathers interpreted the purpose of life in historical terms. . . . Basically history is destructive" and, in concert with similar processes, destroys "the sanction that the past has in religion, politics, education and morals nowadays." Noting that its growth is "subtly linked" to that of science, Plumb demonstrates that history as we know it is not to be found even among the most venerated Greek or Latin texts, nor, in his judgment, in those of any other society. No classical historians, he says, ever "disentangled themselves from the past, from its myth or its social use."[6] Only Thucydides perhaps saw the problem, but as M. I. Finley put it, Thucydides "tended to abandon history" in order to give meaning to history: inventing funeral orations, etc.[7] Even the massive Chinese archives cannot qualify: "Chinese history never developed the process of self-criticism and discovery, the relentless testing of generalization, the purposeful search for documentation to prove hypotheses which marks Western history."[8] But it could be argued that the Hebrew prophets, in their revisionist visions and attacks on the "official" past of Israel, invented the forerunners of such self-critical processes; they were not history's only demythologizers, but perhaps its most fanatical and impressive ones, giving rise to a tradition which might have allowed Thucydides to solve his problem. Curiously, Plumb does not recognize this Hebrew contribution; like other bemused Westerners with classical educations or orientations, he can think only of Greeks and Romans as intellectual ancestors. Yet he is right on the verge of insight, especially when he notes the tardy development of the discipline of history among past societies. Only the "cold power" of a mythological society, the utility of a frozen past for supporting the culture, can explain such tardiness, which emphasizes once again that cold societies

6. J. H. Plumb, *The Death of the Past* (Boston: Houghton Mifflin, 1970), 17, 14, 20.

7. Quoted *ibid.*, 20 n. See M. I. Finley, "Myth, Memory, and History," *History and Theory* IV, 3 (1965), 281–302, where he affirms that the Greeks lacked what we call the sense of history, since for them myth was the "great teacher": "the only people in antiquity who were somehow 'modern' in this respect were the Hebrews . . ." (p. 294).

8. Plumb, *The Death of the Past*, 109.

are normative, and that the hot or historical societies must be explained as resulting from severe disruptions. The tardiness of history is roughly analogous to the process of domestication of plants and animals: we know now that the conditions were ripe for the development long before it happened, so that lack of opportunity cannot explain the nonoccurrence. The prehistoric societies must have sensed in some way that domestication, or history, would let alienation's nose into the tent. Octavio Paz notes that "primitives distrust history because they see in it the beginning of the separation, the beginning of the exile of man adrift in the cosmos."[9] Our history, in all senses, stems from the time when that risk was accepted.

History is not "true"—neither in contrast to myth nor in some absolute sense—but is rather a continual sifting of events to find the meaning of "what really happened." Such sifting, carried on not with expectationless "objectivity" but with the impartiality of a Hebrew prophet, will yield insights of many kinds, although those who have no taste for it see the monumentality of the task as productive only of ambiguity. This is the price that must be paid: many societies, otherwise quite capable of managing the enterprise, have shied away. The relevant example, in parallel to China, is Egypt. In an important passage (quoted by Speiser), Frankfort says:

The Egyptians had very little sense of history or of past and future. For they conceived their world as essentially static and unchanging. It had gone forth complete from the hands of the Creator. Historical incidents were, consequently, no more than superficial disturbances of the established order, or recurring events of never-changing significance. The past and the future—far from being a matter of concern—were wholly implicit in the present; and the odd facts enumerated above—the divinity of animals and kings, the pyramids, mummification—as well as several other and seemingly unrelated features of Egyptian civilization—its moral maxims, the forms peculiar to its poetry and prose—can all be understood as a result of a basic conviction that only the changeless is truly significant.[10]

9. In Paz, *Claude Lévi-Strauss*, 85; see also p. 89: "One could even say that only the modern West has identified itself fully and frantically with history."
10. Frankfort, *The Birth of Civilization in the Near East*, 9.

Whereas our assumption, of course, is just the opposite: in our science, our history, and our philosophy, causation and significance are in the mode of change. The ideology of the cold society in Egypt, with its links to the prehistoric past arranged as unchanging features of a *logos,* presents itself as our opposite in many ways: history and myth *are* different.

Occasionally we entertain the fantasy of lightening the oppressiveness of our history by going back to take that alternate route, through mythology, for human societies. Today we see many wavering between the zany version of pastoralism called the "counter-culture" and the apocalyptic of revolutionism: they propose to appropriate these Biblical modes to go back on the one hand to nature, on the other to culture, and so to mythologize these. The prevalence of these escapisms, with or without pacifying opiates, does tell us much about the bankruptcy of the secular-humanist tradition, which appropriated the Bible's demythologizing powers without assuming the burden of its insights. But could we go back in any sense if we decided we wanted to? No doubt we have much to learn from the cold societies, about all the world *can* mean, in contradistinction to our modes of ascertaining meaninglessness. But the Eden myth is still the problem: once self-conscious, we know about nakedness, and we cannot get back to taking the world and its meanings for granted. We call this growing up, because for us aging involves laborious instructions in meaninglessness, although in cold societies adults are not necessarily so trained. But even if there is nothing inevitable in such a regimen, the mere possibility of demythologizing would haunt our efforts to reconstruct ourselves on Edenic models. And we would be troubled by the fear of losing our place in history: the double sense depends on history's likeness to a book we're reading; we want to know how it comes out.

Although Plumb has little sense of the Hebrews and their work, he is instructive on that phase of the Biblical idea of history that became the Christian *mythos*: his key term for it is "narrative."

This sense of narrative and of unfolding purpose bit deeply into European consciousness. It brought easy acceptance of the idea not only of change but also of development. . . . The past acquired a dynamic, almost a propulsion, which it did not acquire elsewhere. It became easy enough for a Christian to regard his own life in the same dramatic terms, as an unfolding, as possessing a purpose, a mission, a destined end. That is the purpose of God, and the purpose of individual life became identical—again unique and revolutionary.

. . . .

And although historians have sought for the origins of aggressive individualism in the Protestant ethic, it is to my mind embedded in the basic historical concepts which emerged in the first centuries of Christian activity.[11]

Thus from the beginning the Christian use of the past could never be as static or frozen as that of the typical mythological society. Like Western literature, Western history is less a thing than a process. Of course, as Plumb points out, this quality did not make the Christian past necessarily less "corrupt": it was capable of becoming a rationalization of such exploitative ideologies as that of Manifest Destiny. Yet it was always, to some degree, in tension with culture itself. Plumb points to Augustine's distinction between the City of God and the earthly city: for Augustine, and for the Middle Ages in general, Rome was always falling, Troy was always burning, because of their sins. "No matter how cataclysmic the ruin of the state might be, this was only to be expected, considering man's sinful nature. . . . [The City of God] grew even as the world decayed. History proved it."[12]

Plumb implies, too, that the worst excesses of imperialist rationalization in the West came when the "religious past donned a secular overcoat."[13] When the sense of "providential destiny" was superficially demythologized into romantic nationalism, mixed with myths of progress and rugged individualism, the result was rapacious expansionism. In recent years we have heard almost a litany of what was destroyed by Western imperialism, but the conclusion that we are more depraved than other peoples will not bear impartial examination. Imperialism is the same everywhere. Certainly

11. Plumb, *The Death of the Past,* 77–78.
12. *Ibid.,* 76–77.
13. *Ibid.,* 88–89.

our heritage lends itself to perversions, because of its very flexibility; and like that of the early city-states, our religion can be forced
to support these perversions. The fact remains that secularization
released the most demonic of the destructive urges: which is to say,
the time of worst abuse was when Christianity made too submissive
a truce with culture.

The sense of the individual's mattering in the scheme of things,
from one point of view, provides our tradition with great energy;
but from another it is psychically burdensome, likely to produce
what we call "guilt." (Of course it can serve too as a recompense:
Robinson Crusoe's sense of "particular providence," the feeling that
he was reserved for some destiny, kept him going. Daniel Defoe
shrewdly picked this up from the sectarian ideas of his time.)[14] In
some provisional ways we arrange to have group psychic power support individuals. Alcoholics Anonymous and encounter groups, for
instance, function like mythological communities, perhaps because
families seem to do it less and less. But the Christian sense of history
prevents any such organizations from becoming solidly institutionalized. The overriding power in the concept of the separate destiny
of the individual still masters us.

That the Christian sense of history was a "narrative" has been
fateful for our literature, in obvious ways. The narrative norm has
dominated so long that the recent attempts to do without it, at
least the serious ones, take on the responsibilities of demythologizations. In Ezra Pound's plotless epic *The Cantos,* an act of tearing
down economic myths takes place: Pound's shorthand battle cry for
this effort was to call epic a "poem including history."[15] As usual
history is the agent of choice for demythologizing. Pound's hatred
of art and literature that simply "tells a story" is an index to the
possibility of narrative's degenerating into something insipid or
shoddy. But what would the novel be without the feeling that every-

14. See George A. Starr, *Defoe and Spiritual Autobiography* (Princeton, N. J.:
Princeton University Press, 1965), esp. 113 and 125; J. Paul Hunter, *The Reluctant Pilgrim* (Baltimore: Johns Hopkins Press, 1965), esp. Chap. 3.
15. Pound, *ABC of Reading* (1934; rpt. New York: New Directions, 1960), 46.

one's life is a "story," if only it can be told? This paradigm goes far back in history, linking saints' legends, allegorized individual lives like *Pilgrim's Progress*, "spiritual autobiography" as in Defoe's work, and the novel *per se*. Meanwhile, the processes of historical analysis are everywhere intertwined with this paradigm: Plumb notes that the Maurist and Bollandist fathers who collected and edited the saints' lives were, in a sense, "the fathers of modern historical scholarship as we know it." [16]

Still another aspect of the narrative paradigm in literature may derive from an even older phase in the Hebrew concept of history. T. S. Eliot related literature not only "[to] the pastness of the past but [to] its presence." [17] The Biblical appearance of this idea was linked to the historicization of cult festivals, as described in the influential work of Gerhard von Rad:

> The festal calendar is, of course, Canaanite in origin, and as such is the expression of a farmer's religion which looks on the processes of sowing and reaping as direct sacral events. Obviously however in Israel, very soon after the settlement, and in spite of the fact that she herself had become a completely farming people, the content of these festivals underwent a change. At Unleavened Bread, the festival which falls at the beginning of the barley harvest, the Exodus from Egypt was commemorated (Ex. XXIII.15), and at the great harvest and vintage festivals the sojourn in the wilderness and the dwelling in booths (Lev. XXIII. 42f). Before this the festivals had been purely agrarian, but Israel "historicized" them. We can scarcely overestimate the importance of such changes, brought about as they were by a unique understanding of the world and of human existence.[18]

Von Rad believes that at the time Israel did not understand its own uniqueness, or it would not have used Canaanite festivals: but the latent hostility of the historical outlook to myth appears in the resistance of the Hebrew farmers to falling into normative agricultural ideological patterns. Geo Widengren comments on the institution of Passover: "From our point of view there is an obvious clash

16. Plumb, *The Death of the Past*, 125.
17. T. S. Eliot, "Tradition and the Individual Talent" (1919), in his *Selected Essays*, 4.
18. von Rad, *Old Testament Theology*, II, 103–104.

here between myth and history, and I think that the traditionists who tried to connect this festival with the great national memories of Israel really felt something of this clash and were intentionally aiming at a 'demythologization' of the annual festival."[19]

But to make the point about literature we must let von Rad continue:

> While, therefore, it is perfectly correct to say that Jahwism is founded in history, this does not, of course, involve any thought of the modern concept of history which, as we know, lays great stress on the idea of relativity and of the transitoriness of all events. The historical acts by which Jahweh founded the community of Israel were absolute. They did not share the fate of all other events, which inevitably slip back into the past. They were actual for each subsequent generation; and this not just in the sense of furnishing the imagination with a vivid present picture of past events—no, it was only the community assembled for a festival that by recitation and ritual brought Israel in the full sense of the word into being: in her own person she really and truly entered into the historic situation to which the festival in question was related.[20]

Not our history but our literature inherits the force of these rituals: in fiction, typically, events are narrated in a past tense and yet with an obvious aim at immediacy. Very briefly we may call this the " 'Oh!' he said" characteristic: the interjection must appear to be uttered now, yet the juxtaposed verb sends the action irretrievably into the past. This dimension of fiction can be manipulated with rich results, exposing a kernel of truth beneath the bromides about literature making the past "live again." What is technically involved in such use of two planes of time in language we are only beginning to understand, but the parallel with the sense of Yahweh's acts cutting through the transience of time is arresting.

YAHWEH'S MIGHTY HAND IN HISTORY

> My father was a wandering Aramaean. He went down into Egypt
> to find refuge there, few in numbers, but there he became a na-

19. Geo Widengren, "Myth and History in Israelite-Jewish Thought," in Stanley Diamond (ed.), *Culture in History: Essays in Honor of Paul Radin* (New York: Columbia University Press, 1960), 481.
20. von Rad, *Old Testament Theology*, II, 104.

tion, great, mighty, and strong. The Egyptians ill-treated us, they gave us no peace and inflicted harsh slavery on us. But we called on Yahweh, the God of our Fathers. Yahweh heard our voice and saw our misery, our toil and our oppression, and Yahweh brought us out of Egypt with mighty hand and outstretched arm, with great terror, and with signs and wonders. He brought us here and gave us this land, a land where milk and honey flow. Here then I bring the first-fruits of the soil that you, Yahweh, have given me.

—Deut. 26:5–10

History is the Exodus from civilizations.

—Eric Voegelin

Von Rad and others regard the passage quoted as perhaps the oldest of the Hebrew "cultic confessions," ritual statements made by worshipers at a festival. As von Rad says, it has "all the marks of great antiquity," the very paucity of events in it being one of the most obvious: for the tendency with such confessions is to grow more elaborate, not less.[21]

The passage sets Israel—both the patriarch (Jacob) and the nation—firmly in seminomadic tradition, even though it was apparently used at a harvest festival; we may note how pastoralism overrides the expectable agricultural symbolism. Moreover, it can be seen how the pastoral character of Israel could become transposed over the ages to Yahweh's act in "leading" Israel out of slavery, so that the metaphor of Yahweh the shepherd could be born. Thus Yahweh's "saving acts," the very armature of the Hebrew beliefs about history, are pastoral motifs in themselves.

The "mighty hand and outstretched arm," the "great terror" and "signs and wonders" are obviously formulaic phrases embodying the sense of personal will in an unearthly, terrifying manifestation that is the core of belief in Yahweh. The will behind events is personal in the Old Testament, which thus extends "Thou-ness" to history in a way that parallels the personalizing of aspects of nature by mythological peoples, from the tribes of the Stone Age to the

21. *Ibid.,* I, 122.

present-day sorcerer, Don Juan.[22] But there is more than a hint of inscrutability behind the portrayal of Yahweh's compassionate response. The old "confession" does not attempt to explain why Yahweh acts, only that he does. The compassion is in the way humans see things: Yahweh's emotions are left unarticulated. Mesopotamian myth knew of gods who injected "great terror" into history, for inexplicable reasons. But the Hebrew belief puts all these characteristics on a new footing.

We know how much the Hebrews took from Mesopotamian myth; the first ten chapters of Genesis have undeniable parallels in Sumerian and later sources. Especially when compared with Egypt, Mesopotamia seems to have had many other ideological influences on Israel. The Hebrew concepts of the afterlife and of kingship are strikingly closer to those of Sumer and its heirs than to those of Egypt. Even the Hebrew prohibition of images may have some precedent in Mesopotamia, where imageless temples and altars have been found.[23]

Insofar as Mesopotamian ideas influenced Biblical concepts of history, the deeper sense of alienation from nature among the Mesopotamians, compared to the Egyptians, may be crucial. The Tigris and Euphrates were apparently more unpredictably and potentially devastating than the Nile. Thus a mistrust of nature sometimes found articulation; even the aggressive expansionism of the city-states may be associated with underlying fear and pessimism.[24] In contrast the Egyptians remained self-contained and relatively static, their anxieties about the gap between nature and culture assuaged by the elaborateness of their cult and the regularity of the Nile.

22. Cf. Frankfort *et al., Before Philosophy*, 14, on the extension of "Thou-ness" to aspects of nature and the phenomenal world: see also the discussion above, in Chapter Two.

23. Giedion, *Eternal Present*, II, 97; H. W. F. Saggs, *The Greatness That Was Babylon* (1962; rpt. New York: Mentor, 1968), 40.

24. See Thorkild Jacobsen in Frankfort *et al., Before Philosophy*, 137–39. His thesis is that cosmic order appeared in Mesopotamia not as something given, but only achieved by imperious will. Such a concept could when diverted lead to imperialism. See also his tracing of the degeneration of "primitive democracy" into aggressive monarchy in Mesopotamia (note 20 in Chapter Three).

Moreover, the Mesopotamian gods, like Yahweh on certain occasions, show a surprisingly destructive side. Enlil was usually a beneficent father and Inanna the goddess of love, but the one could become "a violent and destructive storm deity" and the other was also a raging, bloodthirsty war goddess.[25] Curiously, however, the vengeful acts attributed to Yahweh do not seem to have disturbed the Hebrews much: what made them regard him with an awe bordering on terror was his absoluteness. Only much later, in Judaic times, did theologues grow squeamish about attributing afflictions and destructive acts to Yahweh, substituting instead the concept of the Satan.[26]

Another aspect of distant but relevant Mesopotamian influence may have had even more far-reaching consequences for the concept of history in the Bible. "The absence of mythology in Israel has been explained by the western Semitic conception of deity as king —as divine ruler who marches into battle before his tribe. YHWH, it is said, was originally a lone warrior, without consort or family, like Moab's Chemosh, or Assyria's Ashur."[27] Yehezkel Kaufmann cites this view only to scorn it: yet some signs in the text might make it germane to early Yahwism, and still other signs indicate that a clash between this archaic concept and the rise of the human monarchs could have been the issue that precipitated the Hebrew sense of history, which had been held in suspension in cultic confessions and the like.

Kaufmann is undoubtedly correct to deny that this conception could explain the absence of mythology: for Chemosh and Ashur were mythologized finally. But if a common west-Semite conception

25. On Enlil, see Kramer, *The Sumerians,* 119; cf. Jacobsen, in Frankfort *et al., Before Philosophy,* 153–57, and Jacobsen, *Toward the Image of Tammuz,* 31. On Inanna, see Kramer, *The Sumerians,* 140–41 and 153, Jacobsen, *Toward the Image of Tammuz,* 28; see also Arvid S. Kapelrud, *The Violent Goddess: Anat in the Ras Shamra Texts* (Oslo: Universitetsforlaget, 1969), esp. Chap. 1.

26. The textbook example is the substitution of "Satan" for "Yahweh" in the events recounted first in II Sam. 24 and later in I Chron. 21. See Albright, *From the Stone Age to Christianity,* 348, 361; Wright, *The Old Testament Against Its Environment,* 91.

27. Yehezkel Kaufmann, *The Religion of Israel,* trans. and abridged by Moshe Greenberg (1937–48; rpt. New York: Schocken, 1972), 61.

of deity was that of kingly battle-leader, might not the Hebrews have visualized Yahweh in this way when they began to fight for the land of Canaan? The "lone warrior" concept would have been acceptable precisely because offensive mythology would not be, at that early date, necessarily associated with it. Not that the Hebrews would be aware that they were borrowing; they seem to have felt unique in having a god as their king, "to go before them and to fight their battles."[28] Mesopotamian kingship, though "lowered from heaven" in mythology, had originated in the functions of war-leaders and was always highly militaristic. The early Hebrews would have seen primarily a contrast between themselves and the pagans, in that their king was not a deified human but a real god.[29]

Samuel objected to the institution of the monarchy precisely on these grounds: "Yahweh your God himself is your king." His anger was dissipated only by Yahweh's instruction to let the headstrong people have their king, to fulfill their iniquity, for "they have re-

28. As the recent work of Frank Moore Cross shows, the concept of "The Divine Warrior" was a widespread mythological element in the Near East, having primarily two forms: one as creator-god, head of a pantheon; the other as "tutelary deity" for a league of seminomads (Cross, *Canaanite Myth and Hebrew Epic*, 38–39). Cross thinks the Hebrews combined the two. But although he is persuasive about the influence of the Canaanite "El," and about the borrowed nature of Hebrew cult in general, he slights the divergence in purpose that the Hebrews may have had for their borrowings: unlike the other nations, they were not essentially syncretistic. One could argue that he does not fully acknowledge the possibilities of cultural hostility implicit in Mendenhall's concept of "withdrawal," which I would contend led to a genuine demythologizing animus.

29. See Speiser, *Oriental and Biblical Studies*, 285–86, on the Mesopotamian connection between kingship as a gift of the gods conferring order and civilization in the place of anarchy and barbarism; cf. Jacobsen, *Toward the Image of Tammuz*, 18, 138, 145–50, and 375: "The 'king,' lugal, in contrast to the en was from the beginning a purely secular political figure, a 'war leader.'"

Mendenhall bases *The Tenth Generation* on the Hebrew concept: "In summary, then, early Israel was the dominion of Yahweh, consisting of all those diverse lineages, clans, individuals, and other social segments that, under the covenant, had accepted the rule of Yahweh and simultaneously had rejected the domination of the various local kings and their tutelary deities—the *baalim*. As a necessary corollary, Yahweh was the one who exclusively exercised the classic functions of the king, as described in the prologue to the Code of Hammurabi and in other early codes [such as] the administration of law internally, the waging of war, and the economic well-being of the diverse population. . . . [Yahweh's] function as a leader in war has frequently been an embarrassment to a liberal theology unaware of the historical context of the whole ideology" (pp. 28–29).

jected Me from ruling over them." So Samuel gave in when the people cried again, "Give us a king to rule over us, like the other nations . . . [to] fight our battles." Many scholars explain these parts of the book of I Samuel as later retrojections, but others judge that they must correspond to real tensions existing at the time.[30] The very lateness of Israel's adoption of monarchy suggests a hostile resistance to any change in the pattern of charismatic leadership of so-called judges, which could well have stemmed from the earlier belief in Yahweh's physical presence at the head of the army. Gideon, the great charismatic judge raised up from obscurity by the "spirit of Yahweh" coming upon him, had refused the offered kingship: "It is not I who shall rule over you, nor my son: Yahweh must be your lord."[31]

Yahweh is said to have manifested himself, in regard to Hebrew warfare, in a variety of forms. If we assume that a general tradition of his presence was passed down through oral legend, it would go through several branches and might well assume a variety of hypostases, being as it was ultimately mysterious. The best-known forms of leadership are the column of fire and smoke, and somewhat later the Ark. Between these conceptions the texts mention several other formulae which sound like variant descriptions of Yahweh's agency: he promises to lead the people with, or send ahead of them, "my terror," "my angel [or messenger]," "panic," "hornets," "the marching sword."[32] Perhaps the "mighty hand" was originally one of this series. The lack of agreement in these hypos-

---

30. I Sam. 12:12, 8:1–22. See Martin Noth, "God, King, and People in the Old Testament," in Robert W. Funk (ed.), *The Bultmann School of Biblical Interpretation: New Directions* (New York: Harper, 1965), esp. 38 n: "A literary polemic against kingship is not found but at a relatively late stage in the Old Testament, even though it may be assumed that the negative attitude toward kingship is much older. The fact that this attitude—not against individual kings but toward the very institution of kingship—could develop at all and express itself, speaks against divine kingship [*i.e.*, the idea of the king as embodiment of the god] in Israel as a universal or even widespread conception." In *The History of Israel*, Noth comments that this attitude was "current among the tribes of Israel before the rise of the monarchy" (p. 165). See also John Bright, *A History of Israel*, 167.

31. Judg. 8:23.

32. See Exod. 13:21–22, 23:20–33, 25:22; Deut. 1:33, 7:20, 9:3, 33:26–29, and Josh. 24:12.

tases might testify in the first place that the people were not permitted to approach too closely the actual manifestation, and that, in later times, the mysterious traditions were fabulously elaborated. The column of fire and smoke, for example, might have been originally a traveling forge, such as the one portrayed on the famous Beni Hasan painting of Semites entering Egypt.[33] Moses is said to have spent almost all of his adult life among the Kenites (Midianites in some passages), nomadic pastoralists whose eponym, from Cain "the Smith," might indicate that they were traveling metalworkers who would have such forges; perhaps from them Moses learned sorcery, another knack of nomadic metalworkers, for his displays before Pharaoh.

The texts from which the traditions of Yahweh's agency can be surmised do not refer only to Exodus times. In much later references Yahweh is still said to lead the army. In a little-noticed passage, Yahweh tells David: "When you hear the sound of steps in the tops of the balsam trees, advance, for that will be Yahweh going out ahead of you to rout the army of the Philistines."[34] We have an urge to gloss over such texts as metaphorical, in the way that we treat the phrase "Yahweh is with you" used to stir up judges like Gideon and Barak. But even if they became metaphorical, such passages might well have derived from the archaic belief in the physical presence of the divine king-warrior.

In another battle in I Samuel, Yahweh is said to "thunder with a great noise" to throw the Philistines into a panic.[35] This might point to still another hypostasis, closely related perhaps to "the terror" and "panic" which Yahweh not only causes but *is*. Such noises might link up with the archaic tradition of battle cry, which later became a part of the acclamation of the king. An army raising its

33. See fig. 17. Note that Josh. 3:4 records a tradition of the people keeping back "a thousand cubits" from the ark which led them.

34. II Sam. 5:24.

35. I Sam. 7:10. Cf. the "great shout" of the Hebrews on seeing the ark come into camp in 4:5; also the tradition of the battle cry prescribed in Num. 10:1–10. The notes to this last passage in the Jerusalem Bible connect the war-cry to the much later ritual acclamation of the king, a natural transference.

battle cry in a canyon, for instance, might produce a multiplying echo that could have been heard as the voice of God; compare Athena "bellowing" before Troy.[36] In Numbers and other places we read of this "sacred battle cry," which among other things might make the garbled story of Jericho's fall somewhat more coherent. There the cry, plus the sound of the *shofar* or ram's horn, a pastoral-warrior emblem perhaps, proved able to knock down the walls by itself. Actually the story as we have it does not resemble anything so much as a ritual, perhaps annually reenacted on the site that symbolized urbanism, megalithic walls, autochthony, etc. The site of Jericho shows signs of having been conquered some centuries before Exodus times, but not again in those times.[37] One might conclude that the "Conquest" of Jericho was really a ritual conducted by Hebrew ancestors among the ruins of the hated city. Such a ritual might have been revivified by the influx of the desert wanderers, especially if they had already sacralized a battle cry, perhaps the name of the new God himself: "Yah!" A horde of nomads charging a Canaanite hill-town behind a mysterious Ark, forge, or whatever, screaming this imperative monosyllable, might well have given rise to the tradition of "the terror."

Historians of Israel have long postulated the formation of a cultic amphictyony, a league of tribes—the sacred number was twelve—around the imported figure of Yahweh, as the effective origin of the nation. Perhaps this bonding could have been suggested by Joshua, or some other leader of the fugitive slaves, on the grounds that the nomads had acquired a new God, identical to be sure with the "God of the fathers" but with a new warrior's name, who could be king over the new nation and lead it in battle. Some such appeal must be hypothesized to explain how the seminomads

36. *Iliad*, XX., 48–50. Mendenhall thinks of a similar analogy: *The Tenth Generation*, 62.

37 Kenyon, *Archaeology in the Holy Land*, 211. Miss Kenyon thinks it possible the destroyers were indeed Hebrews, but a pre-Exodus group. If so they might have instituted a ritual at the site. See also Miss Kenyon's chapter on "Jericho" in D. W. Thomas (ed.), *Archaeology and Old Testament Study*, 266 ff., esp. 273: "the placing at Jericho of a dramatic siege and capture may be an aetiological explanation of a ruined city." See fig. 18.

skulking around the Canaanite hills became eager to join their putative cousins. If this horde had already destroyed some cities, that
validated the new God.

We should then possibly think of the Exodus wanderers, and the
nation formed around them, as a kind of divinely led militia. Two
of the oldest texts in the whole Bible, according to some theories,
would support this hypothesis: The Song of Miriam and the Song
of Deborah. Both glorify Yahweh as God of battles. Miriam is said
to sing:

> Yahweh is a warrior;
> Yahweh is his name.
>
> .   .   .   .
>
> Yahweh will be king for ever and ever.[38]

The Song of Deborah is accompanied by a prose gloss in which
Deborah urges Barak and his army with the cry "Up! Yahweh
marches at your head." In the song, Yahweh's march into Canaan
is a warrior's progress through the land, and he coerces the "stars
in their courses" to aid Israel.[39]

Both songs imply that the horde fought as a guerrilla militia
rather than a disciplined army, perhaps even the women taking
part: both songs are named for women, and a woman allied with
the Hebrews (a Kenite, in fact) kills the Canaanite general in the

---

38. Exod. 15:3, 18.

39. Judg. 5 contains The Song, chapter 4 the prose gloss. Eric Voegelin, using
a different translation, says that the stars fought *for* Sisera, in aid of the "meleks"
(kings or, as he says, "celestial rulers") of Canaan (*Order and History*, Vol. I,
Israel and Revelation, 203). If this is correct, "the war between Sisera and the
Israelites is depicted as a battle between the city-gods of Canaan and Yahweh"
(*ibid.*, 203 n). Cf. the hints in Exodus (esp. 12:12) that the Passover and Exodus
were part of a combat of Yahweh the warrior against Pharaoh and the other
"gods" of Egypt. The Pharaoh in Gen. 41:44 talks like a god (cf. Exod. 6:1, 7:1;
note that Moses and Pharaoh argue over whether the Israelites are to "serve"
Pharaoh or Yahweh, that Israel is Yahweh's "firstborn son" to be redeemed by
the sacrifice of the firstborn of Egypt [4:22–23], that Pharaoh forbids Moses to
"see his face" again, lest he die [cf. 33:23]). See also Voegelin, p. 74, on Pharaoh as
"god incarnate" compared to whom the Christian conception (where the idea of
"the King" as an "ordinary man of low social status" is raised to its highest
power) is "an inkling of the scandal which Christianity must have been for men
emerging from cosmological civilizations."

Song of Deborah.[40] The natural enemy of this horde would be royal armies with chariots. In the Song of Miriam, Yahweh wins the victory by throwing horse and rider "into the sea"—or in the prose mythological elaboration, by parting the waters and then closing them again.[41] The battle in the Song of Deborah was fought in the plain near Megiddo, a site so strategic throughout history that it has given its name to Armageddon. Normally the guerrillas would not fight in the plain, since there the chariots could decimate them. In premonarchic times, the Hebrews controlled the hill country and the Canaanites dominated the plain (an ironic reversal occurred in 1948–1967, when the technologically superior Israelis won the old Canaanite lands and the Arabs stayed in the hill country).[42] But in this battle Yahweh and "the stars" seem to have caused a flash flood, well known to be a danger in dry countries, which mired the chariots and gave Israel the victory.

Very possibly the role of Yahweh as battle-leader was behind the conception of "holy war." The rules of this warfare stated that every thing and person in captured cities was to be destroyed: a barbarous practice, but one which prevented the guerrilla horde from turning into nomadic raiders like the archenemy cousins the Amalekites, Ishmaelites, and Midianites. No one can make war for spoil under the rules of holy war; all potential booty and slaves must be "devoted" to destruction. At critical junctures in the stories of Hebrew warfare, severe penalties were meted out for transgressions of this rule. Achan tried to hide away some treasure from Jericho (including a mantle from "Shinar," *i.e.*, Sumer, symbol of high culture), for which he and his clan paid with their lives.[43]

40. Judg. 5:24–27; cf. 4:17–22. Note that the prose version improves the credibility by having Jael slay Sisera lying down instead of standing up.
41. Exod. 15:1, 4; cf. 14:21–29.
42. See Judg. 1:19; the tradition surfaces again in I Kings 20:23 (cf. 20:28). There the Aramaeans know of the belief that Yahweh as warrior was "a god of the mountains. . . . But if we fight [the Hebrews] on level ground, we will certainly beat them." See also Baly, *The Geography of the Bible*, 145, 119, 154, on the way in which ancient geographical patterns figured in the 1948 war.
43. On holy war, see Deut. 20, and the study by Gerhard von Rad, *Der heilige Krieg im alten Israel* (4th ed., Gottingen: Vandenhoeck & Ruprecht, 1965). Achan's story is in Josh 7.

Saul lost his mandate for kingship for keeping an Amalekite king alive, no doubt to grace a self-glorifying victory parade. The implied early sacralization of warfare would fit the conception of Yahweh as king, present among his people in battles. The whole complex of rules would act as a unifying force, one which would make the amphictyony a sacred military organization: complaints in the early texts may allege that some tribe spoiled the united front of the "whole people" by failing to show up; this is treated as a dire offense against Yahweh.[44] This rule itself would further distinguish Israel from its anarchic nomad cousins, whose sheikhs were notorious for bringing their clans to a battle only if they felt like it.

The amphictyonic system worked well enough when it had only the Canaanites to deal with, for their city-states rarely banded together against the Hebrews. But the coming of the Philistines made a new military order imperative. Dependence on charismatic leadership and a militia army might have reduced the Hebrews to slavery under these new, technologically advanced invaders, who had superior iron weapons. Thus, where Judges 1:19 tells us of a stand-off in which the Canaanite chariots kept the swarming Hebrews from conquering the best arable areas, the plains, the Philistines reversed the impetus and took the initiative: they were able to penetrate the hills with their armies and soon had the Hebrews on the run.

The story of Samuel, Saul, and David tells how the Hebrews escaped the new threat. But between the lines, especially in the parts about Saul, signs of a clash over the form of leadership recur: Saul is portrayed as frequently at odds with religious functionaries. To allay the conflicts Saul tried to pass himself off as another kind of charismatic leader, or at least we have several texts suggesting such a conclusion, while at the same time he attempted to raise what was surely an appendage of monarchy, a standing army. "Any strong man or man of valor that caught Saul's eye he recruited into his service."[45] Castes of professional warriors were exactly what Is-

44. See esp. Judg. 5:16–17; cf. Judg. 21:8–10.
45. I Sam. 14:52. See Alt's analysis of the relation of Saul's kingship to the

rael did not want, if she was sacrally bound to the archaic military order of a divinely led militia. Charismatic leadership could not coexist with warrior castes, though there are hints that Gideon provided himself with a standing army.[46] But such a cadre was the normal military arm of a human king, and what better excuse could there be for it than the Philistine threat?

Saul's role in religious affairs suggests that he tried to usurp the prerogatives of the priestly leaders. Two legends are offered to explain the saying "Is Saul also among the prophets?" Both attribute ecstatic activity to him; such trances could well have been an accepted sign of charisma, in which the "spirit of Yahweh" possessed the leader with warlike frenzy, but in this context we may suspect that the proverb hints at an attempt by Saul to make a claim that the religious leadership and divine sanction had passed to him. More direct usurpations are hinted at in the two explanations offered of Saul's loss of mandate from Yahweh: one was a violation of holy-war rules, as mentioned, and the other involved his attempt to offer a sacrifice himself when he should have waited for Samuel to do it. Both stories indicate a struggle reminiscent of the temple-dynastic conflict in early cities.[47]

Saul failed, but he may have taught David how to succeed, for David managed to get both a standing army and the blessing of acceptance as a charismatic leader. David's standing army did not involve the raising of a warrior caste within Israel, with the resulting jealousies and fears, but was instead composed essentially of Philistine mercenaries accumulated at a time when David was driven into exile by Saul.[48] Also, in pursuit of David, Saul had slaughtered many of the Hebrew priests, thereby eliminating much potential

---

charismatic tradition in "The Formation of the Israelite State" and "The Monarchy in the Kingdoms of Israel and Judah," in *Essays on Old Testament History and Religion.*

46. Notice his elimination of the less animalistic warriors in Judg. 7:1–8.

47. The two violations are recounted in I Sam. 13:8–15 and 15:7–35; cf. the ecstatic acts in 10:1–2, 11, and 19:23–24. See also the reference to Adams' theory on militarism vs. temple in note 5 to Chapter Three herein.

48. See Alt, *Essays on Old Testament History and Religion,* 271–88.

later resistance to the monarchy; still others took refuge with David.[49] So Saul's persecution of David may itself have been the efficient cause of David's success in winning religious support.

The deepest complication in this story may turn on the identity of Saul's tribe, that of Benjamin. The name itself seems to be older than that of Israel. No one knows exactly what kind of people it designates in the old Mesopotamian texts where it is found, but they seem to have been troublesome: possibly the same kind of outlaws-nomads-freebooters who were called *Habiru*.[50] Benjamin means literally "sons of the south" or "of the right hand": the latter could mean "south," but it also might imply warriors, those dextrous with arms.[51] The portrait of Benjamin in the Joseph story seems to have nothing to do with restless, perhaps mercenary troublemakers: the story tells of a tender stripling, darling of his father's old age. Yet on his deathbed Jacob gives an oracle allotting fates to his sons; this doubtless archaic text conforms to the extra-Biblical notices of the *banu-yamina*:

> Benjamin is a ravening wolf,
> in the morning he devours his prey,
> in the evening he is still dividing the spoil.[52]

To follow the fortunes of Benjamin we must consider the hair-raising story that ends the book of Judges. Whatever its origin, it was intended at some point to serve as a cautionary tale about anarchy, illustrating the last verse: "In those days there was no king in Israel, and every man did what was right in his own eyes." Yet its thrust, in the context of the struggle over the kingship, perhaps was to discredit Saul's origins. The story tells of a Sodomitical crime attempted by some Benjaminites against a traveler; the act was a violation of sexual mores and of the laws of hospitality as well.

49. I Sam. 22:6–23; cf. II Sam. 8–17.
50. See H. G. May in *Peake's Commentary on the Bible,* 116; also see George Mendenhall, "Mari," in Edward F. Campbell, Jr., and David Noel Freedman (eds.), *The Biblical Archaeologist Reader II* (New York: Anchor, 1964), 16–17; also Georges Roux, *Ancient Iraq* (N.p.: Penguin, 1966), 175–76 and 180.
51. Albright, *Yahweh and the Gods of Canaan,* 79.
52. Gen. 49:27.

Frustrated in their desire to assault the man sexually, the Benja-minites abuse his concubine instead and leave her for dead. The traveler is then said to unite the nation against Benjamin by send-ing around the body of his concubine cut into twelve parts. So the "whole people" forms an army to come down against Benjamin. Here occurs a key point: though they outnumber the Benjaminites sixteen to one, the army of Israel loses the battle at first, one rea-son being that the army of Benjamin includes seven hundred ambi-dextrous warriors—with two right hands as it were—who can "sling a stone at a hair and not miss it." Finally, by ambush, Israel con-quers its brother tribe, then has to worry about preventing its total extermination, so that number of tribes in the sacred amphictyony will not drop below twelve. In a confused ending fresh wives from other sources are provided for the six hundred remaining Benja-minite warriors, so that the tribe can flourish again.[53]

One motive in this story seems clears: to portray Benjamin as a rapacious band that must be disciplined and then domesticated with new wives. The inference is tempting, that at some time Benjamin was on the way to becoming a warrior caste, as its mercenary repu-tation might suggest. Now one frequent practice of ancient warrior castes was homosexuality (Sparta, Turkey), due to the isolation of the young men. Whereas other Near Eastern countries tolerated this form of sex, the Hebrews were extremely contemptuous of it, and their name for the male cultic prostitutes of Canaan was "dogs."[54]

In the story, Benjaminites are portrayed as pugnacious homo-sexuals, as well as skilled fighters, but when their tribe is shattered they are presumably no more a threat sexually than militarily. The soldiers with their new wives apparently return to ordinary Israel-

53. Judg. 19:1–21:25; see vv. 20:11 and 16. Note that the army of Israel loses an astounding total of 40,000 men in the war, while 25,000 Benjaminites are killed: also the village of Jabesh-Gilead (except for marriageable maidens) is exterminated for failing to show up for the crusade. All this for one concubine? Historically the story is incredible, but that does not make its motives less inter-esting.

54. Deut. 23:18.

ite life and sexual mores. The next time we hear of Benjamin, it has apparently reconstituted itself, and it furnishes Israel's most ambitious soldier to that date, Saul, who addresses his officers as "you men of Benjamin."[55] Later, under David, rebellions are led by Benjaminites: perhaps simply disgruntled adherents of Saul, but perhaps also throwbacks to the role of the "ravening wolf" among the tribes.[56] From all this we might have guessed that Benjamin would be the likely source of men willing to tamper with the militia form of warfare and to replace it with a standing army that would fulfill the old aspirations of tribe as warrior caste. This would help explain why Saul failed: the military ambitions of a Benjaminite would arouse mistrust.

Saul himself is a confusing figure: in one chapter he is astonished at being chosen king by Yahweh, for he is an insignificant young man from an obscure family (and he calls his tribe "the least of the tribes of Israel"). When they come to crown him he hides among the baggage.[57] But in other passages he is no stereotype of a reluctant leader: he is a head taller than anyone else, seizes the leadership with great zeal, and turns up with a full-grown warrior son, Jonathan. Obviously inconsistent traditions have been combined, and similar anomalies occur in the stories of Samuel and David.[58] But in Saul's case the double image seems to be related to the crisis

55. I Sam. 22:7; cf. II Sam. 2:15, 25, and 31.
56. II Sam. 20; cf. 16:5–13. See Alt, *Essays on Old Testament History and Religion*, 248.
57. I Sam. 9:21, 10:16 and 22. Note those who "despise him" in 10:27.
58. I Sam. 9:1–3, 10:9–12 and 23–24, 11:6, 13:1–2. The anomalies about Samuel and David may be illustrated by 7:2–12, where Samuel is judge and leader of the nation, contrasted to 9:6–19, where he is an obscure "seer" whose name Saul does not even know. Similarly, David appears as a mere stripling, unknown to Saul, in the Goliath story, 17:55–58, although Saul had specifically sent for him, to his father, in 16:18–23, to serve as henchman, companion, armor-bearer, and lyre-player. Note that in the latter passage Saul "loved him greatly," while Jonathan "came to love him as his own soul," made a *pact* to love him, and gave him armor (18:1–4). When Saul and Jonathan are killed David's lament calls them "loved and lovely," and states that Jonathan's love was "more wonderful than the love of a woman" (Sam. 23, 26). I hope I will not be thought a scandal-monger if I suggest that warrior homosexuality might be relevant to these traditions: as it might, also, with the prohibition against contact with women for soldiers on active duty (see I Sam. 21:4–5, II Sam. 11–11). This "law" is not likely to have been a practice of a militia horde. On the contrary, the laws of holy war given in

in military leadership, leaving us with the question: was Saul really "raised up" by Yahweh like the judges, or was he an ambitious warlord?

The whole story can be read as centering on this crisis. It begins when there is no judge to lead the nation, and the priests are in control; but they are decadent, and they lose the Ark to the Philistines, proving that Yahweh is no longer present in it. (On hearing the news of this capture a wife of one of the sons of Eli names her newborn baby *Ichabod,* meaning "the glory has departed": the glory, *kabod,* was a literal physical effulgence supposed to radiate from God.[59]) Samuel inherits the mantle from the priests, and his judge-like rule is satisfactory, but his sons too are degenerate, so the people call for a king.[60] Saul takes over as war-leader: his successes are great, but soon are overshadowed by those of one of his own men, David. Saul drives David into exile, and into the service of the Philistines: the Bible unblinkingly records this astonishing fact, surely true since there would be every reason not to invent it. Saul kills eighty-five priests at Nob, on the pretext that they had sheltered David, and puts their city to the sword. But Saul loses Yahweh's favor, his mandate, and his life. David comes out of exile to dominate the Hebrew political scene and soon is accepted as king, ridding himself of Saul's sons and generals either by great good luck, or by cleverly engineered assassinations, depending on how you look at it.[61]

After David gains the throne, we read that "his sons were

Deut. 20 seem purposefully heterosexual: they specify that the bridegroom who has not consummated his marriage is to leave the army in order to go home and do so (v. 7).

59. I Sam. 4:19–22.

60. I Sam. 8:1–4. The theme of unworthy or degenerate or rebellious sons haunts the whole story, serving as an antidynastic note. Cf. Eli's (2:12, 22–25, 4:1), Saul's (except for Jonathan, and even he gets abuse from his father over David), and David's. Alt's *Essays on Old Testament History and Religion* make many points about resistance to the dynastic principle in these affairs (see pp. 263 ff., 278, etc.)

61. David in Philistine service, I Sam. 21:11 ff., 27, 29; Saul's massacre of the priests, 22:6–23; assassinations, II Sam. 1:5–16, 3:22–39, 4, 21:1–14. David spares only one crippled Saulide, whose handicap made him no threat to claim the role of warrior-king.

priests." [62] We don't hear of him slaughtering religious leaders. No doubt he took care to nourish the sacral traditions that Saul had in effect driven into his camp; his shrewdest maneuver in this line was to bring the Ark to his new capital, Jerusalem. In the procession he dances in front of the Ark in a frenzied way, appropriate to charisma, even exposing his nakedness so as to be despised by his wife Michal, Saul's daughter. (Nakedness was shameful among Semites, but since Sumerian times priests had practiced sacral nudity in certain rites, as witches did later.) [63] Perhaps Michal was moved not by prudery alone: it must have galled her to see David acquiring all the benefits of religious traditions over which her father had come to grief.

Having appropriated the Ark, David had established continuity with the old traditions, yet he did not have to conform to them in such a way as to remind men that Yahweh was supposed to lead the people himself. The presence of Yahweh was still associated with the Ark (one unfortunate dies when he touches it), but now it was safely ensconced in Jerusalem. [64] All of the mysterious traditions about the Ark, persistently connecting it to war-cries and other military rituals, its role in leading the people across the Jordan to the Promised Land, against Jericho, and all its other functions now belonged to David's service. The God of the Ark, and thus David's God, was *Yahweh Sebaoth*, the Lord of Hosts: whatever this name may have meant originally, in David's story it was glossed to mean "the lord of battles," "the god of the armies of Israel." [65] From its beginning, where Hannah prays to him for a son, this was the dominant title of Yahweh in the story of Samuel and the Kings.

Thus David managed to make himself seem the heir rather than the antagonist of the ancient military traditions of Israel. Still plenty of murmuring went on, and some rebellions occurred, but Yah-

62. II Sam. 8:18.

63. II Sam. 6; for sacral nudity, see Saggs, *The Greatness That Was Babylon*, 49 and 337; Albright, *Yahweh and the Gods of Canaan*, 121, 123, and 146.

64. II Sam. 6:6–8.

65. I Sam. 17:45. See Psalm 24:7–10 and Cross, *Canaanite Myth and Hebrew Epic*, 71, 99.

weh seems to have been on the side of the big battalions. Evidently David's standing army, assembled around a body-guard of "Chereth-ite and Pelethite" mercenaries recruited from the Philistines, was powerfully intimidating. After some years of soft living, David was faced with the rebellion of his son Absalom, and fled with only the mercenaries and a few others faithful to him: but Absalom's failure to chase them down immediately allowed the advantage to swing back to David. Obviously the mercenaries' reputation for ferocity was enough to convince wavering Hebrews that David would win the struggle in spite of his adversity. In the stories we have, this group's exploits are mixed with those of an even more fearsome cadre called "David's mighty men." Clearly David had not relied on religious sanction alone for his success: he provided himself with all the available fighting talent.[66]

David must have used his period of service among the Philistines to good advantage, not only in recruiting soldiers but in learning Philistine strategy, for he seems to have defeated them with relative ease and reduced them to a vassal state. But neither what he learned nor the details of his battles against the Philistines are recorded, so it is unlikely that this episode was invented as some sort of ration-alization of David's military genius. On the contrary, every critical argument would suggest that the story must be substantially true, and that it was of the utmost imporance for the germination of the Hebrew sense of history, because there was little attempt to gloss it over, and thus it testifies to the antimythologizing tendency in Is-rael. Although such flexible loyalties were well known in the an-cient world (Alcibiades is a notorious example), they would hardly be attributed to a mythologized national hero. This episode sets the stage for the unsparing treatment of David's guilt in the Bathsheba affair, and for the portrayal of the multifold problems arising from his attitude toward his children.[67] Merely the inclusion of sinful and shameful episodes does not guarantee a story's authenticity, of

66. II Sam. 8–18, 15:1–23, 17:1–14 *et seq.;* the "mighty men," 23:8–39. See Alt, *Essays on Old Testament History and Religion,* 271–75.

67. II Sam. 11, 12:1–25, 13:1–19:9, I Kings 1.

course, since these occur in myth: but the profile of David's career that we are given in the Bible is so unlike what we are told of heroes in legend that the conclusion is inescapable: if anything at all in the story was historically true, then a great deal of it (perhaps almost all of it after David's youth) is likely to be true also.

This is not to say that contradictions and garbled episodes do not occur in the story. Indeed, it is precisely their appearance that testifies to the basic historicity of the narrative. The plenitude of solecism, anomaly, and self-contradiction in the Bible is the best evidence for the slow but steady development of the Hebrew sense of history, for it demonstrates that writers would not cheerily alter their sources to conform to predetermined patterns of expectation. On the contrary, the writers were obviously conditioned not only to regard their sources as canonical, which was a great step in history-writing, but also to expect the unexpected, the incongruous, and the unlikely: precisely the signs of an inscrutable God's intervention in history. Yahweh's acts must always, in the eyes of men, possess a certain arbitrary quality. Paul does not hesitate to use God's arbitrariness (he quotes Exodus 33:19, "I have mercy on whom I will, and I show pity to whom I please") as a sufficient explanation of apparent flaws in the apportioning of justice in the fates of men; such confidence in God's grace was consonant with the position that God's wisdom was foolishness in this world.[68] Tertullian's famous *credo quia absurdum* means essentially the same thing: I believe it because it is ridiculous—in the eyes of the world. The nucleus of the whole Judaeo-Christian sense of history shows through clearest on this point: precisely because, as Aristotle implies, history does not manifest the *logos*, the eternal patterns of things, it acquires validity from our Western point of view.[69] Whereas myth will always conform to eternal patterns, history struggles against them, not always successfully, of course. The es-

68. Romans 9:6–33, I Cor. 1:17–31.
69. See Patrides, *The Grand Design of God*, 2–3. Cross makes an old but recurrently useful point in this connection: actual events could break the concept of eternal patterns. See continued discussion in note 82 of this chapter.

sential differences of history from myth include this sense of the unexpected. As Joyce's Stephen Dedalus puts it, in a way much like Tertullian, the church (and the world) are founded "upon incertitude, upon unlikelihood."[70] That truth is stranger than fiction may be a cliché, but it chimes with the *skandalon* of the incarnate god suffering the most shameful form of death.

Enough of the confusion and uncertainty that must have infected Israel in those days of living under the Philistine threat is preserved in the story to give it just that episodic quality that made Aristotle spurn history for poetry. Only by reconstructing such plausible issues as the conflict over kingship can we find a real unity in it; otherwise David makes a strangely halting progress toward the throne. Our hypotheses can supply a logic missing in the text itself, for the account is so full of detail, and so lacking in reflective explanatory schemes, that many decide the author must have been an eyewitness from the court.[71] Two of the most likely candidates are Abiathar, the priest who fled to David after the massacre at Nob, and Ahimaaz, son of another priest who had joined David's entourage. They are sometimes implicated in the action in ways that suggest personal knowledge. Both figures mediate David's assumption of religious leadership in the nation; significantly, Solomon on his accession has Abiathar, last priest of the house of Eli, deprived of his priesthood and sequestered.[72] This act was the final step in the assumption of sacral power by the kings, bringing to an end the long resistance of the religious leadership against the new order and culminating the first great phase of Hebrew history-writing.

Actually this innovation of the monarchy was in several senses a regression, a retreat by Israel away from the independence its "withdrawals" from the high cultures had established: by passing the kingship to humans they became "like other nations." For a time

70. James Joyce, *Ulysses* (New York: Random House, 1934), 205. Stephen is talking about paternity, a "legal fiction" as he calls it: see below, pp. 233–47, on the relation of history to paternity.
71. See L. H. Brockington in *Peake's Commentary on the Bible, s.v.*, "II Sam. IX," and "II Sam. XVII, 15–20."
72. I Kings 2:26–27.

the petty empire enjoyed success, then was caught up and eventually destroyed in the power struggles of the larger empires in the area. Some prophets seem to have regarded the institution of kingship as a sin that led inexorably to final destruction: clearly they had a *prima facie* case, though it is hard to say what would have happened to Israel without a king.[73]

In the event, Solomon made the Hebrew kingship into a monarchy indistinguishable from many others in the Near East. No war-leader himself, he became a man of the palace, a busy administrator, cementing his father's conquests by a foreign policy that featured marriages with princesses of many neighboring powers, even haughty Egypt.[74] But he did keep a mighty standing army, sufficient to intimidate, marked by the presence of vast numbers of war chariots: such a thing had never been heard of in Israel before, since the chariot had always been the symbol of Israel's enemies. When Joshua captured a large number of these in the Canaanite wars, he burned the chariots and hamstrung the horses.[75] Two hundred or so years later David did exactly the same thing, which testifies to the continuing hold of the archaic traditions of warfare and to David's care to conform to them when possible.[76] Everywhere else David appears as a genius of military opportunism, but he could

---

73. On the prophets against kingship, see below, pp. 208–11. See Mendenhall, *The Tenth Generation*, esp. 15–19, 28–31, and 224–26. He identifies David as an "Old Testament Constantine" who presided over Israel's regressive "reassimilation to Late Bronze Age religious ideas and structures," in effect dissolving "religion into politics" (p. 16) and thus repealing the effect of the "revolution" that the early "kingdom of Yahweh" manifested. Mendenhall ably demonstrates that this "kingship of Yahweh" was something very different from the usual identification by a people of its national interests with a god or a cosmic order. He also argues that such recognition of an ethical authority above, and often in conflict with, the state, is politically vulnerable. The threat is Caesarism: "the age-old paganism in which the military leader is the great benefactor who is thereby entitled to the gratitude and obedience of the populace. . . . Politics has made little progress since, and the process of political revolution is usually based upon the blind devotion of masses in hope of gaining wealth by following a leader who promises everything" (pp. 30–31).

74. I Kings 3:1, 11:1–3. See Bright, *A History of Israel*, 191.

75. Josh. 11:1–9.

76. II Sam. 8:4.

make no use of these alien contrivances except to keep a few for parades.

David's sons, in contrast, were shamefully quick to pick up the Near Eastern monarchic style, including the use of chariots. When Absalom wanted to appear a more kingly man than his father, he procured a chariot and fifty men to run ahead of it.[77] Adonijah, trying to seize the kingship when David was old, did the same.[78] But the supreme charioteer in Hebrew history was Solomon, who "built up a force of chariots and horses; he had fourteen hundred chariots and twelve thousand horses; these he stationed in the chariot towns and near the king in Jerusalem. . . . A chariot was imported from Egypt for six hundred shekels, a horse for a hundred and fifty. These were exported through the King's agents to all the kings of the Hittites and to the king in Aram in the same way."[79] In other words, not only did Solomon assemble so many chariots that he had to build stable towns around the country, but also he became the middleman in the Near Eastern horse and chariot trade! No doubt he made a fortune.

Such easy accessions to the ways of emperors show why Solomon is such a fitting symbol of ambivalence toward culture in the Bible. Some of the prophets of later ages continued to use his amassing of chariots as an indictment against him (though in general the nation quickly got so used to chariots that they appear as angelic manifestations, without offensive connotations, in the stories of Elijah and Elisha).[80] Samuel had been made to warn the people, in a probably retrojected passage, about the tyrannies of a king: he would "take your sons and assign them to his chariotry and cavalry, and they will run in front of his chariot."[81] Deuteronomy 17:16–17, a supposedly Mosaic law, is even more explicit as a condemnation:

77. II Sam. 15:1.
78. I Kings 1:5.
79. I Kings 10:26–29.
80. II Kings 2:11–12; but cf. Isa. 31:1, Hos. 10:13, and other passages in the prophets which bring out the old hostility to chariots, monarchic armies, and trust in man rather than God.
81. I Sam. 8–11.

"Ensure that [a king] does not increase the number of his horses, or make the people go back to Egypt to increase his cavalry, for Yahweh said to you, 'You must never go back that way again.' Nor must he increase the number of his wives, for that could lead his heart astray. Nor must he increase his gold and silver excessively." Wives, idolatry, wealth, chariots, and the Egyptian chariot trade: irrefutable references to the mechanisms of prosperity with which Solomon seduced the Chosen People to complete their acculturation and to become a Near Eastern state, "like the other nations." Both passages were barely disguised attacks on his memory.[82]

Even Solomon's vaunted wisdom was a product of his importing culture; much of Proverbs, for instance, was lifted from Egyptian works belonging to the "wisdom" genre, an old tradition in the Near East.[83] Hence the books of Wisdom in the Bible are somewhat

---

82. We must assume here, of course, that these passages were written by the so-called Deuteronomist *ca.* 621 B.C. See Bright, *A History of Israel*, 207.

(Continued from note 69): Against the evolutionist view that history replaces myth as a society "matures," Cross says: "The movement from dominantly mythical to dominantly historical patterns is not a natural or inevitable tendency, as is evidenced by the perennial resurgence of mythic forms and language in biblical religion: in the royal theology, in apocalyptic, in Gnosticism, in Qabbalah. The reason for this [mistake] lies in the refusal of many form critics or historians of tradition to raise the question of actual historical memory lying behind cultic patterning of the Exodus, Covenant at Sinai, and Conquest. The thrust of historical events, recognized as crucially or ultimately meaningful, alone had the power to displace the mythic pattern. Even then we should expect the survival of some mythic forms, and the secondary mythologizing of historical experiences to point to their cosmic or transcendent meaning" (*Canaanite Myth and Hebrew Epic*, 87). But, while recognizing that it is "natural to mythologize (and re-mythologize) rather than historicize, and acknowledging the role of real events in overcoming this tendency, we might also say that all would be insufficient without the mythologizing animus derived from cultural hostility. The Bible is dotted with assertions that "we do things this way because the nations do them the other way." That seems a more powerful force even than real events, or at least serves as a catalyst to allow the events their full power of signifying. See also Roland de Vaux in J. Philip Hyatt (ed.), *The Bible in Modern Scholarship* (Nashville: Abingdon, 1965), 24. Other contributors to this volume make many related points.

83. See W. Baumgartner in H. H. Rowley (ed.), *The Old Testament and Modern Study* (New York: Oxford University Press, 1951), 210–211; cf. Cross, *Canaanite Myth and Hebrew Epic*, 239: "Another index of Solomon's departure from the ways of his father and assimilation of foreign styles of kingship may be

compromised: they are not informed by a rigorous Yahwist vision but rather by an essentially foreign ethic of prudent calculation designed to lead to prosperity.[84] If Solomon really wrote any of those books, he was the Ben Franklin of his day, and as repellent to perceptive Yahwists as Poor Richard to D. H. Lawrence. However, there was a more sinister side to Solomon's program of culture. It appears to have been ancillary to an effort to reorganize the country into administrative districts, in order to supersede the old tribal organization and thus disorient resistance to future monarchic schemes; massive forced labor and a military draft were the other signs of this effort.[85] Although in his father's day hostility to a homegrown standing army had been so great that a plague in Israel was ascribed to the "sin" of taking a census—the preliminary step to a draft—Solomon was undeterred and built up his army without letting opposition develop.[86]

Solomon, in short, showed tendencies and desires of a despot. This puts his building of the Temple in a new, Ozymandian light. For this project he had to import Phoenician (North Canaanite) builders and architects, since the Hebrew antipathy to monumental building excluded such professions from Israel.[87] The work was

---

found in his cultivation of wisdom. Solomon expended his energies not in the primitive, exuberant Yahwism of David but in the pursuit of cosmopolitan and tolerant wisdom in the fashion of the foreign courts."

84. Baumgartner remarks that most wisdom proffers "the class ethics of a feudal aristocracy" (Rowley [ed.], *The Old Testament and Modern Study*, 210).

85. See I Kings 5:27; J. Mauchline in *Peake's Commentary on the Bible, s.v.,* "I Kings IV"; Cross, *Canaanite Myth and Hebrew Epic,* 240; Alt, *Essays on Old Testament History and Religion,* esp. 293: "We begin to realize how in the kingdom of Israel the balance began to swing from the Israelite to the Canaanite side [with Solomon's innovations, districts, chariot cities, etc.]. It is the old superiority of the civilization of the plains over the mountains which was once more coming into play."

On the pattern of Solomon's excesses, especially with forced labor, see Bright, *A History of Israel,* 199–202.

86. II Sam. 24; see Cross, *Canaanite Myth and Hebrew Epic,* 240 and n; Alt, *Essays on Old Testament History and Religion,* 289. Speiser, *Oriental and Biblical Studies,* 171 ff. develops another aspect of the census, but agrees it was military.

87. II Sam. 5:15 ff. Cross calls the Temple "Canaanite" (*Canaanite Myth and Hebrew Epic,* 238); Mendenhall calls it "utterly pagan" (*The Tenth Generation,* 86). Bright points out that the "bronze sea" and the altar may have repre-

done, we are told in I Kings 6:7, without pick, hammer, or any iron tool: this may have been an observance of a sacral code of immense antiquity, since Jericho's walls and Egypt's pyramids had been constructed that way. If so, it means that Solomon was importing megalithic beliefs along with the workmen and the cedars from Lebanon. A hint of apostasy here would not be surprising, for Solomon's imported wives did indeed "lead his heart astray" into idolatrous worship of the syncretized cults they brought with them from their native countries.[88] Solomon's Temple was accepted by the people, but in its historical dimension it was a sellout to the high cultures. From this point of view Solomon the wise looks rather naive: but of course he didn't have the advantage of having the Bible to read.

Opposition to the kings and their projects was not lacking. Though the kings had their own prophets, guilds of yes-men culled from bands of wandering ecstatics, the great writing prophets carried along a tradition of smoldering hostility to the new, regressive order. It is curious that archaeology has uncovered no Hebrew royal inscriptions, whereas other Near Eastern kings were devoted to these self-advertisements. Writing in Israel seems to have been the property of the anti-Ozymandian party.[89]

---

sented prominent pagan notions: the underground sea of fertility-power and the mountain of the gods (A History of Israel, 197). For a more detailed discussion, see Albright, Archaeology and the Religion of Israel, 138–50.

88. I Kings 11:4 ff. We are told that Solomon became a "follower of Astarte," Milcom, Chemosh, and other foreign gods. However, his wives may not have to bear the brunt of the blame. An earlier note says, curiously, that "Solomon loved Yahweh: he followed the precepts of David his father, except that he offered sacrifice and incense on the high places" (3:3). Obviously his syncretistic tendencies were there all along, as part of his imperialist presumptions.

89. Millar Burrows comments on the lack of royal inscriptions in Robert C. Dentan (ed.), The Idea of History in the Ancient Near East (New Haven: Yale University Press, 1955), 101–102. Cross compares the relations of kings and prophets to a hostile symbiosis, which reminds us again of the function of the pastoral theme in the Bible. He says, "It is fair to say that the institution of prophecy appeared simultaneously with kingship in Israel and fell with kingship. This is no coincidence: the two offices belong to the Israelite political structure which emerged from the conflict between league and kingdom. While prophecy was not an institution of the league, the charismatic principle of leadership which ob-

Sometimes the prophets appear as advisers or even sponsors of a king, but their function was always double-edged, taking its pattern perhaps from Samuel's role in Saul's career. Nathan also appears as a figure at David's court, but was a gadfly to him all the same, who trapped him into denouncing himself, in the Bathsheba story, with his parable of the poor man's lamb stolen by the rich man.[90] Elijah's fearless hostility to Ahab and to his Baal-worshiping foreign wife Jezebel brought the latent hostility into clear view:[91] thereafter Isaiah, Jeremiah, and the rest stand in some adversary or admonitory role to their kings.[92] Hosea made his opposition a key to his reading of history: he outspokenly blamed Israel's troubles on "the wickedness at Gilgal," where Saul was crowned. According to Hosea, Yahweh himself proclaimed that the kings had been set up without his sanction or blessing.[93]

The opposition to idolatrous and despotic tendencies among the monarchs grew so strong that it curiously vitiated history-writing. The writers of the Bible were mostly Judahites, since the Northern Kingdom destroyed by Assyria became the Ten Lost Tribes and disappeared from history; the writers treat Northern kings as hopeless idolaters, worshipers of the "golden calves" created in the shrine at Bethel, and thus of no interest to good Yahwists.[94] Some Southern kings had fits of Yahwist reformism: notable was Josiah, who initiated the Deuteronomic reforms about 621 B.C.[95] But others were

---

tained in the era of the Judges survived in its liveliest form in the office of the prophet" (*Canaanite Myth and Hebrew Epic*, 223).

90. II Sam. 12:1–14. Note the pastoral overtones.

91. I Kings 17–21; cf. the equally fearless acts of the prophet Micaiah in 22:1–38.

92. Isa. 36–39; cf. II Kings 18–20. See also Jer. 26, 36–38; Ezek. 19, 34, 35c.

93. Hos. 12:15 and 8:4 (cf. 8:14, 5:1–2).

94. I Kings 12:26–13:10; 13:33–34 *et seq*. The only Northern king to merit extensive treatment, besides Ahab the villain, was the Yahwist usurper, Jehu (II Kings 9–10), but even he retained the "golden calves" (10:29). Alt and other analysts have suspected that in fact usurpation was more prevalent in the North precisely because of the continuing force of the conflict between charismatic and dynastic principles.

95. II Kings 22–23:30; cf. Jehoshaphat, I Kings 22:41–51. See Christopher R. North, *The Old Testament Interpretation of History* (London: Epworth, n.d.), 101.

more Solomonic: the notorious Manasseh brought in full-scale "Molech worship," Phoenician rites featuring infanticide.[96] This grisly idolatry was the final degradation, representing the whole process which led the Yahwist prophets to denounce their own culture and its attempts to sophisticate itself.

The fact that in the Bible the Northern kings are dismissed and the Southern ones judged by an increasingly simplistic formula shows that history-writing in Israel was dominated by the critical viewpoint, not by the urge to record events. Many of the kings— Omri is a well-known example—were fairly important in the history of the Near East, but were almost ignored, because of their idolatries, by the Bible-writers.[97] Our notion of a documentary record is thus merely a by-product of the Hebrew impulse to set down the narrative of a great cultural watershed in Israel's existence. The essence of history, looked at in this way, would not be the desire to tell *wie es eigentlich gewesen*, "how it really happened," in Leopold von Ranke's famous phrase, but rather the assumption of a vantage point beyond culture itself, implicitly alienated from it. Since the crisis that produced monarchization and superseded the old conception of Yahweh as war-leader king was synecdochic for the whole question of culture in Israel, as Solomon's tendencies demonstrate, the history we find in the Bible is basically concerned with the pos-

96. II Kings 21. Manasseh also restored "high places," "altars to Baal" and "a sacred pole" in imitation of Ahab, plus altars to the "whole array of heaven" (in the Temple itself, where he also introduced male prostitutes in imitation of Rehoboam, son of Solomon: I Kings 14:24) and a carved image of Asherah. For good measure he revived "soothsaying and magic" and "necromancers and wizards." His reign caused Yahweh to announce, according to the prophets, that "I will scour Jerusalem as a man scours a dish" (21:13).

A Jewish tradition holds that Isaiah was martyred in Manasseh's reign (see *The Jerusalem Bible*, p. 1124).

97. See Speiser, *Oriental and Biblical Studies*, 196–97: "For the Scriptures were never intended to be a mere chronicle of events, a story of certain states, or even the biography of a nation. The reader who is interested in such things is told time and again where he can find them: in the *Book of the Wars of the Lord*, the *Book of Jasher*, the *Chronicles of the Kings of Israel*, the *Chronicles of the Kings of Judah*. The aim of the biblical authors was of a wholly different order."

Omri gets five verses (I Kings 16:23–28). Yet Assyrian records for 150 years call Israel the "land of Omri" (see J. Mauchline in *Peake's Commentary on the Bible*, s.v., "I Kings XV 33–XVI 34").

sibility of judgment of culture's strivings and achievements. Even where the writers are unquestioningly pro-Israel and promonarchic, they write from a viewpoint that projects beyond culture. Thus, though the kings succeeded in presiding over Israel's sophistication and in diminishing the opposition to culture, the prophets' and historians' point of view itself preserved the old order.[98] To write history, for a Hebrew, was in some sense to take Yahweh's view of things into account: the literal belief in his watchfulness and interventionism, the intense sense of his personal presence and will and care, seem to have led to the habit of seeing things, as it were, with his eyes. Not that any of the writers ever deify themselves! They don't even assume what we would call an "omniscient" point of view. But they do identify with Yahweh's interests; they do judge by standards they could attribute to him, as best they understand his purposes; and thus they produce that distancing, that habit of judgment and criticism that is the complement to the sense of immediacy postulated by von Rad as the effect of the Hebrew historicization of cult festivals. In the stories of the later kings, the distancing so dominated as to dissipate the immediacy; and it was left to the prophets, in their revisionist project, to revive the style of the earlier writers, so as to recapture at once the pitiless critical attitude and the sense of urgency, of immediate relevance and vibrancy in events. As they punctured the fatuous and complacent illusions of the post-Solomonic, cultured Hebrews, and told them that their history guaranteed them not peace but punishment, the prophets created a rhetoric which forces writer and reader into an intense but estranged personal encounter. From this style Western literature has profited greatly.[99]

98. See above, note 89; Wright, *The Old Testament Against Its Environment*, 57; J. H. Hexter, *The Judaeo-Christian Tradition* (New York: Harper, 1966), 43; North, *The Old Testament Interpretation of History*, 92 ff.; Cross, *Canaanite Myth and Hebrew Epic*, 223–24; Millar Burrows, in Dentan (ed.), *The Idea of History in the Ancient Near East*, 118.

99. See below, Chapter Five, on the relations between alienation, distancing, "point of view," and the practices and possibilities of literature. The recent attack on "perspectivism" led by Marshall McLuhan should be stood on its head:

LITERATURE OUT OF HISTORY: GENESIS TO JOB

> [Biblical] literature consists very largely of historical narratives, all presented under a dominant conception of the meaning of history. Yet it is not a single, uniform idea. . . . Back of the rather sophisticated presentation of history in the Old Testament lie early popular traditions and legends. Some of these have been taken up into the later historical literature and preserved almost intact; others are preserved merely in fragments or faint echoes. Sometimes the old tradition and the later interpretation can be easily distinguished; sometimes it is difficult or impossible to disentangle them. In some cases an earlier motive can be dimly seen behind the particular purpose for which the story is used by the historian. The story of Cain and Abel, for example, reflects the conflict between pastoral and agricultural societies, but as the story is used in Genesis this motive is replaced by the later writer's interest in the history of sin and judgment.
>
> —Millar Burrows

The changing motives to which Burrows refers give rise to texts having what we might call "layers of purpose." Sometimes these go in different, unrelated directions, and sometimes they cohere in a movement toward a new form, a synthesis of narrative and parable, derived from history but issuing finally in a great work of self-conscious fiction, the Book of Job. As such it is highly unusual in the Old Testament, but it is compelling enough to stand as the culmination of the Old Testament's literary dynamic.

At about the same time the "Court History" of David was being written, about 950–900 B.C. by most accounts, another great strand in the Hebrew narrative of history was being prepared. According to the much-criticized but as yet unreplaced "documentary hypothesis" of Biblical scholars, a writer labeled "J" was at this time organizing ancient traditions into a story of Yahweh's appearances and control of events in the pre-Mosaic age. Whereas Exodus 6:3 held firmly that Yahweh had not been known by that name until

---

the alienation involved is inevitably ours, for better and worse, and brings recompenses that "immediacy" knows nothing of.

the time of Moses, J was in possession of another tradition—that Yahweh-worship went back to the time of Enosh, grandson of Adam —and he went on to identify the God of the Creation legend and Eden story as Yahweh.[100] In other words, J followed out the logical impulse consequent on the view of Yahweh as Lord of History.

J's work is already informed, even at its early date, by some of the basic components of the conception of history: the narrative continuity, the search of events for meaning, the idea of canonicity, or reverence for the exactness of the source. This last is an element in J's work at variance with the usual mechanisms of transmission in myth; it may owe something to ritual's care for exact wording, and even to old beliefs in word-magic, but these are distant influences at most. E. A. Speiser demonstrates how canonicity is implied in J, and his subtle reasoning is worth repeating. First he summarizes the archaeological finds that have made it clear that Genesis does, in several crucial places, possess real historicity: the theft of the *teraphim* by Rachel, the bypassing of primogeniture in the Jacob story, and the wife-sister motif in three stories of Abraham and Isaac, cannot be explained with reference to the social conditions of tenth-century Israel when J wrote, but accurately reflect habits of the Patriarchal Age (ca. 1800 B.C.) that J purports to describe. Each of the problematic passages was found to have ample precedent in documents dating from those earlier centuries in Northern Mesopotamia. But as Speiser points out, the clue to canonicity is that these once-purposeful passages were already mysterious to J, or whoever first wrote them.

The full meaning of these episodes . . . had already been lost to the narrator himself; otherwise he would surely have taken the trouble to enlighten his readers just as he did so often elsewhere. . . . In these circumstances, why were the narratives in question included at all? The manifest

---

100. Enosh, Gen. 4:26. For a summary of J's importance, see Millar Burrows, in Dentan (ed.), *The Idea of History in the Ancient Near East*, 112. For J and the historians, see Gerhard von Rad, *The Problem of the Hexateuch and Other Essays,* trans. E. W. T. Dicken (New York: McGraw-Hill, 1966), 51, 71, etc.

J is properly a document, not an author, but the differences are set aside here purely for convenience. *Someone* wrote the words.

fact that the narrator no longer knew the explanation, yet set down the details—details which prove to be authentic reflections of a forgotten civilization—can mean but one thing: his aim was not to question or to reason why, but only to record faithfully what tradition had handed down to him. ... The lives of the patriarchs had already become part of an oral canon.[101]

Clearly J was not slavish in his practices, for his work bears the marks of an interpretation as well as a recording of history; yet where the oral canon gave him fixed narratives to work with, he included them in full detail—though the presuppositions of the events were already lost to him. This kind of canonicity is not the same as the preservation of cultural detail that we find in Homer and in oral poetry generally. J's interest was not in preserving the folkways of a culture at all; his concern was the meaning of the story in the sense of its revelation of Yahweh's plan in history. There is nothing comparable in Homer, no "meaning" in that sense of the word at all.

The result was that almost all the Biblical narratives acquired a historical cast even when they were plainly legendary. No one has made this point more emphatically than Erich Auerbach. To him we owe the point that the very brokenness and lack of homogenization in the Biblical text differentiates it clearly from legend, which he says is discernible from its form alone:

Even where the legendary does not immediately betray itself by elements of the miraculous, by the repetition of well-known standard motives, typical patterns and themes, through neglect of clear details of time and place, and the like, it is generally quickly recognized by its composition. It runs far too smoothly. All cross currents, all friction, all that is casual, secondary to the main events and themes, everything unresolved, truncated, and uncertain, which confuses the clear progress of the action and the simple orientation of the actors, has disappeared. ... The tendency to a smoothing down and harmonizing of events, to a simplification of motives, to a static definition of characters which avoids conflict, vacillation, and development, such as are natural to legendary structure, does not predominate in the Old Testament world of legend.[102]

101. Speiser, *Oriental and Biblical Studies*, 205–206.
102. Auerbach, *Mimesis*, 16–17.

Look at the last words carefully. Auerbach is under no illusion that Genesis is actual history: his point is that the historicizing style, aided no doubt by the occurrence of gaps and anomalies in the text, dominates even passages which are undoubtedly unhistorical. The patriarchs are obviously composite figures, made out of many separate traditions. But because of the Hebrew reluctance to homogenize, in other words because of canonicity, they take on a historical shape in spite of themselves: "Abraham, Jacob, or even Moses produces a more concrete, direct, and historical impression than the figures in the Homeric world—not because they are better described in terms of sense (the contrary is the case) but because the confused, contradictory multiplicity of events, the psychological and factual cross-purposes, which true history reveals, have not disappeared in the representation but still remain clearly perceptible."[103] What we are witnessing in Genesis, and in parts of the David story, is the birth of a new kind of historicized fiction, moving steadily away from the motives and habits of the world of legend and myth. It works something like a *pointilliste* painting: its very raggedness and incoherence forces the beholder into an extra effort of imagination, giving the work a quality of dramatic vividness—and yet at the same time distancing is accomplished. Strangeness is inherent in canonicity, as Speiser describes it: the world portrayed is not familiarized for us, as in Homer, but kept "in darkness," to use Auerbach's phrase. "God is always so represented in the Bible, for he is not comprehensible in his presence, as is Zeus; it is always only 'something' of him that appears, he always extends into depths. But even the human beings in the Biblical stories have greater depths of time, fate, and consciousness than do the human beings in Homer." He characterizes Homer's style as that of a vividly lighted foreground, in which nothing is unexpressed and unexternalized, and contrasts it to the Bible's reticent, laconic, obscure, disjointed narratives. The Biblical style calls for interpretation, whereas Homer positively resists it: "Homer can be analyzed, as we have essayed to do here, but he cannot be interpreted."[104]

103. *Ibid.*, 17.
104. *Ibid.*, 9, 11.

We would not dream of doing literary things Homer's way, but the Old Testament style seems life itself to us. "Odysseus on his return is exactly the same as he was when he left Ithaca two decades earlier. But what a road, what a fate lie between the Jacob who cheated his father out of his blessing and the old man whose favorite son has been torn to pieces by a wild beast!—between David the harp player, persecuted by his lord's jealousy, and the old king, surrounded by violent intrigues, whom Abishag the Shunnamite warmed in his bed, and he knew her not! . . . They show a distinct stamp of individuality entirely foreign to the Homeric heroes."[105] This is what we call realism; our fictions are made in its image. As Homer's can be called a mythologizing style, so is this demythologizing.

The many ideas of history that appear in the Old Testament are in effect unified, though they range from literal beliefs that Yahweh leads his people in battle with his "mighty arm" to the sophisticated interpretation of God's "hidden hand" in history that appears in texts as diverse as Deutero-Isaiah and the Joseph story. Joseph says to his brothers, "The evil that you planned to do me has by God's design been turned to good, that he might bring about, as indeed he has, the deliverance of a numerous people."[106] In the revisionist rewriting of history undertaken by the prophets, two themes dominate: the faithless people have forfeited Yahweh's care and will be punished, yet this punishment will somehow come to good in the end, as in Joseph's saying.[107] The question of evil, of disasters to be suffered by guilty and innocent alike, becomes the overriding concern of the Bible in its depiction of the coming of the enemy powers, Assyria and Babylonia. In order to face the threat, the prophets

---

105. *Ibid.*, 14–15.

106. Gen. 50:20; cf. 45:5. "Deutero-Isaiah" refers to Isaiah, Chaps. 40 ff., by common agreement among scholars regarded as composed in the time of Cyrus and the Persian victory over Babylon, *ca.* 539 B.C., or about two centuries later than the original Isaiah.

107. Cross also finds two themes in the Deuteronomic history, but couches them in terms more specifically related to the history of kingship: *Canaanite Myth and Hebrew Epic*, 279 and 281.

exaggerate both Israel's guilt and the horrors it will have to undergo. Isaiah luxuriates in describing the desolation that the land will become, and all the prophets use images borrowed from the systematic inflictions of terror that the imperialist armies used as weapons. (One device was to put captives to death in calculatedly terrifying ways: the Assyrians favored impalement, giving rise to a typology that leads on to the Roman preference for crucifixion.)[108]

The culmination of this rhetoric comes in Deuteronomy, in a passage undoubtedly influenced by the prophets: Chapter 28 enumerates blessings for keeping the law and curses for breaking it, but the visionary vividness of the curses far overshadows that of the blessings. The horrors of invasion, deportation, and slavery were not only familiar but haunting; here is a portion:

You will never be anything but exploited and plundered continually, and no one will come to your help. Betroth a wife, another man will have her; build a house, you will not live in it; plant a vineyard, you will not gather its first fruits. Your ox will be killed before your eyes and you will eat none of it; your donkey will be carried off in your presence and not be restored to you; your sheep will be given to your enemies, and no one will come to your help. Your sons and daughters will be handed over to another people, and every day you will wear your eyes out watching eagerly for them, while your hands are powerless. A nation you do not know will eat the fruit of your soil and of your labour. You will never be anything but exploited and crushed continually. You will be driven mad by the sights your eyes will see. Yahweh will strike you down with foul boils on knee and leg, for which you will find no cure, from the sole of your foot to the top of your head.[109]

This passage, apparently suggestive to the author of Job, may well have been written in Judah in 621 B.C., or exactly a hundred years after just these disasters had fallen on the Northern Kingdom. Very likely these horrors were rehearsed to prepare the Southern Kingdom psychically for what was so obviously coming; there may have been an effect like that which Freud postulated for anxiety dreams: by giving images to our free-floating fears, we can "cathect" them.

108. Mendenhall notes the same progression from impalement to crucifixion (*The Tenth Generation*, 120), relating it to ancient concepts of transgression against society, wrath, and expiation.
109. Deut. 28:29b–35.

From such passages we can see that the later Bible-writers do not visualize history as necessarily pleasant just because Yahweh is in control of it.

The Book of Job takes up the question of evil in an even more dramatic way. By the time it was written, probably, the nation had supped full with horrors, and was slowly rebuilding. But the disasters of the Assyrian and Babylonian days were perhaps even more terrifying in retrospect than they had been in presence. Job asks why Yahweh troubles him with bad dreams: perhaps an allusion to the nightmare memories of Hebrew persecutions. In meditating on suffering and guilt, the author of Job comes to a daring conception: Job suffers not because of his sins but because of his righteousness. Job's friends offer the clichés that had grown up to obscure the starkness of the Yahwist vision: you must have sinned, for only the wicked suffer, etc. But Job mercilessly demythologizes these assurances. Job cannot comfort himself with any bromides about Yahweh's care for man; indeed he complains of feeling that he is always being watched: "Will you never take your eyes off me, long enough for me to swallow my spittle?"[110]

Job dramatizes the ultimate test for Yahwists: how to accept that overbearing Will in the face of all human notions of justice. Whoever could pass this test could face with reasonable equanimity the anxieties of history with its incessant injustices, in which the innocent not only suffer equally with the guilty, but sometimes even more. Jeremiah long before had complained to his God: "Why is it that the wicked live so prosperously? Why do scoundrels enjoy peace?"[111] The author of Job simply asked the obverse. He reached the end of culture's hopes of pleasing God, emphasizing how puny was even human righteousness when juxtaposed to the Creator of good and evil: but only after reaching for the limit of human anguish that this alienation must cause.

In one way the Book of Job seems a parable, in another way a

---

110. Job 7:19.
111. Jer. 12:1b. See Gerard Manley Hopkins' sonnet "Thou art indeed just, Lord, if I contend."

drama. Helen Gardner places the book, and the "Suffering Servant" songs of Deutero-Isaiah, "very close to tragedy" in feeling; indeed she concludes that it is "not wholly improper to set [Job] beside Greek tragedy as a work of literary art," not only because of its "quasi-dramatic" form but because it preserves the tragic ambiguity of suffering, and "rejects any attempt to explain human suffering in terms of the guilt or sin of the sufferer."[112] What Miss Gardner then goes on to show is how Western conceptions of the components of tragedy are indebted more to our religious heritage than to the Greeks: the differences between Greek and Shakespearean tragedy are due, she says, to the "revolution in religious thought" which she identifies with Christianity and, more generally, with the Biblical idea of history:

We are accustomed to take for granted the emergence in post-classical times of the notion that tragedy is essentially narrative. With the death of a living theatrical tradition the notion of tragedy as the "imitation of an action" becomes the notion of tragedy as a "certain story," and a story of "*him* who stood in great prosperity," the life-story of an individual. From the presentation of crisis it becomes the presentation of process. It is surely an interesting change. I cannot think it is unconnected with the Biblical stress on history as meaningful, on the fact that the sacred books of Christianity contain so much historical narrative and so many life-stories.[113]

She compares the action of a Greek tragedy, which as we say "begins in the fifth act," with the untying of a knot, whereas the action in later Western tragedies is the telling of a story. "There is an irreducible narrative element in all Elizabethan tragedies, and preeminently in Shakespearian." While Miss Gardner uses the Gospels as her primary source, she sees them in the context of the whole Bible. It is true of Christianity, as she says in this passage, that "no other religious tradition builds into its confession of faith the narrative of a life lived from the cradle to the grave at an actual period of history, and finds in this a revelation." But we should remember that Christians used to interpret the Book of Job as a foreshadowing allegory

112. Helen Gardner, *Religion and Literature* (London: Faber, 1971), 58–60.
113. *Ibid.*, 74. The influence of Augustine's *Confessions* is often brought up in this connection.

of the life of Christ; in terms of the need for suffering, it and the Servant Songs provide the paradigms by which the Gospels were interpreted.

In the relevant Biblical texts, *history* and *story,* which after all are cognate forms, come together. The Book of Job was produced in response to the agonizing questions of Hebrew history. Fiction opens a new dimension in searching history for meaning, via the function of parable. From Nathan to Jesus, the parable is used to probe history and point up a latent meaning in it. In Miss Gardner's view, the great works of English drama were similarly indebted to intense meditation on the paradigms of the individual, his deserts and his destiny: "As the 'Guilt Culture' of the Archaic Age lies behind the appearance of Attic tragedy, so the growing obsession of the religious imagination and of religious thought and devotion with sin and death and judgment in the later Middle Ages lies behind Elizabethan Tragedy, providing what Professor Gombrich has taught us to call the *schemata* by correction of which great artists explore the world."[114]

The whole sense of Hebrew history has, especially in the light of Job, a strangely mixed affective character. On the one hand it is resolutely optimistic: God is good, creation is good, and his plan in history will come to good. Yet even in the wish-fulfilling forms of messianism and apocalypticism, there is a powerful suspicion that suffering is necessary and that failure is the end of all human effort. This is not the Greek idea that suffering enables man to learn. Rather for Yahwists the tortures that men inflict on each other or that nature inflicts on them are seen as somehow man's lot. Yet they face this without assurances of any compensatory afterlife, and without counseling themselves to despise earthly pleasures and material things. They did not believe that man's soul was imprisoned in his body, awaiting liberation. A good life on earth, followed by rest, was the only reward they looked for, yet they believed that history entailed suffering.[115]

This hopeful resignation in the Hebrew idea of history was trans-

114. *Ibid.,* 102.
115. Though the churchgoing public tends to ignore the fact, Old Testament

formed into a Christian vision by the Russian mystic Nicolas Berdyaev, whose *apologia* thus embodies the essence of Biblical continuity.

Man's historical experience has been one of steady failure and there are
no grounds for supposing that it will ever be anything else. Not one single
project elaborated within the historical process has ever proved successful.
None of the problems of any given historical epoch whatsoever have been
solved, no aims attained, no hopes realized. . . . One may speak of revolutions as capital events in the destiny of mankind, as phenomena of inner
and inexorable determination subserved by all that went before, but the
fact remains that they have never solved the problems with which they
were confronted.

What is astounding is that Berdyaev sees this limitless vista of failure at the end of a long discourse on the meaningfulness of history.
Nor does he exempt his own religion:

Christianity also was a complete and utter failure. The enemies of Christianity take a malicious pleasure in indicating this very fact as the capital
objection against Christianity. They repudiate Christianity because it did
not succeed on earth. . . . It is true that Christianity shared the collapse of
every other historical process. Two thousand years have not sufficed to
realize the ideals of Christian faith and consciousness. They will never be
realized within the framework of human time and history.[116]

Yet, concludes Berdyaev, neither Christianity nor history is meaningless. A Yahwist, if any were left, might agree. And Western literature has felt this sense of things to its core. As Helen Gardner says,
King Lear "displays suffering as the universal law of life," so that
men are bound together by it: in the play the prosperous quarrel,
but the sufferers come together.[117]

---

scholars generally agree that the conception of afterlife in the text (until some
very late passages in Daniel, etc.) posits a tenuous, powerless existence in Sheol,
"The Pit." At death one was "gathered to his fathers" to sleep. Hebrews' prayers
to Yahweh repeatedly remind him that they will no longer be able to praise him,
once they're dead: see Isa. 38:18, Ps. 88:9–12, Ps. 6:5, and so on.

For a suggestive treatment of this and other aspects of the problem, see David
Noel Freedman, "The Biblical Idea of History," *Interpretation*, XXI (1967), 32–49.

116. From Nicolas Berdyaev, *The Meaning of History* (1923), conveniently
quoted in Ellmann and Feidelson (eds.), *The Modern Tradition*, 526–27. It is the
key passage in Berdyaev's book.

117. Gardner, *Religion and Literature*, 88.

DIVINATION AND SACRIFICE

A spirit that will make it fertile must be fixed in the soil. The
Khonds sacrificed human victims to ensure the fertility of the
earth. The flesh was shared out among the different groups and
buried in the fields. Elsewhere the blood of the human victim was
sprinkled over the earth.

—Henri Hubert and Marcel Mauss

To take a stand upon one single meaning of the ziggurat is to be
quite out of tune with the mentality of the period. A number of
ideas are woven into the phenomenon: the rock as the first thing
to emerge from primeval chaos; the mountain, which, whenever it
arose, represented the center of the universe; the earthly throne of
the god; and—what seems to come closest to the Sumerian outlook
on life—the ziggurat as the monumental site for the offering of
sacrifices.

Just as most of the symbols of prehistory circled around the
idea of fertility, most of the concepts of Sumerian culture and its
successors circled around the idea of sacrifice.

—S. Giedion

In the first chapter a point was made about the world view of those
who practiced divination being "diametrically opposed" to that of
modern science.[118] The point is equally true of history and provides
a more relevant contrast than such oppositions as linear with
cyclical time, etc. For the divinatory attitude postulates that a de-
terminism exists without freeplay, in which all events exist in eternal
patterns, recurring in endless variations but always leaving micro-
cosmic clues in the very structure of appearances in the world, which
if properly interpreted can predict the associated events.

Thus, by looking at a sheep's liver, or configurations of altar
smoke, or even a pattern of arrow shots, the diviner can intuit the
structure of the *logos* as it bears upon the day or event in question.[119] This belief accords with what Lévi-Strauss says of savage

118. See note 41 to Chapter One herein.
119. Cf. Ezek. 21:26. Much divination sought simply to learn the will of the
gods, especially in Mesopotamia: this kind was not inherently inimical to Yahwism, or at least could have been subsumed under the desire to learn Yahweh's will.
But wherever it became a mantic art, or "science of cosmic secrets" as Yehezkel

thought, that for it the appearances of the physical world are the elements of a message.[120] Like a book, the world can be read if we can learn its language, for it is a series of interlocking structures, in many scales, each of which can be inferred from the others.

Lévi-Strauss could also point out that this view of the world is oriented more along the synchronic axis than the diachronic. Events are seen as caused not by the events before them but by their relationship in an eternal pattern. A man's sickness and death would be less the result of his medical history than of the pattern "written in the stars" for that day. Our view of causation is not, on the face of it, superior: but it is certainly different.[121]

Divination affirms continuity throughout all realms of existence; for in this view nothing is really fortuitous or meaningless, at bottom. It implies a cosmic ecology of universal interdependence. But history withdraws from these assumptions, emphasizing instead the predominant role of one or another factor, usually in a diachronic sense. Like science, it must begin by turning its back on what is immediately observable to the senses, stressing instead what may be "gone." It demythologizes the sense of universal interdependence and meaning.

Even the Roman historians reveal an attitude different from ours in regard to causation, more like that of the practicers of divination.

Kaufmann calls it, divination posited a *logos*, a principle of order, to which man could acquire access, and this clashes with Yahwism in every way. "The basic idea appears to be that the system of signs and portents functions autonomously, as a part of nature through which one learns about both the will of the gods and the cosmic order which transcends them" (Kaufmann, *The Religion of Israel*, 43). Astrological divination in particular assumes this character, since "the influence of the stars follows natural and eternal laws" (p. 47). Thus pagan prophecy represents "a human faculty of sensing hidden things irrespective of the gods" (p. 49).

The *logos* is an order-creating utterance: in myth it is typified by what Albright calls the "Sumerian *gish-khur,* the outline, plan, or pattern of things-which-are-to-be, designed by the gods at the creation of the world and fixed in heaven to determine the immutability of their creation" (*From the Stone Age to Christianity,* 177). This concept, he says, anticipates "the Platonic idea." (See also his pp. 369 ff. on the mixture of Semitic and Hellenic ideas in the use of *logos* in New Testament and other later times.)

120. Lévi-Strauss, *The Savage Mind*, 268.

121. As Lévi-Strauss demonstrates in the last chapter of *The Savage Mind*; see esp. 256 and 263.

For them events are "overdetermined." Moses Hadas says of Tacitus: "His *Weltanschauung* has been criticized as immature and full of irreconcilable contradictions. Following the tradition of Polybius he explains events by natural causes, and when natural causes fail he invokes accident or Fortune. But Tacitus refers events to transcendent causes also; he speaks of the gods, their grace and their wrath . . . [leading to] odd combinations of the immanent and transcendent in explaining events: Varus succumbs to destiny and the strength of Arminius (*Annals* 1.55); a famine is averted by the grace of God and a mild winter (*Annals* 12.43)."[122] This was not Tacitus' sloppy thinking, but a continual habit of the ancient world. In Homer victory or death in war is always in question, as to whether the strength of men or the help of the gods—or finally the decree of Fate—has prevailed. (Patroclus tells Hector that he's only third in line as the cause of Patroclus' death, and the skillful use of such "over-determinism" was the source of Greek tragedy's deepest effects.)[123] Such habits of thought were normative for thinkers with the divinatory attitude, but they irritate us.

While there is some divination reported in the Bible, its contexts are revealing. Invariably it is a priestly function, of special use to kings. The great user of divination is Saul: perhaps it was an aspect of his attempt to coerce the religious powers. Ironically he is also credited with harrying diviners, sorcerers, and witches from the land, although more likely this occurred during the Deuteronomic reform of King Josiah. But divination never meshed with the Yahwist world view. So also with dream interpretation: Daniel and Joseph have great powers, but only by special gift of Yahweh, as part of his belittling of mythological cultures and their claims. The Hebrews never allowed oneiromancy, or anything else for that matter, to become an independent form of access to the divine.[124]

122. *Complete Works of Tacitus*, xvi.

123. *Iliad*, XVI., 849 ff. For "overdeterminism" in Greek thought, see Dodds, *The Greeks and the Irrational*, 30–31 and 51–52.

124. See Lev. 19:26, 31; Deut. 18:9–20. For Saul's and David's use of divination, see I–II Sam.; for Josiah, see II Kings 23:24. Cf. Kaufmann, *The Religion of Israel*, 87–94, esp. 91.

In world view and in ritual practice divination linked itself to sacrifice: "Extispicy [reading of the entrails] was tied to the sacrificial cult" in Mesopotamia.[125] Both were attempts to out-maneuver or cajole the divine will. But sacrifice in the Near Eastern context had other important aspects and rationales, which helped to complete the picture of Hebrew ambivalence toward it.

To see these clearly we must go back all the way to the Stone Age figurines and the doubleness of life and death for which they stand, the fertility-fatality complex as I have called it. Nowhere does the Old Testament extend any recognition to the life-out-of-death presupposition of sacrifice. That was left to Christianity: "Verily, verily I say unto you, Except a grain of wheat fall into the earth and die, it abideth by itself alone; but if it die, it beareth much fruit."[126] As the Letter to the Hebrews so eloquently argues, Christ's was the sacrifice to end sacrifice: this formula was consonant with the Christian tendency to appropriate rather than blankly oppose mythic insights.[127] But the Hebrews felt more threatened by myth, and by sacrifice, because their neighbors were famous for human sacrifice, especially infanticide.

When we compare the bulbous Mother-figurines of the Stone Age with the voluptuous Canaanite Astartes we are first inclined to observe that men's taste improved over the centuries. But actually the seductive goddesses bespeak a deep cultural shift, probably due to population pressures predictable in agricultural societies, from fertility rites to antifertility rites. Those Astartes are blood-thirsty: they demand the lives of children. If population limitation was a cause, it might also explain such Canaanite habits as ritual prostitution and homosexuality, both ways of sterilizing reproductive urges.[128]

125. Hallo and Simpson, *The Ancient Near East,* 159.
126. John 12:24.
127. Heb. 9:26, 10. This argument stands on the old precept: "Without the shedding of blood, there is no forgiveness of sins" (cf. 9:22). The complex ideology behind this precept can be explained in numerous ways, of course. For an especially challenging view, see René Girard, *La Violence et le sacré* (Paris: Grasset, 1972).
128. See figs. 19 and 2 to compare the Paleolithic Venuses with the Astartes.

We cannot assume that the Hebrews were more humanitarian or squeamish than their neighbors, but the zealous Yahwists hated and feared the possibility of syncretism which acceptance of infanticide would signal. Similarly they execrated ritual prostitution and homosexuality. Biblical rhetoric usually denounces idolatry in sexual terms, a fact which has given the Hebrews a mistaken reputation for puritanical prudery: the generic phrase is "whoring after other gods." Hosea and other prophets many times compare the nation to a harlot; Jeremiah says: "So shameless was her whoring that at last she polluted the [whole] country; she committed adultery with lumps of stone and pieces of wood. [The allusion is to the Canaanite *masseboth* and *asherim*, stone and wood pillars symbolizing sexual divinities.]"[129]

He also calls Israel a she-camel in heat, and its men "well-fed, lusty stallions, each neighing for his neighbor's wife."[130] Isaiah and Ezekiel, using similar metaphors, become almost scabrous. Ezekiel constructs an elaborate allegory of the two kingdoms, Israel and Judah, as two sisters:

Son of man, there were once two women, daughters of the same mother. They became prostitutes in Egypt, when they were girls. There their nipples were handled, there their virgin breasts were first fondled. . . . She had played the whore in the land of Egypt, when she had been infatuated by profligates big-membered as donkeys, ejaculating as violently as stallions.[131]

The reference to Egypt recalls the tradition, missing in Exodus but recorded in Joshua 24:14, that the Hebrews had worshiped alien gods there: "Put away the gods that your ancestors served beyond the River and in Egypt, and serve Yahweh."[132]

On survivals of ancient population-limitation practices, see Darlington, *Evolution of Man*, 59–60 and 105. Ritual prostitution was, with some lapses, nonfertile: the highest type involved anal intercourse. See Michael C. Astour, "Tamar the Hierodule," *Journal of Biblical Literature*, LXXXV (June, 1966), 191 n.

129. Jer. 3:9. On the *massebôth* and *asherim*, see de Vaux, *Ancient Israel*, Vol. 2, *Religious Institutions*, 284–88.

130. Jer. 2:24 and 5:8.

131. Ezek. 23:2–3, 19–20.

132. Cf. Ezek. 20:18: "[Yahweh] said to their children in the wilderness: Do not

Actually the Hebrews warmly approved of sexuality that led to reproduction. In this time when the Canaanites practiced anti-fertility rites, the Hebrews still had an obsession with fertility, and a fear of impairing reproductiveness in any way. A quaint law in Deuteronomy forbids wives to aid their husbands in fights by seizing their opponents' genitals: the penalty was loss of the offending hand.[133] Other laws forbid eunuchry in the congregation, while the cleanliness laws are primitive attempts to preserve childbearing powers; the story of Onan tells of Yahweh's fatal wrath against anyone who rejected the duty of the levirate, to raise up children by a dead brother's wife (Onan, however, did not die for masturbation, as so many generations were told and as the dictionary still implies, but for *coitus interruptus*).[134] These fanatical beliefs in reproductive duties had their benefits: when the population was decimated, as by Babylonian or Roman armies, the people replenished their numbers in amazingly few generations.[135] No wonder Tacitus thought the Jews "singularly prone to lust"—sneering meanwhile at their failure to expose unwanted infants.

The fact that the Hebrews did not allow population pressure to drive them into accepting infanticide (only a comparative few ever practiced Moloch-worship) shows that such pressures can only bring out a tendency already latent in the peoples around the Hebrews. After Freud, after the experiments with overcrowded rats, after all we know about the orgiastic pleasures of aggression and of vigilante fantasies in all reaches of the political spectrum, we can no longer be surprised by combinations of violence and eroticism. Freud went so far, in a speculation too dark and ominous for his positivist followers, as to grant the destructive instincts an equal place with the

---

live by your ancestors' standards, do not practice the observances they practiced, do not defile yourselves with their idols."

"Beyond the River" in Josh. 24 refers to Mesopotamia, and the origin of Abraham's tribe from Ur.

133. Deut. 25: 11–12.

134. Eunuchry (a common condition of male cultic prostitutes), Deut. 23:2; cleanliness, Lev. 12 and 15; Onan, Gen. 38.

135. See Abraham Schalit, in Toynbee (ed.), *The Crucible of Christianity*, 75, and the editorial note by Toynbee on p. 76.

creative ones and to suggest that they could become strangely linked. The mythological world, like our literature, is steeped in the great theme of love and death.[136]

André Leroi-Gourhan has recently completed the most comprehensive survey of European cave art since that of the great pioneer in the field, the Abbé Breuil. For our purposes Leroi-Gourhan's most significant finding is that the mysterious "spear and wound" marks found with and on the great painted animals are not expressions of hunting magic, as was long believed. Leroi-Gourhan, by noting the systematic manifestations of these marks, concludes that they form a typology of differentiated signs, in other words a written language, organized around the basic binary opposition of male and female. But though the classification system may have served as an arbitrary form of organization, an opposition without real content such as we see still in modern languages' genders or in "strong" and "weak" verbs, there is a metaphorical side effect almost as fateful for human thought as the creation of language itself. Tentatively, even somewhat reluctantly, Leroi-Gourhan states it: "In other words, it is highly probable that Paleolithic men were expressing something like 'spear is to penis' as 'wound is to vulva.' "[137] The linkage led to belief that the powers were twinned, and the reverence for the powerful beasts portrayed would have reinforced it: they were symbols at once of death, in their power to gore and trample men, and of life, in their role of breeders and nourishers—of their own species and of men.

Into this kind of "ambiguity of the sacred" fall the veneration of stones, as fertility objects and as weapons; the variations of such

136. Freud's speculation is in *Beyond the Pleasure Principle.* On love and death, there is a host of texts ranging from Denis de Rougemont's *Love in the Western World,* which concentrates on the *Liebestod* as in the Tristan legend, to brief poetic insights such as Whitman's memory of the "low and delicious word" whispered by the sea: "death" ("Out of the Cradle Endlessly Rocking"). At this point, we could pursue many standard references: to the seventeenth-century use of the word *die* as a euphemism for orgasm, to D. H. Lawrence's fascinations, and so on.

137. André Leroi-Gourhan, *Treasures of Prehistoric Art,* trans. Norbert Guterman (New York: Abrams, 1967), 173.

cults as that of the bull; the goddesses of seductive love and battle-lust, such as Inanna and her numerous avatars in the Near East; the doubleness of the wall-images of Çatal Hüyük; and the whole history of the altar of sacrifice, where life is taken that it may be given. The epitomizing image is the Paleolithic Venus of Laussel, a pregnant woman holding a beast's horn: the symbol of lethal penetration is also the symbol of sexual penetration, representing imminent death and renewed life at the same time.[138] So potent a symbol was the horn that even in the Bible ("He exalts the horn of his Anointed") it stands for supreme power and strength.[139]

Lévi-Strauss reads myths as linked series of theme-and-variation-like speculations on the most immediate sensory givens of the world: raw and rotten, fresh and cooked, etc., a "logic of sensations," as he calls it.[140] But it is possible to read the myths he has collected, as in *The Raw and the Cooked,* as binary speculations organizing themselves around the fateful pairing of life against, and out of, death. For instance many are concerned with the "poisonous" and yet fructifying powers of excrement.[141] In this way they resemble noth-

138. See fig. 11. Especially fascinating are the goddesses of love, lust, and fertility who become also incarnations of war and battle-lust. Sometimes they perform acts of carnage themselves: see Pritchard (ed.), *The Ancient Near East,* 4 and 122 ff.; also Kapelrud, *The Violent Goddess,* 49–54: "Anat seems to represent cruelty and violence, in a way unlike that of Baal," he says (p. 53), in differentiating her from merely martial personifications.

The joy of slaughter that seems to us incongruous in the myths of Hathor, Anath, and the rest could be traced to some merely quotidian sources. Thorkild Jacobsen says of Inanna-Ishtar: "To her typing as a young marriageable girl she probably owes her role as incarnation of the rage of battle, for in early Sumer, as still among the Bedouins, it appears to have been the accepted function of young unmarried girls to encourage and egg on the young warriors in battle with praise and taunts" (*Toward the Image of Tammuz,* 28). But this might be carts before horses. Further exploration is needed: some hints can be obtained from the sly treatment of Joan Baez as a Maud Gonne-Great Goddess figure in William Irwin Thompson's *At the Edge of History,* 55–59 (cf. p. 39, where the Love-Hate ambivalences of the "kill-for-peace" syndrome are juxtaposed). See also Albright, *Yahweh and the Gods of Canaan,* 130–31, and the beginning of the section below, on "Mothers and Fathers."

139. I Sam. 2:10b.

140. Lévi-Strauss, *The Savage Mind,* 12; cf. Lévi-Strauss, *The Raw and the Cooked,* 240.

141. Lévi-Strauss, *The Raw and the Cooked,* 49, 62–63, 71, 123, 134–36, 178–79, 185, 270–71; cf. 103–104, 124, etc. Cf. Paz, *Claude Lévi-Strauss,* 47–48.

ing so much as children's mythologies of what happens inside the body, in those great mysterious systems of alimentation and reproduction. Lévi-Strauss himself repeatedly comments on such related connections as that between eating and sex, both possessing the great doubleness: to eat is to destroy and to give new life; to have sex may also be both (cf. the orgasm as "little death").[142] From Lévi-Strauss's point of view the important conclusion is that human thought is essentially algebraic, with the first oppositions continually spawning others. Yet we might also consider the relevance of the great theme itself, especially as the Hebrews would have reacted to it.

By the time of the Canaanites, the latency of death's presence within sexual themes was known in a myriad of ways, but the Hebrew mind rejected ritualized aspects of the sex-death connection wherever it encountered them. We find in other societies, of course, not only infanticide, but many variant forms of human sacrifice, each with after-the-fact rationales dutifully collected by Sir James Frazer and others: the sacrifice of the priestess after sacred copulation was good for the crops, the ritual killing of the king prevented his and the country's powers from waning, and so on.[143] Less spectacularly, animal sacrifice acquired its rationales as food for the gods, or whatever. The common factor remained the twinning of the powers of life and death.

For the Hebrews, as we might expect, sacrifice was a divisive and

142. Lévi-Strauss, *The Savage Mind*, 105; Lévi-Strauss, *The Raw and the Cooked*, 269. It must be said that Lévi-Strauss explicitly rejects "reducing" the myths to "an explanation of love and death" (*The Raw and the Cooked*, 340), but compare the myths represented by the specimen on p. 155.
See also Kirk, *Myth: Its Meaning and Functions in Ancient and Other Cultures*, 72.

143. See "The Slaying of the Corn Spirit" and "Putting the King to Death" in *The Golden Bough*, in James Frazer, *The New Golden Bough*, ed. Theodor H. Gaster (New York: Criterion, 1959), 223–33 and 425–44. My point is that these adduced "motives" seem insufficient for human sacrifice, though they provide aetiological explanations or "Just-So Stories" once the practice was instituted.
See also Saggs, *The Greatness That Was Babylon*, 354–62; Henri Hubert and Marcel Mauss, *Sacrifice: Its Nature and Function* (1898: rpt. Chicago: University of Chicago Press, 1964), esp. 72. Cf. p. 34: "The act of slaughter released an ambiguous force—or rather a blind one, terrible by the very fact that it was a force. It therefore had to be limited, directed, and tamed; this was what the rites were for."

demoralizing topic. Though long a part of their cult, it seems to have been offensive to zealous Yahwists: Yahweh could not be made into a fertility / fatality god. Amos, Isaiah, and later prophets attacked the rituals openly: Amos portrays Yahweh saying "I hate and despise your feasts, I take no pleasure in your solemn festivals. . . . I reject your oblations, and refuse to look at your sacrifices of fattened cattle."[144] Isaiah is even more eloquent:

> "What are your endless sacrifices to me?"
> says Yahweh.
> "I am sick of holocausts of rams
> and the fat of calves.
> The blood of bulls and of goats revolts me . . .
> Bring me your worthless offerings no more,
> The smoke of them fills me with disgust
>
> .   .   .   .
>
> Your hands are covered with blood,
> wash, make yourselves clean."[145]

Scholars rightly insist that these attacks are aimed at the use of sacrifice for hypocritical purposes and do not demand the eradication of the cult itself. The prophets lived in an era of Solomonic acculturation, when rich men competed with their neighbors in the showiness of their sacrifices, using wealth gained by "grinding the faces of the poor."[146] But such images as Isaiah creates almost make us smell the rising stench, and it is hard to see how devoted Yahwists could take much pleasure in sacrifice after he spoke.

What the Yahwists may have recognized was that the form of the rituals closely resembled, and probably derived from, Canaanite practices. Father Roland de Vaux, the authority on Israel's institutions, makes the point: "If we set aside sacrifices of babies [as Canaanite but not Hebrew], then, according to the biblical evidence, Canaanite sacrifices do not seem to be materially different from those which were offered to Yahweh."[147] No doubt the prophets felt

---

144. Amos 5:21–22.
145. Isa. 1:11–18.
146. Isa. 3:15.
147. de Vaux, *Ancient Israel,* Vol. 2, *Religious Institutions,* 438.

it was suitable for the Canaanites to try to bribe their gods, according to the traditional formula *do ut des*. But they despised the idea of cajoling Yahweh. To be sure, sacrifice could be practiced as a genuine sign of contrition, as part of the expiation of guilt. But the prophets saw that the rich were trying to buy off Yahweh, to smooth over injustice and exploitation: to them this was repugnant in the extreme. Thus sacrifice runs through the Old Testament as another skein of ambivalence, and shows again the Yahwist tendency to demythologize its own institutions.

Some scholars think that the story of Abraham and Isaac, together with such texts as Exodus 13 ("consecrate to me all the firstborn") and Judges 11 (the story of Jephthah), represent relics of a barbarous period when Yahwists practiced infanticide. More likely the introduction of Yahwism coincided with the end of infanticide among the Hebrews, with such texts serving as deflections and rationales. But in any case the practice soon became identified as "of the nations" and thus abhorrent.[148]

One frequent variant, with ideological roots going back to Paleolithic burial in the cave or under the house, was the foundation sacrifice: a king raising a city wall, or a temple, or a palace, might kill his own child and plant the first stone over the corpse.[149] Jericho was rebuilt, in Biblical times, with such a sacrifice (I Kings 16:34, *cf.* Joshua 6:26). Kings in Biblical times were also known to sacrifice their children to avert national disaster or to remove some curse. A king of Moab sacrificed his son in the face of a Hebrew invasion; whether from fear or repulsion, the Hebrews withdrew (II Kings 3:27).

That the villains in these stories were kings suited Yahwist preconceptions perfectly. It may even be that the name of the hated "Moloch," the putative deity to whom apostate Hebrews "passed their children through the fire," is a variant of the common Semitic word for king (in Hebrew *melek*).[150] De Vaux holds this opinion:

148. See the discussion *ibid.*, 441 ff.
149. See Saggs, *The Greatness That Was Babylon*, 34.
150. Another theory holds that *molk* was simply the name of a Phoenician type of sacrifice. See Albright, *Yahweh and the Gods of Canaan*, 236.

"These offerings, then, were held to be offerings to a king-god, a Melek. . . . The form *molek,* which predominated in these texts, is to be explained by a change of vocalization telling the reader to say *bosheth* (disgrace, shame)."[151] Such a change was usual with names having a *-baal* element; *Ishbaal,* "man of Baal," was changed to *Ish-bosheth,* "man of shame."[152] (Saul named several sons with Baal names; even Gideon's real name was Jerub-baal.) Another related name was that of a similarly despised pagan deity, *Milk-qart* (or Melcarth), meaning "King of the City," the city being either Tyre or the City of the Dead, the underworld.[153] If the suggested associations between kingship, infanticide, necrolatry, and urbanism are as close as they seem in this name, then it was a sinister ideogram of all that the Hebrews knew as pagan evils.

MOTHERS AND FATHERS

In the lands from India to the Mediterranean there is a substratum of primordial religions, pre-Indo-European and pre-Semitic earth gods, spirits of wood and water of pantheistic or animistic nature. There was especially about the eastern end of the Mediterranean from very olden times a cult of the Magna Mater, or Earth Goddess, who became Ishtar, Astarte, Demeter or some other goddess of later religions. These seem to have walked the earth for a long time. . . . The principle of fertility was in the female, the male was irrelevant or subordinate.

—Carl Sauer

If the societies which worshiped Astartes are descended from a union of two kinds of cultures, one matriarchal and autochthonous

---

151. de Vaux, *Ancient Israel,* Vol. 2, *Religious Institutions,* 446.

152. II Sam. 2:8, in the Hebrew text, has "Ish-bosheth" but cf. I Sam. 14:49, and the notes in the Jerusalem or New Oxford Annotated Bibles.

153. See Donald Harden, *The Phoenicians* (2nd ed.; New York: Praeger, 1963), 85–86, and Albright, *Yahweh and the Gods of Canaan,* 128, 145–46, and 243. (Cf. Albright's *Archaeology and the Religion of Israel,* 29.) See also Lewis Mumford in Kraeling and Adams (eds.), *City Invincible,* 225–26, on the cemetery as the prototypical form of the city: note the overtones of autochthony, recycling of ancestors, etc., as in Chapter Two. The comparatively callous-seeming Hebrew attitude toward the dead is thus a rejection of pagan custom and ideology.

and the other patriarchal, nomadic, and ferocious, then the goddesses' curious combination of seductiveness and vengefulness might
be further highlighted. To the older, sedentary societies the new-
comers brought "the war chariot and the cavalryman, new forms of
war and conquest, military aristocracy," thus providing the pattern
of the early cities with their decline of authochthony into chauvinism, their rigidified social classes and petrified forms of archaic
mythological traditions, and their expansionist enterprises. By
merger and imposition their pantheons of gods were formed, and
they took in the archaic maternal deities to complement their
warrior-father-fertility gods.[154]

The belief in a matriarchal substrate in certain human societies is
an old and recurrently rejected one, but it does not have to rest on
the controversial works of the authors with whom it is so often
identified (J. J. Bachofen, R. Briffault, Erich Neumann). Sauer derived his belief from the work of the great geographer Eduard Hahn,
who found his evidence in the traces of animal domestication. One
of the most puzzling features of the process was that the species
chosen do not seem logical choices on economic grounds alone. "The
selection was not based on propinquity to man, nor on sharing his
habitat. It was not based on declining abundance, for most of the
domestication took place near the margins of the natural range
occupied by the species. It was not based on docility: antelopes,
gazelles, and deer, easily tamed and much kept for diversion, provided no domesticate except the reindeer. . . . Rather, one might say
that animals were chosen that were not easy to take, which were not
common, and which were difficult to make gentle—the wild mountain goats and sheep that avoid the vicinity of man, the formidable

154. See the discussion in Chap. V of Sauer, *Agricultural Origins*, esp. 88–89,
93, and 96–97; also Shepard, *Man in the Landscape*, where the conflict of patriarchal with matriarchal societies is discussed in terms of an "antagonism toward
farming and women and female gods" (p. 102)—in other words, pastoral demythologization. As Shepard notes in discussing breeding techniques: "Paternity
is the intelligent application of a cause, not an enigma" (p. 103). Thus, compared
with the mysteries ritually celebrated by autochthonic agriculturists, the rites of
pastoralists might well assume a demythologizing, even a historical, character:
perhaps in the way von Rad postulates for Passover.

wild cattle and buffalo."[155] If need and convenience are ruled out, the evidence points toward religious motives as the basis of domestication. Sauer's consideration of Hahn's theses on milking patterns, etc., reinforced his belief in an "elder maternal society [underlying] the high cultures of the ancient West."

Sauer scoffs at the materialistic and mechanistic models of human evolution which consider only economic factors, stressing the killing of animals for meat and the primacy of hunting; these propose human bands patterned after baboon societies, which are male-dominated, promiscuous, food-snatching instead of sharing, and so on. Instead he suggests we consider the primacy of woman, in her sedentary, child-rearing, food-assuring roles, as the key to human development. She created the "enduring family," with its all-important kinship ideologies (frequently still matrilineal among primitives) and learned the secrets of fire, around which hearth the "home" was organized. "Women were the original food chemists and botanists," developing not only cooked food but the pharmacopeia, including, for example, the fish poisons that have helped sustain fisher-foragers for millennia in Southeast Asia and South America.[156] All the productive arts of the Neolithic Revolution, which made civilization possible, were her concern: it is hard to agree after considering these facts, that male-dominated societies are somehow "in the nature of things."

Sauer's speculations were given concrete exemplification when James Mellaart excavated Çatal Hüyük. In this impressive ancient site the cult of the Great Goddess was dominant, and the social structure apparently reflected it: the women's beds are larger than the men's, for instance.[157] This town cannot be written off as that of some backwater group with bizarre Amazonian ideas, either: its cul-

155. Sauer, *Agricultural Origins*, 90.
156. Sauer in Washburn (ed.), *Social Life of Early Man*, 262; cf. Sauer, *Agricultural Origins*, 88–89. Sauer openly identifies woman with the "sedentary bent" in culture (fire-using, growing, collecting, domestic arts) and man with mobility: with hunting for pleasure, for instance, not for provision. In pastoralism, it may be, some previously domesticated male traits assume a new dominant role, which may involve demythologizing the maternal aspects of the culture.
157. Mellaart, *Çatal Hüyük*, 60; cf. pp. 182–84, 201–202, 225–27.

ture was the most formidable of its day and preserved an amazing number of links to Paleolithic practices and traditions, which implies that it was the heir of the great mythico-cultural traditions. In fact Çatal Hüyük had so many ties to the past that it appeared archaic in comparison to other Neolithic sites.

The art of wall-painting, the reliefs modelled in clay or cut out of the wall-plaster, the naturalistic representations of animals, human figures and deities, the occasional use of finger-impressed clay designs like "macaroni," the developed use of geometric ornament including spirals and meanders, incised on seals or transferred to a new medium of weaving; the modelling of animals wounded in hunting rites, the practice of red-ochre burials, the archaic amulets in the form of a bird-like steatopygous goddess, and finally certain types of stone tools and the preference for dentalium shells in jewelry, all preserve remains of an Upper Paleolithic heritage.[158]

Not even this list is complete: flexed burials, hand-prints on the walls and other features also suggest cave art and traditions. In at least one burial the brain was carefully removed, and Mellaart speculates that in the art, headlessness was associated with death: "The absence of heads is a pictorial convention to indicate corpses."[159] These points, and the probable practice of excarnation by vultures (exposing the corpses so that the flesh would be removed) point toward the widespread "two-stage" funeral rites, noted from New Guinea to prehistoric North America, which may go back to extremely ancient practices, frequently involving head-worship and brain-eating. Finally, the houses were low and were entered from the roof; the shrines were underground, and the doors into them were small, floor-level holes. Rachel Levy would call these cave-houses.

If Çatal Hüyük was such a concentrated distillation of the mythological consciousness, then the apparently matriarchal shape of the society is most telling. Mellaart concludes that the social structure and the mythology reflected each other, as they usually do. "The divine family then was patterned on that of man; and the four aspects are in the order of importance: mother, daughter, son and

158. *Ibid.*, 226.
159. *Ibid.*, 167.

father." It is possible, he speculates, that the hypostases can be reduced to two: "The Great Goddess and her son and paramour. Later parallels from Crete and Bronze Age Greece would tend to confirm this conception of the Divine family," he adds.[160] Not only were the women superior, there were more of them, as the burials show. How their interests dominated is shown in the lack of penis or vulva representations, even in erotic scenes: direct portraiture of sexual organs, as Mellaart observes, is "invariably connected with male impulse and desire. If Neolithic woman was the creator of Neolithic religion, its absence is easily explained and a different symbolism was created in which breast, navel and pregnancy stand for the female principle, horns and horned animal heads for the male."[161] This of course is that very symbolism that dominated the cave-art, which curiously lacks phallic portrayals but in which pregnancy and other attributes of female sexuality are plentifully represented.

At Çatal Hüyük too, fertility was intertwined with fatality: associated with, sometimes merged with, the breast-symbols are the horns, jaws, and other lethal motifs from the animal cults. The wall-paintings feature winged vulture-goddesses excarnating the dead, reminding us of Le-hev-hev in Malekula, where the rites of death open the door to newness of life.

If it is correct to portray this matriarchal element as an indispensable component in the mythological consciousness, then the Hebrew insistence on patriarchal symbols and motifs takes on added meaning as a form of rejection of the mythologized culture complexes. In the great centers the warrior- and father-gods had made their peace with the mother-goddesses, combining through syncretism and compromising nomadic values with sedentary ones. But the Hebrews typically would have no compromise: they insisted that their God had neither consort nor pantheon and no sexual adventures. Some abortive attempts to marry Yahweh to Anath or other goddesses may have occurred, though the evidence is most tenuous, but the opposi-

160. *Ibid.*, 201.
161. *Ibid.*, 202.

tion was monolithic.[162] Whether such intransigence is the effect or perhaps the cause of Semitic ethnology cannot be known. Among the Hebrews, at any rate, little derogation of women seems to be implied by the refusal to accept goddesses, or even to have a word for them in the language. Miriam, Deborah, and Jael were primordial war-heroines of Israel; Sarah, Rebekah, Rachel and Leah, Tamar, and Dinah play a more than incidental part in the patriarchal stories. In contrast to, say, Athenian or Arabic women, the women in the Bible are important and autonomous, although foreign women are treated as particularly dangerous agents of idolatry, and the rich women of prophetic times, the "cows of Bashan," earn scathing contempt from Amos and Isaiah as instigators of greedy consumption and concomitant exploitation.[163]

In any event the idea of paternity in the Bible seems to have been elaborated as part of the pattern of opposition to high-culture ideology. Any reader can see the immense emphasis placed on fathers and sons in the Bible; it can of course be read as mere sentimentality, but a more enlightened view can see it tying together several strands of opposition not only to goddesses, but to what they represent and are associated with. Jeremiah's last work as a prophet was to denounce apostates who wanted to worship the Queen of Heaven; this aspect of the Goddess demonstrates that she was tied in with the astronomical lore and cults for which Babylon was famous, and which Giorgio de Santillana and Hertha von Dechend believe to be the very basis of myth.[164] Similarly the opposition to golden calves, to the bull-pillars of Bethel, and so on, has its context in the relation of the bull-cult, which was prominent at Çatal Hüyük, to that of the Great Goddess. The bull was consistently associated with the *hieros gamos,* the sacred marriage. Even Dumuzi the shepherd-

---

162. See, *e.g.,* S. H. Hooke, *The Siege Perilous: Essays in Biblical Anthropology and Kindred Subjects* (London: SCM Press, 1956), 182.

163. Amos 4:1–3; cf. Isa. 3:16–26, Solomon's wives, Jezebel, etc. The possibility arises that Miriam, Deborah, and the rest could have been warrior-goddesses originally: most unlikely, but in any case they would seem to have been strenuously demythologized early on.

164. Jer. 44; see note 63 to Chapter Two herein.

god was given a "wild bull" form for his *hieros gamos,* "essentially
a fertility rite of spring, the king's potency in the consummation of
it being coincident with the shooting up of the flax, the grain, and
the verdure of the steppe."[165] All these facets of cultic practice were
of course opprobrious to zealous Yahwists. One can see why in the
Bible the bull stands for idolatry, while the lamb is salvation.

The refusal to envision Yahweh's control of fertility as a sexual
process requiring a consort must have had origin or reinforcement
from the repulsiveness of cultic rites and their animalistic associations. One particularly offensive Egyptian deity, whose attributes
illuminate still another reason that the Hebrews rejected the whole
complex, was the archaic Min-Kamutef, "one of the few Egyptian
gods who certainly stems from the reservoir of prehistory," according to S. Giedion.[166] He shows several signs of primordiality: though
"ithyphallic," often represented as a man holding his erect phallus,
he was sometimes inscribed with archaic signs indicating both sexes;
also he was ambiguously bull and human. *Kamutef* means "Bull of
his mother," which implies, as Giedion says, that he begets himself:
at the annual Min festival, when the Pharaoh was celebrated as Min
the giver of fertility and procreative power to men, beasts, and
plants, the priest said: "Hail to thee, Min, who impregnates his
mother! How mysterious is that which thou hast done to her in the
darkness." Thus he stood for the king's perpetual regeneration as a
living god, and was even called "the king's father."[167]

---

165. Jacobsen, *Toward the Image of Tammuz,* 29. On bull-cults see Albright,
From the Stone Age to Christianity, 299–301.

166. Giedion, *Eternal Present,* II, 82 (cf. pp. 83-89); cf. his *Eternal Present,* I,
200–207.

167. Henri Frankfort, *Kingship and the Gods: A Study of Ancient Near Eastern
Religion as the Integration of Society and Nature* (Chicago: University of Chicago
Press, 1948), 188–89. Not only was he "Bull of his mother": he was associated
with a white bull in a "complex of beliefs regarding cattle," and "his shrine was
crowned with a pair of bull's horns." Grain was offered to the white bull in the
royal procession at the harvest festival. Cf. Albright on the moon-god in Sumer:
he was addressed in a "very early hymn" as "mighty young bull . . . with lapis-
lazuli beard [cf. fig. 9] . . . fruit which begets itself . . . womb which bears everything" (*From the Stone Age to Christianity,* 193).
Lévi-Strauss's analysis of the Oedipus myth as reflecting a clash of autochthonic

Min, as a hypostasis of "self-creation" and "self-genesis," could well have been descended from the son-paramour figure of the Great Goddess. If so he must stand for the implied demotion of the father in the scheme of things that is normative in autochthonous, matriarchal societies. Though procreative and phallic in himself, by being self-engendering he denies that aspect of fatherhood which implies that every human being is contingent, dependent on one among a host of casual sexual encounters. Here we must see that the bond to the mother is felt as "natural," whereas any relationship to the father must be a matter of mutual acknowledgment—even for Stephen Dedalus.[168] Min-Kamutef stands for a rejection of the relation, not an acknowledgment: he corresponds to that element in the Oedipus complex in which, as Freud saw, the child wishes to become its own father, to be self-creative.

This mythological theme is probably more widespread than we imagine. Its basis, obviously, would be that metaphysical anxiety in all of us which makes us fearful of admitting that we are contingent and dependent, not wholly autonomous beings.[169] Many of the powers of myth are deployed to assuage this anxiety, on a collective as well as an individual level: for the role of myth in asserting the

---

vs. sexual ideologies might appear, with Min in mind, to include (as he claims) the Freudian reading: denial of and hostility toward the father.

Min was no doubt extremely repugnant to the Hebrews. A triadic figure (fig. 20) shows what Albright calls "the basic pantheon of Tyre" in Egyptianized form: the naked goddess Qudshu ("Holiness") or Astarte (or Anath) as sacred prostitute, between Min and Resheph. Hebrew reaction to this image would see it, like the name Melcarth, as an ideogram: sex and sacrifice, blood-lust and fertility, entwined with a heavy overlay of the infantile desire for self-generation.

168. Joyce, *Ulysses*, 204–205. Stephen says: "Fatherhood, in the sense of conscious begetting, is unknown to man. . . . Paternity may be a legal fiction. Who is the father of any son that any son should love him or he any son?" But he affirms that *"amor matris,* subjective and objective genitive, may be the only true thing in life." Stephen asserts that Mariolatry is a concession to the feeling that motherhood is natural, fatherhood conventional: the "cunning Italian intellect flung [the cult of Mary] to the mob of Europe" to disguise the fact that the Church is founded upon the "void" of paternity (see note 70 above). The "void" is the opposite of any *logos,* of course: history is another such "non-center."

169. See Niebuhr, *Nature and Destiny,* 16, 178–79, 182–83. As Niebuhr says, our anxiety stems not from our dependence but from our ability to know or envision something beyond it: if we were merely contingent we should not know it.

"givenness" of a culture is simply the collective form of what Min (and Oedipus in that sense) stands for in relation to the individual. We can all be badly frightened when we realize how ephemeral we are, and acknowledging our fathers, our dependence on "an instant of blind rut" as Stephen calls it, can force us to face our transience. But through myths of autochthony, de-emphasizing the father's role in conception, as through conceiving a society as an eternal recycling of ancestors, we can persuade ourselves that we are "cosmically" integrated with the permanences of nature.

In this light the Hebrew insistence on paternity as the only allowable social continuity is another form of demythologization; though a "myth" in its own way, it moves against the grain. It demands that we acknowledge our dependence and thus our transience. It rebukes our desire to create ourselves, to give ourselves a permanence on which to rest our being. Psalm 100 puts it perfectly: "It is He that hath made us and not we ourselves." The Bible mocks our desires to glorify, mythologize or even deify ourselves by "founding" our existence in the nature of things—all of which we might well do if we had the opportunity, as the Roman emperors did.[170] The connection of Min-Kamutef to the Pharaoh is telling: he who was an incarnate god could of course not have his existence tied to the chancy process of human reproduction initiated by another person. The enormous psychic power of a mythological culture, focused centripetally on the ruler, must make him conceive himself as autonomous and self-generated, never contingent or dependent. Sometimes myth can be too reassuring.

The "feeling of immortality in early youth" of which William Hazlitt wrote is a familiar and relatively innocuous form of compensation for the metaphysical anxiety. As we grow older and more anxious, we are more inclined to acknowledge our mortality and dependence, but we may turn philosopher and search for an unconditioned ground of Being on which we can rest, at least intel-

170. See Chapter Three on the self-deifiers (note 20). The motif of pastoral resistance to or "withdrawal" from the great imperial-urban centers becomes the theme of history, giving point to Voegelin's remark cited as epigraph to this chapter (*Order and History*, Vol. I, *Israel and Revelation*, 133).

lectually. Thoreau desired to work his feet down through the mud of illusion, superstition, and convention, till he could stand on the Real, saying "This is, and no mistake!"[171] Though it seeks to do away with all myths, this kind of "Real" is simply one more myth, a concession to and an assuagement of our metaphysical anxiety.

In this way, the Bible's concept of paternity is exactly parallel to its idea of history. Both demythologize the limitless aspirations and pretensions of man and his culture, and their "quest for permanence." In these, even in the noblest forms, the Bible sees an inevitable end: man building Babel or seizing the fruit, "making himself as a god." History deflates expectations, telling us that failure is the end of human action; paternity makes us aware of how vulnerable we are, how enmeshed in each other, no matter how masterfully we manipulate our lives. It teaches us that no man can erect metaphysical barriers against the chances of the world. We are conceived in them just as surely as we are born *inter urinam et faeces.*

To acknowledge one's father is to acknowledge one's mortality, and when that is recognized, a dimension of meaning drains from the world and from our acts in it. Camus had to discover this for himself since he apparently could not read Ecclesiastes.[172] What purpose has striving for riches, or wisdom, or fame, when the mere possibility—not even the certainty, just the mere possibility—of death undercuts the meaning of all striving? Meaning can only be restored to human activities if we become fathers ourselves (both sexes of course are included), beings that stand for contingency but also for care. Hence the desire of the Hebrew couple for the son, hence the joy of Sarah and Hannah and the others when the reproach of barrenness is taken away. Of course there is a quest for immortality, but it is the preservation of the name, that which is inherited from the fathers, that is the goal, not the immortalization of the

171. Henry David Thoreau, *Walden,* end of the second chapter, "Where I Lived, and What I Lived For."

172. Qoheleth, after confessing that all his great achievements have lost their savor, or become "vanities," tries to comfort himself with his hard-earned wisdom: but "wise man, alas, no less than fool must die" (2:16). "Hence I have come to despair of all the efforts I have expended under the sun" (Eccles. 2:20).

individual.[173] Thus paternity, and the Western "overvaluation of the diachronic" implicit in it and in history, represents a counterforce to what Min-Kamutef stands for: it represents the arbitrary as opposed to the supposedly necessary.

Hebrew society was not sentimentally deluded about inbred harmonies between parents and children. Deuteronomy threatens death for the disobedient son, but in fact the tensions over children's struggles for independence are manifest everywhere.[174] Adam and Eve are the first disobedient children, but all of Genesis can be read with that scheme in use. Abraham had to leave the city of his fathers to find his patriarchal destiny; later he had to be willing to put to death his only son in order to become the father to his people. A recurrent theme in Genesis is that of "the Younger Son," in which Yahweh's mysterious acts in history give preference where human expectation, symbolized by primogeniture, cannot fathom it.[175] So the patterns of Genesis, and of the rest of the books, are not simply prescriptions for social order through the subordination of sons to the social structure: they recognize both the creative and destructive aspects of filial tensions.

---

173. In *Memory and Tradition in Israel* (Napierville, Ill.: Allenson, 1962), Brevard S. Childs remarks on an old theory that the Hebrew word for "male," *zakhar*, was related to the verb *zakhar*, "to remember." Thus "the male was conceived of as the sex through which the memory of parents and ancestors was propagated" (pp. 9–10 n.). Even if folk etymology is it significant.

It may be added, with much cogency, that the quest for immortality is not so easily subordinated in late texts such as the book of Daniel. But foreign influence may be determinative on those.

174. Deut. 21:18–21; cf. 27:16, Exod. 21:17, and of course Exod. 20:12.

175. The "Younger Son" theme appears in the stories of Jacob and Esau, Isaac and Ishmael, Cain and Abel, Ephraim and Manasseh, the degradation of Reuben, the favoring of Joseph and Benjamin, Perez and Zerah, perhaps others in Genesis: certainly also in the stories of Moses, David, and Solomon. David is chosen by Yahweh while still an insignificant lad, in contrast to his prepossessing brothers (I Sam. 16:1–13: "God does not see as man sees; man looks at appearances but Yahweh looks at the heart.").

See also note 51 to Chapter One herein. Mendenhall points out that, as in the Cain-Abel story, "pastoralism in ancient (pre-camel) times was presumably an occupational specialty of the younger family members" (*The Tenth Generation*, 164).

René Girard would give the whole theme an entirely different reading.

In the story of the Kings, unworthy sons are a leading motif; the virtue of the fathers guarantees no privileged status to the children, apparently. That this theme runs counter to the rationale for monarchy is probably not coincidental, any more than was the association of Min-Kamutef with kingship. David receives from Yahweh two promises: one, that his house will be established, and two (after David steals Bathsheba and kills her husband), that his children will raise up trouble for him, so that his dynasty will never be free from the sword.[176] David could conquer many peoples, but he could not rule his children, who were his delight and his scourge. The probable historicity of the narrative does not detract from the efficacy of the motif, especially in David's complex and poignant relation with Absalom.

The royal sons were all too often given to fratricide, a common failing in Near Eastern dynasties that could easily be read as a Min-like attempt to do away with the father and establish oneself as self-generated. For a brother also is a reminder of contingency, as the universal reaction of young children to siblings shows. Absalom's rebellion was preceded by his murder of Amnon, just as Cain's was implied in his slaying of Abel. Solomon seizes the first excuse to have his elder rival Adonijah executed. All follow the pattern of Gideon's son Abimelech (a suspicious name meaning "my father is king," which suggests that Gideon was not so unwavering in his belief in the kingship of Yahweh as the text reports); Abimelech set some kind of record, for he murdered seventy brothers to try to seize a crown, only to wind up having a woman drop a millstone on his head. To die at a woman's hand was the most shameful form of death, "as a fool dies," so Abimelech's ambition led to a suitable reward.[177] The theme of fratricide plays around the stories of the

176. II Sam. 7:11–16, 12:7–12. Notice that in the earlier passage (though some scholars consider it a late addition) Yahweh speaks of making David's successor his adopted son: "I will be a father to him and he will be a son to me." This differs from deification of the king, although later Messianic concepts came perilously near that.

177. Judg. 9. Note that in this chapter occurs one of the rare Old Testament parables, and it is antimonarchic.

three early leaders who raised monuments to themselves: Gideon, Saul, and Absalom, all "failed" kings.[178]

It might well be argued that the kind of animalistic mating combat that Freud postulated to lie behind father-son relations reflected not so much his observations of nature as his Biblical reading. He too must have seen the creative / destructive potentials of the struggle between generations. Where the Oedipus story could suggest to him the meaning of the desire for self-creation, the Bible could teach him the necessity for conflict and the equal necessity for resolution through a kind of inner acknowledgment of paternity and contingency. This possibility cannot impoverish Freud's contribution to intellectual history, though it will surely undermine the absolutist pretensions of Freudianism. (For the same reason, to read the distinctions made in sociology between *Gemeinschaft* and *Gesellschaft,* or organic and mechanistic social organizations, against the background of the pastoral-urban conflict in the Bible, can only enrich the reverberations of meaning in the idea.)[179]

But if we insist that after all there was some biological basis for Freud's thought, we may still be persuaded to see it in a Biblical context by considering David Bakan's book on *The Duality of*

178. Gideon's ephod, a "snare" to which all Israel prostituted itself (Judg. 8:27), becomes more ominous in view of Abimelech's name, "my father is king." Saul "raises himself a monument" while violating the laws of holy war against the Amalekites (I Sam. 15:12). Surely he was concerting an effort to become an autonomous arbiter of the nation's war-powers—in short, an emperor.

Absalom fathered three sons (II Sam. 14:27) but none seem to have been alive when he revolted (18:18). Were his imperialist ambitions sharpened by the failure to achieve the Hebrew ideal of a son to carry on the name? Here the cairn that he "raises" is explicitly a substitute: the "royal" inscription is an avatar of Min.

Absalom's hated brother Amnon also raises the interesting possibility that incest was seen—obscurely, perhaps—as a royal prerogative, as among the pharaohs (and, of course, many pantheons in myth). Again, Min would be a powerful symbol: he "does it" to his mother "in the darkness." Amnon's incest turned into a tragic farce: but see II Sam. 13:13, which suggests that David might have been willing to indulge his sons in this "innovation."

179. See Chapter Three herein, and Paul Wheatley, "The concept of urbanism" in Ucko, Tringham, and Dimbleby (eds.), *Man, Settlement and Urbanism,* 602–603. The petrifaction of Near Eastern imperial cities, as well as the feverish pattern of Western (especially American) city-growth is illuminated by Wheatley's summaries.

Human Existence. Briefly, Bakan sees human acts falling into two large patterns of motivation: one he calls "agentic," for it is dominant, achieving, mastering; the other is "communal," for it is conservative and unifying.[180] He makes out a suggestive case for considering these as typically masculine and feminine behavior, but his analysis could easily be transposed to a contrast of alienated Western and integrated mythological cultures. The paternalistic forms in Western history with their conflicts and changes would affirm its heritage from Hebrew patriarchy. Even the suffocating aspect of paternalism is relevant; father knows best but the child has to learn for himself, whereupon he goes through the process in the next generation. This is not ancestor-worship, but a pattern of lived ambivalences.

On these points there is a certain contrast between Old and New Testaments, but there is also a continuity. If the ultimate Hebrew problem was how to face suffering, failure, and evil, the metaphor of Yahweh as Father to the disobedient Children of Israel had to be elaborated as He who chastens those whom he loves. Hosea does this most notably:

> When Israel was a child I loved him
> and out of Egypt did I call my son.
> But the more I called to them,
>   the further they went from me . . .
> They will have to go back to Egypt,
> Assyria must be their King,
> because they have refused to return to me.[181]

Jeremiah sees the loving care that motivates punishment when he

180. David Bakan, *The Duality of Human Existence* (Boston: Beacon Press, 1966), 14–15, 124, 152–53. The diacritical theory of meaning (as opposed to the referential), the influence of which pervades this work, would agree with radical feminism and with Leroi-Gourhan's reading of the Paleolithic cave-signs that the difference of male and female is not a matter of two opposed "natures" but rather is that made by a primary diacritical or differentiating mark, the phallus. (For similar reasons, sexual desire may be held not to be a magical attraction on the analogy of magnetism, but a complex project of mediated desire, involving concepts of lack, otherness, etc. I refer the reader to the works of Jacques Lacan and René Girard.) But after this concession, it is still possible to argue Bakan's case, as transposed above.

181. Hos. 11:1–5.

merges the paradigms of paternity and pastoralism. In Chapter 31 he foretells the return of fallen Israel as a result of Yahweh's guidance; Yahweh says:

> I will comfort them as I lead them back;
> I will guide them to streams of water,
> by a smooth path where they will not stumble.
> For I am a father to Israel
> and Ephraim is my first-born son.
> Listen, nations, to the word of Yahweh.
> Tell this to the distant lands,
> "He who scattered Israel gathers him,
> he guards him as a shepherd guards his flock."[182]

But the New Testament offers other kinds of elaborations. "For God so loved the world that he gave his only begotten son"; this text reveals the depth of purpose behind what Yahweh asked of Abraham; equally revealing is the insistence that only through the Son is the Father made manifest: "No one has ever seen God; it is the only Son, nearest to the Father's heart, who has made him known." The author of the Gospel of John had stored all these metaphors in his heart and pondered on them. Finally he has Jesus say of himself: "I tell you most solemnly, the Son can do nothing by himself; he can do only what he sees the Father doing: and whatever the Father does the Son does too."[183] This image is drawn from the homeliest level of family life. Jesus implies of course that the Son performs a mediating role, bearing the divine act into a world rigorously sundered from it, the Yahwist boundary finally crossed. Yet on the other hand the saying equally insists on the nonautonomy of the Son's act; he can only be imitative, therefore dependent. In the end the Hebrew sense of the contingency of beings refills the metaphor.[184] Jesus is significantly called Son of Man as well as Son of God. The theme of paternity could hardly issue in a richer conception, and it too "makes" history.

182. Jer. 31:9–10. If paternity is a theme that implies demythologization, so is pastoral: see note 154 above.
183. John 5:19.
184. Cf. Chapter Five herein, where metonymy and metaphor play the roles suggested here by paternity (at least of the Biblical type) and maternity (as represented by what Min-Kamutef stands for).

Chapter Five The Bible and Literature: Against Positivism

> The Old and New Testaments are the Great Code of Art.
> —Blake
>
> Of making many books there is no end.
> —Eccles. 12:12
>
> For oure book seith, "Al that is writen is writen for oure doc-
> trine," and that is myne entente.
> —Chaucer's Retraction

THE EPISTLE TO THE HIGHBROWS

Positivism is discourse containing an implicit assumption that we
have an easily accessible standard of "external reality" against which
to measure any of our utterances. Usually it tends to assume, also,
that only the thinking of the most recent epoch (variously defined)
has been usefully guided by the application of this standard, and
that all previous discourse is tainted with superstition. From technology it borrows the assurance that the latest "state of the art" is
the best, forgetting the tendency of all eras to take their own ways
of thinking for granted. We might do well to ask if the bulk of
modern discourse which assumes its own enlightenment has not
compounded hubris with complacency. Will not much of our
thought seem quaint and fatuous in the next century? We have no
doubt corrected certain errors. But anyone who has ever dealt with

printed texts knows that to correct one error is to invite others.

Twentieth-century positivism is not more benighted than others, but its special errors are indicative. Typically it congratulates itself on being liberated from theologization, while its very notions of "reality" and "truth" are, fairly obviously, covert theologizations. Positivism is associated with the discrediting of metaphysics in our time, but often it simply borrows a naive version of what it denounces. In the medieval view, if you weren't worshiping the true God you were surely worshiping some false one: to be human, they thought, was to worship, to elevate some principle into the realm of the sacred. Those who worship success, or money, are hardly even worth pointing to, especially since the once-almighty dollar has declined; but consider how many votaries "the natural" has today. It would not be difficult to delineate more devious and complex fetishes in modern discourse. Relevant here would be the sacralization of methodology in the sciences and pseudosciences. Many practitioners of specialties seem to assume that asking the proper questions, in the proper order, as in a quest-ritual or Ali Baba story, will magically open doors to stunning new knowledge. Hence the cult of the expert and of the "trained" mind. These assumptions are undercut by T. S. Kuhn's assertion that normal science is mostly puzzle-solving, and that the really creative advances require major distortions of current methods. To question methodology we need not subscribe to Romantic myths of "inspiration"; rigor remains a value, but to face the possibilities of the future we need more heuristic means. For one thing, we need to be able to skew our visions of "reality": we learn to do this neither from textbooks nor from fieldwork.

From the Biblical point of view all our idols are only projections of ourselves and of our vaulting ambitions, and against them only remorseless desacralization can prevail. We have to be repeatedly reminded how transient and fallible we are and how self-glorifying are our works, no matter how noble in conception. This message cannot be given once and for all, but must be ceaselessly renewed, in every age. When prophecy ceased, the message had to take differ-

ent forms. The contention of this final chapter is that serious literature—as opposed to trivial, not to comic—is one of the forms the renewed message takes.

More traditional derivations of literature, and explanations of its
liveliness and importance in our culture, betray an anxiety to have
it all seem "natural." What can be more "human" than the urge to
tell tales around the campfire? however few of us ever feel that urge.
The Dean, when required to justify the Freshman English course,
usually resorts to some such model, although his language will of
course be general enough to conceal the poverty of his inspiration.
But if we are habitually self-deceived about the givenness of our
ways of doing things, we should *a fortiori* beware of trying to nat-
uralize literature. For in fact it might well be defined as a series
of unnatural acts.

"Why books?" as Ezra Pound put it. "This simple first question
was never asked." Pound's own answers are incidentally quite revealing, especially since a strong reaction against a YMCA-and-Sunday-
School childhood left him powerfully intolerant of orthodoxy in
religion. In spite of his overmastering prejudice against the "Old
Testy-munk," he insisted on the unsettling function of literature in
a way that reveals an essential continuity with the urgencies of the
Biblical prophets. Good literature, he said, worries "lovers of order":
"they regard it as dangerous, chaotic, subversive," because its exacti-
tudes show no mercy to society's self-inflating tendencies. In other
words, it shows us what idols we worship, and that they are idols.
This is not a "natural" act of man in society. Nor does literature's
exactitude mean reflecting back to us our preferred self-images. We
tend to forget the hortatory emphasis of Hamlet's "holding the mirror up to Nature." Mirrors, as in the *Mirror for Magistrates,* are
meant to show us our faults—and our ephemerality. Inferior or
merely popular art may avoid the task, but serious art must play
Yorick's skull: in the lady's chamber it reminds her "let her paint an
inch thick, to this favor she must come."[1]

If we have misconceived the mimetic function of literature, we

1. *Hamlet,* III, ii, 20–21 and V, i, 181–182; T. S. Eliot (ed.), *Literary Essays of
Ezra Pound* (New York: New Directions, 1954), 20–21.

make no improvement by switching to a theory that it is natural to "express oneself." Beginning with the prophets, we find a continuous record of the association of writing with cost and pain: there is little evidence that the act can simply be derived from the pleasure principle. Perhaps all writers feel a sense of what Hamlet's mirror entails, even if they reject the beliefs behind it: for literature or any writing can constantly remind us of our own mortality, simply because it can outlast us. The most casual scribble may turn up, generations later, in an attic or, for that matter, in an archaeological dig. We are delighted to discover Sumerian grocery lists. Thus when William Carlos Williams makes poems out of grocery lists, or out of notes to his wife about raiding the icebox, he obliquely recognizes writing's potential escape from the transience of its occasions. It is not immortal, but it is less mortal than we are. To paraphrase Oscar Wilde on statues ("if they know nothing of death, it is because they know little of life"), the disturbing *memento mori* function of any writing has to do not with its participation in the realm of nature, but in its severance from it.

If writing's connection with natural values is tenuous, its unnatural aspects are plainly obvious. On the one hand, it suits the needs of those who can't think of "what they should have said" until days later: the constitutionally alienated. On the other hand, for most people it is harder than speaking precisely because it is less a reflex action. Instead of placing us in a "normal" stance for social intercourse, the process of writing tempts us to assume a strange, aloof vantage point. (The "omniscient" point of view in fiction should really be seen as alienated.) Yet since the act itself hints at our transience, we have difficulty maintaining the pose. No wonder we face a blank page with apprehension; the agonies of decision about what to say, and how to say it, are not allayed by the peculiar, even ominous, finality of the words once written. For that finality is never the comforting fixedness of ritual order: no matter how apposite a phrase is, the possibility of bettering it always arises. The unending, implacable contingency of revision makes even the *mot juste* a psychic torture. Writing is a dreary horror to the average man, but great artists suffer even more. Flaubert described his labors as

Augean, the effects on him as nauseating. Perhaps the strangeness of
the whole process is epitomized by Joyce's day-long struggle to write
two sentences—for which he already had all the words; only their
combination daunted him.[2]

A powerful recent trend urges us to recognize the conventional,
not the natural, basis of our arts. Like a language, an art seen from
without is arbitrary, though a certain necessity comes to inhere as it
functions as a system. It proceeds by adaptations of conventions, of
paradigms that govern "works." Probably E. H. Gombrich's analyses
of art history have argued this line most forcefully, so suggestively
that we are virtually compelled to transpose them to literature. One
consequence of conventionality is the relevance of the diachronic, of
the historical use and influence of the conventions. About this Gombrich is quite unapologetic; he remarks that "there is, you might say,
a symphonic element in art. Every theme that turns up has a relation to what goes before and is sometimes even seen as having a
relation to what comes after; and the theme acquires its meaning
partly from this relation within the history of art. At least this is
true of Western art, though not of all other arts." The cultural heritage may be disguised or hidden, but it cannot be ignored. The
place of individual works of literature within immediate and distant
"traditions" testifies to the same relentlessly historical factor in its
meaning; even the nihilistic and antitraditional has its tradition in
our culture. Only an act of pure spontaneity could escape this
participation; programmatic spontaneity is obviously farcical, and
Gombrich compares it to "trying to forget": the ultimate psychological futility.[3] But no one sits down to write the purely
spontaneous novel or poem anyway. Literature is only produced out
of conventions, by arduous labor, ever since Adam's curse. T. S.
Eliot stated the consequences satisfactorily enough for most of us:

2. See Frank Budgen, *James Joyce and the Making of Ulysses* (1934; rpt.
Bloomington: Indiana University Press, 1960), 20. On alienation and writing, see
James A. Boon, *From Symbolism to Structuralism: Lévi-Strauss in a Literary Tra-
dition* (Oxford: Blackwell, 1972), 197.

3. Gombrich, *Art and Illusion*, 174, and "Interview: Ernst Gombrich," *Diacritics*, I (Winter, 1971), 48.

No poet, no artist of any art, has his complete meaning alone. . . . The existing monuments form an ideal order among themselves, which is modified by the introduction of the new (the really new) work of art among them. The existing order is complete before the new work arrives; for order to persist after the supervention of novelty, the *whole* existing order must be, if ever so slightly, altered; and so the relations, proportions, values of each work of art toward the whole are readjusted; and this is conformity between the old and the new. Whoever has approved this idea of order, of the form of European, of English literature will not find it preposterous that the past should be altered by the present as much as the present is directed by the past.[4]

Nor should anyone aware of the Biblical roots of the idea of history find preposterous the notion of an "ideal order" which is yet an ongoing process, one in which the present alters the past. The relevance here of Biblical paradigms is unsurprising, not because Eliot was a Christian—he was unconverted when he wrote this—but because they have in fact shaped the progression of our literature.

The Biblical element in Western literature does not raise the question of a "myth of origins" in the usual sense, still less that of a return to an ideal state. (Eliot's "ideal order" has an epistemological, not an ethical, flavor.) The chimera of lost innocence that haunts the efforts of explaining by origins is a creature of the classical world, though it was supported by importing extra-Biblical notions into Genesis. In the Bible, we must repeat, there is never any question of returning to Eden. The future is in God's hand, but its form is extremely vague; the metaphors of "salvation" remain unfixed except in subsequent theologization. (Even these will appear nearly commonsensical if we consider what would be implied by asserting their opposite, as in the perversely self-pitying fantasies of negative apocalypticism.)

Many use the Bible as a "myth of origins," of course. But what the Bible bequeaths to the West is not only a book, which can be used as a myth, but some quintessence of the act of writing. We are all in the debt of Jacques Derrida for opposing "writing" to "the book";

4. T. S. Eliot, "Tradition and the Individual Talent" (1919), *Selected Essays,* 4–5. See, however, note 32 below, on the differences between highly stylized "conceptual" arts and ours.

the latter can be theologized into timeless truths, becoming a "bulwark of logocentrism."[5] But there is something else in the Bible, typified perhaps by the scene of Isaiah's commission as a prophet. Yahweh says: "Go, and say to this people, 'Hear and hear again, but do not understand; see and see again, but do not perceive.' "[6] These words evoke the function of the parable, the form which can dramatize the most urgent kinds of meaning for those thirsting for it, which yet seems baffling or trifling to those wise in their own conceits. These may say "we've heard all this before; what does it mean?" Serious literature at all levels is built around this function, of revealing and concealing at the same time. It has nothing for those who share the positivist creed that "everything that can be expressed can be expressed clearly," and thus that interpretation should yield something plain and obvious. In effect literature seems to be straining with signification, yet we are never confident that what it is saying can be reduced, for more than certain superficial purposes, to a descriptive statement of meaning. In this it follows parable, which contains, in spite of its oral modality, the problematic of writing, a sudden alienation from meaning: the one thing literature's words cannot mean is what they "say" in ordinary discourse.

Prophecy, as Isaiah and the other great prophets use it, is discourse in essentially the same mode as parable, and these typify the enduring heritage of the Bible's literary forms. Neither of these kinds gives itself up to casual inspection; of them, as of literature, we must ask questions.

The devotion of Henry James was to the literary form most elaborated by the 19th century: the prose fiction, which is to say, the enigma. . . . Always, the "story" has been a hermetic thing. Of the first hearers of the Parable of the Sower, it was those closest to the Parabolist who wanted afterward to know what it meant. . . . Part of the primitive fascination of a story is this, that we often cannot be sure why it has been told. Often we can: it may say, I am Odysseus, this happened to me: share my self-esteem;

5. See Jacques Derrida, *De la Grammatologie* (Paris: Minuit, 1967), 30–31 and *passim.*
6. Isa. 6:9.

or, This may happen to you, King Pentheus, be prepared; or, This happened here in Athens: know how to feel. Or often: You will wish this might happen to you. But devoid of arteries from *me*, or *you*, or *here*, why does that tale's heart beat? A sower went out to sow his seed. . . ; or, A governess went to Bly, where there had been servants named Quint and Jessel, undesirable people, and the two children. . . . Why are we being told *that*?[7]

This is Hugh Kenner on the literary state of things left by James to Ezra Pound's generation. But it also serves to establish the general debt of "fiction" to the Biblical imagination. Kenner disqualifies prose fictions from the use to which Homer was put, on Eric Havelock's showing, in ancient Greece: "Know how to feel." The comments on lack of "arteries" and on the wonderment of those *closest* to the Parabolist, should also be noted. Fiction does not tell us how to play our roles in society (more often it insists precisely that they are "roles"); nor does it reveal a magical *gnosis* that can give us another kind of social identity, as members of an esoteric brotherhood. If we follow this line of thought from social meaning to the nature of any kind of meaning, we are on the Biblical track.

The Bible's "influence" is not to give us genres or archetypes which can be endlessly refilled with extraneous materials; instead it plays a role which demands that we acknowledge how precarious is our grasp of any meaning in the world at all and that we force ourselves to probe the words and forms before us in a never-ending labor. Like the dynamic incompleteness of language itself, the gap or lack that gives it an endless, never-catching-up-to-itself character, the Bible sets the problem of retracing urgent but unfixable messages, located in a series of texts which come to no real end or conclusion. Writing posits an original disjunction, a violent removal from immediacy of meaning: "L'écriture universelle [serait] l'alienation absolue," as Derrida paraphrases Rousseau.[8] Writing is actively prior though historically posterior to speech; it conveys to us a sense

7. Hugh Kenner, *The Pound Era* (Berkeley: University of California Press, 1971), 23–24.
8. Derrida, *De la Grammatologie*, 429. On the prophets and writing, see Lindblom, *Prophecy in Ancient Israel*, 163–65.

that we must become thoroughly unsure of understanding before we can understand. "Derrida represents a position that stresses the dearth of meaning, the occlusion of truth. He engages the interpreter in a labor of deciphering, of transcription that could lead to no refuge of historical empathy in the manner of *Geistesgeschichte*, to no act of participation and communion as intimated by certain phenomenological and hermeneutic approaches."[9] So does Isaiah.

These recent approaches against which Derrida can be defined stress communion, empathy, as in familiar discourse. They make much of the "hermeneutic circle," meaning roughly that we must know what is going to be said before we can understand it. That this takes place in speech is undeniable, but it is obviously not quite the same in writing, precisely because of the lack of gesture and other tonal indicators. Those who read the Bible via these recent approaches are making it into oral myth, or would like to. They believe that "when language is operating properly interpretation or translation is unnecessary," thus allying themselves with cultic oral- ists like Marshall McLuhan, and those who produce, like Susan Sontag, manifestos against interpretation.[10] For them writings are *faute de mieux* substitutes for the full reality of the oral. However, even in theological studies objections to this view are rising. For instance we may take preunderstanding, which allows the comple- tion of the hermeneutic circle; a critical view can find preunder- standing to be dangerously near preconceived ideas, even prejudices, those fateful mental sets that are vital in human functioning but more appropriate, and more dominant, in cold societies than in hot or historical ones. One summary puts it: "Exegesis guided by pre- understanding is lacking in objectivity and can only establish what

9. Alexander Gelley, "Form as Force," *Diacritics*, II (Spring, 1972), 13. Derrida has the happy function of reminding us to be critical without being constructive.

10. Dan Otto Via, Jr., *The Parables: Their Literary and Existential Dimen- sions* (Philadelphia: Fortress, 1967), 33. Those familiar with these problems will recognize that I am overlooking certain values of "preunderstanding" for the purpose of heightening contrasts; Via's discussion will restore some of the com- plexity. But it must be affirmed that two opposite trends are in motion: for a persuasive display of the oralist argument, see Father Walter Ong's *The Presence of the Word* (New York: Simon and Schuster, 1970). See also Fredric Jameson, *The Prison-House of Language* (Princeton, N. J.: Princeton University Press, 1972), esp. 175–76.

it already knows. Historical sources are not allowed to say their own word and express their alien subject matter, but rather sources of the greatest variety are all made to speak the same language."[11] That is, the intransigent discontinuities of history are Procrusteanly forced into myth. This distorts the irreducibly literary character of the Biblical tradition.

Whoever has struggled to achieve a critical understanding of a literary text will probably not overestimate the utility of preunderstanding. Far more important is some sudden jarring into a new context, which may even take place accidentally, making the schemata previously used to read the work seem arbitrary and flexible, able to take new shapes or to efface themselves before newer schemata. Preunderstanding and familiarization are necessary for reading to take place, but can never substitute for interpretation and insight that arise from bringing together elements not previously familiar with one another.[12]

These claims do not imply that the Bible was ever the sole repository of writing or interpretation. By developing a powerful literature that moved away from myth, and toward the ambiguities which for instance tragedy thrives on, the Greeks approached the problematic of language in their own way. That this development was a process of demythologization is implied in several testimonies: most recently, Gerald Else, noting "the relative poverty of Attica in myths," comments: "This quasi-vacuum or low density of mytho-

11. Via, *The Parables,* 49.
12. Familiarization is in any case overrated in the usual conceptions of the learning process. Evidence is beginning to accumulate showing that the crucial steps are, in fact, alienations. Cf. Roman Jakobson: "When we observe the highly instructive process of a child's gradual advance in the acquisition of language, we see how decisively important the emergence of the subject-predicate sentence is. It liberates speech from the here and now and enables the child to treat events distant in time and space or even fictitious. This capacity [is sometimes labeled] 'displaced speech'" (*Scientific American,* September, 1972, p. 80). Also the Soviet psychologist L. S. Vygotsky reports that, with adult instruction, children master "scientific" concepts better than they deal with "spontaneous" and everyday matters: in spite of the fact that "the advantage of familiarity is all on the side of the everyday concepts." See L. S. Vygotsky, *Thought and Language,* ed. and trans. Eugenia Hanfmann and Gertrude Vakar (Cambridge, Mass.: MIT Press, 1962), 106–107.
Familiarity is inarticulate (the Cordelia principle).

logical tradition in Attica was perhaps in the long run her greatest asset for the development of a tragic drama based on . . . *a new penetration of the myths from within,* a new way of facing directly up to them and asking their general import in terms of human experience. This would have been much more difficult if tragedy had begun with accredited Attic myths," for if Athens had been full of autochthonous beliefs it could not have made the psychic withdrawal needed for the "new penetration."[13] To interpret, even in this creative way, is to demythologize; the myths no longer retain their mythic quality under this new handling. Bruno Snell points out that though in the forerunners of tragic drama "mythical events were communicated to the people as an immediate present experience," tragedy as a developed form substituted probing and questioning of the myths: "Tragedy is not a faithful mirror of the incidents of myth; instead of accepting them as historical reality, as they are accepted in the epic, tragedy traces the ultimate causes in the actions of men, and consequently often pays but little attention to concrete facts."[14] Indeed, as he goes on to discuss the "primitive religious concepts," the "fertility magic and ritual mummery" that engendered the satyrs' choruses, Snell notes that these had to be superseded in the growth of tragedy:

The popular character and the religious function of tragedy would never, by themselves, have sufficed to make tragedy what it is, to advance it beyond the stage of a masked procession such as may be found anywhere and at any time. For the popular religious festival which is so prominent among primitive societies to achieve the unique quality which has given Attic tragedy its importance far beyond its own time, something else was needed. This indispensable element which explains why we continue to occupy ourselves with tragedy is none other than the very principle in which Aristophanes discerned the undoing of tragedy. It is the Socratic "knowledge," the element of reflexion.[15]

Eric Havelock defines this Socratic reflection as "the separation of

13. Gerald Else, *The Origin and Early Form of Greek Tragedy* (1965; rpt. New York: Norton, 1972), 38–39. See also Else's discussion of "myth-and-ritual" theories of origin, pp. 3 ff.
14. Snell, *The Discovery of the Mind,* 90, 106.
15. *Ibid.,* 121–22.

the knower from the known," the indispensable alienation against which Aristophanes, and Nietzsche, protested in vain.[16] The former foresaw its culture-dissolving effect, and mourned. "Aristophanes," says Snell, "fails to understand that a man's opposition to the traditions, and his appeal to another authority—be it reason or the voice of conscience—are fully as moral as obedience to custom; some have since considered it an even higher type of morality."[17] Those who do have been following the prophets, not the Greeks. For, to a large degree, Greek literature remained under the sway of myth, particularly since history proved unsuitable as an alternate source. "Attempts to write historical tragedy were early abandoned by the Greeks, since history was less susceptible to intellectual elaboration, and to play, than myth. Thus myth remained the proper domain of artistic reality, particularly after myth had lost its standing as factual reality."[18] Hence, as already argued, Aristotle's preference for poetry over history was an expression of subservience to myth; the preference assumes philosophy, knowledge of the *logos,* to be the goal of both inquiries, and the classical *logos* is none other than the philosophized version of the archaic cosmic continuum. Thus history, full of "time and chance" as Ecclesiastes put it, reveals the logic of the eternal structure of things less efficiently than poetry, which can make virtue of the necessity opposed to history's contingency. But our poetry does not work that way. It portrays not what Alcibiades might have said or done if events more perfectly mirrored the *logos,* but what Don Quixote or Bouvard and Pécuchet or Vladimir and Estragon might do in agonized reaction to a world where nobody can find out what the *logos* is.

If Helen Gardner is correct to contrast Greek and Western tragedy as "crisis" *vs.* "process," the one untying a knot and the other telling a story, and if, as has been suggested, the Biblical feeling for narrative is tied up with a sense of awe at the way God's destiny continually violates human expectation, so that Tertullian's famous *credo*

16. See note 29 to Chapter One herein; Snell, *The Discovery of the Mind,* 119 ff.
17. Snell, *The Discovery of the Mind,* 133.
18. *Ibid.,* 112.

is a fitting extension of the Biblical attitude toward history, then the
heritage of the Western forms from the Greek ones should not be
exaggerated.[19] Snell points up the difference by observing how
strange the Greeks would have thought the story of Gideon and the
fleece.

> But Gideon's demand that the natural sequence of events should be
> reversed, and the readiness of the believer to have his faith reinforced and
> refreshed by the paradoxical, such things are not to be found among the
> Greeks. The saying ascribed to Tertullian: "credo quia absurdum" is not
> Greek; it goes against the very grain of Greek thought, and deliberately
> so. According to classical Greek notions the gods themselves are subject
> to the laws of the cosmos, and in Homer the gods always operate in
> strictest conformity with nature. . . . Nor is the Greek deity capable of
> creating a thing out of nothing; that is the reason why the Greeks have
> no Genesis of their own.[20]

Whereas Yahweh erupts into history, creates and changes, the
Greek gods conform to expectations drawn from study of the *logos*:
"It would not be far from wrong to say that the supernatural in
Homer behaves with the greatest regularity."[21]

For those who do not know Snell's work, it must be said that he
aims to establish our debt to the Greeks, not to the Hebrews. "European thinking begins with the Greeks. They have made it what it is:
our only way of thinking," and so on.[22] But his comparisons with the
contrary tendencies of the Hebrews are sometimes doubly revealing
of the constitutions of Western thought. For instance, he skillfully
and persuasively demonstrates "the rise of the individual in the
early Greek lyric": Sappho, for instance, still looks at love as a
visitation from a divine power, but is capable of seeing herself as an
individual—not in the fact that she loves, but in the emotional
turmoil it produces in her. By calling love "bitter-sweet," Sappho
"discovers the area of the soul and defines it as fundamentally distinct from the body."[23] That Snell finds the necessary kind of think-

---

19. See notes 112–14 to Chapter Four herein.
20. Snell, *The Discovery of the Mind*, 29.
21. *Ibid.*
22. *Ibid.*, vii.
23. *Ibid.*, 60. Finding this concept of reflection on one's own experience lacking

ing, *i.e.*, looking at oneself from a removed viewpoint, to be available first in literature, is most suggestive. But it would be helpfully complemented by an analysis of the processes of self-alienation in Hebrew writings. In transcribing suffering in poetry (as in Job, the Servant Songs, many Psalms), the Bible-writers cause one to doubt the validity of Dr. Johnson's assertion about *Lycidas*, that "where there is leisure for fiction there is little grief."[24] But at the same time the poems attain a curious self-distancing.

> Lay your scourge aside,
> I am worn out with the blows you deal me.
> You punish man with the penalties of sin,
> Like a moth you eat away all that gives him pleasure—
> Man is indeed a puff of wind!
>
> (Ps. 39: 10–11)

The Western concept of individualism so intrinsic to our literature is a compound in which an Oriental sense of man's nothingness, as above, leavens the Greek tendency to self-assertion; as the story of Babel reminds us that the Acropolis is properly a ruin. In prophets like Jeremiah and Ezekiel, personal anguish is mixed with a fading of the self before the implacable demands of God's purpose. Fittingly, these two prophets are the ones to state most clearly the doctrine of individual responsibility that supersedes collective and familial guilt: "Each is to die for his own sin. Every man who eats unripe grapes is to have his own teeth set on edge."[25]

On the question of Greek influence, we must always remind our-

---

in Homer, Snell shows how it came about through the practice of alienation: "The early lyrists try to reproduce those moments in which the individual is all of a sudden snatched out of the broad stream of life, when he senses that he is cut off from the ever-green tree of universal growth [a green bay, perhaps? Cf: the idea of the cosmic continuum in Chapter Two]. . . . Though the individual who detaches himself from his environment severs many old bonds, his discovery of the dimension of the soul once more joins him in company with those who have fought their way to the same insight. The isolation of the individual is, by the same token, the forging of new bonds" (p. 65).

24. "Life of Milton," in *Lives of the Poets*, World's Classics ed., p. 112.

25. Jer. 31:30, cf. Ezek. 18:1–4. G. E. Wright maintains that the concept of individualism in the Bible is far older, however, and is even implicit in the covenant: see his *The Old Testament Against Its Environment*, 69.

selves that the preservation of Greek traditions in the West was
ancillary to religious thought. Also, the influence was filtered
through Virgil, Ovid, Cicero, and the like, far down into our recent
history. Thus its role in forming the conventions of our literature,
while crucial, cannot be understood by direct examination of the
originals. We tend to forget this and to overplay their role, ignoring
the alignment of the Greek insights with Biblical vectors. Yet had
it not been for Christianity the Greek achievements would have remained rooted in the place where they had grown. Werner Jaeger
emphasizes how much the Greek poets' and intellectuals' work was
"deeply sunk in the soil of social and political life," so much so that
"the history of Greek culture coincides in all essentials with the history of Greek literature."[26] If, as Gombrich suggests, the Greeks
invented art when they took images out of sacred contexts, a parallel
process had to occur in literature: a deracination had to take place.
Plato may have begun it, and the poverty of myths in Attica pre-
conditioned it, but "it was the Christians who finally taught men to
appraise poetry by a purely aesthetic standard—a standard which
enabled them to reject most of the moral and religious teaching of
the classical poets as false and ungodly, while accepting the formal
elements in their work as instructive and aesthetically delightful."[27]
So the demythologizing and decentering operation that Christians
performed on Greek poetry, taking it out of "social" context, was
vital to its acceptance into our canon.

These conclusions may appear strange if we have been taught to
think only of that side of Christianity which is associated with the
question, "What has Athens to do with Jerusalem?" But there was
always another side to Christianity, willing to use pagan writings
(despoiling the Egyptians of their gold, Augustine called it in reference to Exodus 12:36) as long as these could be interpreted, moral-
ized, and thus demythologized. The Greek thinkers could be looked
at as having gone as far as unaided reason could go. Paul began it on

26. *Paideia: The Ideals of Greek Culture,* trans. Gilbert Highet (1935; rpt.
New York: Oxford University Press, 1965), xxvii–xxviii.
27. *Ibid.,* 35.

the Areopagus: "As certain of your own poets have said . . ." (Acts 17:28).[28]

THE MYTH OF MYTH

> There is nothing sacred about literature, it is damned from one end to the other. There is nothing in literature but change and change is mockery.
>
> —William Carlos Williams

Literature makes use of paradigms, verbal structures that can be usefully varied, and these can be likened to structures in myth, *topoi* and motifs and so on. In this aspect literature inherits from many sources, the Bible included, a hoard of devices: at the higher levels of organizations, these structures have a strong totalizing tendency and will arrange themselves into patterns that suggest an incorporation of wholes of experience into their domain. Almost any systematizing or totalizing thinking is mythic in that sense, myth here representing ways to deal with confusing or inchoate experience, or simply to believe in many things of which we can have no direct individual knowledge. Hence the validity of referring to complexes of dubious assumptions, superstitions, and suspicions as myths, along with the "storified" beliefs of ancient and primitive cultures. They share that totalizing tendency, going far outside the bounds of verification or falsification.

The Bible's relation to this aspect of literature is demonstrated by Northrop Frye. He sees as the dominating and encyclopedic myth of our culture "the Judaeo-Christian myth as set out in the Bible . . . stretching from creation to apocalypse," supplemented from classical and other sources. This is no doubt true, as far as it goes. But in spite of the fact that Frye recognizes the "revolutionary quality" passed on from Hebrew monotheism to Christianity, the importance of which is "hard to overstate," he cannot see that this makes us essentially different from typical mythological societies.

28. In addition to Jaeger on the subject, see C. N. Cochrane, *Christianity and Classical Culture* (1940; rpt. New York: Oxford University Press, 1968), Chaps. VI and X, esp. p. 360. See also Augustine, *On Christian Doctrine*, 75–78 (II, 60–63).

"When a mythology crystallizes in the centre of a culture, a temenos or magic circle is drawn around that culture, and a literature develops historically within a limited orbit of language, reference, allusion, belief, transmitted and shared tradition."[29] That does not precisely describe the Greek experience, much less the Western one. Whenever demythologizing intrudes, then the "coldness" of such a society thaws, the magic circle becomes broken in many places.

For all the importance of the myths and conventions on which our society or literary tradition plays variations, their full description would not comprehend the energies of art. What is the force that puts the forms to use? Why is this force conceived, even for instance in so apparently un-Biblical an aesthetic as Ezra Pound's, as a continuing urge to "make it new"? Why is Pound so dismissive of those who merely conform to the conventions of a period, the "diluters" as he calls them?[30] He does not really believe in progress, nor think that Homer, Ovid, Catullus, or Villon are to be superseded. Like Eliot, he distinguishes between the "really new" work and the novelty, but also between imitation of the schemata, mere dead repetition, and creative "quotation," an opposition vital to *The Cantos*. For Pound was anything but a naive revolutionary; he taught the value and importance of the concept of "tradition" to his friend Eliot.[31] What he desired was a use of the past and its schemata so as to emphasize new creative possibilities. He awaited the coming of a "Renaissance": perhaps he would have subscribed to Gombrich's version of the process that produced the original Renaissance.

[The] dry psychological formula of schema and correction can tell us a good deal, not only about the essential unity between medieval and post-

29. Northrop Frye, *The Critical Path* (Bloomington: Indiana University Press, 1971), 37, 48, 35. Frye has gained some precision by replacing an earlier version that began "Once a mythology is formed," but still neglects the possibilities of what Derrida would call "decentering." On the other hand, cf. p. 107: "Occasionally we find it suggested that breaking up closed myths of concern [his term for that side of myth concerned with social cohesion] may be part of the historical function of Judaism" [read "the Bible"].

30. Eliot (ed.), *Literary Essays of Ezra Pound*, 23–24.

31. See my *Ezra Pound: The Image and the Real* (Baton Rouge: Louisiana State University Press, 1969), Chap. 5.

medieval art but also of their vital difference. To the Middle Ages, the schema is the image; to the postmedieval artist, it is the starting point for corrections, adjustments, adaptations, the means to probe reality and to wrestle with the particular. . . . [Postmedieval art's] symptom is the sketch, or rather the many sketches which precede the finished work and, for all the skill of hand and eye that marks the master, a constant readiness to learn, to make and match and remake till the portrayal ceases to be a secondhand formula and reflects the unique and unrepeatable experience the artist wishes to seize and hold.

It is this constant search, this sacred discontent, which constitutes the leaven of the Western mind since the Renaissance and pervades our art no less than our science.[32]

What drives this "sacred discontent"? We must ask, unless we wish to resort to saying it is "natural." Gombrich and others have successfully eroded the notion that style is a slow progression toward more and more realistic form. The schemata of earlier ages were quite sufficiently real to those ages. The testing and probing of these was not done with an eye toward attaining a uniform, univocal, final style of reality: there is no such thing; any style can only emphasize a few of the possibilities in representation. Rather the testing seems to have its own raison d'être.

We look in vain to Aristotle or classical theorists for illumination of this mysterious probing energy, even if we find revealing examples of it in Sappho, the dramatists, or Plato. Their world admitted this power only as something anomalous. But in the prophetic mode of writing, and in its canonization by the people it excoriated, we find a consistent readiness to dismantle the schemata of myths and *idées reçues*. This is precisely the remarkable characteristic of the Bible considered among other ancient texts. Not only

32. Gombrich, *Art and Illusion*, 173. This is where "preunderstanding," whose value Gombrich would understand as a requirement for perceiving anything (for the "innocent eye" has no function), yields to something further. In the arts we could call "conceptual" (primitive, Egyptian, medieval) what is achieved is basically a conformation to minimally varied precepts of style: in ours the concept of the individual work assumes primary importance. Gombrich admits that all art is "conceptual" (p. 87), for "without some starting point, some initial schema, we could never get hold of the flux of experience" (p. 88), yet the difference of our art from the others is indubitable.

To cite an older critical vocabulary, "archetype" must not simply be opposed to "signature": the archetype itself must be individualized. The strategy of West-

does it probe and mock the vauntings of pagan kings, and of fools who say in their heart "There is no God," and of those who assert their superiority in the belief that "We have Abraham for our father": it even corrects and reshapes its own verbal formulas. The motto for this function would be the refrain of the Sermon on the Mount: "Ye have heard it said . . . but I say unto you," etc.

The whole Bible rejoices in the sense of a new word, of breaking free from redundant patterns. When Ezekiel and Jeremiah want to establish the aforementioned doctrine of individual responsibility, they do it by attacking the proverb that runs "The fathers have eaten sour grapes, and the children's teeth are set on edge." When Job rejects the comfort of his counselors, he does it by mocking their traditional sayings and orthodoxies. Long before Jesus, Isaiah dared to put a new, shocking meaning upon the very promises of Yahweh to Abraham: "Israel, your people may be like the sand on the seashore, but only a remnant will return." Jesus proposed, in place of the recitation and elaboration of legalistic precepts, new and direct exhortations, new simple prayers which depended not at all on the heathen habit of piling up ritualistic phrases. For God was not to be coerced by formulas, and by every little word we are to be justified, or not. Not what goes into a man's mouth may defile him, but what comes out.

With a scornful fervor that matches Ezekiel's denunciations of the prideful musings of the city of Tyre, or Isaiah's mockery of the deluded boasting of the king of Assyria, Amos humiliates those in Israel who tell each other "The day of Yahweh is coming." The whole thrust of the work of the prophets was against man's tendency to misappropriate words for his own ends. The prophets hunt down every rationalizing hypocrisy, expose to plain sight every verbal refuge. Those who say "Peace! Peace!" when there is no peace are no better than the pagans who will execute God's righteous wrath on them.[33]

---

ern art is not replication of the theme, but variations on it. The present alters the past, the variations make something new of the theme.

33. Ps. 14:1; Matt. 3:9 and 5; Job 12:2, 13:12, 16:2, etc.; Isa. 10:22, Matt. 6:7, 13:36–37, 15:11; Am. 5:18 ff.: Ezek. 13:10.

If we look at the Bible's demythologizing of verbal formulas as prefiguring the urge to "examine the schema and test its validity [as] since the time of Leonardo, at least, every great artist has done,"[34] we may see something about those crucial events of the West, the Renaissance and the Reformation, and why they come together. What was each one but a great schema-testing? The upsurge of new artistic energies coincides with a rise in individualistic Bible-reading. Now it is the writers, as Ezra Pound points out, who do what the prophets and Jesus would have us do: probe and criticize the language we inherit, the universe of verbal forms that shapes our acts whether we will or not. And the key point goes back to Eliot's sense that the present alters the past. No expression is allowed to become "timeless truth": there is no such thing for us. The historical element, the dynamism, in Western life produces not only readiness to change and openness to the future, but also a drive to explore and re-explore the potentialities of meaning in the past. The most obvious example is the application of historical criticism to the Bible itself, an activity which in this light appears founded on firmly Biblical premises. It gives us not a "true" reading of the text, but new heuristic insights gained by testing the schemata, and by shifting our perspectives in new, unfamiliar ways.[35]

The Russian Formalist critic Victor Shklovsky gave currency to the term *defamiliarization* (*ostraneniye*, making strange) as the essence, the literariness, of literature. He founded it on a simple psychological explanation, the deadening effect of habit, or what he

---

34. Gombrich, *Art and Illusion*, 174.

35. See Amos N. Wilder, *Early Christian Rhetoric: The Language of the Gospel* (Cambridge, Mass.: Harvard University Press, 1971), esp. the insistence on "the new utterance" in pp. 5–12 and the attack on "empty phrases" noted on p. 23. Wilder takes an oralist line in general, but cf. p. 14 on the continuity of writing and speech. Here the point is simply that early Christianity did not become a heaping of schemata: "one did not hoard its formulas" (p. 13). The Christian feeling of a "new dynamics in human speech," Wilder says, "brought forth not only new vocabulary and oral patterns but also new literary forms and styles" (pp. 9 and 7). "We can, therefore, appreciate the special incentives to the literary arts that Christianity has always provided. . . . [For it is] a religion of the Book and this has had its corollaries for its total cultural thrust" (p. 12). The Christians were the first to make extensive use of what we call today "books," *i.e.*, codices (p. 8).

called "automatism" in perception.[36] As such his idea was a revival of the Romantic animus against "custom," which can lie upon us "with a weight, / Heavy as frost, and deep almost as life!"[37] Coleridge wrote that Wordsworth's object in the *Lyrical Ballads* was to "give the charm of novelty to things of every day, and to excite a feeling analogous to the supernatural, by awakening the mind's attention to the lethargy of custom, and directing it to the loveliness and the wonders of the world before us; an inexhaustible treasure, but for which, in consequence of the film of familiarity and selfish solicitude we have eyes, yet see not, ears that hear not, and hearts that neither feel nor understand."[38]

That the "lethargy of custom" and the "film of familiarity and selfish solicitude" have a more than psychological origin is witnessed by Coleridge's adaptation of the lines from Isaiah's lines on hearing and seeing but not understanding. He plays a variation on them that reminds us of the one Jesus played: let those who have ears to hear, hear.[39] Shklovsky cites riddles and erotic euphemisms as simple examples of defamiliarizing technique, in which the revealing-concealing pattern is manifest: these indicate an object or meaning not by naming it but by avoiding the name.[40] But the Christian and Coleridgean variants on Isaiah suggest that he might have put forward the parable as the basic form. In this sense parable contains the kernel of the rudimentary difference between fiction and more common forms of discourse: the fiction is barred from commenting directly on itself or naming its own meaning; it exhibits what might be called a peculiar inhibition of the metalinguistic function. If an author breaks into his work and comments *in propria persona*, we take in the comment as part of the fiction. Though highly skilled authors play games with this rule (as they do with all rules) by con-

---

36. See Jameson, *The Prison-House of Language*, 50–51 *et seq.* See also Lee T. Lemon and Marion J. Reis (trans. and eds.), *Russian Formalist Criticism: Four Essays* (Lincoln: University of Nebraska Press, 1965), 4, 11–13, etc.

37. Wordsworth, *Ode: Intimations of Immortality*, 127–28.

38. *Biographia Literaria*, Chap. XIV, second paragraph.

39. Matt. 11:15, 13:9 and 43, Mark 4:9 and 23, Luke 8:8, 14:35. Jesus explicitly quotes Isa. 6:9 in Matt. 13:14, Mark 4:12, Luke 8:10.

40. Lemon and Reis (eds.), *Russian Formalist Criticism*, 18–21.

structing self-reflexive works, these aspects too become part of the work rather than externally grounded statements about it. (Authors are notoriously deceptive guides to the meanings of their own works anyway, causing D. H. Lawrence to remark "Never trust the artist, trust the tale," because they are too painfully aware of the problem of meaning to assign their own works to any formula.[41])

Defamiliarization is made to operate against taking things for granted. But the aim is at the seeing, not the object. "An image is not a permanent referent for those mutable complexities of life which are revealed through it; its purpose is not to make us perceive meaning, but to create a special perception of the object—*it creates a 'vision' of the object instead of serving as a means for knowing it.*"[42] Of course "meaning," denotation in the referential sense, is not the aim of art. Shklovsky's point is paralleled by Gombrich's analysis of representational art not as portrayal of an object, but as "image," a new reality in its own right, a vision perhaps: art is image-making, and our art tends to be *about* image-making. Ezra Pound also makes a relevant comment by quoting approvingly an unnamed Russian who tried to explain Vorticism, the movement that he and Wyndham Lewis created in 1914: " 'I see, you wish to give people new eyes, not to make them see some new particular thing.' "[43] The Russian might as well have been Shklovsky, who insisted that realism, in the sense of more and more transparent portrayals of objects, was not the goal of art: "The forms of art are explainable by the laws of art; they are not justified by their realism."[44] The search for realism never ends with the goal achieved: "The paradox in the evolution of French painting from Courbet to Cézanne is how it was brought to the verge of abstraction in and by its very effort to transcribe visual experience with ever greater

41. Lawrence, *Studies in Classic American Literature*, 13.

42. Lemon and Reis (eds.), *Russian Formalist Criticism*, 18. Italics in the original. Cf. p. 12: *"Art is a way of experiencing the artfulness of an object; the object is not important."*

43. "Vorticism" (1914), reprinted in Ellmann and Feidelson (eds.), *The Modern Tradition*, 148.

44. Lemon and Reis (eds.), *Russian Formalist Criticism*, 57.

fidelity."[45] Several similar evolutions have occurred in literature, notably in Modernism. The recurrent tendency of representationalism to transcend itself makes the bourgeois theory of art as portrayal hard to maintain.

Defamiliarization appears to be simply the creative application of principles long known to artists and to critics as well, about the heuristic value of "new ways of looking at things": sudden changes of context, viewpoint, and so on. We seek these constantly in the Western world, which is why we thrive on alienation or "making strange." But our literary history can make it clear, if nothing else will, that "things" as such are transformed even by the most realistic portrayals, and that therefore their unmediated delivery cannot be art's function. Art may lie in concealing art, but that makes it even more visible by implication, so that we see the art itself as the object. Ortega, in *Meditations on Quixote,* contributes an obvious but helpful point: in a novel "the real things do not move us but their representation—that is to say, the representation of their reality— does."[46] The objects and persons in a typical novel, or painting, if met in life, would not necessarily interest us: might even bore us. But in the work they may be endlessly fascinating. How is this sense of their "reality" achieved in a manifest fiction? One way to look at it might be to substitute *signification* for *reality* in Ortega's phrase. A work of literature functions as a language, so to speak, and its signifiers include more than the words themselves: things represented (objects, events, persons, feelings) are important only as they signify, as they become in a sense linguistic units with a syntax of their own. The work essentially defines the words that are in it, gives them the contexts that make them meaningful, and does so by constructing a *langue,* a selection from the common code or vernacular, which is also a *parole,* a speech act. The provision of a context identical to the work itself depends on things becoming utterances (a

45. Clement Greenberg, *Art and Culture: Critical Essays* (Boston: Beacon, 1961), 171.

46. José Ortega y Gasset, *Meditations on Quixote,* trans. Evelyn Rugg and Diego Marín (1914; rpt. New York: Norton, 1961), 144.

principle illustrated at its simplest level by Andy Warhol's signed soup cans).[47] A concordance of a book is not the book because it lacks what is created by syntactical relationships: and these are the events, which themselves come to function as signifiers, and thus acquire a reality independent of their homologues in so-called real life.

The point may be carried further by considering feelings or emotions, which in art are again not ends in themselves. Some think the goal of all art should be to melt the "seas of pity" that "lie / Locked and frozen in each eye," but if we become raw nerve ends of sympathy, as I. A. Richards remarks, into what convulsion will the evening paper throw us nightly?[48] Shklovsky's view avoids sentimentalistic conclusions by proposing that emotions are signifiers too. "Art, then, is unsympathetic—or beyond sympathy—except where the feeling of compassion is evoked as material for the artistic structure."[49] An artist may want us to feel a particular emotion, but only as part of the symbol-system which the work as a whole creates.

Another arena in which defamiliarization is relevant, on Shklovsky's showing, is in the differentiation of plot from story in our literature. By his line of thought plot becomes primary: the story is like the object, not important for its own sake. It is not so simple as E. M. Forster thought: for him "the king died, and then the queen died" was a story, whereas "the king died, and then the queen died of grief" was a plot.[50] Causation is doubtless a crucial element, revealing the demythologizing presence of history, so that even Aristotle preferred the plot that is linked like a historical chain to the episodic or mythlike story.[51] But Shklovsky's work, as on *Tristram Shandy*, for example, highlights the ways in which plot may retard, displace, and dismantle the story, and make a mockery of

47. See Kenner, *The Counterfeiters*, 77–79.

48. I. A. Richards, *Practical Criticism* (1929; rpt. New York: Harcourt, Brace, n.d.), 242–43 and 248–49; W. H. Auden, "In Memory of W. B. Yeats."

49. Lemon and Reis (eds.), *Russian Formalist Criticism*, 44.

50. E. M. Forster, *Aspects of the Novel* (1927; rpt. New York: Harcourt, Brace, n.d.), 86.

51. *Art of Poetry*, x.

normal ideas of causation. In Boris Eichenbaum's summary of
Formalist methods, "the discovery of various techniques of plot
construction (step-by-step structure, parallelism, framing, the weaving of motifs, etc.) clarified the difference between the elements used
in the construction of a work and the elements comprising its material (its story, the choice of motifs, the characters, the themes, etc.)"[52]
Shklovsky considered Don Quixote not a character but "a result of
the business of constructing the novel."[53] (This view has the heuristic value of forcing us to think of the problem of a work as that of
finding a subject adequate to its language, rather than vice versa.)
More consequentially still, the insistence on the priority of plot and
its defamiliarizing of the story demonstrates the distance of literature from myth. Because it is passed orally from generation to generation and culture to culture, myth tends to reduce itself to normative structures: individualistic plot-construction and the values it
can engender are unavailable. Myth either is simply a story, or in
Lévi-Strauss's even more reductive view, the story is merely a vehicle
through which the repeated themes make themselves heard.[54] By
taking this stand, Lévi-Strauss can say that the variants of a myth
are all one: if the order of incidents and events is rearranged in
some versions, it doesn't matter, for the meaning of the myth consists not of their relation in the narrative but in a set of logical
patterns. Thus there is no plot at all, but a fugal structure: in the
Oedipus myth, elements of "overrating of blood relations" (as incest)
are ranged against those of "underrating" these relations (fratricide),
and complemented by a similar opposition of autochthonous *vs.*
sexual themes in relation to the origin of men. There is no beginning or end (the Greek stories are untraceable to one event that sets
them off, for some other event always lies behind an origin) and no
development as we know it, no concept of the *work*.

52. Lemon and Reis (eds.), *Russian Formalist Criticism*, 119.
53. *Ibid.*, 121.
54. In the essay on the Oedipus myth Lévi-Strauss opposes "telling" the myth,
using the serial order of narrative, to "understanding" it, which can only be done
by ignoring the "diachronic" structure so as to see the relations among the
"mythemes" (*Structural Anthropology*, 209–11).

Thus Lévi-Strauss's essay on Oedipus has the incidental effect of making the distance between myth and literature almost too obvious, though Octavio Paz for instance seems to feel challenged to tie them together in some ways. Of one essential difference, however, he is as a poet keenly aware: myths are translated with relative ease, whereas literature is not. The poetry, in Frost's definition, is what gets lost in translation. With some works, for some purposes, translation is possible, of course: but as Paz says, paraphrasing Lévi-Strauss, a poem "is not only untranslatable into other languages but also into the language in which it is written. The translation of a poem is always the creation of another poem," a principle honored by Pope, Pound, Lowell, and others. This fact has to do with another realm closed to myth: that of nuanced verbal values, overtones, word-play, and figures of speech. Many of these, as it happens, are parts of "deconstructive" activities: satire, parody, ironies of all kinds—in other words, much of what we think of when we say "literature." Thus our literature is language-oriented, obsessed indeed with its own linguistic possibilities, in a way that myth is not. The existence of this realm of values justifies the obsessions of textual criticism with the *ipsissima verba*. Literature begins with a concern for a text, for exact words; oral-formulaic poetry is a step toward it, and away from myth.[55]

Thus, in formal attributes, myth and literature emphatically divide. Lévi-Strauss sums it up in his phrase "myths have no authors," by which he points not only to the obvious fact that they are anonymous, communal, timeless, and fluid, but that they lack the unifying consciousness, sometimes identified with "the subject,"

---

55. Paz, *Claude Lévi-Strauss*, 60. Cf. Lévi-Strauss: "Myth is the part of language where the formula *traduttore, traditore* reaches its lowest truth value. From that point of view it should be placed in the gamut of linguistic expressions at the end opposite to that of poetry, in spite of all the claims which have been made to prove the contrary" (*Structural Anthropology*, 206).

We could say, using structuralist language, that literature searches the order of the signifier for meaning as history searches the order of past events (see above, the discussion of schemata). Myth searches language in a different way, and for different ends. It only begins to approach literature's possibilities in the oral-formulaic structures of Homer and other epic singers.

from which or in which all works of literature are projected.[56] Even an anonymous work of literature has a hypothetical author; every part of a text has a "voice," or at least a "point of view," whose provenance can be inquired.

Finally, to raise the point for one last time, myth and literature divide in their relation to culture. Literature is a solvent. When Homer became "literature," Greek culture began to erode. When Dante turned the myths of the Middle Ages into a poem, those myths were questioned. Ortega cites Cervantes as one who realized that literature not only probes the pretensions of the culture in which the work occurs, but those of culture in an ideal sense. The materiality of the realist novel is a "critical power before which, providing it is declared sufficient, man's pretension to the ideal, to all that he loves and imagines, yields; the insufficiency, in a word, of culture, of all that is noble, clear, lofty—this is the significance of poetic realism. Cervantes recognizes that culture is all that, but that, alas, it is a fiction."[57]

The relevant analogy for myth and literature would seem to be Gombrich's comparison of representational art to islands, rising from a sea of conceptual, so-called "primitive" art.[58] The West is an island of literature in a sea of myth. Lévi-Strauss's work forces us to respect the profound otherness of myth, and not to treat it as either *arché* or *telos* of literature. Hopefully we will no longer be tempted to gloss over the differences, to treat literature as failed myth, or myth as some idealization of what we hope literature could be. Let us consider the implications of Gombrich's geographical metaphor:

56. See Lévi-Strauss, *The Raw and the Cooked*, "Overture," pp. 12, 18, etc.; also Eugenio Donato, "Of Structuralism and Literature," *Modern Language Notes*, 82 (December, 1967), 571–72. "As Lévi-Strauss says, and who should know better than him, a myth can be characterized by the fact that it is a linguistic utterance that does not have a subject—a myth 'speaks itself.' Myths, therefore, can be considered within the spectrum of various modes of linguistic speech as that which is furthest and most different from a literary one."

57. Ortega, *Meditations on Quixote*, 144.

58. In Gombrich's essay "Meditations on a Hobby Horse," reprinted in his book by that name (1963) and in *Classic Essays in English*, ed. Josephine Miles (2nd ed.; Boston: Little, Brown, 1965), 419.

swimming on the ground is more ridiculous if less disastrous than walking on the water.

THE BELIEF IN FICTIONS

What's Hecuba to him, or he to Hecuba,
That he should weep for her?
—*Hamlet*

It is difficult to believe in fictions, that is, to remember that they are fictions. Coleridge's phrase "the willing suspension of disbelief" throws the emphasis on the wrong side. Unless the convention is handled in a painfully amateurish way, we will fall in with it; even children mime dialogues into which we will imaginatively enter. Illusionist painting, as Gombrich points out, is nothing miraculous, and any careful craftsman can learn the tricks: in literature the imagination is even more willing to help out (or rather, help us *in*). Those poor souls who send money to soap opera heroines in trouble are not so very different from the rest of us, as actors know who have become identified with their roles.[59] We must be excruciatingly vigilant to keep reminding ourselves, when reading, that the work is fictional, for our visceral responses alone cannot make the distinction. Even metaphysicians acknowledge that fictional characters may be more real to us than our neighbors, and we all know how much easier it is to sympathize with them, indeed to be really moved by their situations, though we are perfectly aware that they are imaginary.[60] It may be, as Oscar Wilde jibed, that he would have a heart of stone who would not laugh at the death of Little Nell, but both

59. Actors in TV doctor shows, it is said, receive great quantities of mail asking for medical advice. Naive skepticism is merely the other side of the coin: some 25 percent of the respondents in a Los Angeles sidewalk survey professed disbelief that astronauts have really landed on the moon. They are participating in a different fiction.

60. "Tolstoi tells the story of the countess who wept buckets at a play while her coachman sat on the box of her waiting carriage, perishing of the cold through the long hours of the performance" (Trilling, *Beyond Culture*, 93). See also Augustine on Dido (*Confessions* I, 13, and III, 2), I. A. Richards on sentimentality in *Practical Criticism*, and Etienne Gilson, *Being and Some Philosophers* (Toronto: Pontifical Institute of Medieval Studies, 1952), 15.

great and worthless novelists have depended on the unfailing sentimentalism of the mass of readers. The critical response to literature,
as opposed to reading used for an anodyne, is therefore something
unnatural, tenuous, difficult to learn and to maintain. There is a
similar order of difficulty in acknowledging, other than intellectually, that we are really going to die.

Jaeger's remark that it was only the Christians who taught men
how to take poetry as poetry tells the story, and shows that the
Christians completed what Plato began through the mechanism of
self-alienation. This moderates the easy response of "getting involved" in the work, and turns it into a mirror for us rather than a
mold. The authors we value most are often the ones who not only
enmesh us in their works, but also subtly manage what Shklovsky
called the "baring of the device": reminding us that what we are
reading or seeing is an illusion, a game, a pretense. This tactic has
the intriguing consequence of allowing us to watch our own reactions. Sometimes a work keeps insisting on itself as imaginary, in the
fullest sense of that word, until we begin to understand that something more than a contrast of reality and appearance is being
demonstrated. As Jorge Luis Borges remarks of the *Quixote,* about
the characters revealing their knowledge of the book they are in,
if the fictitious can be readers then the readers can be fictitious.[61]
Here the Yahwist roots of literature are most fully exposed. When
Shakespeare promises us that the "great Globe itself," the theater, the
audience, and the world, will fade away and leave not a rack behind,
he voices the fundamental Yahwist insight into the constructedness
of created things.[62] Not only the fictions but we ourselves are made:

61. Jorge Luis Borges, *Labyrinths: Selected Stories and Other Writings* (New
York: New Directions, 1964), 196.
62. *The Tempest,* IV, i, 148–58. Fredric Jameson, in comparing Brecht's
Verfremdungseffekt with Shklovsky's *ostraneniye,* comments: "For Brecht the primary distinction is . . . between that which is perceived as changeless, eternal,
having no history, and that which is perceived as altering in time and as being
essentially historical in character. The effect of habituation is to make us believe
in the eternity of the present, to strengthen us in the feeling that the things and
events among which we live are somehow 'natural,' which is to say permanent.
The purpose of the Brechtian alienation-effect is . . . to make you aware that the
objects and institutions you thought to be natural were really only historical: the

and something made is not real in its own right, but in that of its maker; so that the easy distinction between real and fictional breaks down.

Fiction, in its literary uses, bears an unsettling resemblance to a historical recounting. It has little relevance to the world of myth: a native informant asked whether the myths of his society were true or fictitious would wonder what the question meant. Bronislav Malinowski says that the myth "in its living primitive form" is "not of the nature of fiction, such as we read to-day in a novel, but . . . is a living reality."[63] For the very concept of fiction does not naturally suggest itself to the human mind; unless practiced assiduously, it is hardly an activity that could be taken for granted. We have no more right to assume that other cultures are as familiar with it as we are, than we have to assume that they are essentially secular. And it can be very useful to consider these two entities, secularism and fiction, as related.

An aside on this point may be helpful. The editor of J. H. Hexter's study of *The Judaeo-Christian Tradition* remarks, truly enough, that "modern Western civilization is radically different from all earlier civilizations, most especially in its secularism, its tendency to relegate religion to a secondary status."[64] Yet, although he is thus aware of the paradox that this secularism is somehow directly obligated to "a past that was deeply religious," he seems to feel no urge to account for the peculiar qualities of a religious tradition that acts in this way. Surely we must conclude that it differed from others?

In the same way, perhaps, the presence of fiction as a live tradition

---

result of change, they themselves henceforth become in their turn changeable" (*The Prison-House of Language,* 58). As Jameson says, the influence of Marx is clear, but what might have influenced Marx?

Cf. above, Barthes on myth, or the discussion of the self-deifying emperors.

63. From Malinowski, *Myth in Primitive Psychology* (1926), quoted in Ellmann and Feidelson (eds.), *The Modern Tradition,* 632. We should be scrupulous not to confuse "multiple truth" in mythological societies with "fiction" as we know it. Ours bears all the marks of coming to birth only as the twin of history: which in the Bible, we remember, has a dissolvent and destructive effect, mocking the "reality" of things taken for granted.

64. Hayden White, in Hexter, *The Judaeo-Christian Tradition,* x and xii.

in the West has its paradoxical generation out of the Old Testament's fanatical insistence on historical truth. Once we examine our past with the question, "Did it really happen?" we have not only the birth of history but that of self-conscious fiction. The Hebrew consciousness searched history for meaning, in terms of God's will. Fiction is a device that allows us to search the possibilities of language in terms of a secularized but not positivistic meaning.

The concept of fiction was resisted by the Greeks, in spite of their flourishing poetry and drama, whereas the Hebrews laid the groundwork for the idea though they had no epic, no drama, and only a restricted, if intense, poetry and prose.[65] There are comparatively few parables *per se*, for instance, in the Old Testament, yet the importance of the concept is shown in the widely accepted analysis of many of the prophets' activities as "acted parables": behavior meant to act out signs corresponding to the prophetic messages. The culmination here comes in the New Testament, for the Gospel portrays Jesus freely and skillfully using parables, both verbal and acted. "Indeed he said nothing to them without a parable."[66] The acted ones, in fact, usually refer to Old Testament paradigms. Throughout most of the Christian centuries part of the rationale for literature was the demonstrable fact that Christ spoke in parables; there was perhaps more in this justification than we think.

Of course parable is not the only form of fiction in the Bible.

---

65. See [Edgar] John Forsdyke, *Greece Before Homer: Ancient Chronology and Mythology* (London: Parrish, 1956), 160–64. Forsdyke comments: "It is easier to understand why these intellectual Greeks rejected fiction in principle than why in practice they accepted so much obvious fiction as historical fact." The reasons for rejecting fiction ranged from "philosophical reverence for truth" to "actual fear of being deceived." Philip Slater in *The Glory of Hera* points out that even today any Greek would rather be the deceiver than the deceived. See his discussion of Greek competitiveness, pp. 36 ff.

My point is that the Hebrews showed no intolerance of fiction as long as it had a sufficiently visionary quality. This criterion we still use, even if we do not recognize it, in separating serious from trivial (or even merely "professional") literature. For us, a person may aspire to be a "professional" musician, actor, or whatever: but if he is a writer, technical skill will never be enough. We judge his inner vision as we would a prophet's message.

66. Matt. 13:34. On "acted parables," see Lindblom, *Prophecy in Ancient Israel*, 165–72.

Many of the Psalms are imaginative recreations of moments of individual anguish, especially the fear of abandonment by Yahweh, or its complement, the sense of being watched. Others are equally dramatized hymns of thanksgiving. Moreover, the genre of the prophetic visions and oracles has been strangely neglected by literary theorists. These rely neither on observations of historical fact nor on mythological affirmations. Whereas the Greeks believed that the gods dealt out to men truths and delusions with a more or less even hand, and that the convictions of individuals were centrally relevant only to themselves, the Hebrews at the same point in history were already developing a belief that Yahweh sent to the prophets true warnings of perils and disasters.[67] If any messages were false they were carried by lying prophets. Yet these true messages are still fictions in the technical sense, imaginative evocations of the fall of princes, destructions of nations, and cataclysms in the earth, or else beatific visions in Isaiah's pastoral oracle of the lion and the ox lying down together, with a little child leading all of nature as a flock.

In the cases where myth does attain something like our fictional quality, as in Homer or the Gilgamesh epic, we find increasing conviction among scholars that these stories have a historical basis. Myth can start from anywhere, of course; but what happens as it develops, and how this development can be differentiated from the growth of fiction in the West, can best be indicated by referring again to Homer, who, as Auerbach says, presents his material with that superb articulation, externalization, and illumination characteristic of a Greek or Egyptian statue. Though his mode familiarizes us with the whole of a complex culture it lacks that immediacy and that historicity so evident in the narratives of Genesis, in which the "ring of truth" is heard not in spite of but in the ambiguity and inconsistency. The continuing theme of the early chapters of *Mimesis* is that classical style, following Homer, became the victim of its own dexterity, ending in the ornate periodic rhetoric of the Latin historians, with their division of styles rigidly tied to a stratified, frozen sense of social class. In the Bible, on the other hand, the

67. See Dodds, *The Greeks and the Irrational*, 10–13.

simple parataxes of the narratives with their underexpressed poignancies—as in David's lament for Absalom—lead straight to the homely, forceful style of the Gospels, where for instance direct discourse is employed in a way unthinkable to classical writers, as ordinary men and women equally with important personages are portrayed as caught up in world-shaking forces.

This is to say that the classical style reflects the petrifaction that put an end to the glittering achievements of the great early civilizations. That a deepening social stratification accompanied the rigidification of mythological traditions has already been extensively argued; this, whereas Homer's fiction at least touches the "real" passions of a warrior aristocracy, the Roman writers can deal with ordinary life only in supercilious comedy and satire, reserving higher styles for higher matters. Christianity shattered this world along fracture lines which made social class irrelevant, just as its writings shattered classical rules of decorum and subordination. Even so learned a writer as Augustine, perfectly at home among the devices of classical style, adapted such devices as parataxis when he wanted vividness. In demonstrating this, Auerbach makes clear how the Bible brought a new kind of life into literature.[68] At the same time, the Christian style inherited that Biblical viewpoint which implicitly judged the culture it portrayed. Whereas Homer and the historians simply accepted their world and its cultures as "given," the Bible and the writers who follow it take a far more critical attitude: the immediacy of their presentation of life accompanies an alienated viewpoint.

Our fiction thus begins with history, and continually twines itself around the concepts of historical truth and meaning. Those of its practitioners who take their art most seriously have stringent views on "the truth" of their writings, though of course their definitions vary. In the eighteenth century a novel may begin by asserting its own truth in contradistinction to all "mere fictions." This amiable

68. See Auerbach, *Mimesis*, esp. 40–41, 61–66, 82: in other editions, the conclusions to the first four chapters. Cf. Amos N. Wilder, *The New Voice: Religion, Literature, Hermeneutics* (New York: Herder and Herder, 1969), esp. 67.

pretense masks an intent that grows more serious as it reappears in the next century. George Eliot felt that she had no more freedom to tamper with her own vision of truth than a witness in a courtroom.[69] The result of this trend, as is widely known, was the proliferation of movements known as Realism and Naturalism, with further reverberation in, for example, Ford Madox Ford's "Impressionism," the law of which was that you could narrate only what you could have known at the time: no long speeches, because you couldn't have remembered them.[70] It becomes apparent that literary truth was getting mixed up with empiricism and the "scientific method." But, although the results do not always do credit to the tradition of literature, all this testifies to the continuing need that writers felt to have their work embody truth. They were not always wise to try to make this truth conform to the notions of their times, and some, like Joyce, wound up playing elaborate jokes with the canons of Naturalism that they inherited (see Hugh Kenner's discussion of Joyce's "counterfeiting").[71] Early in his career Joyce commented that "he is a very bold man who dares to alter in the presentment, still more to deform, whatever he has seen and heard."[72] This is a deliciously ambiguous declaration, for as an artist Joyce was very bold. Nonetheless, even when he was practicing Daedalian arts in an outrageously mechanical manner, Joyce's work can only be understood with the Biblical concepts of historical truth behind it. Our litera-

69. George Eliot, *Adam Bede,* Chap. 17; see the discussion by J. Hillis Miller, "Three Problems of Fictional Form," in Roy Harvey Pearce (ed.), *Experience in the Novel: Selected Papers from the English Institute* (New York: Columbia University Press, 1968), 26 ff. Miller observes that the novel uses "an overlapping or interaction of real and imaginary which is like those optical illusions which may be seen as right-side-up or upside-down, inside-out or outside-in, depending on how they are looked at, and come, as one looks, to vibrate with dizzying rapidity between the first orientation and the second" (p. 29).

70. See Frank MacShane (ed.), *Critical Writings of Ford Madox Ford* (Lincoln: University of Nebraska Press, 1964), "On Impressionism," esp. 36–43 and 67: " 'You must render, never report.' You must never, that is to say, write: 'He saw a man aim a gat at him'; you must put it: 'He saw a steel ring directed at him.' Later you must get in that, in his subconsciousness, he recognized that the steel ring was the polished muzzle of a revolver."

71. Kenner, *The Counterfeiters*, 69–71 and 98 esp.

72. *Ibid.*, 98; cf. Kenner, *The Pound Era*, 49.

ture never has the pure freedom of invention that myth displays. In myth, if the hero needs wings, he simply grows them. In our tradition, by contrast, everything tends to be overdetermined, and Joyce's ingenious elaborate contrivances are the best testimony to this. Kenner has remarked that if we consider Flaubert, Joyce, and Beckett as a kind of Apostolic Succession, we deal with men who went to great pains to give the appearance that they could not improvise a tale by the fireside, not if their lives depended on it.[73] In so doing they pay an oblique and comic but nevertheless profound homage to the Biblical idea of truth.

American authors are particularly liable to treat truth in literature puritanically; Ernest Hemingway, whose convictions about the need and difficulty for fiction to re-create "the way it was" are well known, was intolerant of the last section of *Huckleberry Finn,* since for him it lacked a truth present in the rest of the novel; it was "just cheating."[74] His belief that he could ascertain varying truth-value in a work which, after all, is a fake, derives surely from the Puritan idea of the autonomous conscience. We commonly underestimate the importance of this concept in our culture, but it has moved from the church, where the listener must test what is said from pulpits by his inner response, to our law courts, universities, and private lives. Behind the juries' decisions on the credibility of witnesses, or the student ratings of the effectiveness of teachers, lies the assumption of the verifiability of verbal messages by conviction alone: it is a primitive "lie detector."

This relic of the prophetic mode plays a part in unifying the obviously disparate elements in what the authors cited meant by *truth,* for though it appears most visibly in Americans the Puritan belief is tied up with the emergence of fiction elsewhere too; the novel is a post-Reformation entity. Some Puritans or their forerunners charged poets with being liars, but from Boccaccio and Sidney to our time the apologists for fiction have ably assuaged their

73. See Hugh Kenner, *Flaubert, Joyce, and Beckett: The Stoic Comedians* (Boston: Beacon, 1962), xviii.
74. Ernest Hemingway, *The Green Hills of Africa,* Chap 1.

consciences against this wrongheaded censure, averring that the rhetorical mode of literature exempts it from the standards applied to common speech. They all point in the direction of Picasso's phrase: "Art is a lie that makes us realize truth." The prophets told many of these lies.[75]

To an involuted Puritan like Herman Melville, the concept of truth hidden under the surface of words became so ominous that it seemed capable of holding a vast cosmic secret, that of innate depravity not only in man but in the power that ordained his world. Melville turns Christianity against itself, appositely using the Job story in *Moby Dick* to imply his message. But this tactic only shows the depth of his indebtedness to the Bible. Consider also his famous exposé of Hawthorne's "blackness," which he praises by comparing it to Shakespeare's:

But it is those deep, far-away things in him; those occasional flashings-forth of the intuitive Truth in him; those short, quick probings at the very axis of reality,—these are the things that make Shakespeare, Shakespeare. Through the mouths of the dark characters of Hamlet, Timon, Lear, and Iago, he craftily says, or sometimes insinuates the things which we feel to be so terrifically true that it were all but madness for any good man, in his own proper character, to utter, or even hint of them. Tormented into desperation, Lear, the frantic king, tears off the mask, and speaks the sane madness of vital truth.[76]

What Lear says is so exactly in the prophetic mode, so obviously drawn from prophetic unmasking of human hypocrisy, gratuitous cruelty, lust and greed in the guise of justice, that his "vital truth" is unerringly identifiable as a Yahwist legacy: "Thou hotly lust'st to use her in that kind / For which thou whip'st her" might have been said by Jeremiah. If we search literature for these flashes of "sane madness," we find many, for as Eliot concluded of Pascal, "A man of great and intense intellectual powers . . . cannot avoid seeing

75. Picasso, see note 46 to Chapter One herein; Sidney, *A Defence of Poesy* (or *Apology for Poetry*), 1595; Boccaccio, Books 14 and 15 of the *Genealogia Deorum Gentilium*, trans. Charles G. Osgood as *Boccaccio on Poetry* (New York: Liberal Arts Press, 1956).

76. "Hawthorne and His *Mosses*," *Literary World*, 1850; reprinted in Edmund Wilson, *The Shock of Recognition* (New York: Grosset and Dunlap, 1955), 192–93.

through human beings," nor can he avoid seeing, in the arbitrariness of their supposedly necessary social structures, a universal tendency toward injustice which he may, if so inclined, trace back to the original constitution of things. Melville thought he could see through the cosmos; but he identifies himself with the prophets when he calls this kind of vision "truth."

We need not be literal-minded in following Melville's hints, however. What of the joyful affirming visions? They too, of course, have antecedents in the prophets. What of comedy? Though most of it depends on the alienated viewpoint, what of the happier kinds? Literature abounds in celebrations simply of the palpability or grittiness of life—yet these in their own way are demythologizations of various pretensions. Well then, what about literary art for the sheer joy of it? Fantasy, which might seem to escape from the duty of truth-telling, reveals its strong affinities to Biblical patterns of history, truth, and fictiveness when analyzed by its most widely respected contemporary practitioner, J. R. R. Tolkien. "For creative fantasy is founded upon the hard recognition that things are so in the world as it appears under the sun; on a recognition of fact, but not a slavery to it. . . . Fantasy remains a human right: we make in our measure and in our derivative mode, because we are made: and not only made, but made in the image and likeness of a Maker." For Tolkien, fantasy stands in a creative relation to our sense of reality, giving rise to a "secondary world" in which truth becomes transmuted into joy through the presence of unexpected reversals in the story:

[Fantasy] does not deny the existence of *dyscatastrophe*, of sorrow and failure: the possibility of these is necessary to the joy of deliverance; it denies (in the face of much evidence, if you will) universal final defeat and in so far is *evangelium*, giving a fleeting glimpse of Joy, Joy beyond the walls of the world, poignant as grief. . . . In such stories when the sudden "turn" comes we get a piercing glimpse of joy, and heart's desire, that for a moment passes outside the frame, rends the very web of story, and lets a gleam come through. . . . The peculiar quality of the "joy" in successful Fantasy can thus be explained as a sudden glimpse of the underlying reality or truth. It is not only a "consolation" for the sorrow of this world, but a satisfaction, and an answer to that question, "Is it true?"

We might see here the influence of the view that art reveals the *logos*, but Tolkien derives the "turn," or *eucatastrophe*, from the Biblical (here specifically Christian) sense of history, taken in the sense not of demonstrable but of unexpectedly self-validating truth:

> But in the "eucatastrophe" we see in a brief vision that the answer may be greater—it may be a far-off gleam or echo of *evangelium* in the real world. . . . The Birth of Christ is the eucatastrophe of Man's history. The Resurrection is the eucatastrophe of the story of the Incarnation. This story begins and ends in joy. It has pre-eminently the "inner consistency of reality." There is no tale ever told that men would rather find was true, and none which so many sceptical men have accepted as true on its own merits. For the Art of it has the supremely convincing tone of Primary Art, that is of Creation.[77]

Of course Tolkien's own religious belief must be taken into account here, but note that he suggests that the Christian story be judged as a fiction or acted parable, so as to see it as "true on its own merits." As a fiction it is dependent on that suggestive improbability, "upon incertitude, upon unlikelihood," that gives the paradoxical conviction of reality. *Credo quia absurdum.*

This view of literature's relation to truth does not dissipate that consciousness of the evasiveness of meaning to which Derrida points. Although Tolkien's way of putting things would seem to him hopelessly nostalgic, Derrida must have a certain fondness for fantasy: his conviction that language signifies regardless of referents leads him to assert that the condition for a true act of language is to be able to say "I am dead."[78] In any case, nothing in Tolkien's words, or in those of the other authors cited, suggests that meaning or truth is anything but a transient, painfully difficult achievement, in literature or anywhere else. Tolkien speaks of "fleeting" glimpses, of far-off gleams, of a momentary passing "outside the frame." The effect he describes turns on a sense of evasiveness of meaning. Surely all would agree, and so would the Bible, that reality is not something we can casually grasp, any more than we can seize the meaning of a text. The limits of the fictitious are not well marked: "Accustomed

77. From *Tree and Leaf* (1964), reprinted in Lincoln (ed.), *Pastoral and Romance*, 204–207.
78. See Macksey and Donato (eds.), *The Languages of Criticism*, 155–56.

as we are to the form letter, the mechanically reproduced signature, the edited Congressional Record, the doctored tape recording, the Xerox copy . . . the documentary film with every scene carefully staged," we are in no position to be facile on this matter.[79] We live surrounded by lesser fictions of our own making, short-lived myths, a fact which is demonstrated more perceptively in fiction than anywhere else. Twentieth-century psychology, with its insistence on the active rather than passive nature of perception, has pretty well validated the old Romantic and Kantian notion of the "creative imagination." We make the world we see out of hints and clues; we do not merely take in what is given from the outside. If our perceptible world is thus a construct, and therefore largely fictional, our explanations of it are no less: what of the role of fiction in science's hypotheses? We speak of chemical "bonds," of elementary "particles": clearly metaphorical language. The "model" of the atom is just that, an extended metaphor, an allegory. Given all this, it should be impossible for us to equate the fictional with the unreal. In the end, as in their early appearances in the Bible, fiction and history murmur to each other: "Mon semblable—mon frère!" And the theme of reconciliation of estranged kin is of the essence of the New Testament, as revealed in the most joyous of all parables, that of the Prodigal Son.

METAPHOR AND METONYMY, NECESSARY AND CONTINGENT, CYBERNETIC AND KERYGMATIC

> Yet I speak of an art . . . weary of its puny exploits, weary of pretending to be able, of being able, of doing a little better the same old thing, [preferring] the expression that there is nothing to express, nothing with which to express, nothing from which to express, no power to express, no desire to express, together with the obligation to express.
>
> —Samuel Beckett

If we look back over our heritage, we find that the massive efforts to translate the Bible (and literature too) into metaphysical concepts

79. Kenner, *The Counterfeiters*, 97.

have invariably exposed some intractability in the material. The Hellenizing Fathers never saw their formulations attain the once-and-for-all validity they sought. To refer again to the words of Kornelis Miskotte, *Being, causality,* and *process* (in the sense of the working-out of givens) are inadequate terms for God and his acts: and the "gravely passionate negations" that disqualify these terms are "simply inherent in the fundamental structure of the Bible."[80] The key point is that such negations are not regretful. The Bible does not depend on that "sad, *negative,* nostalgic, guilty, Rousseauist" sense of loss, of falling away from "the nature of things," that Derrida dispraises in Lévi-Strauss, nor the latter's "ethic of presence . . . of nostalgia for origins . . . [for] archaic and natural innocence." The laments of the prophets for Israel's faithlessness are not of that kind. Nor is there a Biblical ethic of "a purity of presence and self-presence in speech."[81] When the prophet says "The heart is more devious than any other thing, perverse too: who can pierce its secrets?" he seems to make finally ludicrous the effort to find communion of souls through speech.[82] His words are preserved in writing, the fitting form for the alienated insight.

If we react to the Bible in a would-be Fundamentalist way, so as to "live like an exile the necessity of interpretation," then we are dreaming "of full presence, the reassuring foundation," believing that time and change have "sullied the original transparency of Revelation."[83] But the Revelation was never transparent. Ezekiel believed that God had given Israel bad laws to test them, and Paul stated flatly that the Law propagated sin. Even in the stories of the kings, the Yahwist Micaiah has a vision of God allowing a spirit to

80. Miskotte, *When the Gods Are Silent,* 14.

81. Derrida, "Structure, Sign, and Play," in Macksey and Donato (eds.), *The Languages of Criticism,* 264.

82. Jer. 17:9.

83. Derrida, "Structure, Sign, and Play," in Macksey and Donato (eds.), *The Languages of Criticism,* 264; Fredric Jameson, "Metacommentary," PMLA, 86 (January, 1971), 15. See again Kenner, on the hermetic nature of parables; also the Gnostic belief that after the resurrection Jesus had tarried to provide the Gnostics with the true esoteric interpretation of his otherwise unintelligible riddles (in the *Apocryphon of James;* see James M. Robinson, *The Nag Hammadi Codices* (Claremont, Calif.: Institute for Antiquity and Christianity, 1974), 10.

animate the mouths of lying prophets, so that Ahab may be tempted to his fall.

These points might give us a new sense of what interpretation is. By now most of us realize that if we try to deal with texts "unmediatedly," we wind up as Know-Nothings, victims of rancid readings born of paradigms and schemata we refuse to recognize as such. The attempt to avoid interpretation altogether brings back to mind Gombrich's remarks on "trying to forget." Apart from the Biblical pattern of vividness and distancing, where meaning is re-experienced yet always already happened, the concept of "immediacy" is debilitating. Nowadays in literary criticism it reappears, full of overtones of mythic communions, serving as pretext for snide remarks about the difference between knowing from "the inside" and knowing from "the outside": part of the familiar litany against alienation. The Gospel comment is "Fools! Did not he who made the outside make the inside too?"[84] Knowledge is a Moebius strip: both "sides" are constructs.

But we must be even more vigilant against another enemy of interpretation, namely the myth of progress. The decay of accepted readings may mislead us into thinking we move ever closer to truth; this delusion is one of the self-glorifications of the autonomous consciousness or "modern mind." What this decay really means, however, is that all readings are misreadings, which time progressively exposes. The situation is analogous to that in detecting art forgeries: those of any given time can if well done fool all of its period's critics, but a mere generation or two suffices to reveal the invariable "period style" in the work of even the most self-effacing forger. A meticulous copy of Vermeer painted in the era of Cezanne differs from one turned out in the age of Pollock. Hence our contempt for nineteenth-century critics is almost unbounded, and we laugh ourselves sick over Nahum Tate's adaptations of Shakespeare. It becomes obvious that paradigms in criticism, and in literature, disintegrate with the same alacrity as those in science. As how should they not, given "sacred discontent"?

84. Luke 11:40.

Paul de Man and many others have insisted recently that literature and criticism are not different in nature, precisely because they are both interpretations involving deconstructive acts. "A literary text simultaneously asserts and denies the authority of its own rhetorical mode. . . . Poetic writing is the most advanced and refined mode of deconstruction; it may differ from critical or discursive writing in the economy of its articulation, but not in kind."[85] De Man's occasion for the assertion was his reading of a passage from Proust, which he analyzed with the help of Roman Jakobson's classification of metaphor and metonymy as the two poles of the linguistic act: without going into Jakobson's argument, it is possible to appropriate these terms to delineate a series of suggestive distinctions.[86]

De Man analyzes his passage from Proust by suggesting that the "poetic" metaphors in which young Marcel, the narrator, evokes the "actual, persistent, unmediated presence" of a summer's day arrogate a metaphysical function to lift themselves above metonymic prose:

Here it is the substitutive totalization by metaphor which is said to be more effective than the mere contiguity of metonymic association. As opposed to the random contingency of metonymy ("par hasard"), the metaphor is linked to its proper meaning by, says Proust, the "necessary link" that leads to perfect synthesis. . . . The passage acts out and asserts the priority of metaphor over metonymy in terms of the categories of metaphysics and with reference to the act of reading.[87]

Metaphor seeks to be a totalizing, closed act asserting shared essence, but metonymy displays endlessness, arbitrariness, hence the basic problematic of language and interpretation.

We can easily see, once de Man shows it to us, that theologizing tendency in Proust's metaphors which Derrida finds in Ferdinand de Saussure, Lévi-Strauss, and others who think they have just freed themselves from theology, and which is ascribed to complicity in the metaphysical heritage. But the words also remind us of the mytho-

85. Paul de Man, "Semiology and Rhetoric," *Diacritics,* III (Fall, 1973), 32.

86. The relevant text is "Two Aspects of Language and Two Types of Aphasic Disturbances," in Roman Jakobson, *Fundamentals of Language,* with Morris Halle (The Hague: Mouton, 1971), 69–96.

87. de Man, "Semiology and Rhetoric," 31.

logical consciousness and its belief in access to power and divinity: especially because metaphor is a fundamental mode of what was for the Hebrews idol-worship. The pagan gods were embodied in forms that were metaphors of their power, "necessary links": *e.g.,* Baal is really in the storm, and it expresses his nature. But Yahweh, we remember, is never in any of his appearances, only behind them, and they are arbitrary not necessary links: they neither express his power nor furnish analogies to it. They tell us not *what* he is, but *that* he is.[88] Yahweh is known only by displacement, *i.e.,* in his acts.

In other words, metaphor tends to invite sacralization, covert or otherwise; but metonymy keeps reminding us of "random contingency" and arbitrariness in the world's relationships. We might say it invited secularization, if that term were free of its own idols. De Man goes on to show that in the Proust passage a sort of subterranean flow of metonymy undercuts the metaphorical edifice being constructed above: hence the work "simultaneously asserts and denies the authority of its own rhetorical mode." For him this confirms Derrida's critique of the "ethic of presence," the metaphysical self-delusion: but might it not be equally well described as an example of self-demythologizing in literature?

De Man's demonstration is intended as a rebuke to certain tendencies of structuralist critics, and he wants to insist that the imperfect fit of grammar to rhetoric opens up again a problem which used to be considered that of authorial intention: "Rhetoric radically suspends logic and opens up vertiginous possibilities of referential aberration. And although it would perhaps be somewhat more remote from common usage, I would not hesitate to equate the rhetorical, figural potentiality of language with literature itself."[89] The structuralists have put in question many former conceptions about the author or the speaker of a literary discourse; yet the problem cannot be settled by eliminating the author, retreating behind a slogan like "language speaks through us," which would be to treat literature as myth. Because of its escape from logical and referential

88. I owe this formulation to Jesse Gellrich.
89. de Man, "Semiology and Rhetoric," 30.

limitations we must in some way deal with the "figural potentiality of language" in literature, often when the linguistic clues alone are ambiguous. Hugh Kenner has done precisely this in *The Counterfeiters,* pointing out for instance that the Epistle "To Augustus" is not satirical at all unless signed "A. Pope." Signed "Ambrose Phillips" it must be read as a "torrent of adulation."[90] Perhaps as important as the author's intention (or even his unconscious tendencies which might, for example, make his images contradict his statements) is the possibility set forth in Isaiah, of going beyond the oracularly ambiguous to messages that must be misunderstood by the complacent. Once literature was aware of the possibility, all its de-totalizing tendencies could come to the fore.

For various reasons the twentieth century is a good time to make these observations, one of them being that the giants of modern literature struggle with language as Jacob wrestled against God, deriving thus his true name. This *agon* was mandatory—whether for Joyce, whose tremendous fluency did not prevent him from spending a day on two sentences and seventeen years on a book, or for William Carlos Williams, labeled by Pound *"the* most bloody inarticulate animal that ever gargled," who revised these apparently artless lines at least seven times:

> Easy girl You'll blow
> a fuse if ya keep
> that up.[91]

Because these authors were so conscious of the opportunities and despairs opened to them by language's Protean slipperiness, they barred themselves from using it simply to "communicate" along utilitarian and uniformitarian lines, eschewing the supposed ideals of fluency and clarity. Even our proliferation of glib "readings" of their work does them a disservice. Their notorious difficulty arose from no coterie impulses, as Tolstoy would have suspected, but rather from a vivid sense of the multifarious contingencies, the com-

---

90. Kenner, *The Counterfeiters,* 93.

91. *Ibid.,* 169; D. D. Paige (ed.,) *The Letters of Ezra Pound, 1907–1941* (New York: Harcourt, Brace, 1950), 131.

plexity and precariousness of meaning, and of the frequency of falls into so-called meanings that are merely old schemata being shuffled around. From their work, we know that we will never be able magically to dispose of the subject-object problem or any of the other forms in which the dilemma of language shows itself.

In Biblical writing, in which metaphor does not predominate, this dilemma of ambiguities, disintegrations, and misinterpretations is kept constantly before us: the people receive the message, and immediately rationalize it away. Because of its ever-present awareness of discontinuity, Biblical writing fails to establish anything like the world of linked analogies and correspondences natural to the divinatory mode and to *la pensée sauvage* in general. A cosmology of hierarchic continuities, as in mythological thought, exhibits strong metaphorical tendencies. The enmeshing and interlocking of structures is coherently expressed in poetic evocation of transferable, substitutable qualities and names. In this world, movement tends to round itself into totalization, impelled by the principle of closure: as Santayana said of himself, it yearns to complete circles. But all this contrasts sharply with a world conceived on metonymic lines: Jakobson relates the contiguities of metonymy to the relatively open, tangential, and untotalized relationships of syntax: this association with prosaic point-to-point movement, rather than with the harmonics of poetic evocation, suggests in turn the modes of narrative and of history: in short, of the Bible, where events break away from old orders along nonhierarchic lines. Where myth is hypotactic metaphors, the Bible is paratactic metonymies.

Giambattista Vico is reported to have said that every metaphor is a short myth. This holds in spite of some necessary updatings and revisions. For although Lévi-Strauss has demonstrated that the mythological thinking called totemism, for example, does not depend on supposed resemblances, but rather on systematically differentiated identifications, we are still in the world of metaphor. A man called a "lion in war" is really being differentiated from other warriors, but in the ancient world, the tendency to hypostasize differences by establishing identifications and mystic participations was always strong; metaphors always seemed on the verge of asserting shared essence and continuity. This is what Bruno Snell finds by examining animal metaphors in Homer and later texts: they still show some traces of Paleolithic animal cults, and in fact reflect a belief that animals are more constant in their natures than men.

The idea that some men are of the same order as certain animals is extremely old; but despite some survivals of primitive beliefs among the Greeks, such as animal-shaped gods, animal disguises in cult, and tales about the animal ancestors of certain clans, the crude concepts of a totemic era, if such a one ever existed, had dropped out long before Homer. And yet, Homer's animal similes are more than merely ways of catching a mood or an impression. . . . The warrior and the lion are activated by the same force [*menos,* the forward impulse]; and thus a man who walks "like a lion" betrays an actual kinship with the beast.

. . . .

The sentence: "Hector is as a lion," besides constituting a comparison, besides focussing the formlessness of human existence against a characteristic type, also signalizes a factual connexion.[92]

This belief in real kinship can be seen as weighty evidence for the implication that mythic immediacy turns on what de Man calls "naive metaphorical mystification." But if de Man is correct, literature works against the grain of that impulse, and performs an act of deconstruction on itself: or as he says elsewhere, it is demystified from the start.

With metonymy, the role of arbitrariness cannot be disguised. It tells not what something is by what essences it shares, but can only

92. Snell, *The Discovery of the Mind,* 201–203. Cf. John A. Wilson in Frankfort *et al., Before Philosophy,* 71, and Thorkild Jacobsen on 215: "It is one of the tenets of mythopoeic logic that similarity and identity merge; 'to be like' is as good as 'to be.'" Lévi-Strauss, in *The Savage Mind,* p. 263, says that "savage thought can be defined as analogical thought"; in *The Raw and the Cooked* he asserts that myth's logic of sensations "makes no clear-cut distinction between subjective states and the properties of the cosmos" (p. 240); on p. 339, he says that "thanks to myths, we discover that metaphors are based on an intuitive sense of the logical relations between one realm and other realms. . . . Metaphor, far from being a decoration that is added to language, purifies it and restores it to its original nature, through momentarily obliterating one of the innumerable synecdoches that make up speech." This is negative and guilty (though highly subtle) Rousseauism.

point to the thing by saying what it is not: hence it is a *via negativa*. It cannot lend itself to elaborate systems of correspondences or chains of identifications. Metonymy, unless it degenerates into mere circumlocutions, stresses contingency not necessity. Now it happens that Lévi-Strauss lays out the similarities and differences of *la pensée sauvage* to Western science in terms of "the distinction between the contingent and the necessary," which serves to distinguish "event and structure." In his view, savage thought approaches science by reaching for structures, but unlike science it constructs these only in the process of constantly rearranging images in myth—images which are left over from exploration and classification of the world "in sensible terms." He tries to show that art is "half-way between scientific knowledge and mythical or magical thought." Thus:

> The creative act which gives rise to myths is in fact exactly the reverse of that which gives rise to works of art. In the case of works of art, the starting point is a set of one or more objects and one or more events which aesthetic creation unifies by revealing a common structure. Myths travel the same road but start from the other end. They use a structure to produce what is itself an object consisting of a set of events (for all myths tell a story). Art thus proceeds from a set (object & event) to the *discovery* of its structure. Myth starts from a structure by means of which it *constructs* a set (object & event).[93]

We could improve this formula along these lines: art looks toward structure only to test and probe it; Lévi-Strauss's description really applies only to medieval or other mythologized arts, for he has missed Gombrich's points about the sacred discontent that dismantles the schema. The "individualizing" trend, the realism, in postmedieval art shows itself in the fact that interested Browning, that Fra Lippo Lippi painted a real girl, not an ideal Virgin: an event, not a structure.

Nonetheless the picture's interest is not in the girl herself. The picture is an anatomy of an event by means of various examined and provisionally used structures. Might it not be said that art, and literature, are opposites of science (as well as myth) in that for them

93. Lévi-Strauss, *The Savage Mind*, 21, 22, 16, 25–26.

the event is "the necessary," while the structures are contingent? Some such reversal of priorities is clear in the Western use of images, with their constant respect for the liveliness, and thus the transience, of events, as opposed to passive acceptance of the schemata. Shklov-sky's points suggest that art tries to capture not the idealized experi-ence but the process of its unidealized perception. In our art and literature, because of the constant demythologizing of structures, the contingent becomes itself what is necessary.

To some extent Lévi-Strauss himself anticipates this line of thought; he goes on about the "integration" of the contingent in three separate aspects of a work of art, "either with the *model* or with the *materials* or with the future *user*." But he does not think of the parallel with Biblical history, dependent on and drawing its very meaning from the contingency of events. By this route we may return to the question of aesthetic truth, even perhaps to Tolkien's notion of the affinity between art and Creation and between the *evangelium* and fiction.

If literature does not model itself on myth (even though it may for its own purposes use a variety of mythic techniques), what is its ulti-mate model? Bultmann and the other theologians who have given the term *demythologization* its currency have usually opposed kerygma to myth, and Paul Ricoeur has told Lévi-Strauss to his face, without receiving a pertinent reply, that structuralism is misapplied to Western materials because we are a kerygmatic not a cybernetic society.[94] The kerygma is the *evangelium,* the preaching of the Gospel, but is also the prophetic mode of proclamation: it has much of interest as a model for literature.

As John Barth might say, the key to the treasure is the treasure. The key here is the contrast of the kerygmatic to the cybernetic. In historical terms, the kerygma presents us not with any metaphysical or positivist truth, measured by something extrinsic, but asserts that a new word, saving yet demanding, has been uttered. Against its background, such an utterance is world-shattering. For in the mytho-logical world, even in the austere form rationalized into the classical

94. *Esprit,* No. 322 (November, 1963), 652–53.

logos, the function of the word can never be really new: it can only validate what has gone before, and is thus cybernetic, a feedback loop that confirms again and again the structure and functioning of things. The kerygmatic *logos* is the exact opposite: it disconfirms structure. The very event is itself the message, a performative utterance in the fullest sense, an "acted parable" whose acting is its meaning. That the Word is made Flesh is itself the Word. Not only can it be said that the man is the message—to paraphrase McLuhan, the message is the message.

In the cybernetic circle, all utterances simply say that the channels are clear, that the cosmic continuum is rocking right along; or at most they are utilized for the great machine's self-adjusting mechanisms. Myths merely think things through (Lévi-Strauss says that myths think themselves in men's minds without their being aware of it) in infinitely variable but kaleidoscopic patterns. No events disturb the function; at bottom there are no events in the mythological world, not in the Biblical-historical sense. As Frankfort remarks, in Egypt only the changeless is significant. The new event would be like the new word: inconceivable. Myth repeats endlessly the refrain that Lévi-Strauss poses for the Oedipus sequences: "Although experience contradicts theory, social life validates cosmology by its similarity of structure. Hence cosmology is true."[95] The Bible never accepted this: in it, social order never replicates cosmology; indeed the last shall be first. Thus the cybernetic circle was broken by the Bible, and the kerygma was the decisive sundering.

Cybernetic communication did not thereby disappear, least of all in the West: our frenetic using-up of myths makes it more needful than ever. We must have some cultural glue to replace what myth provided; we now get it from the operation of great cliché-circulators —magazines and newspapers, TV entertainment and TV commercials and TV news, the educational system, the platitudes of the business world, the social whirl. From all these arenas comes good "news" that appeals to our self-image, while the bad conforms to

95. Lévi-Strauss, *Structural Anthropology,* 212; cf. Lévi-Strauss, *The Raw and the Cooked,* 12.

conventional alarmisms. They all act to "bring us together" and avoid confrontation with self.

There are those who will object that the cult of "pop" evades this structure by being subversive. There are even busy gurus who make good money on lecture circuits telling audiences that their vulgar tastes in entertainment have profound social implications. But this is to mistake charisma for kerygma. Soap operas and rock music and *Playboy* may fill social needs, may even be enjoyable occasionally, but their function is really to reinforce in-group self-esteem. A noted pop spokesman, Greil Marcus, sums it up: "POP is a sense that someone else is missing something, but you're not."[96] Pop asserts the exuberance of the young and mocks the incomprehension of elders, but its antisocial quality is all on the surface, consisting basically of the cruelty that any group of children normally shows to outsiders. Its defining image is that of Tom Wolfe's Pump House Gang. Thus it is of a piece with that literature which Stanley Fish calls "rhetorical," as opposed to "self-consuming."

A presentation is rhetorical if it satisfies the needs of its readers. The word "satisfies" is meant literally here; for it is characteristic of a rhetorical form to mirror and present for approval the opinions its readers already hold. It follows then that the experience of such a form will be flattering, for it tells the reader that what he has always thought about the world is true and that the *ways* of his thinking are sufficient. This is not to say that in the course of a rhetorical experience one is never told anything unpleasant, but that whatever one is told can be placed and contained within the categories and assumptions of received systems of knowledge.[97]

To be sure, the *Narrenfreiheit* of pop is a safety valve for fretfulness among the populace, and it can give the appearance of being subversive. But the people, the mass, is never revolutionary (sometimes a mob will run amok with a prophetic idea, as Norman Cohn shows in his *Pursuit of the Millennium*). Mass culture seeks mass homeostasis. Today's young terrorists frustratedly find that they are hated

96. Quoted in John Gordon Burke (ed.), *Print, Image, and Sound: Essays on Media* (Chicago: American Library Association, 1972), 66.
97. Stanley Fish, *Self-Consuming Artifacts: The Experience of Seventeenth-Century Literature* (Berkeley: University of California Press, 1972), 1.

by the workers they claim to fight for. The frustration helps explain their witless violence.

Serious literature is a different proposition. Typically it does not proclaim orgiastic or portentous aims, but much more modest ones: perhaps nothing more than the desire to lock words together in such a way as to sharpen our sense of the way language interacts with the world. Yet it is not cybernetic or rhetorical; even in its most innocuous forms it asks us to question our experience rather than take it for granted: it sets ajar, however slightly, our settled verbal universe. Compare Wallace Stevens' lines: "It was snowing / And it was going to snow"[98] with some pseudorevolutionary rant from the world of Pop. Which one is in Fish's terms "self-consuming"? The nostalgic evocation in the Stevens image, the sense that we've seen those afternoons before, does not prevent it from belonging to that kind of art that "undermines certainty and moves away from clarity, complicating what had at first seemed perfectly simple, raising more problems than it solves."[99] Whereas the other is "self-satisfying": it flatters our vigilante fantasies about being street-fightin' men, or whatever.

As Ricoeur says, Lévi-Strauss thinks that all communication is cybernetic, mythological or not: what we say to each other never really means anything, but serves to fulfill and adjust social and natural structures we're hardly conscious of. We do need the cybernetic: some evidence shows that persons deprived for long of its kind of "news" can suffer acute anxieties, symptoms of sensory deprivation. But if all communication were cybernetic, what Reinhold Niebuhr asks of determinisms would be equally relevant here: if this were true, how would we know it? That such a view can be proclaimed shows the possibility of another kind of communication, the kerygmatic, and of course Lévi-Strauss is one more in the long series of those who borrow the prophetic mode without acknowledging it. Despite his views about the content of it, the fact (or even possibility) of his message is the message.

98. "Thirteen Ways of Looking at a Blackbird." Stevens is a prime example of a poet who preaches a revelation. That the revelation is agnostic does not disqualify it from the prophetic mode.

99. Fish, *Self-Consuming Artifacts*, 378.

A tendency to see all communication as cybernetic may easily arise from overabsorption in studying the habits of oral cultures; for although the kerygma is frequently treated as a phenomenon dependent on oral, face-to-face persuasion, its inner life is in writing, and oral cultures thoroughly exemplify the cybernetic. Father Walter Ong, normally a partisan of the oral, tells us that "an oral culture does not *put* its knowledge into mnemonic patterns: it *thinks* it in mnemonic patterns. There is no other way for it to proceed effectively. An oral culture does not merely have a quaint liking for proverbs or 'sayings' of all sorts: it is absolutely dependent on them. Clichés constitute its thought. Constant repetition of the known is the major noetic exercise."[100] In such a world, the kerygma literally cannot be heard; where the individual is perfectly integrated into his culture and its constantly circulated but minimally varied knowledge, no "new word" can penetrate. The kerygmatic cannot come to birth without long preparation by the earlier-remarked demolition of cliché, formula, and proverb, so that the prevailing self-satisfaction of oral culture can be undermined. Failure to grasp this point seems largely due to our recurrent habit of sacralizing orality, roughly parallel to the elevation of "the natural." Derrida's analysis of "grammatology" has sufficiently exposed this tendency, with most persuasive (graphic?) demonstrations from the writings of Lévi-Strauss. As with the Nambikwara, so with the oral: in spite of strenuous efforts Lévi-Strauss cannot resist projecting them onto a metaphysical plane. Oedipus-like, he flees this fate, but runs right to it.

Yet his own classifications can remind us that, in the kerygma as in literature, the event is what is necessary, whereas the structures, or at least the schemata through which the kerygma can be apprehended, are contingent and provisional. The Messianic and other expectations are useful *preparatio*, but are not the "Christ-event" as

100. Ong, "Agonistic Structures in Academia Past to Present," *Interchange*, V (1974), 2. Cf., *e.g.*, James M. Robinson, "Kerygma and History in the New Testament," in Hyatt (ed.), *The Bible in Modern Scholarship*, 119: "Rather than the saving event simply being described as it happened, to some extent it happened as it was described. . . . The saving event cannot be shelled out as a brute fact behind the language witnessing to it." Cf. also Walker Percy's treatment of "news" (kerygma) as opposed to "knowledge" in the title essay of *The Message in the Bottle* (New York: Farrar, Straus, and Giroux, 1975).

the theologians speak of it; nor are they metaphors for it: in the end, they lead to it only by a kind of pointing rather than a sharing of essences, for the very definition of that event is that it exceeds all possible expectations. Of course Snell's point about believers ready to have their faith refreshed by paradox is relevant; but this readiness is not a form of preunderstanding.[101]

Moreover, although word, event, and meaning all coincide in the kerygma as in some ideal act of language, interpretation is apparent from the beginning, not made necessary by any defect in the message, yet somehow intrinsic to the act all the same. For the message is no more self-evident than it was predictable. Precisely because it exceeds the most grandiose expectations, yet appeared in the humblest manifestations imaginable, those who should have been ready to hear the Word failed to understand it.

Where myth is an encoding, the kerygma is a decoding. Only interpretation can reveal the sacred in the banal.

The last formula can describe our fiction too. Note the habit of the novel of finding the rich significance of epic events in quotidian, even trivial material. Paz has remarked: "It is well known that epic poetry uses myth as its raw material or argument and that the decline of the epic genre (or rather: its metamorphosis into the novel) is due to the relative decline of myths in the West."[102] The novel uses not myth but a "random [n.b.] fusillade of information."[103] Often it has the appearance of a *tour de force,* when it emphasizes the randomness. But even where it finds something like the sacral (in the form of its power to signify) in banal and random event, the novel is a demythologizing because of its tacit relation to epic predecessors.

The novel shows that mythologization is not needed to make things into utterances, or the book into a *langue*. For in certain ways it seems to work toward proving that events or things can be stripped of all metaphysical pretensions whatsoever, and still func-

101. See note 20 above.
102. Paz, *Claude Lévi-Strauss*, 77.
103. Kenner, *The Counterfeiters*, 65.

tion. In this sense one of the goals of fiction is that vision that haunts Beckett as it haunted Flaubert, and Henry James, and James Joyce: the story in which "nothing happens."[104] The achievement of works like *Waiting for Godot* stands as a rebuke to the adventure story, but also to something far more important and insidious—our tendency to assert that we can easily or habitually measure the significance of events.

Just this inclusion of interpretative tendencies marks our literature as different from myth and strikingly like kerygma. For myths stand in a wholly inimical relation to interpretation: we who are so eager to interpret myths thereby denature them, as Lévi-Strauss recognizes.[105] We may repeat Auerbach's comment: Homer may be "analyzed but not interpreted." Myth and interpretation meet like matter and antimatter.

To complete this train of thought we must consider the nature of the event which the kerygma articulates. In the first place its eruption into history distinguishes it from myth, which takes place in "dreamtime," or Mircea Eliade's *illud tempus,* or Giedion's "eternal present."[106] But as a consequence the event must suffer the metaphysical deprivation that history entails: Jesus must be both God and man, not merely a god in a man's disguise. Ultimately this "puts in question" the status of the event as a Transcendental Signified (Derrida's term). Thus it is far easier to say, with Eliot's Magus, that there was an event than to say what the event was. One could suggest that those who believe that, because it happened in history, its nature can be established are incipient positivists. If we could even say the event was "true," in the sense in which the positivist thinks his so-called facts are true, then we could set about legalistically determining the probabilities as to its nature. But the whole point

---

104. Cf. Kenner on the "Stoic Comedians," and Jean Rousset, "*Madame Bovary* or the Book about Nothing," reprinted in Raymond Giraud (ed.), *Flaubert: A Collection of Critical Essays* (Englewood Cliffs, N. J.: Prentice-Hall, 1964), esp. 113.

105. Lévi-Strauss, *The Raw and the Cooked,* 12.

106. Cf. Leach, *Genesis as Myth,* 29; Giedion, *Eternal Present, passim;* Mircea Eliade, *The Sacred and the Profane: The Nature of Religion,* trans. W. R. Trask (1957; rpt. New York: Harper, 1961), 80.

of the event would seem to be that it entered the world of contingency fully and unhesitatingly. Precisely this quality made it a rupture with all the old structures of the metaphorical-mythological world. Even the metaphor of "Sonship," as already argued, firmly implies dependence and contingency. Thus, to view the event as the "reassuring foundation," the "full presence," is to conceive it in a way tending toward positivism.[107] That positivism as such is a creature of a simplified notion of the Biblical insistence on historical truth cannot be denied, but what reason is there to take the parent at the perverse child's valuation?

The dilemma is an old one in the Judaeo-Christian tradition: whether to regard the event primarily as that which founds and centers new structures or as that which broke away so radically from former structures as to put in question all possible new ones. If the first view were correct, we might conceive the event's meaning as the removal of successive layers of concealment or illusion: but in the event, the veil of the Temple was torn asunder, not removed so as to reveal what was behind it. As the tomb was empty, so was—or should have been, by Yahwist precept—the Holy of Holies.

By this reasoning we should proceed, perfectly respectfully, to see the kerygma as a fiction: in several ways, including Tolkien's, or as all but the least sophisticated New Testament scholars now do. Such a process opens fearful chasms under the feet of positivistically-minded believers. Every fictionalizing of the kerygma produces unrest. The authorities of Elizabethan England, wisely in their own eyes, pretty nearly banned Biblical subjects from their drama, obviously deducing that the Medieval play-cycles with their dramatizations of the Bible must have had something to do with the turbulence of the Reformation.

Naturally such conceptions of the kerygma, whatever their motive, pose a danger to institutions and those who feel safe only within them. Yet there surely exists a momentum in the Biblical tradition that continually asks for the meaning, *i.e.*, for a new interpretation

107. Derrida might call this theme The Event as Empty Tomb. My effort here is to reaffirm that positivism is one of the forms of the self-inflated "autonomous consciousness."

of what has come to pass. That this line of thought is not often in evidence in non-Biblical societies is a sufficient indication. The result of contemplating the kerygma as a fiction is to see it as the proclamation of *an* event rather than an *event*. A slight shift of emphasis provides the bridge to literature's use of the kerygma as model. As our art is not interested in objects for themselves, but in the form of their manifestation, so the "content" of the event itself fades before the mere possibility of it, all that it might be.

There is no disguising the fact that this liaison of kerygma with fiction would be a scandal in the world's eyes. And why not? Why not make it sound more scandalous? We could say that kerygma is literature's secret life, its closet fantasy. Literature yearns to become that which it cannot be; it desires the status not of timeless myth but of the "new word," the timely revelation, the Good News ("that stays news," as Ezra Pound would say). We have already alluded to the suggestion that fiction and reality can heuristically swap identities: when fiction does this, it imagines itself as kerygma.

The metaphor is outrageous, as it should be to cauterize those totalizing pretensions that metaphors seems to cherish. But Paul insisted that Christ was a *skandalon* anyway, while literature's reputation has frequently been suspect—if the linkage seems farfetched, remember Tertullian. The real scandal, of course, is interpretation; it is the spreading stain that pollutes the untroubled waters of positivist faith. Michel Foucault says: "If interpretation can never accomplish itself, it is simply because there is nothing to interpret."[108] Looked at hard, the "raw datum" of perception, the "given" of reality, or any other form of Transcendental Signified evaporates. It cannot be found behind the veil.

The relation of kerygma to fiction is, however, a verifiable proposition along more conventional lines. We have already observed, following J. H. Plumb, that there exists a series of connections between Biblical narratives, saints' lives, history, and the novel. The kerygmatic impulse is evident there, as it is in the difference between the works of Dante and Homer, or Spenser and Vergil. Chaucer,

108. Quoted by Donato, in Macksey and Donato (eds.), *The Languages of Criticism*, 96.

before telling his own Tale of Melibee, uses the Gospel-writers as precedent for the variations in his version: "And alle accorden as in hire sentence, / Al be ther in hir tellyng difference." We take this as a conventional pious analogy, forgetting that Chaucer not only in his Retraction but in the Nun's Priest's Tale borrows the Pauline assertion that all writing can teach us, is for "our doctrine." Thus even a *fabliau*, in a certain setting, has continuities with the supreme Teaching. Chaucer's words hint that literature is a series of transformational variants on kerygmatic kernel sentences.

We can make our own parable. The kerygma is like a stand of wheat; deracinated and transplanted from its Near Eastern setting, it may hybridize and eventually flourish in nearly unrecognizable forms, far from its native place. We might say it travels well. Certainly it is a hardy perennial.

If the kerygma shows a certain aptitude for becoming fiction, it is not thereby diminished. The ancient stand of wheat may flourish nonetheless, even though it has given rise to numerous progeny. Chaucer comments on this when he has Absalom and Januarie sing lecherous lays made from garbled fragments of the Song of Songs; not the corruptibility of the Biblical text but merely the singers' witlessness is shown. The Word is the stronger for being mocked. Thus the transformation not only fails to taint the kerygma: continuity is underscored, for the process testifies to the revealing power of fiction.

In our time, Derrida treats positivistic writings as if they were fictional: a most heuristic gesture. The truth of literature must lie in the possibility of its taking anything as fictional. Paul de Man, in the course of an analysis of the polarities of modernity and history in literature, remarks that "man himself, like literature, can be defined as an entity capable of putting his own mode of being into question," which would be the ultimate form of fictionalizing and deconstructing.[109] We need only add that we owe this view of man as problematic to the Bible, not to mythology.

109. "Literary History and Literary Modernity," in de Man, *Blindness and Insight*, 165.

The way in which de Man reaches his formulation is relevant. He has to account for Nietzsche's youthful rejection of history, in favor of the vital present, the modern. De Man concludes that Nietzsche, and European literature, end in a paradox: "The continuous appeal of modernity, the desire to break out of literature toward the reality of the moment, prevails and, in its turn, folding back upon itself, engenders the repetition and the continuation of literature. Thus modernity, which is fundamentally a falling away from literature and a rejection of history, also acts as the principle that gives literature duration and historical existence."[110] De Man has caught Nietzsche in the act of exhibiting the doubleness that is peculiar to Western literature, and which redoubles itself in different forms: immediacy and distancing, uncertainty and finality, and so forth. The recurrence of the pattern gives literature its endlessly equivocal character: a past which is yet present, a fiction which is somehow true, a message which reveals and yet conceals, effacing and yet highlighting its own meaning so that interpretation is always already present: as de Man puts it, "The ambivalence of writing is such that it can be considered both an act and an interpretative process that follows after an act with which it cannot coincide."[111] Those writers who have pondered this doubleness of their act most fruitfully often dramatize themselves as both narrator and spectator. This variant of " 'Oh!' he said" is used from Dante and Chaucer to Proust. Indeed Proust extends it so far that the theme of his work may be said to be "watching the voyeur."

As Paul Valéry observed, in ordinary discourse words consume themselves and disappear, but literature's words cling to a form of existence which resists the loss or change of even a syllable, a tenacious self-preservation unjustified by positivist thinking. They are the words which will not pass away.[112] Such words put in question the claims of previous utterances, yet use them at the same time. As Eliot said, the advent of the really new work alters the whole of the

110. *Ibid.*, 162.
111. *Ibid.*, 152.
112. Matt. 24:35, Mark 13:31, Luke 21:33; Paul Valéry, *The Art of Poetry*, trans. Denise Folliot (New York: Vintage, 1961), 64–65 and 72.

existing order, if ever so slightly. Western art already obeys Ezra Pound's injunction to "make it new." In so doing it follows the bent of the writings which recapitulate themselves in the phrase "Behold! I make all things new."[113]

113. Rev. 21:5.

Bibliography

Adams, Robert M., and Thorkild Jacobsen. "Salt and Silt in Ancient Mesopotamian Agriculture." *Science*, 128 (November 21, 1958), 1251–58.

Aharoni, Yohanan. *The Land of the Bible: A Historical Geography*. Trans. A. F. Rainey. London: Burns and Oates, 1966.

Albrektson, Bertil. *History and the Gods*. Lund: Gleerup, 1967.

Albright, William Foxwell. *Archaeology and the Religion of Israel*. Fifth ed. New York: Anchor, 1969.

———. *Archaeology, Historical Analogy, and Early Biblical Tradition*. Baton Rouge: Louisiana State University Press, 1966.

———. *The Biblical Period from Abraham to Ezra*. Rev. ed. New York: Harper, 1963.

———. *From the Stone Age to Christianity*. Second ed. New York: Anchor, 1957.

———. *New Horizons in Biblical Research*. London: Oxford University Press, 1966.

———. *Yahweh and the Gods of Canaan: A Historical Analysis of Two Contrasting Faiths*. New York: Anchor, 1969.

Alt, Albrecht. *Essays on Old Testament History and Religion*. Trans. R. A. Wilson. New York: Anchor, 1968.

Altmann, Alexander, ed. *Biblical Motifs*. Cambridge: Harvard University Press, 1966.

Anati, Emmanuel. *Palestine Before the Hebrews: A History, from the Earliest Arrival of Man to the Conquest of Canaan*. New York: Knopf, 1963.

Anderson, Bernhard W. *Understanding the Old Testament*. Second ed. Englewood Cliffs, N.J.: Prentice-Hall, 1966.

Anderson, Bernhard W., and Walter Harrelson, eds. *Israel's Prophetic Heritage*. New York: Harper, 1962.

308   BIBLIOGRAPHY

Anderson, Edgar. *Plants, Man, and Life*. Berkeley: University of Califor-
     nia Press, 1967.
Anderson, G. W. *The History and Religion of Israel*. New Clarendon
     Bible, Vol. I. London: Oxford University Press, 1966.
Astour, Michael C. "Tamar the Hierodule." *Journal of Biblical Literature*,
     LXXXV (June, 1966), 185–96.
Auerbach, Erich. *Mimesis: The Representation of Reality in Western
     Literature*. Trans. Willard Trask. New York: Anchor, 1957.
Augustine. *On Christian Doctrine*. Trans. D. W. Robertson, Jr. New York:
     Bobbs-Merrill, 1958.
Bakan, David. *The Duality of Human Existence*. Boston: Beacon, 1966.
Baly, Denis. *The Geography of the Bible*. New York: Harper, 1957.
Barr, James. "Theophany and Anthropomorphism in the Old Testament."
     Congress Volume: Oxford (Supplements to *Vetus Testamentum*, Vol.
     VII) , Leiden, 1960. Pp. 31–38.
Barrett, C. K., ed. *The New Testament Background: Selected Documents*.
     New York: Harper, 1961.
Barthes, Roland. *Mythologies*. Trans. Annette Lavers. New York: Hill
     and Wang, 1972.
Beardslee, William A. *Literary Criticism of the New Testament*. Philadel-
     phia: Fortress, 1970.
Before Philosophy. See Frankfort.
Bercovitch, Sacvan. *Typology and Early American Literature*. Amherst:
     University of Massachusetts Press, 1972.
Berdyaev, Nicolas. "The Historical Meaning of Christianity," in *The Mod-
     ern Tradition*. Ed. Richard Ellmann and Charles Feidelson, Jr. New
     York: Oxford University Press, 1965.
Biblical Motifs. See Altmann.
Black, Matthew, and H. H. Rowley. *Peake's Commentary on the Bible*.
     Rev. ed. London: Nelson, 1962.
Boccaccio, Giovanni. *Boccaccio on Poetry*. Ed. Charles G. Osgood. New
     York: Liberal Arts Press, 1956.
Boon, James A. *From Symbolism to Structuralism: Lévi-Strauss in a Lit-
     erary Tradition*. Oxford: Blackwell, 1972.
Bottéro, Jean, ed., with Elena Cassin and Jean Vercoutter. *The Near East:
     The Early Civilizations*. Trans. R. F. Tannenbaum. New York: Dela-
     corte, 1967.
Braidwood, Robert J. *Prehistoric Men*. Rev. ed. Chicago: Chicago Natural
     History Museum, 1964.
Braidwood, Robert J., and Gordon R. Willey, eds. *Courses Toward Urban
     Life*. Chicago: Aldine, 1962.
Brandon, S. G. F. *History, Time, and Deity*. New York: Barnes and Noble,
     1965.
Bright, John. *A History of Israel*. Philadelphia: Westminster, 1959.

Brothwell, Don, and Eric Higgs, eds. *Science in Archaeology: A Survey of Progress and Research.* Rev. ed. New York: Basic Books, 1970.

Brown, Norman O. *Love's Body.* New York: Vintage, 1968.

Brumm, Ursula. *American Thought and Religious Typology.* New Brunswick, N.J.: Rutgers University Press, 1970.

Buber, Martin. *I and Thou.* Trans. R. G. Smith. Second ed. New York: Scribner's, 1958.

————. *On the Bible: Eighteen Studies by Martin Buber.* Ed. Nahum N. Glatzer. New York: Schocken, 1968.

————. *Two Types of Faith.* Trans. N. P. Goldhawk. New York: Harper, 1961.

Bultmann, Rudolf. "New Testament and Mythology," in *Kerygma and Myth.* Ed. Hans Werner Bartsch. Trans. R. H. Fuller. New York: Harper, 1961.

————. *Jesus and the Word.* Trans. L. P. Smith and E. H. Lantero. New York: Scribner's, 1958.

————. *Primitive Christianity in Its Contemporary Setting.* Trans. R. H. Fuller. New York: Meridian, 1956.

Bultmann, Rudolf, and Karl Jaspers. *Myth and Christianity: An Inquiry into the Possibility of Religion without Myth.* Trans. Norbert Guterman. New York: Noonday, 1958.

Burrows, Millar. "Ancient Israel," in *The Idea of History in the Ancient Near East.* Ed. Robert C. Dentan. New Haven: Yale University Press, 1955. (American Oriental Series Volume 38.)

The Cambridge Ancient History. Third ed. 2 vols in 4. London: Cambridge University Press, 1970–75.

Campbell, Edward F., Jr., and David Noel Freedman. *The Biblical Archaeologist Reader II.* New York: Anchor, 1964.

————. *The Biblical Archaeologist Reader III.* New York: Anchor, 1970.

Carcopino, Jérome. *Daily Life in Ancient Rome.* Ed. Henry T. Rowell. Trans. E. O. Lorimer. New Haven: Yale University Press, 1964.

Castaneda, Carlos. *Journey to Ixtlan: The Lessons of Don Juan.* New York: Simon and Schuster, 1973.

————. *A Separate Reality: Further Conversations with Don Juan.* New York: Simon and Schuster, 1971.

————. *Tales of Power.* New York: Simon and Schuster, 1974.

————. *The Teachings of Don Juan: A Yaqui Way of Knowledge.* New York: Ballantine, 1969.

Charity, A. C. *Events and Their Afterlife: The Dialectics of Christian Typology in the Bible and Dante.* Cambridge: Cambridge University Press, 1966.

Childe, V. Gordon. *New Light on the Most Ancient East.* New York: Praeger, 1953.

————. *What Happened in History.* Baltimore: Penguin, 1964.

Childs, Brevard S. *Memory and Tradition in Israel*. Napierville, Ill.: Allenson, 1962.

———. *Myth and Reality in the Old Testament*. Second ed. London: SCM Press, 1962.

City Invincible. See Kraeling.

Clark, Grahame, and Stuart Piggott. *Prehistoric Societies*. Harmondsworth: Penguin, 1965.

———. *Aspects of Prehistory*. Berkeley: University of California Press, 1970.

Clements, R. E. *Abraham and David: Genesis XV and Its Meaning for Israelite Tradition*. London: SCM Press, 1967.

Cochrane, C. N. *Christianity and Classical Culture*. London: Oxford University Press, 1968.

Cohn, Norman. *The Pursuit of the Millennium*. Second ed. New York: Harper, 1961.

Cole, Sonia. *The Neolithic Revolution*. London: British Museum, 1967.

Coulborn, Rushton. *The Origin of Civilized Societies*. Princeton: Princeton University Press, 1959.

Covensky, Milton. *The Ancient Near Eastern Tradition*. New York: Harper, 1966.

Cox, Harvey. *The Secular City*. New York: Macmillan, 1966.

The Crucible of Christianity. See Toynbee.

Culler, Jonathan. *Structuralist Poetics: Structuralism, Linguistics, and the Study of Literature*. Ithaca: Cornell University Press, 1975.

Culture in History. See Diamond.

Cross, Frank Moore. *Canaanite Myth and Hebrew Epic: Essays in the History of the Religion of Israel*. Cambridge: Harvard University Press, 1973.

Cullen, Patrick. *Spenser, Marvell, and Renaissance Pastoral*. Cambridge: Harvard University Press, 1970.

Daniélou, Jean. *From Shadows to Reality: Studies in the Biblical Typology of the Fathers*. Trans. W. Hibberd. Westminster, Md.: Newman Press, 1960.

———. *The Lord of History*. Trans. N. Abercrombie. London: Longmans, 1958.

———. *Primitive Christian Symbols*. Trans. D. Attwater. Baltimore: Helicon, 1964.

Darlington, C. D. *The Evolution of Man and Society*. New York: Simon and Schuster, 1969.

Dawson, Christopher. *Religion and Culture*. New York: Meridian, 1958.

Derrida, Jacques. *De la Grammatologie*. Paris: Editions de Minuit, 1967.

Diamond, Stanley, ed. *Culture in History: Essays in Honor of Paul Radin*. New York: Columbia University Press, 1960.

Dodds, E. R. *The Greeks and the Irrational*. Berkeley: University of California Press, 1963.

The Domestication and Exploitation of Plants and Animals. See Ucko.

Driver, S. R. *An Introduction to the Literature of the Old Testament*. Cleveland: World, 1956.

Dumézil, Georges. *The Destiny of the Warrior*. Trans. Alf Hiltebeitel. Chicago: University of Chicago Press, 1970.

Eichrodt, Walther. *Theology of the Old Testament*. 2 vols. Trans. J. A. Baker. Philadelphia: Westminster, 1961.

Eissfeldt, Otto. *The Old Testament: An Introduction*. Trans. P. R. Ackroyd. New York: Harper, 1965.

Eliade, Mircea. *The Sacred and the Profane: The Nature of Religion*. Trans. W. R. Trask. New York: Harper, 1967.

Else, Gerald. *The Origin and Early Form of Greek Tragedy*. New York: Norton, 1972.

Empson, William. *Some Versions of Pastoral*. New York: New Directions, 1960.

Enslin, Morton Scott. *Christian Beginnings*. 3 parts in 2 vols. New York: Harper, 1965.

Every, George. *Christian Mythology*. London: Hamlyn, 1970.

Finley, M. I. "Myth, Memory, and History." *History and Theory*, IV, 3 (1965), 281–302.

Fish, Stanley. *Self-Consuming Artifacts: The Experience of Seventeenth-Century Literature*. Berkeley: University of California Press, 1972.

Forsdyke, [Edgar] John. *Greece Before Homer: Ancient Chronology and Mythology*. London: Parrish, 1956.

Frankfort, Henri, and H. A. Frankfort, John A. Wilson, and Thorkild Jacobsen. *Before Philosophy: The Intellectual Adventure of Ancient Man*. Baltimore: Penguin, 1961.

Frankfort, Henri. *The Birth of Civilization in the Near East*. New York: Anchor, n.d.

———. *Kingship and the Gods: A Study of Ancient Near Eastern Religion as the Integration of Society and Nature*. Chicago: University of Chicago Press, 1948.

Frazer, Sir James. *The New Golden Bough*. Ed. Theodor H. Gaster. New York: Criterion, 1959.

Freedman, David Noel. "The Biblical Idea of History." *Interpretation*, XXI (1967), 32–49.

Freedman, David Noel, and Jonas C. Greenfield, eds. *New Directions in Biblical Archaeology*. Garden City: Doubleday, 1971.

Frye, Northrop. *The Critical Path*. Bloomington: Indiana University Press, 1971.

Fuller, Reginald H. *The New Testament in Current Study*. New York: Scribner's, 1962.

Funk, Robert W., ed. *The Bultmann School of Biblical Interpretation: New Directions*. New York: Harper, 1965.

Gardner, Helen. *Religion and Literature*. London: Faber, 1971.

Gelley, Alexander. "Form as Force." *Diacritics*, II (Spring, 1972), 9–13.

Gerhardsson, Birger. *Memory and Manuscript: Oral Tradition and Written Transmission in Rabbinic Judaism and Early Christianity*. Trans. E. J. Sharpe. Lund: Gleerup, 1961.

Giedion, S[igfried]. *The Eternal Present*. Vol. I: *The Beginnings of Art*. Vol. II. *The Beginnings of Architecture*. New York: Pantheon, 1962–64.

The Epic of Gilgamesh. Trans. N. K. Sandars. Baltimore: Penguin, 1960.

Girard, René. *La Violence et le sacré*. Paris: Grasset, 1972.

Glueck, Nelson. *Rivers in the Desert: A History of the Negev*. New York: Farrar, Straus, 1959.

Gombrich, E. H. *Art and Illusion: A Study in the Psychology of Pictorial Representation*. Second ed. Princeton: Princeton University Press, 1961.

————. "Meditations on a Hobby Horse." In *Classic Essays in English*, Josephine Miles, ed. Second ed. Boston: Little, Brown, 1965.

Grabar, André. *Christian Iconography: A Study of Its Origins*. Princeton: Princeton University Press, 1961.

Grant, Frederick C. *The Gospels: Their Origin and Their Growth*. New York: Harper, 1957.

————. *Hellenistic Religions: The Age of Syncretism*. New York: Bobbs-Merrill, 1953.

Grant, Michael. *The Ancient Mediterranean*. New York: Scribner's, 1969.

————. *The Jews in the Roman World*. New York: Scribner's, 1973.

Grant, Robert M. *Gnosticism and Early Christianity*. Rev. ed. New York: Harper, 1966.

————. *A Short History of the Interpretation of the Bible*. New York, Macmillan, 1963.

Gray, John. *Archaeology and the Old Testament World*. London: Nelson, 1962.

————. *Near Eastern Mythology*. London: Hamlyn, 1969.

Greenslade, Stanley L., ed. *The Cambridge History of the Bible*. 3 vols. Cambridge: Cambridge University Press, 1963–70.

Grousset, René. *The Empire of the Steppes: A History of Central Asia*. Trans. N. Walford. New Brunswick, N.J.: Rutgers University Press, 1970.

Gunkel, Hermann. *The Legends of Genesis: The Biblical Saga and History*. Trans. W. H. Carruth. New York: Schocken, 1964.

Guthrie, W. K. C. *The Greeks and Their Gods*. Boston: Beacon, 1955.

Habel, Norman. *Literary Criticism of the Old Testament*. Philadelphia: Fortress, 1971.

Hahn, Herbert H. *The Old Testament in Modern Research*. Rev. ed. Philadelphia: Fortress, 1966.

Hallo, William W., and William Kelly Simpson. *The Ancient Near East: A History*. New York: Harcourt, Brace, 1971.

Harden, Donald. *The Phoenicians.* Second ed. New York: Praeger, 1963.
Harrelson, Walter. *From Fertility Cult to Worship.* New York: Doubleday, 1969.
Harrison, Jane. *Prolegomena to the Study of Greek Religion.* New York: Meridian, 1955.
Harrison, R. K. *Old Testament Times.* Grand Rapids, Mich.: Eerdmans, 1970.
Havelock, Eric. *Preface to Plato.* New York: Grosset and Dunlap, 1967.
Hawkes, Jacquetta. *Prehistory.* Vol. I, Pt. I of UNESCO, *History of Mankind.* New York: Mentor, 1965.
Hawkins, Gerald S., with John B. White. *Stonehenge Decoded.* New York: Dell, 1965.
Heaton, E. W. *The Hebrew Kingdoms.* New Clarendon Bible, Vol. III. London: Oxford University Press, 1968.
Heidel, Alexander, ed. *The Gilgamesh Epic and Old Testament Parallels.* Chicago: University of Chicago Press, 1949.
Henderson, Ian. *Myth in the New Testament.* London: SCM Press, 1952.
Henn, T. R. *The Bible as Literature.* New York: Oxford University Press, 1970.
Hexter, J. H. *The Judaeo-Christian Tradition.* New York: Harper, 1966.
Hooke, S. H. *Middle Eastern Mythology.* N.p.: Penguin, 1968.
———. *The Siege Perilous: Essays in Biblical Anthropology and Kindred Subjects.* London: SCM Press, 1956.
Hubert, Henri, and Marcel Mauss. *Sacrifice: Its Nature and Function.* Chicago: University of Chicago Press, 1964.
Hyatt, J. Philip, ed. *The Bible in Modern Scholarship.* Nashville: Abingdon, 1965.
Ivić, Milka. *Trends in Linguistics.* Trans. M. Heppell. The Hague: Mouton, 1965.
Jacobsen, Thorkild. *Toward the Image of Tammuz and Other Essays on Mesopotamian History and Culture.* Ed. W. L. Moran. Cambridge: Harvard University Press, 1970.
Jaeger, Werner. *Paideia: The Ideals of Greek Culture.* Vol. I. Second ed. Trans. G. Highet. New York: Oxford University Press, 1965.
Jakobson, Roman. *Selected Writings, Vol. II.* The Hague: Mouton, 1971.
Jameson, Fredric. *The Prison-House of Language: A Critical Account of Structuralism and Russian Formalism.* Princeton: Princeton University Press, 1972.
Jeremias, Joachim. *Rediscovering the Parables.* New York: Scribner's, 1966.
Johnson, Aubrey L. *Sacral Kingship in Ancient Israel.* Cardiff: University of Wales Press, 1967.
Jones, Alexander, ed. *The Jerusalem Bible.* Garden City: Doubleday, 1966.
Kapelrud, Arvid S. *The Violent Goddess: Anat in the Ras Shamra Texts.* Oslo: Universitetsforlaget, 1969.

Kaufmann, Yehezkel. *The Religion of Israel.* Trans. Moshe Greenberg. New York: Schocken, 1972.

Kees, Hermann. *Ancient Egypt: A Cultural Topography.* Ed. T. G. H. James. Trans. I. F. D. Morrow. Chicago: University of Chicago Press, 1961.

Kenner, Hugh. *The Counterfeiters: An Historical Comedy.* Bloomington: Indiana University Press, 1968.

——. *The Pound Era.* Berkeley: University of California Press, 1971.

——. *Flaubert, Joyce, and Beckett: The Stoic Comedians.* Boston: Beacon, 1962.

Kenyon, Kathleen. *Amorites and Canaanites.* London: British Academy, 1963.

——. *Archaeology in the Holy Land.* Third ed. New York: Praeger, 1970.

Kermode, Frank, ed. *English Pastoral Poetry: From the Beginnings to Marvell.* London: Harrap, 1952.

——. *The Sense of an Ending: Studies in the Theory of Fiction.* New York: Oxford University Press, 1968.

Kirk, G. S. *Myth: Its Meaning and Function in Ancient and Other Cultures.* Berkeley: University of California Press, 1970.

Knox, Ronald. *Enthusiasm: A Chapter in the History of Religions.* Oxford: Oxford University Press, 1950.

Kraeling, Carl, and Robert M. Adams, eds. *City Invincible: A Symposium on Urbanization and Cultural Development in the Ancient Near East.* Chicago: University of Chicago Press, 1960.

Kramer, Samuel Noah. *History Begins at Sumer.* New York: Anchor, 1959.

——. *Sumerian Mythology.* Rev. ed. New York: Harper, 1961.

——. *The Sumerians: Their History, Culture, and Character.* Chicago: University of Chicago Press, 1963.

——, ed. *Mythologies of the Ancient World.* New York: Anchor, 1961.

Kuhn, T. S. *The Structure of Scientific Revolutions.* Second ed. Chicago: University of Chicago Press, 1970.

Lamberg-Karlovsky, C. C., ed. *Old World Archaeology: Foundations of Civilization.* San Francisco: Freeman, 1972.

Leach, Edmund. *Genesis as Myth and Other Essays.* London: Cape, 1969.

Lee, Richard B., and Irven De Vore, eds. *Man the Hunter.* Chicago: Aldine, 1968.

Lemon, Lee T., and Marion J. Reis, eds. *Russian Formalist Criticism: Four Essays.* Lincoln: University of Nebraska Press, 1965.

Leone, Mark P., ed. *Contemporary Archaeology.* Carbondale: Southern Illinois University Press, 1972.

Leroi-Gourhan, André. *Treasures of Prehistoric Art.* Trans. Norbert Guterman. New York: Abrams, 1967.

Lessing, Erich, ed. *The Bible: History and Culture of a People.* London: Herder and Herder, 1970.

Lévi-Strauss, Claude. *The Raw and the Cooked: Introduction to a Science of Mythology,* I. Trans. J. and D. Weightman. New York: Harper, 1969.

————. *The Savage Mind.* Chicago: University of Chicago Press, 1966.

————. *Structural Anthropology.* Trans. C. Jacobson and B. G. Schoepf. New York: Anchor, 1967.

————. *Totemism.* Trans. R. Needham. Boston: Beacon, 1963.

————. *Tristes Tropiques.* Trans. John Russell. New York: Atheneum, 1970.

Levy, G[ertrude] Rachel. *Religious Conceptions of the Stone Age and Their Influence Upon European Thought (The Gate of Horn).* New York: Harper, 1963.

Lincoln, Eleanor Terry, ed. *Pastoral and Romance: Modern Essays in Criticism.* Englewood Cliffs, N.J.: Prentice-Hall, 1969.

Lindblom, J. *Prophecy in Ancient Israel.* Philadelphia: Fortress, 1965.

Loew, Cornelius. *Myth, Sacred History, and Philosophy: The Pre-Christian Religious Heritage of the West.* New York: Harcourt, Brace, 1967.

Löwith, Karl. *Meaning in History.* Chicago: University of Chcago Press, 1949.

Lovejoy, Arthur O., and George Boas. *Primitivism and Related Ideas in Antiquity.* Baltimore: Johns Hopkins University Press, 1935.

Macksey, Richard, and Eugenio Donato, eds. *The Languages of Criticism and the Sciences of Man: The Structuralist Controversy.* Baltimore: Johns Hopkins University Press, 1970.

Malefijt, Annemarie de Waal. *Religion and Culture.* New York: Macmillan, 1968.

De Man, Paul. *Blindness and Insight: Essays in the Rhetoric of Contemporary Criticism.* New York: Oxford University Press, 1971.

————. "Semiology and Rhetoric." *Diacritics,* III (Fall, 1973), 27–33.

Man, Settlement, and Urbanism. See Ucko.

Man's Role in Changing the Face of the Earth. See Thomas, William L., Jr.

Marshack, Alexander. *The Roots of Civilization: The Cognitive Beginnings of Men's First Art, Symbol, and Notation.* New York: McGraw-Hill, 1972.

Marx, Leo. *The Machine in the Garden: Technology and the Pastoral Ideal in America.* New York: Oxford University Press, 1964.

May, Herbert G., and Bruce M. Metzger, eds. *The New Oxford Annotated Bible.* New York: Oxford University Press, 1973.

May, Herbert G., ed., with G. N. S. Hunt. *Oxford Bible Atlas.* Second ed. London: Oxford University Press, 1974.

May, Rollo, ed. *Symbolism in Religion and Literature.* New York: Braziller, 1961.

Meek, Theophile James. *Hebrew Origins.* New York: Harper, 1960.

Mellaart, James. *Çatal Hüyük: A Neolithic Town in Anatolia.* New York: McGraw-Hill, 1967.

————. *Earliest Civilizations of the Near East.* New York: McGraw-Hill, 1965.

Mendenhall, George E. *The Tenth Generation: The Origins of the Biblical Tradition.* Baltimore: Johns Hopkins University Press, 1973.

Milburn, R. L. P. *Early Christian Interpretations of History.* New York: Harper, 1954.

Miller, J. Hillis. *The Disappearance of God: Five Nineteenth-Century Writers.* New York: Schocken, 1965.

————. *Poets of Reality: Six Twentieth-Century Writers.* Cambridge: Belknap Press of Harvard University, 1966.

Miller, Perry. *The New England Mind: The Seventeenth Century.* Boston: Beacon, 1961.

Miskotte, Kornelis H. *When the Gods Are Silent.* Trans. J. W. Doberstein. New York: Harper, 1967.

Moscati, Sabatino. *The World of the Phoenicians.* Trans. A. Hamilton. New York: Praeger, 1968.

Neill, Stephen. *The Interpretation of the New Testament, 1861–1961.* New York: Oxford University Press, 1966.

The New English Bible. N.p.: Oxford and Cambridge University Presses, 1970.

Niebuhr, Reinhold. *The Nature and Destiny of Man.* New York: Scribner's, 1964.

Nilsson, Martin P. *A History of Greek Religion.* Second ed. New York: Norton, 1964.

Nineham, D. E., ed. *Studies in the Gospels: Essays in Memory of R. H. Lightfoot.* Oxford: Blackwell, 1955.

Nisbet, Robert A. *Social Change and History: Aspects of the Western Theory of Development.* New York: Oxford University Press, 1969.

Nock, Arthur Darby. *Conversion: The Old and the New in Religion from Alexander the Great to Augustine of Hippo.* London: Oxford University Press, 1933.

————. *Early Gentile Christianity and Its Hellenistic Background.* New York: Harper, 1964.

North, Christopher R. *The Old Testament Interpretation of History.* London: Epworth, n.d.

Noth, Martin. *The History of Israel.* Second ed. Trans. P. Ackroyd. New York: Harper, 1960.

————. *The Old Testament World.* Trans. V. I. Gruhn. Fourth ed. Philadelphia: Fortress, 1966.

Nystrom, Samuel. *Beduinentum und Jahwismus: Eine Soziologisch Religiongeschictliche Untersuchung zum Alten Testament.* Lund: Gleerup, 1946.

Olson, Charles. *Selected Writings.* Ed. Robert Creeley. New York: New Directions, 1966.

Ong, Walter. *The Presence of the Word.* New York: Simon and Schuster, 1970.

Oppenheim, A. Leo. *Ancient Mesopotamia: Portrait of a Dead Civilization.* Chicago: University of Chicago Press, 1964.

Orlinsky, Harry M. *Ancient Israel.* Ithaca: Cornell University Press, 1954.

Ortega y Gasset, José. *Meditations on Quixote.* Trans. E. Rugg and D. Marín. New York: Norton, 1961.

Otto, Rudolf. *The Idea of the Holy.* Trans. J. Harvey. New York: Oxford University Press, 1958.

Owst, G. W. *Literature and Pulpit in Medieval England.* Second ed. Oxford: Blackwell, 1961.

Parkes, Henry Bamford. *Gods and Men: The Origins of Western Civilization.* New York: Vintage, 1959.

Patrides, C. A. *The Grand Design of God: The Literary Form of the Christian View of History.* London: Routledge, 1972.

Paz, Octavio. *Claude Lévi-Strauss: An Introduction.* Trans. J. S. and M. Bernstein. Ithaca: Cornell University Press, 1970.

Peake's Commentary on the Bible. See Black.

Percy, Walker. *The Message in the Bottle.* New York: Farrar, Straus, 1975.

Pericot-Garcia, Luis, John Galloway, and Andreas Lommel. *Prehistoric and Primitive Art.* New York: Abrams, 1967.

Pfeiffer, John E. *The Emergence of Man.* New York: Harper, 1969.

Piggott, Stuart. *Ancient Europe: From the Beginnings of Agriculture to Classical Antiquity.* Chicago: Aldine, 1965.

Plumb, J. H. *The Death of the Past.* Boston: Houghton Mifflin, 1970.

Pritchard, James B. *The Ancient Near East: An Anthology of Texts and Pictures.* Princeton: Princeton University Press, 1965.

Von Rad, Gerhard. *Der heilige Krieg im alten Israel.* Fourth ed. Göttingen: Vandenhoeck & Ruprecht, 1965.

————. *Old Testament Theology.* 2 vols. Trans. D. M. G. Stalker. New York: Harper, 1965.

————. *The Problem of the Hexateuch and Other Essays.* Trans. E. W. T. Dicken. New York: McGraw-Hill, 1966.

Raikes, Robert. *Water, Weather, and Prehistory.* London: John Baker, 1967.

Redfield, Robert. *The Primitive World and Its Transformations.* Ithaca: Cornell University Press, 1953.

Renfrew, Colin. *Before Civilization: The Radiocarbon Revolution and Prehistoric Europe.* New York: Knopf, 1973.

————, ed. *The Explanation of Culture Change: Models in Prehistory.* N.p.: Duckworth, 1973.

Robinson, James M., and John B. Cobbs, eds. *The New Hermeneutic.* New York: Harper, 1964.

Roston, Murray. *Prophet and Poet: The Bible and the Growth of Romanticism.* Evanston, Ill.: Northwestern University Press, 1965.

Rostovtzeff, M. *The Social and Economic History of the Hellenistic World.* Oxford: Clarendon, 1941.

Roux, Georges. *Ancient Iraq.* N.p.: Penguin, 1966.

Rowley, H. H. *From Joseph to Joshua: Biblical Traditions in the Light of Archaeology.* London: British Academy, 1964.

————. *From Moses to Qumran: Studies in the Old Testament.* New York: Association Press, 1963.

————, ed. *The Old Testament and Modern Study.* Oxford: Clarendon, 1951.

Rylaarsdam, J. Coert, ed. *Transitions in Biblical Scholarship.* Vol. VI of *Essays in Divinity,* ed. Jerald C. Brauer. Chicago: University of Chicago Press, 1968.

Saggs, H. W. F. *The Greatness That Was Babylon.* New York: Mentor, 1968.

Sahlins, Marshall D. *Tribesmen.* Prentice-Hall Foundations of Modern Anthropology Series. Englewood Cliffs, N.J.: Prentice-Hall, 1968.

Sandmel, Samuel. *The Hebrew Scriptures: An Introduction to Their Literature and Religious Ideas.* New York: Knopf, 1963.

De Santillana, Giorgio, and Hertha von Dechend. *Hamlet's Mill: An Essay on Myth and the Frame of Time.* Boston: Gambit, 1969.

Sarton, George. *A History of Science, Vol. I.* New York: Norton, 1970.

Sauer, Carl. *Agricultural Origins and Dispersals.* New York: American Geographical Society, 1952.

————. *Land and Life: A Selection from the Writings of Carl Ortwin Sauer.* Ed. John Leighly. Berkeley: University of California Press, 1965.

————. *Northern Mists.* Berkeley: University of California Press, 1968.

Scholes, Robert, and Robert Kellogg. *The Nature of Narrative.* Oxford: Oxford University Press, 1966.

Schonfield, Hugh J. *A History of Biblical Literature.* New York: Mentor, 1962.

Sebeok, Thomas A., ed. *Myth: A Symposium.* Bloomington: Indiana University Press, 1965.

Van Seters, John. *The Hyksos: A New Investigation.* New Haven: Yale University Press, 1966.

Seznec, Jean. *The Survival of the Pagan Gods.* Trans. B. Sessions. New York: Harper, 1961.

Shepard, Paul. *Man in the Landscape: A Historic View of the Esthetics of Nature.* New York: Knopf, 1967.

Sherwin-White, A. N. *Racial Prejudice in Imperial Rome.* Cambridge: Cambridge University Press, 1967.

Slater, Philip E. *The Glory of Hera: Greek Mythology and the Greek Family.* Boston: Beacon, 1968.

Smith, George Adam. *The Historical Geography of the Holy Land.* 25th ed. New York: Harper, 1966.

Smith, Hallett. *Elizabethan Poetry.* Ann Arbor: University of Michigan Press, 1968.

Smith, Morton. *Palestinian Parties and Politics That Shaped the Old Testament.* New York: Columbia University Press, 1971.

Snaith, Norman H. *The Distinctive Ideas of the Old Testament.* New York: Schocken, 1964.

Snell, Bruno. *The Discovery of the Mind: The Greek Origins of European Thought.* Trans. T. G. Rosenmeyer. New York: Harper, 1960.

Social Life of Early Man. See Washburn.

Speiser, E. A. *Oriental and Biblical Studies.* Philadelphia: University of Pennsylvania Press, 1967.

———, ed. *At the Dawn of Civilization.* Vol. I, First Series, of *World History of the Jewish People,* ed. B. Netanyahu. New Brunswick, N.J.: Rutgers University Press, 1964.

Starr, Chester G. *A History of the Ancient World.* New York: Oxford University Press, 1965.

Tarn, W. W. *Hellenistic Civilisation.* Third ed. London: Arnold, 1952.

Tax, Sol, ed. *Anthropology Today: Selections.* Chicago: University of Chicago Press, 1962.

Thomas, D. Winton, ed. *Archaeology and Old Testament Study.* Oxford: Clarendon, 1967.

———, ed. *Documents from Old Testament Times.* New York: Harper, 1961.

Thomas, William L., Jr., ed. *Man's Role in Changing the Face of the Earth,* Vol. I. Chicago: University of Chicago Press, 1956.

Thompson, William Irwin. *At the Edge of History.* New York: Harper, 1972.

Tillich, Paul. *A History of Christian Thought.* Ed. Carl E. Braaten. New York: Harper, 1968.

Toliver, Harold E. *Pastoral Forms and Attitudes.* Berkeley: University of California Press, 1971.

Toynbee, Arnold, ed. *The Crucible of Christianity.* New York: World, 1969.

Trilling, Lionel. *Beyond Culture: Essays on Literature and Learning.* New York: Viking, 1968.

Turner, Victor. *Dramas, Fields, and Metaphors: Symbolic Action in Human Society.* Ithaca: Cornell University Press, 1974.

———. *The Ritual Process: Structure and Anti-Structure.* Chicago: Aldine 1969.

Ucko, Peter J., and G. W. Dimbleby, eds. *The Domestication and Exploitation of Plants and Animals.* Chicago: Aldine, 1969.

Ucko, Peter J., Ruth Tringham, and G. W. Dimbleby, eds. *Man, Settlement, and Urbanism.* London: Duckworth, 1972.

De Vaux, Roland. *Ancient Israel*, Vol. I, *Social Institutions*. Vol. II, *Religious Institutions*. New York: McGraw-Hill, 1965.

Via, Dan Otto, Jr. *The Parables: Their Literary and Existential Dimensions*. Philadelphia: Fortress, 1967.

Voegelin, Eric. *Order and History*, Vol. I, *Israel and Revelation*. Baton Rouge: Louisiana State University Press, 1956.

de Vries, Jan. *The Study of Religion: A Historical Approach*. Trans. Kees Bolle. New York: Harcourt, Brace, 1967.

Washburn, Sherwood L., ed. *Social Life of Early Man*. Chicago: Aldine, 1961.

Waters, Frank. *Masked Dancers*. Denver: Sage, 1950.

Weber, Max. *Ancient Judaism*. Trans. H. H. Gerth and D. Martindale. Glencoe, Ill.: Free Press, 1952.

Weiser, Artur. *The Old Testament: Its Formation and Development*. Trans. D. Barton. New York: Association Press, 1961.

Wellard, James. *By the Waters of Babylon*. London: Hutchinson, 1972.

White, Lynn, Jr. *Machina Ex Deo: Essays in the Dynamism of Western Culture*. Cambridge: MIT Press, 1968.

Wilder, Amos N. *Early Christian Rhetoric: The Language of the Gospel*. Cambridge: Harvard University Press, 1971.

————. *The New Voice: Religion, Literature, Hermeneutics*. New York: Herder and Herder, 1969.

————. *Theology and Modern Literature*. Cambridge: Harvard University Press, 1958.

Williams, George Huntston. *Wilderness and Paradise in Christian Thought*. New York: Harper, 1962.

Williams, Raymond. *The Country and the City*. New York: Oxford University Press, 1973.

Wilson, John A. *The Burden of Egypt: An Interpretation of Ancient Egyptian Culture*. Chicago: University of Chicago Press, 1951.

Woolf, Hans Walter. "The Kerygma of the Yahwist." *Interpretation*, XX (1966), 131–58.

Wright, G. Ernest. *The Old Testament Against Its Environment*. London: SCM Press, 1957.

————, ed. *The Bible and the Ancient Near East: Essays in Honor of William Foxwell Albright*. New York: Anchor, 1965.

Wright, G. Ernest, and David Noel Freedman, eds. *The Biblical Archaeologist Reader*. Chicago: Quadrangle, 1961.

Wright, G. Ernest, and Reginald H. Fuller. *The Book of the Acts of God: Contemporary Scholarship Interprets the Bible*. Garden City: Doubleday, 1960.

Yadin, Yigael. *The Art of Warfare in Biblical Lands*. 2 vols. New York: McGraw-Hill, 1963.

Index

Abel, 120, 122, 128, 243n, 244
Abiathar, 203
Abimelech, 244, 245n
Abraham: leaves "the city," 119, 126, 133; kinship and nomadism of, 140; mentioned, 213, 215, 232, 243, 247, 266
Absalom, 201, 205, 244–45, 280
Adam, 152, 213, 243
Adams, Robert M., 107, 112, 113, 121, 127, 133
Adonijah, 205, 244
Afterlife, 186, 220
Agriculture: and autochthony, 76; in Near East, 120–25; different patterns of, 135–37; and cereals out of weeds, 146–47; mentioned, 105, 165, 183, 185. *See also* Farmers; Hybridization of plants
Ahab, 168, 209, 288
Ahimaaz, 203
Akhenaten, 101
Albrektson, Bertil, 55n, 175n
Albright, William F.: on "archaic demythologizing," 13n; on syncretism, 53n; on Sumerian *logos*, 223n; mentioned, 77n, 229n, 232n, 233n, 239n, 240n
Alcibiades, 201, 259
Alcoholics Anonymous, 182
Alexander the Great, 92, 106, 116, 117n

Alienation: spread by prophets, 11; of God from people, 11n, and "objectivity," 16–21; and adaptation to change, 39; healed by myth, 41, 99, 166; and subject-object problem, 47; of Hebrews from nature, 62; treated by Lévi-Strauss, 67–69; and "questing," 69, 90, 103; and "distant" past, 79; and megalithism, 86; role in rigidification, 106, 186; and history, 179; in Job, 218; and point of view, 251; and writing, 251, 254–55; and parable, 254; and lyric, 261; and *ostraneniye*, 270; and Biblical style, 280; and comedy, 284; mentioned, 287, 288
Alt, Albrecht, 133, 207, 209n
Amalekites, 128, 194, 245n
Ambiguity of the sacred, 81, 86, 95–96, 225, 228–29
Amorites, 153
Amos: and "Day of Yahweh," 26, 266; mentioned, 16, 19, 129, 231, 238
Anati, Emmanuel, 62, 152
Ancestors, 78–79, 88, 241, 242, 246
Anderson, Edgar, 147, 165
Animals: in mythology, 60–68; and marriage with humans, 61, 91–94; in cult of dead, 79, 82; power of, 93; petrifaction of cults, 108; in metaphor, 293. *See also* Totemism

Antinomianism, 12n, 55
Anxiety: normative in West, 41; in high cultures, 102, 106, 155; expressed by pastoral, 145; metaphysical, 240–42; and the "cybernetic," 298; mentioned, 46, 48–49
Apuleius, 95
Aquinas, Thomas, 18
Arcadia, 163, 169
Aristophanes, 258
Aristotle, 103, 202, 259, 265, 271
Ark: Hebrew, 4, 130, 189, 200
Armageddon, 193
Artuad, Antonin, 37
Arthur, King, 92
"Aspiring mind," 158–60
Assyria, 26, 115, 116, 187, 209, 216–18, 266
Astronomical knowledge, 86, 88–89, 238
Athena, 191
Atlantis, 100
Auden, W. H., 271n
Auerbach, Erich, 25–26, 214–16, 279–80, 301
Augustine, St., 36n, 181, 219n, 262, 275n, 280
Augustus, Caesar, 66, 102
Autochthony: ideology of, 62, 70n, 74–77; and Venus-figurines, 91; and metamorphosis, 95; eroded in great cities, 107, 114; and megalithism, 109; persists in countryside, 114n; repudiated by Rechabites, 132; and pastoral, 135; repudiated by J, 161; mentioned, 234, 240–41
Autonomous conscience, 282
Autonomous consciousness, 37, 45, 48, 57. See also Positivism

Baal, 24, 56, 123, 141, 209, 210n, 233
Babel, Tower of, 5, 90, 110, 119, 158, 242, 261
Babylon, 6, 112, 115, 118–19, 216, 218
Bakan, David, 245–46
Barak, 190, 192
Barth, John, 295
Barthes, Roland, 42–43, 53, 79, 117, 277n
Bathsheba, 201, 209, 244
Battle cry, 190–91
Beckett, Samuel, 259, 282, 286, 301

Bedouin, 29, 123, 128–29, 132n, 137, 143
Behaviorism, 46, 52
Benjamin, 196–98, 243n
Berdyaev, Nicolas, 221
Bergounioux, F. M., 84
Berossus, 101n
Binary opposition, 144–45, 167, 228–30
Blake, William, 20, 248
Blanc, Alberto C., 84–85
Boccaccio, 282
Borges, Jorge Luis, 276
Brain-eating, 83–84
Brecht, Bertolt, 276n
Bristlecone pines: and dendrochronology, 39, 86
Brown, Norman O., 10
Browning, Robert, 294
Buber, Martin, 65n
Buddha, 101
Bull, 97, 229, 238–39
Bultmann, Rudolf, 12, 57, 295
Burrows, Millar, 208n, 211n, 212, 213n
Bushmen, 70

Caesarism, 204n
Cain, 5, 48, 120, 122, 126, 128, 190, 243n, 244
Camels, 128
Camus, Albert, 242
Canaanites: high places of, 25, 87; language of, 32; and syncretism, 54–56; as "native," 77; armies of, 115, 194; means "merchants," 124; chthonic, 153; and Passover, 183; infanticide and antifertility practices of, 197, 210, 225–27, 230–33; build Temple, 207; mentioned, 29, 97, 126n, 192, 204
Carroll, Lewis (C. L. Dodgson), 157, 161, 171
Cassirer, Ernst, 57
Castaneda, Carlos, 18, 23, 65, 94, 143, 186
Castro, Fidel, 175
Çatal Hüyük, 95–96, 229, 235–37, 238
Caves, 72, 85, 93, 232, 236
Census, 207
"Centering," 114
Cervantes, Miguel, 274. See also Quixote, Don

Chain of Being, 64
Chariots, 115, 193–94, 204–206, 234
Chaucer, Geoffrey, 170, 248, 303–305
Cherubim, 32
Chesterton, G. K., 41
Childe, V. Gordon, 8, 28, 33
China: concept of history in, 179, 180
Choukoutien, 84
Chthonic cults and powers: dispossessed by Yahweh, 74; animals, 82; in Palestine, 152–53; mentioned, 71–72
Churinga, 79, 88
Cities: hostility to, 5–6; vs. nomads, 29; require alienation, 43–44; imperialism and rigidification of, 107; and social stratification, 112; and nature, 167; mentioned, 119, 124, 233, 234, 245
Clarke, Grahame, 79, 91n, 102
Codices (books), 267
Cohn, Norman, 176, 297
"Cold societies," 14–15, 48, 58, 78–79, 85, 101, 108, 177–79, 256, 264
Coleridge, Samuel Taylor, 268, 275
Comedy, 284
Communism, 39, 176
Conceptual art, 265n, 274
"Corporate personality," 148
Cosmic continuum: and myth, 27; 60, 64, 67; and the dead, 81; model for cities, 113; and "cybernetics," 296; mentioned, 4, 141, 163, 259, 261n
Crete, 97–98
Cross, Frank Moore, 13n, 55n, 56n, 132n, 188n, 200n, 202n–206n, 207n, 208n, 211n
Crucifixion, 217
Cultural change: and sectarian beliefs, 1–3; demythologizing and, 14–15; frenzy for, 37–39, 43; builds civilizations, 101; insignificant in Egypt, 179–80; mentioned, 48, 69, 108, 145, 156–57, 173
Cuneiform literature, 27
"Cybernetic" effects, 155, 156, 296–99

Daniel, 115–16, 117–18, 224
Dante, 90, 274, 303, 305
Darwin, Charles, 46, 75
David: as "Hebrew," 125; as pastoral symbol, 129; as pastoral king, 130–31; acquires kingship, 198–205; mentioned, 3, 32, 83n, 162, 168, 190, 194, 195–96, 209, 212, 215, 216, 243n, 244, 280
Da Vinci, Leonard. *See* Vinci, Leonardo da
Dead, cults of the, 61, 77–85, 88, 90, 233
Dead Sea, 142
Dead Sea Scrolls, 132
Deborah, Song of, 192–93, 238
"Decentering," 49, 157, 240n, 262, 264n, 302
Deconstruction, 273, 289, 293, 304
Defamiliarization, 268–70
Defoe, Daniel, 182
Demythologizing: and Bible's effect, 12; of Hebrews and neighbors, 29; against heretics, 35; in intellectual change, 36; and psychic trauma, 48–49; of space and building, 73; in pastoral, 111, 125, 138, 155–57, 234n, 235n; in cities, 114n; causes more myth, 165–66; and history, 180–84, 223; Passover as, 183–84; and fiction, 216, 300; against sacrifice, 232; and paternity, 234n, 235n, 241, 242, 247n; and Greek literature, 257–58, 262; and verbal formulas, 266–67; mentioned, 17, 22, 59, 101, 264, 290, 295, 300
Derrida, Jacques, 99n, 114n, 253, 255–56, 285, 287, 289–90, 299, 301, 304
Desert, 11, 125, 128–29, 132, 134–35, 137, 142–45, 153–54, 167
Deutero-Isaiah, 216, 219
Deuteronomy, 205–206, 217, 227, 243
De Vaux, Roland. *See* Vaux, Roland de
Diacritical theory of meaning, 246n
Differentiation, systematic, 10–12, 49, 51, 113, 140, 167, 228, 246n, 292
Dionysius the Areopagite, 30
Divination, 27, 81, 222–25, 292
Division of labor, 10, 109, 122, 145, 154
Documentary hypothesis, 212
Dodds, E. R., 19n, 279n
Dodgson, C. L. *See* Carroll, Lewis
Domestication, 65, 68, 89, 97, 120, 136, 145, 150, 179, 234–35
Dominance: as Western tradition, 40; as human tradition, 147

Dreams, 8, 10, 11, 48, 81. *See also*
    Oneiromancy
Duck, Stephen, 166, 172
Dumézil, Georges, 9
Dumuzi (Tammuz), 122–23, 238–39

Ecclesiastes, 5, 18, 242n, 259
Ecclesiasticus, 145n
Eden *(edin)*, 44, 121, 140, 159, 161,
    180, 213, 253
Egypt: as symbol of slavery, 6, 64; atti-
    tude toward nature, 58; animal cults
    in, 63–64, 82, 92; and the dead, 81,
    109–11, 144; plagues of, 148n;
    change in, 179–80; Hebrew apostasy
    in, 226; mentioned, 29, 53, 130–31,
    145, 151, 155, 184–85, 204, 205–206,
    208, 239–40, 296
Eli, 199, 203
Eliade, Mircea, 114n, 301
Elijah, 19, 24, 129, 141, 168, 205
Eliot, George, 281
Eliot, T. S., 48n, 183, 252–53, 264, 267,
    283, 301, 305–306
Else, Gerald, 257–58
Emperors: self-deification of, 117; men-
    tioned, 102, 110, 115–16, 204, 241
Empson, William, 157, 161, 170–72
Enosh, 213
Epic, 300
Esau, 152, 243n
Ethos, 72
Europa, 93
Exodus: and idea of history, 25, 185;
    as pastoral, 127; Yahweh as leader
    of, 190; mentioned, 64, 111, 140, 142,
    183, 192, 202, 212, 226, 232, 262
Ezekiel: and "bad laws," 3, 287; on
    ancestors, 78n; on Tyre, 118; on
    shepherds, 131n; sexual rhetoric of,
    226; and individual responsibility,
    261, 266; mentioned, 32

"Fact," concept of, 171, 301
Fall of Man, 44, 49, 159
Familiarization, 17, 44, 257, 268
Fantasy, 284–85
Farmers: and shepherds, 119–25, 128,
    135–37, 139, 140, 141; new foods of,

156; and Passover, 183; mentioned,
    16, 29, 76, 88, 152, 165
Faust, 159
Fertility: and fatality, 61, 87, 96, 98,
    225, 228–29, 237; and animals, 62; in
    places, 80; in burial cults, 82; and
    ancestors, 88; Hebrew idea of, 90,
    227; subverted by emperors, 117n;
    and sacrifice, 152, 222; curse on
    ground, 161; in Temple fixtures,
    208n
Fiction: and history, 184, 215–16, 220,
    277–78; Kenner on, 254–55, 286; and
    kerygma, 302–303; mentioned, 251,
    268, 275ff., 300, 304, 305
Fish, Stanley, 297–98
Flannery, Kent, 83n, 121n, 139, 149,
    155
Flaubert, Gustave, 252, 259, 282, 301
Ford, Ford Madox, 281
Ford, Henry, 175
Forgeries, art, 288
Formalism. *See* Russian Formalism
Forsdyke, [Edgar] John, 278n
Forster, E. M., 271
Foucault, Michel, 99n, 303
Frankfort, Henri: on Yahweh, 4; on
    social disorder as theme, 11; on
    mythopoeic as concrete, 22; on He-
    brews against images, 30; on ancient
    cultures embedded in nature, 58n;
    on "I-Thou" relations, 64–65; on
    desert experience, 134–35, 141, 143,
    151; on Egypt as changeless, 179,
    296; on Min, 239; mentioned, 6,
    107n
Franklin, Benjamin, 50, 53
Fratricide, 244
Frazer, Sir James, 230
Freud: and anxiety dreams, 8, 217; and
    unconscious, 10; self-contradictory,
    46; civilization from murder, 48; on
    Oedipus complex, 240, 245; men-
    tioned, 227
Fromm, Erich, 41
Frye, Northrop, 263
Fuller, Buckminster, 74n

Galileo, 26
Gardner, Helen, 219–21, 259
Genesis: denatured myths of, 13; con-

trast to Homer, 25–26, 214–15; and
"Younger Son" theme, 34n, 243;
against cities, 112; and kinship sys-
tems, 139–40; and historical writing,
212–15, 279; mentioned, 32, 66, 74,
80, 121, 127–29, 152, 161, 186
Giants (Anakim, Nephilim, etc.) , 87n
Gideon, 3, 17, 189, 190, 233, 244–45,
260
Giedion, S[igfried]: on animals, 60, 63,
94; on vertical as sacred, 74n; on
sacred building, 85; on Min, 239;
mentioned, 107n, 222, 301
Gilgamesh, 166, 279
Gilson, Etienne, 275n
Girard, René, 225n, 243n, 246n
Gnosticism, 95, 164, 287n
Golden calf, 97
Gombrich, Ernst H.: on schemata, 220,
264–65; on "sacred discontent," 264–
65; on conceptual art, 265n, 274; on
images, 269; mentioned, 83n, 252,
262, 275, 288, 294
Great Goddess. *See* Mother goddess
Greek traditions: use of myth to edu-
cate, 20, 254–55; sense of culture,
23, 30; and science, 28n; syncretism,
53–54, 95n; chthonic, 71–72, 76; hybrids in myth, 93, 97–98; and metaphysics, 163–64, 286–87; historians,
178; and suffering, 220; women in,
238; and literature, 257–63; mentioned, 272, 274, 278–79. *See also*
Homer
Grousset, René, 138
Gunkel, Hermann, 13n

Hagar, 129
Hammurabi, 32, 125, 188n
Hannah, 11, 90, 242
Harrison, Jane, 71, 93
Hathor, 93
Havelock, Eric, 20, 72, 255, 258–59
Hawkes, Jacquetta, 65n, 81n, 91n
Hawkins, Gerald, 108n
Hawthorne, Nathaniel, 283
Hazda (nomads) , 139
Hazlitt, William, 241
"Hebrew": as term, 125, 133, 196
Hemingway, Ernest, 282
Hera, 93

Hermeneutic circle, 256
Herod, 106n, 154
Hexter, J. H., 174, 211n, 277
Hieros gamos, 98, 238–39
History, Hebrew sense of: and actual
events, 25, 202n–206n; and Meso-
potamia, 55, 174, 186–87; unsparing
of heroes, 201; anti-*logos*, 202, 222–
23; Yahweh's point of view, 209–11;
style and themes of, 214–20; and
paternity, 242–43, 247. *See also* Lit-
erature; Demythologizing; Aliena-
tion
Hitler, Adolf, 175
"Hoe culture," 135–36, 146, 152
Homer, 20, 81, 103, 214–16, 224, 254–
55, 260, 264, 273n, 274, 279, 280,
293, 303
Homosexuality. *See* Sex
Hopkins, Gerard Manley, 218n
Horns, 98, 229
Hosea, 209, 226, 246
"Hot society," 14–15, 179
Huckleberry Finn, 172, 282
Humanism, 20, 37, 41, 180
Hunter-collector societies, 105, 119–20,
150, 154
Hybrid animals: in myth, 92–94, 96–97
Hybridization of plants, 146–47, 304

Ichabod, 199
Images: Hebrew hostility to, 30, 56,
186; Gombrich and Shklovsky on,
269
Imdugud, 96
Immediacy, 184, 211, 288, 293, 305
Impalement, 217
Imperialism, 89n, 106–19, 126–27, 181,
186n, 217, 234
Incest. *See* Sex
Indeterminacy principle, 22, 40
Infanticide, 104–105, 225, 230, 231–33
Innocence, 160–62
Interpretation: Bible demands, 2, 215;
discussed, 252–58 *passim*, 287–305
passim. *See also* Literature
Io, 93
Isaac, 133, 213, 232, 243n
Isaiah: on king of Assyria, 115; on
Peaceable Kingdom, 160–62, 168, 279;
against sacrifice, 231; and parable,

254; on remnant, 266; mentioned, 4, 7n, 32, 118, 209, 210n, 226, 238, 256, 268, 291
Ishmael, 128, 243n
"I-Thou" relations, 64–65, 185

"J," 160–61, 212–14
Jacob, 133, 134, 140, 185, 196, 213, 215, 216, 243n, 291
Jacobsen, Thorkild, 4n, 27n, 70, 113n, 117n, 121n, 122–23, 162n, 186n, 188n, 229n, 293
Jaeger, Werner, 262, 276
Jael, 132n, 192–93, 238
Jakobson, Roman, 144n, 257n, 289, 292
James, Henry, 254–55, 301
Jameson, Fredric, 49n, 256n, 268n, 276n, 287n
Jehu, 56, 209n
Jephthah, 232
Jeremiah: against Temple, 3; reluctant, 17; against fetishism, 24–25; on wicked rewarded, 218; sexual rhetoric of, 226; merges paternity and pastoral, 246–47; on individual responsibility, 261, 266; mentioned, 50, 118–19, 209, 238, 283
Jericho: world's oldest city, 5; walls of, 6, 109, 119, 208; skulls, 82–83; chthonic, 153; fall as ritual, 191; and infanticide, 232; mentioned, 101, 133, 193, 200
Jerusalem, 5, 6, 200, 205, 210n
Jesus: against prosperity, 1; against Temple, 3, 119; denounces cities, 6; vs. kinship, 12, 44; and pastoral, 129–30; and desert, 144, 153; and parable, 220, 254, 278, 287n; and sonship, 247; and verbal formulas, 266–67; mentioned, 118, 225, 268, 301, 303
Job, 6, 212, 217–20, 266
John the Baptist, 129, 153
John, Gospel of, 130, 131, 247
Johnson, Samuel, 166, 261
Jonathan, 198
Joseph, 111, 196, 216, 224, 243n
Joshua, 115, 153, 191, 204
Josiah, 209, 224
Joyce, James, 73, 203, 240, 252, 281–82, 291, 301

Judahites, 34, 97, 209
Judges, book of, 33, 194, 196–98, 232
Judges, charismatic, 33, 131, 189
Justin Martyr, 35

Kaufmann, Yehezkel, 187, 223n
Kenites, 128n, 132n, 190, 192
Kenner, Hugh, 171n, 255, 281–82, 286n, 287n, 291, 301n
Kenyon, Kathleen, 82–83, 153n, 191n
Kerygma, 295–304
Kings: Hebrew, 16, 34, 56, 90n, 115, 130–31, 168, 187–211, 232–33, 244
Kinship systems, 10, 12, 51–52, 69, 79, 84, 122, 140
Kirk, G. S., 70, 230n
Knox, Ronald, 106n
Kramer, Samuel Noah, 162n
Kuhn, T. S., 26n, 249

Lacan, Jacques, 246n
Lamb, 239
Lattimore, Owen, 138n
Law: Hebrew, 3, 14, 90, 287
Lawrence, D. H., 20, 172, 207, 228n, 269
Lawrence, T. E., 154
Leach, Edmund, 59–60, 75–76, 91, 301n
Leda, 93
Leisure, 124n
Leroi-Gourhan, André, 228, 246n
Lévi-Strauss, Claude: and "mediation" of myths, 7; and unconscious, 9; on "hot" and "cold" societies, 14–15; *la pensée sauvage*, 21, 27, 58, 293n, 294–95; and indeterminacy, 40; on New World cities, 43n; on structures in myth, 52; on nature, 58–60, 66–68, 116; on sacred place and order, 70–71, 72, 74n, 100; on Oedipus myth, 76–77, 239n, 272–73, 296; on cannibalism, 83; on *churinga*, 88; on marrying animals, 91–92; on dissolving "man," 99n; on totemism, 140, 292; and Jakobson, 144n; on history, 176–77; in prophetic mode, 298; mentioned, 18, 42, 44, 48n, 56, 222–23, 229–30, 274, 287, 289, 299, 301
Levy, [Gertrude] Rachel: 61, 65n, 72, 79; on megalithism, 86–90; on

"Stone Men" of Malekula, 96; mentioned, 91n, 92–94, 236
Lévy-Bruhl, Lucien, 57
Lindblom, J., 7n, 128n, 129n, 255n, 278n
Literature, concept of: and criticism of culture, 3, 45, 142, 250, 274, 283–84, 297–98; identifying with characters, 20, 271, 275–76; and negative knowledge, 26, 31, 260, 283, 294, 298, 301–302; in Hebrew culture, 26, 31, 212–20, 261, 279; and myth, 95, 99, 263–64, 272–74, 290, 292–96; imbued with pastoral, 157; as entertainment, 172, 276, 297–98; and historical narrative, 182–84, 211, 212, 214–16, 219–20, 253, 277–86, 295, 305; and parable, 220, 254–55, 268, 278, 286; love and death in, 228n; unnaturalness of, 250ff, 305; demands interpretation, 215, 254–55, 291–92, 300–301, 303, 305; not understood by familiarization, 257, 267–72, 298; and demythologizing, 257–59, 262, 290, 295, 298, 300; and self-consciousness, 45, 260–61, 290–91; and varied schemata, 264–65, 292, 299, 304; and authors, 268, 274, 290–91; functions as language, 270–71; language in search of a subject, 272; and exact words, 273, 305–306; and deconstruction, 273, 289, 293, 304, 305; as Yahwist, 276, 284; relation to secularism, 277–78; shatters classical world view, 280, 292, 295–96, 302, 306; and prophets, 279, 282–83; and improbability, 215–16, 279, 285, 303, 305; and fictional idea of truth, 280–81, 284, 304–305; and kerygma, 295–304; paradox of, 305
Logos, 180, 202, 222, 259, 260, 296
Longevity, 148, 162
Löwith, Karl, 40n, 176
Luke, 12, 131
Luther, Martin, 36
Lyric, 260–61

Machpelah traditions, 80
McLuhan, Marshall, 211n, 256, 296
Magic, 63, 210n, 294
Malinowski, Bronislaw, 277

De Man, Paul, 69, 289–90, 293, 304–305
Manasseh (king), 210
Manasseh (son of Joseph), 243n
Mantuan, 169
Marcus, Greil, 297
Marie Antoinette, 166, 172
Marlowe, Christopher, 159
Marshack, Alexander, 89
Marx, Karl, 40, 46, 175
Masada, 154
Mauss, Marcel, 52n, 222, 230n
Megalithism, 73, 85–89, 108–109, 119, 152, 208
Megiddo, 193
Melcarth (*Milk-qart*), 233, 240n
Mellaart, James, 95–96, 109, 121n, 235–37
Melville, Herman, 283–84
Mendenhall, George: on Hebrew self-criticism, 3n; on myth, 9n; on imperialism, 116n; on "withdrawal," 123–27; on Yahweh as king and war-leader, 188n; on battle cry, 196n; on Caesarism, 204n; on Temple as pagan, 207n; on crucifixion, 217n; on pastoralism and younger sons, 243n; mentioned, 132n, 133, 191n
Merchants, 118, 124
Mesopotamia: source of Genesis myths, 13, 32; kingship as militaristic, 112, 188; salinization, 113; and concept of history, 174–75, 186–87; divination in, 222n, 225; mentioned, 29, 96, 126–27, 130n, 145ff, 151, 213
Metalinguistic function, 268
Metalworking, 190
Metamorphosis, 61, 81n, 94–95, 97, 98
Metaphor and metonymy, 247n, 289–90, 292–94, 300, 302
Methusaleh, 148
Micaiah, 209, 287
Michal, 83n, 200
Middle Ages, 35–36, 41, 100, 170, 181, 249, 265, 274, 302
Midianites, 128, 129, 132n
Milk, 155–56, 235
Mill, John Stuart, 41, 48
Miller, J. Hillis, 37, 281n
Milton, John, 2, 131n, 170, 261
Min, 82, 239–41, 243, 244, 245n, 247n

Minotaur, 97–98
Miriam, Song of, 192–93, 238
Miskotte, Kornelis H., 15, 57–58, 287
Mithraism, 95, 97, 98
Mohammed, 31, 101
Moloch, 210, 227, 232–33
Moses, 17, 19, 64, 80, 128n, 129, 168, 190, 213, 215, 243n
Mother goddess, 62–63, 76, 90–93, 235–38, 240
Mousterian culture, 39, 84–85, 156
Müller, Max, 89
Mumford, Lewis, 113n, 233n
Myth: and social stability, 2, 4, 7–11, 51, 79, 236–37, 296; as transmission vehicle, 8–9, 50–52, 79, 85; in Hebrew society, 13–14; in West, 14, 42–43, 296–97; in pejorative sense, 17; and "multiple truth," 26, 36, 53–54, 277; origins from nature, 27, 58ff; ingested by Christianity, 35; charter myths, 70n; mediation of shepherd/farmer, 122; and history, 176–77, 179–80, 202–203, 206n; and tragedy, 257–58; and "subjects," 273–74; and art, 294; mentioned, 62. See also Literature
Mythography, 35

Nambikwara, 67–68, 299
Narmer, 92
Narrative, 177n, 180–83, 219, 259, 292
Nathan, 130, 168, 209, 220
Natufian culture, 62, 120–21, 152
Nature: alienation from, 22; and culture, 22, 79; role of in myth, 58ff, 101, 185–86; and divinity, 66–68; overvalued, 162–67, 249; motherhood and, 240; and logos, 260; mentioned, 102, 140, 141
Nazirites, 172
Neanderthal man, 57, 80, 84
Nebuchadnezzar, 117
Negative knowledge: in Hebrew culture, 3, 15–19, 80, 90; in West, 19–22, 26–27; via negativa, 30, 294; of emperors, 110; symbolized by desert, 144ff; and metonymy, 290, 294; mentioned, 304. See also Literature
Neolithic revolution, 89, 101, 102, 120, 139, 235

New Guinea, 84
Niebuhr, Reinhold, 45–47, 145, 240n
Nietzsche, Friedrich, 259, 305
Nihilism, 36–38, 49, 252
Nilsson, Martin P., 106n, 115n
Nimrod, 158
Nineveh, 118
Noah, 132
Nock, A. D., 105n
Nomads: enemies of cities, 29; withdrawal as freedom, 141; symbiosis with culture, 146; and disease, 148–49; and "conquest" of Palestine, 153; and metalworking, 190; mentioned, 127–29, 134–35, 137–40, 234
Noth, Martin, 124n, 143n, 189n
Novel, 183, 300, 303

Ockham, William of, 26, 36
Odysseus, 216, 254
Oedipus, 240–41, 245, 272–73. See also Lévi-Strauss, Claude
Olson, Charles, 1, 99
Omri, 210
Onan, 227
Oneiromancy, 224
Ong, Walter, 256n, 299
Oppenheim, A. Leo, 101n, 107, 113n, 126–27
Oral mode, 17, 164, 254, 256, 272–73, 287, 299
Origen, 13
Orphism, 95
Ortega y Gasset, José, 270, 274
Otium, 158–60
Otto, Rudolf, 143
Ovid, 95, 160, 262, 264
Oxygen, 39
Ozymandias, 111

Panofsky, Erwin, 163
Parable, 218, 220, 244n, 254, 268, 278, 286, 304
Parataxis, 280, 292
Paris: judgment of, 159, 168
Pascal, Blaise, 48, 283
Pasiphae, 93, 98
Passover, 183–84, 192n, 234n
Pastoralism: symbolism of, 125, 127, 134, 154, 168–69; and cultural change, 156–57, 180; poetry, 157ff;

demythologizes, 172–73, 234n, 235n; and history, 185, 241n; and younger sons, 243n; and cities, 245; and paternity, 247; mentioned, 119ff, 135–37, 191. *See also* Shepherd

Paternity, 233–34, 238, 240–47

Paul, 12, 14, 21, 25, 30, 100, 118, 202, 262–63, 287, 303

Paz, Octavio, 68n, 179, 273, 300

Peking man, 84

Percy, Walker, 299n

Peter, 118

Pharaoh, 6, 89n, 130, 134, 192n, 239, 241

"Phatic function," 52

Philistines, 131, 190, 194, 199, 201, 203

Picasso, Pablo, 31, 283

Pig (pork), 82

Piggott, Stuart, 79, 91n, 102, 154

Plants, 65, 165. *See also* Domestication, Hybridization of plants

Plato, 20, 101, 262, 265, 276

Plot, 271–72

Plumb, J. H., 177–78, 180–81, 183, 303

Pop, 297–98

Pope, Alexander, 273, 291

Positivism, 37, 248–49, 254, 278, 285, 295, 301–302, 304–305

Pound, Ezra, 182, 250, 255, 264, 267, 269, 273, 291, 303, 306

Prehistory: idea of, 54–55, 103

Primitive societies: not self-critical, 16; and nature, 23; and the dead, 78; woman in, 235; art in, 265n, 292; mentioned, 18, 51–52, 57–58, 68, 165. *See also* "Cold societies"

Prophets: against culture, 7, 10, 17–18, 31–32, 36; against "wisdom," 21; against nature, 24; heirs of charismatic judges, 33, 208n–209n; vs. priests, 55; vs. kings, 115, 130, 168, 208–209, 211; and wilderness, 127n, 129; and history, 176n, 178; on horrors of invasion, 216–17; 249–50, 254, 259; and verbal formulas, 266–67; and fictions, 279, 283; mentioned, 127, 287

Proust, Marcel, 289–90, 305

Proverbs, 206

Psalms, 129, 241, 261, 279

Pyramids, 85–86, 109–10, 208

Quixote, Don, 259, 270, 272, 276

Qumran, 132, 154

Rachel, 83n, 213, 238

Rad, Gerhard von, 134, 183–84, 185, 193n, 211, 213n, 234n

Ranke, Leopold von, 210

Rechabites, 131–32, 172

Reformation, 267, 282, 302

Renaissance, 157–60, 164, 168, 169–70, 264–65, 267

Renfrew, Colin, 86n, 108n

Revelations, book of, 6, 118, 306

Richards, I. A., 271, 275n

Ricoeur, Paul, 60, 295, 298

Rift valleys, 149–50

Robinson, James, 287n, 299n

Rome (Roman traditions) : and Christian Church, 35; syncretism, 54; historians, 178, 223–24, 279–80; mentioned, 6, 92, 104, 116, 118, 133, 217

Rousseau, Jean-Jacques, 24, 66, 68n, 69

Russian Formalism, 267–72

Sacred space, 61, 69–74, 114, 141

Sacrifice, 90n, 152, 222, 225, 229–33

Sahlins, Marshall, 52n

Saints' legends, 183, 303

Salinization, 113

Samuel, 168, 188, 189, 194–95, 198–99, 209

Santayana, George, 292

Santillana, Giorgio de, 88, 238

Sappho, 260, 265

Sarah, 90, 129, 238, 242

Sargon of Akkad, 107, 117n

Sarton, George, 27

Satan, 187n

Sauer, Carl: on voyaging, 74n; on pastoralism, 120, 135–37, 149, 152, 163; on maternal culture, 233, 234–35; mentioned, 97n

Saul: vs. sorcery, 19; pursues David, 125, 129; accession of, 131, 168, 194–96; failure of, 198–200; and divination, 224; and Baalism, 233; mentioned, 209, 245

Saussure, Ferdinand de, 48n, 289

Schemata, 220, 257, 264–65, 267, 288, 292, 294–95, 299

Science: and demythologizing, 12, 37;
    alienating knowledge, 19, 69; vs. sav-
    age thought and myth, 21–22; and
    nature, 24; vs. divination, 27–28;
    scientism, 28; helps recover myth,
    103; and fiction, 286; mentioned,
    222–23
Scipio Africanus, 92
Sebaoth (title of Yahweh), 200
Secularism, 24, 40n, 176, 180, 181–82,
    277–78
Self-consciousness, 43–49, 61, 260–61
Self-consuming, 297–98
Self-criticism, tradition of: in West,
    3–5, 14, 20, 38; in Hebrew culture,
    10, 34; morbid variants of, 41, 46;
    Lévi-Strauss on, 68–69; and history,
    178; mentioned, 16, 57, 99
Seters, John van, 53n
Sex (sexual life, practices) : in myth,
    62, 228–30, 237–39; and "sperm-
    redundancy" of man, 75; sodomy,
    bestial, 91–93; erotic figurines, 152;
    in Eden, 161; homosexuality, 197–
    98, 198n, 210n, 225–26; rhetoric of
    prophets, 226; ritual prostitution,
    226n; incest, 239–40, 245n
Shakespeare, William, 117, 157, 159,
    164, 168, 170, 219, 221, 250, 276, 283,
    288
Shamans, sorcerers, 18–19, 22, 27, 94,
    190
Shaw, George Bernard, 2, 65
Sheep, 137, 149
Shepard, Paul, 98, 119, 121n, 124n,
    143n, 158n, 161n, 234n
Shepherd: and farmers, 29, 120–28,
    152, 166–67; Yahweh as, 129, 130,
    185; symbolism in Bible, 129–31; in
    poetry, 159; mentioned, 76, 111, 119
Shepherd, Jean, 172n
Shklovsky, Victor, 267–72, 276, 295
Sidney, Sir Philip, 282
Sinai, 74, 80n, 140, 143
Slater, Philip E., 92n, 278n
Smith, Hallett, 158, 159
Smith, Morton, 34, 55n
Snake, 82
Snell, Bruno, 43, 53–54, 258–59, 260,
    293, 300
Snyder, Gary, 98, 100

Social disorder, 11–12, 296
Social stratification, 109, 112–14, 234,
    280
Sodom (and Gomorrah) , 5, 118, 196
Solomon, 31, 32, 110, 130, 203–208,
    243n, 244
Song of Songs, 160
Sontag, Susan, 256
Sorcerers. See Shamans, sorcerers
Speech acts, 270, 296
Speiser, E. A., 5n, 113n, 124n, 174–75,
    179, 188n, 210n, 213–14
Sterne, Laurence, 271
Stevens, Wallace, 298
Stone(s), 87–88, 119, 228
Stonehenge, 73, 86, 109
Structuralism, 48n, 99n, 290
Subject-object problem, 46–47, 65, 99,
    273–74, 292
Sumer: syncretism, 53; attitude toward
    nature, 58, 101, 186; hybrids in
    myth, 93, 96–97; cities of, 112, 121–
    23, 133, 140; Dilmun myth, 162;
    sacral nudity, 200; logos, 223n, 239n,
    251; mentioned, 88–90, 107, 155, 186,
    193
Syncretism, 31, 52–56, 95, 105, 106, 134,
    188n, 208n, 226, 234, 237

Tacitus, 30, 104, 224, 227
Tamburlaine, 159
Tammuz. See Dumuzi.
Temple, 3, 74, 110, 119, 207–208, 210n
Tent, 128, 130, 131
Teraphim, 83n, 90, 213
Tertullian, 35, 202–203, 259–60, 285,
    303
Thompson, William Irwin, 100n, 119,
    126n, 229n
Thoreau, Henry David, 242
Thucydides, 178
Tillich, Paul, 35
Tolkien, J. R. R., 284–85, 295, 302
Tolstoy, Leo, 275n, 291
Totemism, 65n, 74–75, 78, 81n, 93,
    292
Toynbee, Arnold, 97n, 145n, 227n
Tragedy, 145, 219–21, 258–59
Translation, 273
Trilling, Lionel, 45, 99, 275n
Tristan (and Isolde) , 164, 228n

"Two stage" funeral rites, 84, 236
Tyre, 118, 233, 240n, 266

Ur, 97n, 126
Ur-kultur, 100

Valéry, Paul, 305
Van Seters, John. *See* Seters, John van
Vaux, Roland de, 226n, 231–33
Venus-figurines, 91, 98, 225, 229
Via negativa. See Negative knowledge
Vico, 292
Vinci, Leonardo da, 26, 267
Virgil, 157–58, 163, 170, 262, 303
Voegelin, Eric, 176n, 185, 192n, 241n
Voltaire, 119
Von Rad, Gerhard. *See* Rad, Gerhard von
Von Ranke, Leopold. *See* Ranke, Leopold von
Voyeurism, 305
Vriezen, Th. C., 11n
Vygotsky, L. S., 257n

War: holy, 6, 135n, 193–94, 198n, 245n; and Yahweh as king and war-leader, 187–95, 204n

Warhol, Andy, 271
Weeds, 146–47, 165
Wheat, 146, 155–56, 304
White, Lynn, Jr., 24
Whitman, Walt, 228n
Widengren, Geo, 183–84
Wilde, Oscar, 275
Wilder, Amos N., 2–3, 267n, 280n
Williams, William Carlos, 73, 251, 263, 291
Wilson, John A., 4n, 53n, 130n, 151n, 293n
Wisdom, 206–207
"Withdrawal," concept of, 125–27, 133, 141, 170, 188n, 241n
Wolfe, Tom, 297
Wordsworth, William, 268
Wright, G. Ernest, 3n, 50, 211n, 261n
Writing, 89, 164, 208, 251–53, 255, 257, 287, 305

Xenophobia, 54

Yeats, William Butler, 28

Ziggurat, 85, 89–90, 110, 113, 222
Zoroaster, 101